Unfinished Business

The Life & Times of Danny Gatton

by Ralph Heibutzki

Backbeat
Books
San Francisco

600 Harrison Street, San Francisco, CA 94107
www.backbeatbooks.com
email: books@musicplayer.com

An imprint of the Music Player Network
Publishers of *Guitar Player, Bass Player, Keyboard,* and other magazines

United Entertainment Media, Inc.
A CMP Information company

CMP

United Business Media

Distributed to the book trade in the US and Canada by
Publishers Group West, 1700 Fourth Street, Berkeley, CA 94710

Distributed to the music trade in the US and Canada by
Hal Leonard Publishing, P.O. Box 13819, Milwaukee, WI 53213

Composition by Maureen Forys—Happenstance Type-O-Rama
Cover Design by Richard Leeds—bigwigdesigns.com
Front Cover Photo by Jeromie Brian Stephens
Back Cover Photo Courtesy of Jan Gatton

Library of Congress Cataloging-in-Publication Data

Heibutzki, Ralph, 1964–
    Unfinished business : the life & times of Danny Gatton/by Ralph Heibutzki
        p. cm.
    Includes bibliographical references (p. 267), discography (p. 255), and
    index.
    ISBN 0-87930-748-X (alk. Paper)
    Gatton, Danny. 2. Guitarists—United States—Biography. I. Title.

    ML419.G368H45 2003
    787.87'165'092—dc21

Printed in the United States of America

03 04 05 06 07   5 4 3 2 1

To "Budgie," my dear wife, Lisa D. Quinlan Heibutzki:
Your love and support mean everything....

My parents, Herbert (1934–2002) and Hildegard Heibutzki (1934–2003):
You were right all along....

Don Hargraves, Anthony Salazar, Tim Easterday, and John Hilla:
Kick down the doors.

Contents

*T*he first time Danny and I ever met in person, he took the trouble to bring up a set of wire wheels to New York City for my '54 Buick Skylark. Now, this was a typical Danny moment, because even though he was playing that night at Riverside Memorial Church, celebrating the cover of *Guitar Player*, he drove up in a snowstorm in his pickup truck to deliver the wheels. There, in front of the church, he and I sat in the back of the pickup, looking over the wheels and making the transaction. I felt more like I was somewhere on a country road in Maryland than Gotham itself, and you could tell that Danny had never left that country road to begin with.

Prior to this meeting, we had had numerous phone calls and had developed a friendship and a plan to do his first *Telemaster* video. Many years before that I constantly kept hearing of him and his guitar prowess, but we had never crossed paths. He even claimed that he left a message on my machine—which I never received—about doing a video. Many years prior to that, I used to get calls to record jingles in New York City, often from people who wanted Danny to do them, but he would tell them, "What're you calling me for? You're from New York, and you've got Arlen Roth up there. Why don't you use him?!" This blew my mind, because no one had ever so consistently given up work so I could get it. Certainly not in the musically competitive atmosphere I had to exist in. This told me two things about this man: He was incredibly generous, and he probably didn't like traveling too much, especially to New York City!

When I did get to spend time with him, though, those were the finest and rarest of occasions. There was no such thing as non–quality time when you were with Danny. When we did his two videos, it was uproarious fun. When we did my album together, I saw how tireless, dedicated, and masterful he was to work with in the studio. When we performed on Conan O'Brien together in 1994, it was a true show of strength, as he had lost his longtime friend and partner, Billy Windsor, just days earlier. But best of all was simply stopping by his beautiful Maryland farm and hanging out

Arlen Roth and Danny in 1994 at the Newburg, Maryland, homestead where they listened to rough mixes for Relentless *in the garage.*

in his garage, fooling around with the cars, drinking some beers, and listening to the roughs of *Relentless* while my two daughters laughed and played with his daughter, Holly. Danny said it wasn't until he saw me with my wife and children that he knew the "real" me, and it served to further cement our friendship. Little did I know then that just six months later I'd lose my best friend. And little did I know then that my wife, Deborah, and oldest daughter Gillian would be killed in a car accident in 1998. Oh, how I could have used Danny's words of friendship and comfort then and now. I hope he knew how many people loved him, and how deeply.

Yes, Danny was a master on his instrument, but that's really only part of the story. As a man, as a *family* man, that's where the real Gatton was. When we spoke on the phone, the conversation would always start with family, then go to cars, and maybe once in a blue moon, turn to music. We both shared a loathing and mistrust for the business after being screwed so many times that we'd lost count. So who wants to talk about that?!

The last time I ever spoke to Danny, I was touring up in New England, and I had come upon a neon "Ford" sign he had told me to try to find for his garage. I called him up and was completely shocked at how down he sounded. The only other time I had heard that dark tone in his voice was when he lost Billy Windsor—except this time it sounded more like it was about money problems. I got back on the road, called him from a pay phone, and he still sounded the same way. Just as we said goodbye, his final words were obscured by the rushing by of a huge tractor-trailer truck. I'll never know those last words, but they seemed to have an encouraging tone anyway.

Unfinished Business is the perfect title for this book; Danny had lots of unfinished business with everyone. As a father who lost his 14-year-old daughter, I can't conceive of how Danny could choose to leave his. I think when someone does something like this, they're already somehow predisposed to it. As if there's a time bomb ticking inside. Danny had an air of mystery about him. There were times when you were with him that he seemed like he could've been a million light years away. His eyes seemed to speak another language, perhaps from another time. All I know is we loved him, and always will. Thank God he left his music behind, and that the legacy and legend will only continue to grow, because it'll take another universe and another eternity for anyone to see the likes of him again.

Founder of the Hot Licks *instructional video series, guitarist Arlen Roth has recorded and performed with artists such as Bob Dylan, Ry Cooder, Paul Simon, James Taylor, Janis Ian, Pete Seeger, Phoebe Snow, and Rick Wakeman. Roth's seven solo recordings include* Toolin' Around, *with Danny Gatton, and* Drive It Home, *a tribute to his late wife and daughter.*

On October 4, 1994, a 49-year-old man lionized as "The World's Greatest Unknown Guitar Player" locked his Newburg, Maryland, home's garage door and shot himself. There was little of the frenzy that had accompanied the suicide of Nirvana frontman Kurt Cobain earlier that year. Danny Gatton's death created few immediate ripples beyond the family and friends who mourned his loss, as well as among the guitar fanatics who'd hung on every lick he'd ever played around the Maryland, Virginia and Washington, D.C., club circuit where he'd made his mark.

The speculation around Danny's untimely departure only deepened an enigma that few outsiders ever penetrated. Predictably, the few publications that covered his death latched onto the only angle that seemed to make sense: the working musician who couldn't weather the ups and downs of an unpredictable profession. What else explained the demise of someone who'd commanded attention from the time he was a teenager for his lickety-split finger speed, omnivorous musical sensibility, and ruthlessly precise chops?

On the surface, Danny's life story seems to follow the predictable arc of artists whose work concedes nothing to trends but fails to strike the public's fancy. The reality is much more complicated, for Danny's ever-inventive and restless mind never stopped exploring new musical idioms. He seldom rehearsed, yet he remained master of the artful segue. Throughout his life, a set that zigzagged from Charlie Christian's "Seven Come Eleven" to Vince Guaraldi's "Peanuts" cartoon theme ("Linus and Lucy") and the frenzied bluegrass of "Orange Blossom Special" remained standard procedure.

Wherever Danny went, other guitarists seemed sure to follow. A list of those admirers—James Burton, Lenny Breau, Vince Gill, Evan Johns, Bill Kirchen, Albert Lee, Arlen Roth, Ricky Skaggs—reads like a scrapbook of the roots musical idioms that Danny so ardently championed. More recently, less obvious names like alternative-rock godfather Lou Reed, Bon Jovi guitarist Richie Sambora, and Guns N' Roses' Slash have also sung Danny's praises. Bill Holloman—who played horns and keyboards with

Danny from 1990 to '93—jokes that if a couple hundred people caught their show, 150 of them would be guitar players, with the remainder "reluctant girlfriends" and "people coming in from the street."

Danny never reached the heights, in pure sales terms: unwilling to invest much time in national touring, he appeared to take greater satisfaction in raising a family and restoring antique cars. His "greatest hits" were homegrown releases like *Redneck Jazz* (1978)—which appeared on NRG Records, the label run by his mother and number-one fan, Norma Gatton.

Danny Gatton swam upstream all his life. While his '60s peers were grooving to psychedelic anthems like "Purple Haze" or playing slam-bang garage rock, Danny was already exploring the outer boundaries of country, rockabilly, and jazz. As rock 'n' roll grew harder and hairier, Danny stuck to the Les Paul fixations that had inspired his teenage listening experiences. Not for nothing did he call his first album as a bandleader *American Music*—a recording that arrived in 1975, a good half-decade before such back-to-the-roots notions became hip.

Danny's increasing propensity to express himself instrumentally also put him squarely at odds against his profession's focus-on-the-frontman ethic. A celebrity-driven culture that prizes ambition over achievement is hardly the natural venue for someone with Danny's level of virtuosity. That he bucked the inclination is admirable; that he paid the price for doing so is undeniable.

Yet Danny's story isn't only a musical one. Unlike many higher-level performers, he managed to sustain a number of lasting friendships outside the business; numerous sources interviewed for this book said they would still have found him worth knowing even if he'd never played a note. His devotion to family and friends is amply documented: for nearly 20 years, the same names appeared onstage or in the studio next to him. And the guitarist who stopped heavyweight players dead in their tracks could make the greenest drummer feel comfortable playing alongside him.

Danny had to deal with his share of demons. A natural introvert, he rarely permitted his feelings to surface, except indirectly. While self-effacing and friendly, he tended to deflect unsettling questions by changing the subject. All his life, Danny's love-hate attitude towards his career was manifested in an ambivalence that tested his most ardent fans. The same man who laughed and joked with friends was equally capable of asking his fellow musicians at pickup gigs, "Don't you just hate this shit?"

Danny's influence didn't lie so much in what he played but how he played it, which fascinates new generations of guitarists wanting to know what being a complete virtuoso means. Such mastery demands dedication to one truism: either live for the music or forget it. Danny grasped this notion better than many of his peers, who also appreciated the infectious energy and spunk that he brought to their projects. Titling an album *Unfinished Business* may have been one of Danny's most audacious and shrewdest moves, if only because the final vote has not yet been tallied—which is the main premise of this book. Danny Gatton's time is here: now let the story unfold.

—Ralph Heibutzki

From Anacostia to
Uptown (1945–1966)

*F*irst and foremost: Understanding Danny Gatton isn't possible without appreciating the mid-Atlantic region where he was born, raised, and made his musical reputation. Just as the Beatles are always considered Liverpool's favorite sons, Danny was indelibly defined by the Maryland, northern Virginia, and Washington, D.C., area that he called home. Most of his life proceeded there with few interruptions, save for the odd foray to places like California, where he briefly moved during the late '70s to attempt a living in the big-time music business.

But Danny never stayed away too long, nor did he stop paying homage to the area where he'd made his mark in clubs like Beneath It All, the Crazy Horse, and Desperado's. He titled his 1990 major-label release *88 Elmira St.* after the place where he'd grown up in Anacostia, Maryland. His best tribute, though, was the cover of *Unfinished Business* (1987)—one of his most acclaimed albums. It's an idealized representation of a twilit night at Danny's home in rural Accokeek, Maryland. Trees form a dense canopy over the garage, where two vintage cars from the '30s and '50s are parked. The right side is crammed full of auto parts, tools, and bric-a-brac; on the left, three wispy figures are jamming away on their instruments, in the shadow of yet another '30s-era hot rod. To all appearances they're just having a ball, safe from life's demands and distractions. That cover neatly summarizes what most fans and friends regard as the major cornerstones of Danny's life: cars, family, and music.

The diversity of Danny's home region is its most striking feature. The steep, angular hills and sharply cut mountains of rural Maryland and Virginia coexist with the tightly wound density of urban environments like Arlington, Virginia, and Washington, which revolve around the hum of business and professional life. And the venues that Danny played reflected

1

that diversity: at one end stood established theatres like Alexandria's Birchmere; at the other, shacks like Sam's Crab House in Clinton, Maryland, still fondly remembered for the beehived and go-go-booted ambiance that marked its brief heyday as a live venue in the '70s.

Danny Gatton was comfortable in both settings, and it was in those theatres and roadhouses that he spent much of his four decades crafting a guitar style celebrated for its intricate fingerpicking, lightning fretwork, and jaw-dropping virtuosity. Music has long been part of the area's life rhythms, and the scene has revolved around that well-respected but underpaid figure: the journeyman musician.

FROM A PROFESSIONAL-MUSIC STANDPOINT, the nation's capital is an isolated outpost. Unlike Los Angeles, Nashville, or New York, it has no music industry presence—there's no one hustling whatever might be the next big thing. As a result, the list of "usual suspects" who have broken out of the Washington scene is a short one; without his two Elektra albums, Danny's name might well have lagged behind those of Roy Buchanan, Emmylou Harris, Nils Lofgren, and Mary Chapin Carpenter.

"Washington's always been kind of an 'unknown hero' situation, although it's a very good music town," says clubowner Jack Jensen, a friend of Danny's for nearly 30 years. "A lot of good musicians came from here, and a lot of good musicians would pass through here. Depending on what part of town you went into, you'd have either rock or country."

Or maybe something else. A low profile seems to have given musicians in the nation's capital license to ignore trends and swim upstream, even if they may not earn more than a passing listen outside of that environment. Local labels have been few and far between, and the days of getting airplay on major radio stations like WHFS-FM—considered the most supportive outlet for homegrown musicians—are long gone.

Not that Danny Gatton cared much. Throughout his life, he always expressed a determination to do things his way. That desire had its roots in his upbringing. Danny's mother, Norma, always encouraged her children to pursue whatever reasonable ideas they had, and she was particularly supportive of her firstborn son. To this day, she remains fiercely proud of his talents and his untiring efforts to keep them before the public.

Born March 4, 1922, in Washington, Norma was working as a telephone operator when she met Dan Gatton, a sheet-metal worker who had played guitar in a dance band before World War II. Dan Senior's father, Arthur Gatton, had played fiddle, as had many of Dan's Welsh forebears. Norma's own father never really took to the Hawaiian guitar he had bought in the islands (having moved there after Hawaii became a U.S. territory). He loved music nonetheless and was happy to supply the sheet music for his wife, Marie, a self-taught musician who owned a baby grand piano. "We stood around every night after dinner and sang," Norma says. "My brother had a nice voice."

Music was a constant presence in Dan and Norma Gatton's southeast Washington apartment long before Danny Wood Gatton, Jr., was born on September 4, 1945. The family's musical world centered on their roll-top console record player and a disc collection that likely planted the seeds for Danny's famously eclectic tastes. "We were exposed to all kinds of music," Norma recalls. "Normally we just liked pop music, but we got interested in country music, so we were buying records of that. When Danny was young, we played all those records." Danny derived hours of enjoyment from the varied discs his parents bought, including trumpeter Harry James's virtuoso version of "Carnival of Venice"—and, more important, its showpiece flip-side, "Flight of the Bumblebee." "I would play that and Danny would say, 'Play it again, Mommy, play "Bumblebee" again!'" Norma says. "That's what Danny listened to when he was just two years old."

Dan Gatton, Sr., in the early '40s playing guitar in the Royalist Dance Orchestra—an experience he enjoyed until his country called for World War II.

When he wasn't absorbing Harry James or Bob Wills's brand of western swing, Danny was losing himself to the latest 45s that his sister Donna brought home and the work of such local guitar heroes as Charlie Byrd, Roy Clark, and Link Wray. His parents also played the big band sounds of Benny Goodman, with Charlie Christian on guitar. On the country side, he fell in with the likes of Chet Atkins and Merle Travis; when it was time for rock 'n' roll and rockabilly, he gleaned plenty of excitement from such hell-for-leather guitarslingers as Duane Eddy, Cliff Gallup of Gene Vincent's band, and Scotty Moore with Elvis. And Les Paul would prove to be a lasting influence.

According to Norma, Danny began playing guitar when he was nine or ten years old, around the time the family moved to 88 Elmira Street in Anacostia. The neighborhood boasted some formidable musicians. Across the street lived Al Perrotta, who wrote music for the U.S. Navy bands. "He had a son named Gussie," Norma says. "I don't know if he was Danny's age or a little older, but he was taking music lessons of some kind." Next to the Perrottas lived the Reids, whose teenage son Jack played guitar. Another neighbor played in the U.S. Air Force Band, and someone else played drums.

Next door at 98 Elmira Street lived Phil Zavarella, who would become a long-standing figure in Danny's life. Phil began working in his father Tony's Arlington, Virginia, music shop in 1965, and for more than 30 years they catered to musicians famous and obscure. (The store's landmark status was confirmed by the namecheck tucked away on the 1980 Evan Johns & the H-Bombs single "Giddy Up Girl.") As he cleaned out the store after its September 2001 closing, Phil pointed out "the Danny Gatton shrine"—an autographed promo poster for *88 Elmira St.*—the last reminder of a tightly knit world of small duplexes that had linked together families like the Gattons and the Zavarellas. "Danny's sister used to baby-sit for my brother and me," Phil recalls. "We were right next door. He was a few years older than me. I remember seeing the guitar cases and peeping in his basement window to watch him practice with bands—all of that good stuff."

Norma and Dan Senior had hemmed and hawed when their son first asked for music lessons. Norma recalls suggesting that he find someone close to home, since she didn't want him to go downtown. The Gattons found a teacher about five minutes from their house in Abe Rosenbloom, whom Danny later recalled as a better violinist than guitarist. "He couldn't play guitar well, although he sure could teach it," Gatton told Dan Forte of *Guitar Player*. "I did have to learn to read, when I took lessons from him, and all the music had the up-and-down pick strokes—that was very important." Danny was also taught to use his little finger properly, which would prove to be vital in his virtuosic style.

Danny with his Martin guitar, about 10–12 years old.

Once the lessons started, "he was into the music—it took over everything," says Norma. "That's all he wanted to do." There was no need to insist that Danny practice. He'd have the guitar in his hands for three or four hours per day after school, Norma told the *Washington Post*'s Richard Harrington, who wrote a 1991 article about Danny, called "The Fastest Guitar in the East." Norma says that the lessons didn't last longer than six months, because Danny found learning by doing more appealing than trying to filter techniques through somebody else's approach. Danny recalled that he quit after a friend showed him how to play "Wildwood Flower." "I said, 'If I can figure that out, I can figure out whatever else I want to play,'" he told Forte.

By seventh grade, Danny had joined his first band, the Lancers, which—like most teen combos—contented themselves with whacking out the Top 40 hits of the day. At 13, he signed up with Sophocles Pappas, who'd mainly established himself as a classical teacher, so the experience didn't go terribly well. Norma recalls Pappas saying, after only the third lesson, "You're wasting your money." When she asked why, he allegedly responded: "Because he only has to hear it once, and he can play it. I cannot teach him."

Danny told *Guitar Player* that he parted ways with his teacher because he didn't really care to study classical music: "I was much more interested in learning 'Sugarfoot Rag.'" Soon afterward, he made his first public appearance at the Cottage City Fire Department, with Dan Senior backing him on rhythm guitar. "They let Danny get onstage one night, and people threw money," Norma told Harrington. "I think that's when Danny's ears went up!"

Phil Zavarella credits Jack Reid as Danny's initial local inspiration, since he'd made it as "a local guitarslinger playing in the honky tonks."

Reid lived right across the street from the Gattons at 89 Elmira; his band the Thunderbirds practiced in the basement. Danny didn't take long to become an enthusiastic participant, as Reid later informed Mark Opsasnick, author of the D.C. scene overview *Capitol Rock*: "By around 1961 it got to the point where Gatton was playing ahead of me. Even at an early age Danny was an extremely good musician and a very, very good technical player. He was determined, and he was getting into taping and dubbing himself, and he would always practice his heart out."

According to Phil, "Jack custom-ordered a 1957 Les Paul Standard, left-handed, with the first left-handed Bigsby [arm] ever made. We marveled at that guitar for over 30 years, and I eventually sold it for Jack. He brought it in here and said, 'I hear this thing's worth a lot of money.' I said, 'Yes and no, Jack, because it's left-handed—that's a problem. If it was right-handed....'"

Reid's instrument wowed the neighborhood because "it was the first guitar that any of us ever saw with humbucking pickups on it," Phil says. "It was supposed to come with P-90s on it, but '57 was the first year that they put 'em on Les Pauls." When Reid quit playing in the late '60s, Gatton borrowed the guitar. "Danny flipped the nut over, strung it up right-handed, and played it for a long time," Phil says. (Reid's name later surfaced among *88 Elmira St.*'s list of acknowledgments, as did fellow Thunderbirds guitarist Gene Newport "for teaching me how to play by ear.")

When Danny started his lessons in 1954, he made do with a cheap Stella archtop—until his father got him a Martin 00-18. He hung onto that guitar until he was 12, when Dan Senior bought him a blonde Gibson ES-350 electric guitar, which suited another burgeoning interest: decoding the overdubs deployed on Bill Doggett's "Honky Tonk" and Les Paul & Mary Ford's pop classic "How High the Moon."

In an interview recorded to promote his second Elektra album, *Cruisin' Deuces*, Danny cited Charlie Christian's playing as "the first real music that I heard that I enjoyed." But nobody stood taller in the Gatton universe than the American guitar pioneer Les Paul, who'd made his name as a brilliant jazz guitarist during the '30s and '40s with a style built around rapid-fire runs, fluttering rhythms, and a freewheeling mixture of country, jazz and swing styles.

The elaborate multi-tracking used by the "Wizard of Waukesha" on records like "How High the Moon" and "Tiger Rag" assured him a place on the Gattons' turntable. "I was absolutely mesmerized by that sound," said Danny in the *Cruisin' Deuces* interview. Norma recalls how her son and Jack Reid spent countless hours trying to figure how the Wizard had worked his magic: "They each had a tape recorder. I don't know how they did it—tape it slow, I guess, and play it [with the] speed up—but they knew what Les Paul was doing. At an early age, they found out. It was amazing." Danny would slow his records to 33 ⅓, then 16 rpm—over and over again, until he could decipher a lick.

Liz Meyer, whose band would give Danny his first local exposure to D.C.'s country-rock audiences, remembers a story Danny liked to tell about his musical beginnings. "When he was hearing Les Paul & Mary Ford, he knew it was a duo, but he didn't know about overdubs—so he learned to play all those parts himself, as a nine-year-old." Whether Danny exaggerated or not, it seemed believable enough when Meyer watched him play, she says.

Norma describes her son as a "nitpicker," which isn't a negative term in her lexicon. She and her husband lived by the credo of "Do it right or not at all"; their son's internalization of those words would become a hallmark of his approach to both recording music and working on vintage cars, if not the way that he learned to live his life. "Danny was meticulous, and I don't fault him for that, because he was doing the right thing," Norma says.

When Danny was 13, his parents took him to Reliable Pawnbrokers on Ninth Street NW in Washington, where he bought a Vega Little Wonder five-string banjo. By the time he got home, Danny told Dan Forte, he could play "Foggy Mountain Breakdown." Though he'd never played a banjo before, Danny allowed, he'd prepared himself by practicing on his Martin with fingerpicks.

Danny's deft exploitation of his right hand to pull off rippling banjo rolls would prove to be a keystone of the hyperkinetic guitar style that would later awe clubbers and concertgoers alike. Danny previewed this mastery when he appeared on a local country music TV show, on which he played "Foggy Mountain Breakdown" so fast that the house band couldn't keep up. Asked how long he'd been playing, he stunned the host by responding, "Seven months."

ONE LAST ADDITION TO the Gatton family arrived amid all this musical activity: Danny's brother, Brent, born March 7, 1960. "I'm 15 years younger. I always figured I was the mistake," he jokes. "My sister was two years older than Danny, so there was a big-time difference there." Brent was too young for the Elmira Street era, of which he has no memories. He became aware of Danny's music as a four- and five-year-old, when his brother rehearsed with various bands in the basement of their home on Bernard Drive in Oxon Hill, Maryland. The Gatton family had moved from Elmira Street to Oxon Hill in 1962. Danny left when he got married, but his parents would remain there until the mid-'80s. (Norma moved to Alpharetta, Georgia, after her husband's death from cancer in April 1984.)

When he wasn't fooling around with music, Danny could be found working on cars. "He would have taken a hot rod instead of a new car, 'cause that's the kind of person he was," Norma says. In some ways, Danny's never-ending automotive tinkering would prove a metaphor for his musical life: both passions melded his natural exploratory bent with an all-consuming desire to hunt down the answer to whatever problem nagged away at him.

Norma fondly remembers the hours Danny spent on "this junky little Ford" he was trying to remodel. Her husband helped, and Norma eventually got involved, too. "I'm not into cars that much, but I upholstered the car for him in red velvet," she says. "I'd never done that, but it turned out real good." That was how the Gatton family operated. "We were helping him all the time, me and my husband," Norma explains. "I didn't get any encouragement as a child, and because of that, I encouraged all of them."

Brent would become aware of Danny's automotive bent when he turned 12 or 13. "Danny was always working on stuff. That's where our main connection was, that's what kept us close, for all the years," he says. Brent saw little of Danny as a teenager, unless they happened to be working on a car. "I didn't have much interest in music. I've never been a big record buyer, or anything like that." Now a singer and drummer, Brent freely admits that he didn't pursue music with the same intensity as Danny. "I took all kinds of lessons, but I never kept up with anything. I guess I had an interest as a kid, but not enough interest to really jump into it and practice full-time." (Brent would later rekindle that interest after meeting his second wife, Sherry, who'd been playing keyboards in bands.)

Danny in 1963 with his first hot-rod 1930 Model A. Throughout his life, Danny's passions would remain divided between playing music and restoring antique cars.

YOUNG DANNY'S WORLD BEGAN to revolve increasingly around the musical lifestyle, even if he didn't see it as a way of making a living. Dan Senior settled into the routine of shuttling his son around the southeast Washington and Maryland stomping grounds that would establish the parameters of Danny's world—where the rites of passage involved procuring a realistic-enough ID to claim the right to play there. "He played Saturday night school dances at the Catholic church," Norma says. "[The band lineups] just kept fading in and out, getting new people, and pretty soon, he's playing in a nightclub. He played some nice clubs. He was talented, what can you say?"

Bobby Hancock, who had been a 14-year-old guitarist with a Top 40 band called the Offbeats, remembers those days well. (Bobby is known as "No Relation" Hancock, to avoid confusion with the better-known but unrelated Billy Hancock, whom we'll meet in short order.) "When I left the band, Danny took my place. He was this skinny little 15-year-old kid, but he was just a phenomenal player. He was a cut above anything I'd ever heard anybody do in my life. Danny always said it was in '58 when he started playing with them, but I think it was more like '60."

Around that time, Danny also met Billy Windsor, who would become his bandmate two decades later. They met through Jack Jensen, who'd played bass in bands with Windsor and who would also become a lifelong friend of Gatton's. "I had a band, and Billy wasn't quite old enough to drive a car," Jensen says. "We lived in St. Mary, in Accokeek, and we started off being weekend warriors in '59, '60, somewhere in there." Windsor played rhythm guitar and sang, but somebody had to cover the lead parts. "There's where Danny came in," Jensen says.

Billy and his future second wife, Donna, knew Danny from their days at Washington's Ballou High School. The future "World's Greatest Unknown Guitar Player" wasn't a strong academic performer, according to his daughter, Holly. "Dad started out at Ballou in D.C., and then his parents moved out to the suburbs, and he attended Oxon Hill High. He didn't like Oxon Hill and missed his friends back at Ballou, so he would play hooky a lot and go hang out with the 'greasers.' The funniest thing is that he, of all people, got kicked out of band! He didn't do all that well academically …[but] even though he wasn't a stellar student, he was a voracious reader as an adult and had an incredible knowledge of Native American history and archaeology." (Danny started at Ballou, then graduated from Oxon Hill in June 1963 after his move there.)

Poised and polished for the camera, the Offbeats, Danny's first professional band, prepare to take the world by a storm in 1962. Left to right: Dick Heintze, John Broaddus, Ron MacDonald, Jerry Wallmark, Ernie Gorospe, and Danny Gatton.

When Bobby's departure left the Offbeats scratching for a new guitarist, his former bandmates—saxophonist John Broaddus, bassist Ernie Gorospe, and drummer Jerry Wallmark—placed an ad in the local teen paper. Danny responded, not knowing that everyone had three to five years on him—not that it mattered. "We had a practice session set up, and Ernie and I had to pick up John at the bus terminal," Wallmark recalls. The rehearsal was in Anacostia, at the end of Sousa Bridge.

When the trio returned to Ernie's house, they heard Danny and bassist Paul Kirkpatrick playing "Honky Tonk"—just like the record, to Wallmark's recollection. "He was a very, very shy kid, and just a phenomenal musician. You just stood there and listened with your mouth open." Bobby Hancock has no trouble ticking off the reasons why Danny stood out, even at such a tender age: "Much more advanced—technique, skill, comprehension, ability. The whole nine yards. There was no question that he had a gift from God, but he worked awful hard at honing that gift, too."

With Danny aboard, the Offbeats played whatever teen clubs and Catholic Youth Organization dances they could find. There were the odd adult venues, too, like the Club Log Tavern in Alexandria, Virginia, which Wallmark remembers as a very small bar. They spent four hours there on Saturday nights. The owner, Carl, constantly complained about the volume, but the band's take compensated for such annoyances, according to Broaddus: "We were making a lot of money, so we put up with that. It was $12 apiece."

Billy Hancock first heard about Danny's phenomenal ability from Mike Boyd, who'd gone to junior high with Gatton. "Mike was really good, a fine guitar player, and he looked up to Danny quite a bit," Billy says. Danny eventually came to see Billy's band at a club called the Devonshire Grill, on Wisconsin Avenue NW. "He looked like a little kid. He came in with some jock-looking guy and [future Jefferson Airplane bassist] Jack Casady, and we exchanged pleasantries."

The Offbeats carried on in their low-key fashion from 1961 to 1964. The band cut its first record for its members' reference only: according to Wallmark, the songs were instrumental renditions of the country standard "Tumblin' Tumbleweeds" backed with "Rainbow Rock." Vocalist Ronnie MacDonald joined shortly afterwards, and the band made another single with a Ray Haney tune "Beggar Man" and a cover of the country-blues weeper "Trouble in Mind" (later covered by piano pounder Jerry Lee Lewis). The 45s were recorded at Washington's Edgewood and Norwood studios, respectively, and scarcely saw much action, even around the local area. (*Capitol Rock* dates the "Beggar Man" single to 1961, while other sources cite the year as 1962.)

Ray Haney was a local TV personality who knew Dick Denham, a DJ at the Rockville, Maryland, radio station WINX. Denham was also an agent, and he helped the band get a gig in downtown Washington at the Champagne Room—where the downstairs bar was a strip joint. "They had exotic dancers before they decided they were going to bring in rock 'n' roll," MacDonald recalls. They started out playing on Fridays and Saturdays, which later expanded to six nights a week. "I didn't do three, because I was in school, and I think that Danny didn't do three," Broaddus says. But Wallmark recalls Danny playing there every night with himself and keyboardist Dick Heintze, who would become one of Danny's most important influences.

The experience lasted only for three or four months, until the Champagne Room went bankrupt. The Offbeats found a new gig at the Mayfair Lounge, which was right across from the Champagne Room (and next to the Warner Theatre) at 13th and F Streets. "That was, for years, a well-known jazz room, with some heavy jazz players," MacDonald says. Unfortunately, that club soon went under, too. By then, Danny was working with a number of bands, says Jensen, who started getting to know him better in 1963–64. He remembers seeing him working at another D.C. club, the Rocket Room. "Danny used to sit in with anybody, 'cause he could. He didn't need to rehearse—say what the tune was and he could fit in."

IN THE OFFBEATS, EVERYONE had input on the material, and Wallmark doesn't remember hearing many arguments about what they'd play and how they'd go about playing it. The band tried to separate itself by mixing jazz numbers with rock 'n' roll and R&B tunes, and nothing fazed Gatton. "Even before we met him, Danny had gotten to a point where the people he was going to for instruction ran out of stuff they could show him," Broaddus says. Gatton had to find inspiration elsewhere, such as jazz guitarist Charlie Byrd, who had a local TV show in Washington. Danny dissected Byrd's solo on "Homage to Charlie Christian," which later appeared on *Unfinished Business*. "From year one, I always figured I could play it all," Danny said in the *Cruisin' Deuces* interview. "I never could understand why certain players would limit themselves to just one style, 'cause I was always obsessed with learning everything."

Dick Heintze, already in his twenties while Gatton was still a shy 14-year-old, exerted the strongest pull of anyone in Danny's immediate circle. His musical roots "went back to some classical greats in Germany," according to Bobby Hancock. "Dick is the guy that Danny always looked up to and learned from." In *Guitar Player*, Danny recalled his late mentor as someone whose piano style was close to that of jazz great Oscar Peterson—"and on B-3 he was better than anybody I've ever heard," he said. "He was scary." Heintze was adept at whatever musical situation he joined, be it the schmaltzy supper-club jazz he'd play with Danny during the late '60s or the hard-rocking stuff he cranked out with Roy Buchanan's early-'70s road bands.

Heintze commanded respect for having any relevant musical skill at his fingertips, including the ability to sight-read and transpose on the spot. His and Danny's favorite game involved upping the ante after every chorus: if Heintze played eighth-notes, Danny had to respond with 16th-, 32nd-, and 64th-notes. No matter how hard Danny tried, however, Heintze invariably won these feverish exchanges. "Man, he was a real fire-breathing monster," Danny told Bill Milkowski in *Guitar World*. Bobby still treasures memories of the two playing jazz at "warp factor ten." "They'd start trading fours, and it was who could outdo the other," he says. "It was indescribable what would happen when those two guys stretched out."

For Bobby Hancock, nothing beat seeing Heintze put his natural abilities to their fullest possible use. "He had perfect pitch. The speedometer broke on his car, and he knew how fast he was going by what note his snow tires were humming. He was an amazing guy." Heintze's extraordinary prowess might well have assured him a bright future, had he not been struck down by the terrible muscle-wasting paroxysms of amyotrophic lateral sclerosis (better known as "Lou Gehrig's Disease"). "Like Danny, he was the most humble guy you ever met in your life," Bobby says. "He played with us one night at a big supper club over in Virginia. He wasn't regularly playing with us at that time, but Danny relished the chance. I didn't play many solos, for obvious reasons." Hancock finally got an opportunity on a simple country song. "Danny looked at me, teasing, and held his nose," Bobby says. "I'm the guy that looks up to Danny, okay? So the next time Danny played a solo, his hero Dick Heintze held *his* nose."

"I knew Dick pretty well in the latter years," Jack Jensen says. "Danny told me that he came from a strict German family. His father was a disciplinarian and really didn't give Dick a lot of credit—whatever he did, though, he turned out to be one hell of a piano and organ player." According to Broaddus, Heintze's father had trained him for ten years, starting at age four.

Listening to Danny's duels with Heintze reminded Bobby Hancock of a unique Gatton practice technique he'd observed years before. "As a little kid, he would use two little Revere tape recorders. He'd lay down a guitar track on one, play that track back while the other recorder was on, and play along with it." While lots of players created their own play-along tracks, Gatton went an extra step. "He'd play just *behind* [the first recorder], creating his own echo—that's where Danny was as a little kid, okay? Most guys would never even think about that."

Bobby owned evidence of these pre-teen recording feats on reel-to-reel tapes that he was allowed to copy, but he no longer has them. Years later, when they were playing in the Danny Gatton Band, they needed to make a demo but didn't have a spare tape. "Danny said, 'Let's use this tape'—one of my tapes, with all his recordings on it. He says, 'You can re-record that other stuff later.' So we used my tape, but I never had the opportunity to re-record it." The episode typifies many of Danny's lost studio moments, although Bobby still has "a real crude [early] tape that Mrs. Gatton sent me," which he cherishes.

Danny was just as unsentimental about his guitars. Bobby recalls a conversation with Dan Senior about what happened after Danny got his hands on his Gibson ES-350. "One of the first things he did, his dad told me, was take it all apart! Danny had to know how it worked. If he'd ever gotten his nose into computers, he'd have been a basket case, because he'd have to figure out that sucker, somehow. That's just how he was. He was very curious." That curiosity extended to guitar setup and tuning. Gatton told Dan Forte that he'd experimented with alternate tunings almost from the start: "I'd get Gibson Sonomatic strings and throw away the big *E*, use the *A* for an *E* and put a banjo string on top." He also liked to drop the low *E* to *D*.

THE EARLY '60s SAW Danny's musical world expand with his discovery of such jazz guitar masters as George Barnes and Wes Montgomery. He found their work much more inspiring than the pop tunes that filled the airwaves. The Beatles and their British Invasion compatriots didn't impress him. "Those bands played very simply, and I wanted to keep progressing as a player," Danny told *Pulse*'s Ted Drozdowski after the release of *Unfinished Business*. "If you don't play something new that's harder than what you can already play, you don't progress."

At 19, Danny caught what seemed like his first big break when Bobby Scott, who had written the hit "A Taste of Honey," suggested he come to New York and pursue a studio musician's career. But the city's ambiance scared Danny off, so he let the invitation drop. Bobby Hancock had been impressed by Danny's skill when they bumped into each other at a party. "I was at a dance one night, not playing," he says. "A couple of guys from the Offbeats were there, and they invited me to a pickin' party! This must have been '65 or '66, something like that. There were a bunch of players there. I just laid back and did my thing." Near the end of the party, Danny pulled out a new Gibson banjo he'd just acquired and Bobby picked up a flat-top. "I used to be a real big bluegrass fan," he says. "I'd never really played it, but I knew it in my head. Danny and I played some bluegrass tunes, and he and I really hit it off doing that."

Danny on a Washington, D.C., gig, circa 1965. Intense concentration on picking and positioning was a hallmark of Danny's performance style from the beginning.

By the mid-'60s, the Offbeats began to splinter as the pressures of real life—or, in MacDonald's case, other musical ventures—came calling. Broaddus quit first, in 1964. "We weren't doing a lot, " he says, "and I didn't have any aspirations to really go anywhere with music." Wallmark feels that Broaddus simply "wanted to play more than we were playing." But that's not the full story, either, according to Broaddus. When he first met Danny, he says, "I didn't realize how good he was; I didn't realize what I was in. I knew he was the best I'd ever seen, but that just speaks to how much I hadn't been around."

MacDonald left shortly after Broaddus, taking Heintze with him. The Off-beats replaced MacDonald with Sonny Gordon, an amateur songwriter who later made the transition to professional —he penned the Leslie Gore hit "Hey Now"—and moved to California, where he got involved with TV writing, according to Wallmark. The Offbeats worked with Gordon for another 12 to 18 months before breaking up in 1966. Broaddus and Gorospe became federal employees; Wallmark joined his brother's mechanical contracting company; and Heintze enlisted in the U.S. Army, where he conducted the orchestra, according to information compiled by Gorospe's son Steve (who runs a website on Danny). "I guess we just got disinterested, plus Danny and Dick Heintze wanted to move on—they needed to play six nights a week," Wallmark says.

In 1965, Danny and Dick Heintze got a gig as the Soul Mates on the Wilson Line, a cruise that ran on the Potomac River. (Casady, Heintze, and fellow Airplane guitarist Jorma Kaukonen had all grown up in Tenleytown, as MacDonald recalled for *Capitol Rock*; Casady had also passed through the ever-shifting Offbeats' lineups in 1962 and 1963.) "They had gambling in those days, and you could drink on the boat," says Roger McDuffie, who had worked in another area band, the Dominoes. They got to know each other after Danny called with an invitation to blow alto and tenor sax for a single available only on the boat, "Moonlight Cruise" b/w "How's Your Sister." "Funny thing is, Danny was into a lot of bass, so he mixed the bass way up," Roger laughs. "When you bought the record, it wouldn't play on anybody's jukebox—it would just go *boom-boom-boom!*"

Danny, Dick, and Roger spent three summers on the Wilson Line, with Jack Casady joining them during their second year, 1966. Although the boys appreciated Casady's towering musicality, they also derived much merriment from sartorial slips like the black tape he sported on his eyeglasses. In time, fate played its own joke: Casady hung around for a summer before he and Jorma Kaukonen, another guitarist on the local scene, went to try their luck in California's rapidly exploding music scene. "Jack wanted us to go out there with him, but we didn't go—we were so young," Roger recalls. "It wasn't six months later when he had that big hit record, 'Don't you want somebody to love!' "

To the boys on the Wilson Line, the breakout success of the Jefferson Airplane's "Somebody to Love" seemed all the more remarkable because it pointed toward a goal that Danny's parents had drilled into him as being unachievable: succeeding as a professional musician. Although there were no guarantees, there was no question that for Danny and his friends, the door of opportunity had creaked open a notch wider. How they wished to answer the next knock was up to them.

Danny & Roy at the Crossroads (1966–1968)

*D*anny's father insisted that he learn a trade, so he followed in Dan Senior's footsteps and became an apprentice sheet-metal worker. In 1964, he was banging sheet metal during the day and playing at night—and then he met 21-year-old Jan Firkin, the daughter of a military man who'd settled in Lynchburg, Virginia, after traveling around the world. Jan's forebears hailed from Germany, England, and Wales, while her maternal grandmother was a full-blooded Cherokee.

Jan started working for the National Science Foundation right out of high school, thanks to a work-study program that allowed NSF employees to attend college. This arrangement enabled Jan to take classes at George Washington University, where she majored in English and minored in French. "She went to classes at night and on her lunch hour for years, but quit a few credits shy of graduation when she had me in 1979," her daughter, Holly, says.

Danny entered Jan's life at the Foundation's building on 18th and G Streets. "He was 19 and installing air-conditioning ducts in the building," Holly says. "Mom was 21. They first crossed paths in the coffee shop. Dad commented on the fact that both of them liked apple pie and coffee for breakfast. But Mom wasn't too enamored of Dad after he tried to kiss her on their first date."

"When I first met him, I didn't like him at all," Jan says. "I thought he was too forward, in my way of thinking, but I was not very experienced. I did not have one date in high school, so anything was forward to me." After their first date, Jan swore to one of her friends that they'd never go out again. What happened, then? "He just charmed me. He was so sweet—he liked nature, and I did, too. We liked very simple things: going down to the water to eat crabs, walking in the woods, and looking for tadpoles."

Danny represented the polar opposite of the people that Jan had met in college, where "it was all about money and business, and no time to stop and smell the flowers."

Danny's maturity sparked the initial attraction. "Mom thought he was about 25, not 19," Holly says. "He was also handsome and a hard worker. She had no idea he was a musician, or she would not have dated him. You know those musicians...." The courtship lasted four years.

Danny and Jan got married on June 17, 1968. Since there was no money for a big wedding, they settled for a simple civil ceremony. Jan went off on her lunch hour, after leaving a note to explain her absence, Holly says. "They drove to Upper Marlboro to a female justice of the peace, but before they got there, my dad turned the car around three times because my mom kept changing her mind about getting married. Finally, on the third time, Dad said if they didn't do it then they were never going to, so Mom made up her mind and they were married." Such left-field charm and bulldog persistence could overcome innumerable objections, as Phil Zavarella recalls: "That was one thing about Danny—if he wanted this, he would have it. He would have it, no matter what it took."

Jan attributes the day's difficulties to reticence about leaving her family, which included nine brothers and sisters. "I got an apartment once. I was there for one day, and then I went back to my mother and father's house. I was really attached to my family, so it was difficult to make that break."

Soon after the wedding, Danny informed his new wife that he wouldn't be cutting sheet metal any longer—he was going to play music full time instead. "I didn't say that Jan wouldn't have married me if she thought I played music full time...but she had no idea that's what I wanted to do for a living," Danny told Richard Harrington. "Fooled her—she's real mad now!"

Danny's reluctance to cut up his hands was understandable enough, especially for a guitarist of his talent, even if he wasn't the first (or last) musician to juggle the demands of a day job. He'd actually gotten a first glimpse of the musician's lifestyle before getting married, when he'd donned a tux for a year-long road trip with soul man Bobby Charles. Danny recalled most of their gigs being in the Midwest, although he also got his first peek at the country music mecca of Nashville, where he dreamed of being a session man.

The excursion produced an album, *Bobby Charles Invades the Wells Fargo Lounge* (1968), which is often touted as Danny's first recorded appearance (a claim belied by his earlier contributions to the Offbeats and Soul Mates singles). More accurately, it's his first appearance on an album, although he got only one real chance to break out, a solo reading of "Malagueña." He's confined to a supporting role on the remaining tracks.

Bobby Charles AND
Kenny Gordon REVUE

Danny (bottom left) in 1966 with the Bobby Charles and Kenny Gordon Revue, with whom he logged his first major road mileage across the U.S.

The cover screams of lounge kitsch: Danny can be seen second from right, cradling his guitar, decked out in the same tuxedo and bow tie that his colleagues are wearing. The dress may have reflected someone's notion of collective discipline, but matching outfits were fast becoming an unhip anachronism in the psychedelic era. Even so, the album's scarcity has ensured a steady demand among collectors, especially on the online auction service eBay. (One auction from June 17, 2002, featured eight bidders, with the winner shelling out $89.)

Danny's oft-stated antipathy toward touring was cemented when he spent a summer on the road with country singer Sonny James. He recounted to Harrington that the first time he'd begun "smelling diesel fuel, wearing somebody else's too-tight clothes, and hawking records between shows, I said, 'This ain't me, Jim.'" He'd uphold that vow for most of his life, except for a few '70s and '80s outings (with James, again, and Roger Miller) and a three-month summer and fall outing for his second Elektra album, *Cruisin' Deuces* (1993).

Even offers from such certified heavyweights as Creedence Clearwater Revival's John Fogerty and Mel Tillis couldn't lure Danny onto the road. Admirable as this stance sounded, it also left Danny without a broad base of exposure outside his immediate stomping grounds—something he'd struggle with throughout his life. Some associates believe that the reluctance to travel implied difficulties in Danny and Jan's relationship. This reasoning also holds that Jan's absence from gigs showed apathy toward Danny's music. Norma, for one, asserts, "She never cared anything about his music, period—still doesn't."

Norma has little more to say about Jan, following litigation that shut down her NRG Records label, which she'd devised as a promotional outlet for Danny's music. (The name came from her initials.) Norma's solitary operation had quietly grown into a profitable business until Jan emerged in control of the Gatton legacy, following a settlement. We will return to that subject later, but it's worth noting here that NRG was an important factor in Danny's life as a recording artist.

Norma says the couple's main interest centered on antiques, and she recalls Jan being particularly fond of rare black artists' works. "She liked to go to flea markets, and so did he. He was looking for his thing and she was looking for hers, so that's the only bind that I see they really had." According to Holly, her parents' antique-collecting penchant didn't begin until they had been married for several years, "although Dad always loved antique cars. They shared a common love of nature and spent weekends out in the woods and parks, hunting for tadpoles and snakes and such." The couple also enjoyed driving around, sight-seeing and eating crabs, which is how the family ended up living in Newburg, Holly says.

Jan's defenders emphasize that she married Danny the man, not Danny the guitar player—a distinction not readily understood by those who played with him. Liz Meyer, whose band gave Danny some of his first major local exposure, sympathizes with Jan's predicament. "His wife was never happy that he was a musician," she says. "She married a construction worker who worked five days a week and brought home a good paycheck—and suddenly morphed into someone who was gone every night, coming home with very little money! She had a good job and was paying all the bills."

Jan disputes that notion. "I didn't think anything about it—I thought it was great, if that's what he wanted to do. It sounded kind of exciting. The money was minuscule: $50, maybe, for a gig. It never bothered me, but it bothered him a lot, because he came from a family where the wife is supposed to stay home. He had old-fashioned values." If anything, Jan felt an obligation to work so her husband could pursue his dream. "I never, ever asked him not to do it, or to find something else. My girlfriends would say, 'This is horrible,' but I didn't think that way."

Other friends say that Danny and Jan's relationship may have been a complex one, but no harder than anyone else's. "She worked a job; Danny played music and pretty much spent the money he made on his stuff," Bobby Hancock says. "They were a typical husband and wife. I think they were very committed to each other. They got married and that was it. They stuck it out, through thick and thin."

Jan's daily commute to Washington (and later to Roslyn, after the office moved) epitomized the physical logistics that she withstood for 38 years, until she retired from her computer specialist's job in 1998. The carpools, construction zones, and traffic jams around the Beltway worsened after the Gattons moved to Newburg in 1988. "It was probably a two-hour ride for her to get to work," Bobby says. "Jan was up at four o'clock in the morning and got home after six o'clock at night. When she was home, he was playing."

Danny spent most of his life trying to reconcile his feelings about the gap between their incomes, with which Jack Jensen sympathized. "Danny felt guilty about that, in a lot of ways—that she was the big provider," he says. "He'd have windfalls here or there, but she was the constant." He would try to reassure Danny by reminding him, "Hey, pal, you're a genius—there's a difference here."

As different as they were, the Gattons shared a fierce desire for privacy. Contacting Danny could be a daunting task because of "all the people always calling his house, bugging him, and wanting a piece of his time," Bobby says. "Very few of us ever had his phone number, and when too many people got it, he changed it again." Many of those calls followed brief encounters at the nightclubs and beer joints where Danny plied his trade. The people who met him in such places assumed that a phone number attached to a casual after-hours conversation presumed a real friendship. It was a tall order for anyone to fill, and Bobby remembers hearing Danny lament: "I'm a king in the bar room and a bum in the grocery store."

Phil Zavarella jokes that the couple met during "the only job Danny held for more than two seconds." On a more serious note, he feels that without Jan's stable, predictable income, Danny might have had a tougher time following his muse. They often discussed this, which led to some surprising conversational turns. "I don't know if I should sugarcoat this," he says, "but I guess I'll just tell it like it is. Music? Danny wasn't into it. Never did anything for him. It was a life of hunger, and thank God for his wife—she was the foundation of that whole thing, because poor Danny was cursed with that artist mentality. It really is a curse, and he talked about it a lot."

Soon after their marriage, the couple moved into an apartment in Marlowe Heights, Maryland. "They were asked to leave after Dad kept the downstairs neighbors up at night walking around on the wood floors after he got home from gigs," according to Holly. They eventually found another apartment in the area, but had to lie about Danny's occupation. "Landlords discriminated against musicians even then," Holly adds. "So they said he was a music teacher." Jan had to swear that Danny wouldn't teach anybody in the apartment.

Danny would tell his friends, "Poor Jan—she married a sheet-metal worker who turned into a musician." "I heard him say that more than once," Bobby says. "In defense of her, he'd say, 'When she married me, I was a sheet-metal worker.' His father had said, 'You can be a player, but you're going to get that skill under your belt.' So he did his sheet-metal apprenticeship, and after he got his journeyman's card he never banged another piece of tin."

According to Jerry Wallmark, the crunch came on Danny's last day as an apprentice. "I guess his boss sent him down for breakfast—like they do with all the apprentices—and he refused to do it. His boss turned him in to the union, and he got reprimanded for it, so Danny says, 'Up yours, I'll see ya later.'" (Jan remembers a different outcome, in which Danny's uncle fired him, allegedly for sleeping on the job.)

At one point in 1969 Danny and Jan went to Seattle, along with Dick Heintze, ostensibly to play on an album being financed by a wealthy woman. As Jan remembers it, the woman was looking for a band to support her featured artist, a piano player, and there might even be an album deal. The affair ended with everyone going home after about three months. "It was like so many other things that he got involved in," Jan says: the gap between promise and delivery amounted to a chasm.

From the start, Jan detected an ambivalence in Danny about what he wanted. She remembers seeing him cry at a gig after he won applause for his breakneck speed on "Orange Blossom Special." And he didn't want any part of family get-togethers. "Norma would try to have him play for the relatives, and he would get furious," Jan says. Other than Danny's uncle, she never met any of his relatives until after Dan Senior's death.

Norma was upset by these dynamics, and she once called to give Jan an earful about them. "She said, 'It's the wife who sets these rules, who sends the birthday cards and the Christmas cards,'" Jan recalls. She responded, "If he doesn't want to buy a birthday card, then I'm not buying it." Jan tried to stay out of the fray, figuring that Danny could handle the situation with his mother—a view that she would hold until nearly a decade later, when a frightening experience with a gun would change everything.

FRESH FROM HIS LOUNGE GIG with Bobby Charles, Danny knew that something had to give: rock's increasing penchant for extended improvisation was leaving the world of the tuxedo band behind, and if the British Invasion's eight-bars-and-out ethic had been bad news for guitar players, the new era promised a bonanza for anyone who could solo over a two-chord vamp. Explosive power trios like Cream and the Jimi Hendrix Experience had freed bassists and drummers to compete with guitarists for the instrumental voice of their bands. No longer would audiences sit for somebody plunking out a bare-bones solo with so many bands pushing the boundaries of modal-based, often mantra-like improvisation—groups like the Paul Butterfield Blues Band ("East-West"), the Doors ("Light My Fire"), the Grateful Dead ("Dark Star"), and Love ("Revelation").

The new era promised a standard of virtuosity unheard of in the '50s, with its never-ending stream of songs based on the I-IV-V chord trinity. How frustrating, then, for Danny and Dick Heintze to spend their nights and weekends grinding out schmaltzy jazz or whatever Top 40 tunes were happening. So it wasn't surprising that they jumped at the chance to rejoin Ronnie MacDonald in 1967 in a new group called the Take Five Combo.

They started in Bethesda, Maryland, and then moved on to a Washington club called the Pall Mall, formerly the jazz club Charlie's. (Paul Lucas had renamed the club after buying it.) Danny's explosive interplay with Heintze quickly became the band's hottest ticket, MacDonald says: "I'd never seen anybody do it with that much precision—exactly the same note, the same phrasing, the same time."

The band's priorities changed after the owner of Tom Sarris's Orleans House eyeballed them. "He came in and said, 'I really like you guys, I want you to play my restaurant. And by the way, I don't want you to play any rock 'n' roll,'" MacDonald recalls. "Danny's eyes got big, and so did Heintze's." Phil Zavarella's brother Mike joined on upright bass, "and Danny and Dick, they were in heaven. We were playing jazz all night long, and we were off at ten o'clock every night. We were there for a year, maybe a year and a half."

Danny in the Take Five band, circa 1969. While blues, jazz, and rock musicians were pushing instrumental expression to the limit, Danny was playing background music for the local "supper jazz" set.

Bobby Hancock was among the regulars at the Orleans House, which was in Arlington. (He recalls the band's name differently, saying it was East Coast Offering or East Coast Express.) Bobby says "supper jazz" was always on their menu. "That would run at least through dinner, and then there would be dancing afterwards." When they weren't holding down the supper-club fort, Danny, Heintze, MacDonald, and Roger McDuffie would do Top 40 covers at Gus & Johns in Clinton, Maryland. Heintze used the organ's foot pedals to cover for the lack of a bassist, and Danny even got down behind the drums sometimes. "Danny played a great shuffle," Roger says.

Local guitarist Joe Tass wasn't impressed by the Take Five Combo—after all, he'd just met Roy Buchanan, widely acknowledged as the man to beat on guitar. But when Tass and some pals were hunting around for gigs, they paused to listen more closely to Gatton's band at one venue. "They were playing 'Never on Sunday,' which is like a cha-cha," he recalls. "There's Dick Heintze, a monster keyboard player, but listening to that I'm saying, 'Damn, they're playing old people's music.'" Danny then swooped through the fast "mandolin parts" he'd devised for the "Zorba the Greek" theme.

"I said, 'Damn, this guy can fuckin' play! What a monster!'" Tass and company departed, figuring that if the management demanded such ability, they'd better find a gig elsewhere.

Phil Zavarella had missed much of this action, having moved to Oxon Hill in 1959. Norma and Dan Senior bought their own home there in 1962, but Danny didn't see Phil for seven more years; when he did, the occasion proved sufficiently memorable to make up for lost time.

Phil had spent much of his high school downtime in Marshal Hall's parking lot. "We used to drive down there, make sure we had enough gas to get back, gamble all our nickels and dimes, and drink beer," he laughs. "One night, this figure came walking into the parking lot: 'Hey, you guys got any extra beer?' I looked: 'Danny?' He goes: 'Phil?' The next 24 hours was just a big drunk fest." The reunion turned into an all-nighter, because Danny's parents were out of town. Phil spent the time perusing his old buddy's guitar collection and catching up on the band's doings at the Orleans House. "They were making $280 a week, in the '60s," Phil says. "They were the fattest musicians in town. And they were getting off when most people were playing their second set."

Soon after, Danny bought a Martin D-28 acoustic from Phil. The transaction was something of a fluke. "I was never a Martin dealer, but I got it through a dealer friend," Phil says. Phil was known for his access to quality instruments. "I had a collection second to none. I had a '59 'burst [Les Paul], which is a $100,000 guitar today. I had three of them—and I had less than $400 in all three. I sold them, brilliantly, at the $10,000 level."

Recalling other missed opportunities, Phil tells a story about trying to get Danny a gig in the U.S. Air Force Band. "Right around '70, we had it all arranged for Danny to get in—but guess what? He didn't read music. Every note they play, even in their jazz bands and their rock bands, is written on a piece of paper." Brent Gatton confirms the story, with Gus Perrotta being the connection. The issue wasn't exactly a new one: while touring with Bobby Charles, Danny had been approached by big-band leader Woody Herman to join his Thundering Herd, a job he'd rejected for similar reasons.

Such stumbling blocks sometimes had a comical effect. One time, according to Phil, Danny was preparing for a session when some sheet music was put in front of him. Without a word, Danny reached over and turned the page upside down. "The guy goes, 'What're you doing, man?'" Phil says. "Danny says, 'That's what you might as well have done with it. I can't read that!'"

Georgetown attorney James "Spike" Ostmann—who helped Norma set up her NRG label—thinks that Danny's shortcomings in that area might actually have been an asset. "I once said, 'Why don't you learn?' He said, 'I don't want to learn, because it would take the magic out of it.' That's an interesting point, because if I hear a song and like it, once I've learned it, it's lost something. It doesn't have that mystery to it."

BUT WHY BOTHER LEARNING to read notes off a music stand when the local scene offered so much steady work? All Danny had to do was look at Roy Buchanan, whose breakout from the bar and roadhouse circuit seemingly exemplified the hard-working journeyman's steady march from nowhere to somewhere.

Especially in the Washington area, Buchanan's name remains forever intertwined with Danny's, and the immediate parallels are obvious. Both men had garnered larger-than-life local reputations before the outside world paid attention; both drove their tone, technique, and instruments to new peaks; both showed some ambivalence toward their profession's demands; both used a natural reserve to keep unfamiliar forces and people at bay; and both died too young amid unfathomably tragic circumstances.

The two men were rivals, which made them the stars of yarns about the lengths they'd go to steal licks. The more adventurous whisperers had them catching each other's gigs in disguises, or having confederates call up and leave a pay phone off the hook—presumably so the cannier rival could incorporate some new six-string dynamite into his arsenal.

The closer the trail gets to Buchanan, the louder the sparrows chirp in the wilderness. Shouldn't Danny have been a guest on the November 8, 1971, PBS-TV special that did so much to break Buchanan nationally? Hadn't his wife, Judy, urged the producers to forget about Danny, dismissing him as a Buchanan copyist? Not so, according to the show's producer, John Adams. "Danny Gatton was never considered," he says. "It was always, at Roy's suggestion, Nils Lofgren. Nils was a protégé of Roy's, in many ways, as was Danny, at one point."

The two men started off on the wrong foot almost immediately, when Danny saw Roy in 1968 at Georgetown's Silver Dollar Saloon. Bobby Jones—who later played drums with Buchanan—hasn't forgotten, because he recalls taking Danny there. "He was the famous Roy Buchanan, and here was the unheard-of, up-and-coming Danny Gatton," Jones says. "Roy was the fellow that never gave away anything from the stage—he didn't play much more than he had to, a lot of the time, particularly if he felt somebody was listening."

Danny sat quietly for a couple of hours and finally said, "All right, Buchanan, if you're supposed to be so great, why in the hell don't you play something?" "Oh, Roy didn't like that at all!" Jones says. "That sort of started a love/hate feud with him. I think Danny went on and tried to out-Roy Roy, which was impossible, but all around Danny was a much better guitar player. He was more clean and precise, and more well-rounded. Roy was more into the blues-type thing; he was a monster, and creative when he was on a roll.... Over the years, they developed a certain mutual respect for each other, but not really a great friendship."

MacDonald remembers the night, because he and Heintze were there. "Roy throws this '54 Tele at him. Danny gets up onstage, picks it up, and says, 'Hold on, this is really out of tune!' You could see the steam coming out of Roy's head." Roger McDuffie, who was also there, remembers telling Danny about Buchanan when they were working together on the boat. "I didn't know what a Tele was in those days," he says. "I told Danny, 'He plays this little white guitar.'" Roger says the Silver Dollar was packed when they arrived. "We're listening for a little while, and then Danny says, 'Well, go tell him to play something good.'"

On hearing this, Buchanan stopped dead to inform the regulars, "We've got a guy in here—what's his name?—a guy named Danny Gatton who told me to play something I know." If Danny could do better, Roy went on, then he was welcome to show everybody—onstage. "Well, here comes Danny," Roger continues. "They went back into this blues, and it was like something you never heard. Danny just burned the sonfoabitch up."

Gatton then put down the guitar and disappeared into the crowd, which was still applauding him boisterously. Roger swears that Danny switched over to playing a Telecaster right away. Other associates like Billy Hancock maintain that Danny didn't make the change until 1971. Before then, Billy had seen him only with archtops, like his Gibson L5, "and he never bent any strings. He was very much a non-rock player."

Guitarist Lance Quinn—who'd later work with Danny on a tour with Robert Gordon—supports that assertion. He was attending college in the mid-'60s when a friend "took me away from Duane Eddy and the Ventures, and into the blues," he says. After busting his dorm curfew to see Buchanan, Quinn became aware of Danny through local word-of-mouth. He saw him at a Virginia club in 1967, playing a Les Paul with a cover band. "He wasn't playing that Tele style that he's so well-known for, but he was just amazing."

Hearing Buchanan undoubtedly had an affect on Danny. For one thing, he told *Guitar Player*, before seeing Roy he'd always used super-low action and medium-sized Fender thin picks. After seeing him, he changed to "jacked-up action and little picks." But to what degree did each man influence the other?

Norma's not sure the question really matters. Although not seeing as much of her son after his marriage ("he was busy with his own life; once in a while, he'd stop by"), Norma was aware of the Buchanan connection and says that her son always respected the other guitarist. Like others who crossed Roy's path, she had little trouble picking up on his fragile emotional state. "I don't know how to define it. I'd feel sorry for him," she says. "It was like there was a sadness around him—melancholy, I'd say. He was a nice person, according to Danny. Danny didn't have any trouble with him."

Sometimes, Buchanan would make the trip out to Danny's Alexandria home, where they'd drink beer, hang out, and even play a little bit. On one occasion, though, Buchanan had an encounter with Danny's baby raccoon. "Roy's wife had given him a new coat for Christmas," says Roger McDuffie. "He had it on the back of a chair, and nobody noticed what the raccoon was doing. The raccoon removed every button from Roy's coat and carried it up to a hole in the ceiling. When it came time to go home, Roy picked up his brand-new coat, and it didn't have a button on it. He was very pissed. It was freezing out. We drove him home—without buttons."

The Gatton-Buchanan relationship was characterized by an uneasy, often frosty, mutual détente. Many of Danny's musical associates have said that he was disappointed in not finding a greater friendship, "but Roy was going into some deep, dark place where Danny couldn't go," Jan says. "From what I've heard, it was just a spiral downward. He became impossible to talk with, from what Danny said. He wasn't in the real world anymore." Jan believes that Buchanan reached the point where normal conversation wasn't possible, whereas Danny was always more approachable. "A lot of people told me—after he died—how accepting he was," Jan says. "But this was also very wearing on him. He would be so tired at the end of a show, but he was always receptive."

Jan remembers someone saying, "You know what? I introduced myself, and a year later he remembered my name—that was so amazing." Unlike his moodier counterpart, Danny rarely refused to talk with people. Although he enjoyed being by himself, "whether he was onstage or offstage, he was for the people," Jan says. "They could come up to him. He couldn't really hide—he wouldn't hide."

Of course, Danny could knock other players sideways, too. John Broaddus recalls an incident from the late '60s when he was playing the Crossroads with a band that included Boogie Nolan, who'd been the hot guitarist from Billy Hancock's neighborhood. "I don't think Danny was that well-known yet—at least Boogie didn't seem to know what he was dealing with," Broaddus says. "We had a keyboard guy, he couldn't make it, so Dick Heintze sat in." Then Danny came by, and Broaddus asked, "Boogie, do you mind if he sits in? He's rather good." No problem, Nolan assured him. "Danny cranked something up. I don't remember what the hell it was, but Boogie wouldn't get onstage. And this guy was really full of himself, too. I don't think Danny was trying to put him down. At that point, he was just trying to do his thing."

Ed Eastridge says, "I don't know what Danny did when he wasn't at the studio—I know the guy must have practiced a lot—but I couldn't picture him sitting down and listening to Roy Buchanan licks." Eastridge adds that Danny's influences were more likely to be horn players or keyboardists; the guitarists that he absorbed came from the jazz realm, like Les Paul and Charlie Christian. Danny also had a strong affinity for country pickers like Roy Nichols—who played lead guitar for Merle Haggard—and rock 'n' roll pioneers like Elvis's main man, Scotty Moore.

The connection between the genres seems odd until you think about where they intersect, Eastridge says. "A lot of jazz players had started out in country music. Back in the '50s, country was real popular. In rural areas, sometimes it was all you could hear on the radio: Grand Ole Opry and stuff like that. I've heard a lot of jazz guys cite country music [as an influence], even black guys." Billy Hancock adds a few names to bolster the case: "Danny knew who Grady Martin was; Merle Travis and Jimmy Bryant, too. Hank Garland was one of his big heroes."

Western swing drew from both genres. "They're into big chords," Eastridge says. "They're into ninths and thirteenths—they like those harmonies. I loved to hear Danny play those things on a Fender lap slide. He was so good on that thing." (A good snapshot can be found on "Lotta Lovin'" from *Portraits*, the compilation of studio and live material that Eastridge assembled after Danny's death.)

Former *Guitar Player* editor Tom Wheeler believes that it's logical to wonder about Buchanan's influence on Danny, but says that's only part of the story. "It's certainly reasonable to point out the ways in which their paths crossed over the years. It would be silly not to," he says. "But it's not like Danny Gatton was unaware of James Burton or Jimmy Bryant—other people who played the Telecaster." Anyone who's ever seen Danny's instructional videos is aware of his rockabilly fingerpicking style on "Mystery Train," where he sets up a steady drone on the low *E* string, freeing his middle, index, and ring fingers to do the lead work. "That style is very much tied up with the Telecaster," Wheeler says. "Not exclusively, but it's associated with it."

Joe Tass asserts that hearing Buchanan did make Gatton alter his style. He met Danny after Roy left the Crossroads for good in 1971. Danny happened to be filling in for a week with a country band, and he said to Tass: "If you like Roy, you'll hate me." (At least he managed to play guitar and bass with Roy, though.) At that time, Danny was playing a Les Paul. "I spent maybe three hours down there, talking to him about guitars, amplifiers, and so forth," Tass says. "Roy could play all those rockabilly jazz licks. Danny got it all from Roy, because [before he heard him] he never played with a lot of treble, never played with that style." (Tass also believes Danny's ambidextrous nature enabled him to gallop so fluently over the fretboard.)

Tom Principato thinks that Danny didn't copy Buchanan but simply assimilated Roy's better qualities into his own style. "Honestly, I don't really see that Danny influenced Roy very much," he says. "I just think that Danny was heavily influenced by Roy, took what Roy started and ran with it. He went a lot farther, in a lot of ways—went on more tangents. Roy wrote the book, and Danny put a new chapter in it."

Principato's friend and '70s-era guitar partner Pete Kennedy believes that Buchanan's most lasting imprint on Danny was the guitar he wound up playing. Kennedy remembers hearing the story while hanging out in Danny's garage one day, getting some repair work done on a guitar. "He told me that when he was growing up, he always played Gibson guitars on the neck pickup. He was interested only in western swing and organ-trio jazz; he had no desire to play country music, or any kind of trebly, twangy-type stuff. But as soon as he heard Roy, something just clicked, and he got the whole Telecaster treble-pickup thing." Once he saw Buchanan at work, Danny broke out his '52 Tele "and immediately mastered that style without ever having played it before, with all the bending in tune," Kennedy says. "I'd say that he definitely got that style from Roy. He didn't have any bones about saying that Roy had been there first."

Danny was following a long, honored line of Tele players like James Burton, Fred Carter, Roy Nichols, and Robbie Robertson. But none of them had played jazz, which made Danny's use of the guitar for that genre so noteworthy, according to Kennedy. "Roy played some jazz chords, but in the context of western swing, rather than coming from a totally jazz perspective." As far as Kennedy could tell, that's why Danny wasn't interested in rock music, although he definitely loved classic '50s artists like the Everly Brothers and Buddy Holly. "I don't think he was into Hendrix or Clapton, because they were coming from a blues perspective, whereas Danny was working his way back through jazz."

Danny's melodic approach also set him apart from his bluesier peers. No matter how fast Danny played, he always played a melody, Kennedy says, while blues tends to be more riff-oriented music. "You find that pentatonic 'box,' as they call it, and play different riffs in that box," he says.

"Danny played by hearing a melody in his head and then playing that melody, so that would take him outside the realm of blues pretty quickly."

Some crucial differences should also be considered. Commercially, at least, Buchanan's never-ending roadwork had gotten him off to a faster start in his career. Danny's stay-at-home policy, on the other hand, meant that a larger audience would wait longer to find out about him. And being a sideman didn't suit Danny's fierce independence, as his few experiences in that arena bore out.

And perhaps Buchanan was less ambiguous about the musician's life. Right from the start, Danny seemed uncertain about where he'd take his natural talent. Phil Zavarella felt few people understood the dedication needed to reach such a consistent level of virtuosity; people like Danny "spent eight, ten hours a *day* on their instruments," he says. Phil and Danny hung around each other a lot, especially in the early '70s. "I went to every gig," Phil says. "Every night he wasn't playing, we were either eating crabs or working on cars." The conversation could take some surprising turns when they talked about music. When Phil asked what crossed Danny's mind during a set, it elicited an unusual response: "Not on what I'm doin'! I'm thinking about what I'm going to do to my car next, or who's going to give me a cigarette out of the audience, or who's going to give me my next beer." Such conversations gave Phil reason to suspect that Danny couldn't reconcile the disconnect between the never-ending compliments and the financial reality of his life. "You hear everywhere that you go: 'You're the greatest thing in the world,'" Phil scoffs. "Well, pay me! Y'know, give me some money for this—I'm over here making 40 bucks, maybe.' He just suffered with that whole thing. I know that, and I believe that."

Other crucial differences come down to style. Buchanan's immersion in the blues-rock tradition remained a constant throughout his professional life, while Danny's nightly genre-go-round was his most obvious calling card. Both men also parted company in how they presented themselves. Buchanan's earliest public statements often suggested a myth-making bent, such as his tale of being approached to join the Rolling Stones following Brian Jones's death in 1969. Danny, on the other hand, felt no need to create a personality cult or cover whatever tracks he'd left in the past. His introversion ruled out a full-bore accounting of every move he'd made, but only if the subject involved himself. Otherwise, he didn't mind opening up his trick bag—or showing how he pulled off a particular lick that he could play in his sleep, with far greater articulation than most questioners could muster.

Danny could never confine himself to one musical style. Bobby Hancock recalls a recording project they did together in the late '60s. "Danny and I went into this little studio in some guy's house over in Virginia. It was a four-track studio, and we laid down a bluegrass album," he says. Danny played guitar, bass, and banjo, while Bobby added guitar and mandolin. The material they put on tape might have given bluegrass purists the shakes: Bobby remembers tackling Lonnie Mack's "Memphis" and Hank Williams's "Kaw-Liga," among other songs. They especially had fun putting a unique spin on the Williams tune. "This was back in the days when everything was psychedelic," Bobby says. "We called it 'Psy-Kaw-Liga'—psychedelic bluegrass! We'd do anything you could think of: take the strings off the neck, make weird sounds. We played all kinds of crazy stuff; Danny and I would play at outrageous speed." (Norma Gatton had planned on reissuing a couple of tracks from that tape on *Caviar and Grits*, an album intended to showcase her son's banjo-, dobro-, and mandolin-picking abilities; it was to be her final release, until the lawsuit scuttled the project.)

That bluegrass project jump-started an informal tradition that continued through Gatton's life. "I guess I've had the opportunity to play with Danny Gatton for fun more than anybody," Bobby reckons. "I used to be in the plumbing business, and he'd come over to my shop in the afternoons. Later, when he had his house in Accokeek, I'd stop by. He was doing his usual thing out in the garage, wrenching on his cars, and we'd go buy a six-pack and break out a couple of guitars."

In some people's eyes, Danny's life appeared to be growing highly compartmentalized, with car buddies over here and music buddies over there. Some relationships did cross over; in addition to Bobby Hancock, there were Jay Monterose, Paul Tester ("Clinton's resident banjo freak"), and Ernie Gorospe. "When we were on the road," Bobby says, "we'd get in at one o'clock in the afternoon and Danny would say, 'Somewhere down this road and up on that mountain, there's a '57 Chevrolet in the garage.' And we'd go find it. Sometimes, the music was a real pain to him. His joy was getting out in that garage and working on those cars. He was in hog heaven."

Danny & Liz (1968–1973)

*B*illy Hancock hadn't seen Danny in a while when they hooked up again after Gatton's return from Seattle in late 1969 or early '70. Billy had done gigs in Boston and New York City before joining Joe Stanley's Saxons, a seven-piece band that had a house gig in Hillcrest Heights, Maryland. Stanley—who played saxophone—had been a presence in the local scene since the '50s. "Danny, who had been with him before, came back and played with him," Billy says. "All we were trying to do was make a living."

Eddie Adcock had met Danny at a southeast Washington bar in 1969 or '70. "It was during the day, and he was setting up," recalls Eddie. "He was not as good as he'd be three or four years later. He had the mind; he just didn't have the fine-tuning. He was a little green." They'd heard of each other, which was reason enough to have a short conversation before going their separate ways. Eddie says that Danny was playing a hollowbody Gibson guitar at the time.

Singer-songwriter Liz Meyer first met Danny while she was gigging with J.B. Morrison at the Childe Harold, a downtown D.C. bar above Dupont Circle. Meyer and Morrison had been there on Wednesdays and Thursdays since the beginning of 1971. The club's owner, Bill Heard, was an heir to the John Deere fortune and had no trouble standing out, even in a scene of eccentrics. He had to have his own place, Meyer says, "because he'd been 86'ed from all the other bars."

Heard "always had a soft spot for music and musicians, especially country music," says Meyer. "Emmylou [Harris] was my roommate in '71. She had played there once or twice, although I don't believe she told me about the place." Meyer says the clubowner was always generous, recalling that when fiddler Jeff Wisor joined up, expanding her act from a duo to a trio, Heard immediately added 50 percent to their pay.

Bassist Johnny Castle has fond memories of the Childe Harold, too. He was playing in a power-rock band, Crank, that opened for all the day's big names, including Jimi Hendrix, the Allman Brothers, and Grand Funk Railroad. "It was an old roadhouse," he says. "A lot of people on their way up came through there. They had music, I think, six or seven nights a week." The up-and-comers included Bruce Springsteen—who'd later win acclaim as rock's poet laureate of the heartland—which makes Pete Kennedy wonder if Bruce heard Danny there. "I can't verify it, but if you listen to 'Born to Run'—it's that twangy Tele thing."

The next person to join Meyer's orbit would stick around only briefly: Ed Eastridge, a bassist whose own background matched Danny's eclectic tastes. Eastridge, who was playing standup bass, had also studied classical guitar and knew a lot about Brazilian music. But nothing prepared him for Danny. "It was the first time I had seen someone play [electric guitar] with the accuracy, speed, complexity, and detail that are the attributes of good classical technique," he says. Eastridge also noticed that Danny had mastered the technique of using the flatpick and his middle and ring fingers together to execute arpeggios.

Eastridge recalls the quartet working as Liz Meyer & White Lightning (named for the song, not the drink). "I left, but everybody else stayed," he says. He quit to rejoin Babe, a blues band from which he'd been on temporary hiatus. "It was a real working-band scene back then. There were so many places to play, you could work six nights a week."

"D.C.'s always been pretty supportive of its homegrown music, and there's always been a real roots-oriented scene," says Brawner Smoot, who wrote for the alternative paper *Unicorn Times*—which Richard Harrington edited—and oversaw Danny's management during the *Redneck Jazz* era. "Because of the roots movement here, there's always been a real intelligent music scene."

The Washington scene benefited from its 18-year-old drinking age, versus the 21-year-old standard of neighboring Maryland and Virginia. In D.C., clubs like the Bayou, Blues Alley, the Cellar Door, Childe Harold, Crazy Horse, Desperado's (formerly the Apple Pie), the Keg, and My Father's Place stood tallest in drawing power and visibility. Numerous alternatives existed, too, like the Brickskeller and the Grog & Tankard—fondly called the "Drunken Bastard," according to Eastridge. And there were numerous smaller "downmarket" bars to fill up a band's date sheet, like the two Chadwick's locations on Capitol Hill and K Street, near the Bayou. Not far from the city's bus depot stood the Rocket Room and joints like the Butterfly and Casino Royale, on 16th Street, which were still amenable to the charms of burlesque. "I didn't play in those clubs," says Eastridge, "but I know Danny did."

The Fireplace, on the corner of P and 23rd Streets, holds a unique place in Danny's history, according to Eastridge. "He told me that he rigged his amplifier up so it would blow the circuit breakers and he could get out of doing the last set." He pauses to laugh. "He wired some short [circuit] into it, or something, because they used to work 'em like dogs."

Gatton didn't mention the club's name to *Guitar Player's* readers, but he told Dan Forte: "I rigged up a vibrato on/off switch from a Fender amp and put an AC plug on one end and plugged it into the external power supply on the back of the amplifier. So when I stepped on it, it shorted out the power.... We'd play a while, hit the switch, then sit there for hours drinking beer with candles on the tables, take the switch and go home." The next day, Danny and his boys would return to find the power restored, but it didn't matter, since nobody had figured out the secret.

When he met Danny in 1971, Pete Kennedy was working at a guitar shop in Falls Church where he did restringing and minor repairs—and passed the tough jobs to somebody else. One day, he says, a customer brought in a "really nice" Gretsch guitar. "He wanted it refretted, and refretting is a very meticulous kind of job. If you don't get it perfect, the guitar won't play properly." Not sure if he was up to the job, Kennedy put the Gretsch aside and tried to avoid thinking about it. A couple of weeks later, the customer called, saying he needed the guitar the next day.

Pressed for a solution, Kennedy called Don Downing, who led a band called Willie & the Hand Jives. Downing was something of a mentor to young musicians, and he knew just about anybody of consequence in the area. "I've got this boy in Prince George's County who does the best repair in the country, believe it or not," Downing said. "If you ever have a guitar that you're thinking of selling 'cause you don't enjoy playing it anymore, leave it with this guy overnight. When he gives it back, you won't want to sell it."

Kennedy was intrigued and immediately gave Danny a call. Gatton told him, "Don't come over before two o'clock, because I won't be awake." When he got there, Kennedy found himself scanning the walls of a tiny apartment on Old Branch Avenue, off Maryland's Route 5. He saw several instruments scattered around, including an old Fender lap steel guitar and a Gibson mandolin. "He pulled out the guitar, put it on his dining room table, and took a look at it. 'Yeah, I can do this, no problem. Come back at four.'" Not sure that he had heard right, Kennedy asked Danny to repeat the time.

When Kennedy returned, he found a guitar with superb action and fretwork that was detailed and precise. Kennedy was soon making regular trips to Old Branch Avenue, dropping off guitars for Danny to fix. Eventually,

Danny invited him to check out his gig at the Web in Herndon, Virginia. The room itself was called the Pussycat Lounge, and it had a straightforward redneck ambiance far removed from the kinds of venues that Kennedy had experienced. He found Danny on break, along with Billy Hancock and a drummer he remembers only as "Junior." They were busy swigging beer— "not pouring it into glasses, just using the pitchers like mugs, and telling all these amazing stories about being on the road."

This was a new experience for Kennedy; the people in his world wore psychedelic clothes and plugged Stratocasters or Les Pauls into large Marshall amps. He saw nothing like that onstage. "I thought, Man, that's an old, beat-up Telecaster, in a weird blond color that I've never seen before," he says. "And that amp looks like a suitcase! Of course, it was a tweed amp, which I'd never seen before—a 4×10 Bassman."

Danny had just gotten a '52 Tele—"the one that had the little name-plate thing on it, and he'd just put the Charlie Christian pickup in it," according to Kennedy. The '52 would soon join its '53 cousin as Danny's guitars of choice. "He was using that Tele and a gray Echoplex—that was the whole rig." Kennedy also noticed a Dobro, mandolin, and banjo onstage, and a Shure microphone for the acoustic instruments.

Kennedy stuck around for his own amusement—after all, these guys had almost seven years on him. "If you were playing in a rock band, you'd never play with guys who had greased-back hair, wore K-Mart clothes, and played these funky old instruments," he says. Looking around the club gave no reassurance; the men's trucker-style dress and women's white go-go boots suggested that the Beatles had never happened. "It was a rockabilly place, but I didn't know that, 'cause I'd never been around rockabilly people," Kennedy says. "I thought, Well, what the heck, I'll sit here by myself in the corner—maybe I'll get a few laughs from these guys twanging away."

But Kennedy wasn't laughing when Danny led the rhythm section into an Elvis Presley medley ("Mystery Train," "That's All Right, Mama," "My Baby Left Me"), which later became a concert standby. Kennedy soon realized that he was hearing a Scotty Moore solo, but augmented by Danny's furious double- and triple-time picking over the steady drone that he kept up on the low *E* string. The performance left Kennedy awestruck. "I was sure this was probably the best guitar player in the whole world. But it didn't make sense: I'd known him for six months, and he'd never even mentioned that he played guitar."

Kennedy was hooked, and he went back every chance that he got. Danny's sets crossed every boundary imaginable, so he heard Buddy Holly rave-ups, straightforward covers of Carter Family and Johnny Cash songs, and frantic romps through Flatt & Scruggs material like "Jimmy Brown, the News-boy of the Town." This eclectic choice of material ran afoul of the club's owner, who laid down an ultimatum: update the set or be fired. "They actually tried playing 'Maggie May'—it was pretty awful. None of them even knew who Rod Stewart was. They went out and bought a record, or the owner gave it to 'em, and they tried to lurch through it the best that they could." Shortly after that fiasco, Danny and his band quit the Web.

"PLAYING WITH LIZ MEYER is really what changed everything for Danny," Kennedy says. "As of '71, when I first heard him, there were two different scenes: the hippie rock-band scene and what Danny was doing, and never the twain shall meet." Meyer first heard of Danny through a jazz guitarist named Bill Brooks. Then, through the grapevine, she and her colleagues learned about a banjo that Danny was selling, and bought it from him. They next saw him at a steak house in Waldorf, Maryland, playing solo guitar to people "all yapping and drinking—it was just a nasty gig, but we were quite amazed by the guy," she says.

Meyer started sharing some informal musical evenings with Danny. She initially saw herself as a singer-songwriter "on the edge between folk and bluegrass," but got more interested in the latter style after the banjo purchase. "J.B. [Morrison] learned to play banjo in the next year or so—that must have been the end of '70 or early '71," Meyer says. "We would go over there [to Danny's house] and play with him a little bit. He was very taken with the kind of stuff I was writing."

Paul Freeman was among the early Gatton converts. He was then a "fledgling sound guy" with ambitions of becoming a guitarist, "same as any hippie kid of that era," he says. He met Danny at the Reading Gaol, on P Street, where they watched Meyer and Morrison's duo act. "Roy Buchanan had just sort of broken," Freeman says. "He'd done his first gig at Gaston Hall. Between sets, J.B. introduced me to this guy who was a pretty unassuming little squat redneck sort of fellow." When Danny said he was selling a pedal steel guitar, Freeman suggested a trade. "I had a Les Paul and sort of broached the subject. He jumped at it."

Freeman collected the pedal steel from Danny, after which they went to Meyer's Tacoma Park, Maryland, home. Danny started playing a Dobro, "which he was more than a little good at," according to Freeman. Gatton further piqued his interest by borrowing Morrison's banjo and playing jazz standards like John Coltrane's "Giant Steps." "The thing that sticks in my mind is total culture shock," Freeman says, thinking of Danny at that stage in his career. "I mean, here's a guy who had no sense of contemporary music as we knew it—the total absence of the Beatles."

Meyer didn't see Danny for another six or eight months. Her music gained strength with Jeff Wisor's addition at the end of 1971. The trio format lasted for about nine months before Danny joined. "Danny just went crazy—we had this great fiddler and a lot of great songs," Meyer says. "He was very enthusiastic." Danny's appearance couldn't have been better timed. Heard approved another raise for the band, which had already been working five or six nights per week. "It was the embryonic stages of the bluegrass-country-rock scene," Meyer says. "We were always playing."

"There were a lot of really great musicians in that band," Eastridge says. "I don't think it lasted that long between Danny and Jeff, but both of them were virtuosos." The band quickly became a showcase for Gatton's talent, and he developed a following. Jan's not sure if the audience changed, "or if he just got a chance to show what he could do, and people were really appreciative," she says. "It just seemed like, overnight, something changed. It amazed me to read some of the articles about how his playing was received, to see the almost fanatical kind of following that developed."

Drummer Dave Elliott retains vivid memories of the Childe Harold's cramped environs, where it didn't take long to exceed the legal capacity of 150 people. "The stage was small, in front of a bay window," he says. "I used to put cinder blocks in the window and set my drums right on the cinder blocks. The steps and front door were to my right, through this glass [partition], and they finally broke the glass and started climbing in, all over the stage."

Eddie Adcock and his wife, Martha, had a band called II Generation that played some of the same gigs as Meyer's group—but were hotter, having had a 20-year head start, courtesy of Eddie's career with the Country Gentlemen. "We were working internationally and well-known everywhere," Eddie says. "We were doing a rock 'n' roll–bluegrass formula—electric guitars and drums—with a lot of bluegrass flavor. Liz didn't have nearly as much bluegrass flavor."

Eddie saw Meyer as an outstanding country-rock songwriter whose material cleverly integrated '60s and '70s influences. "The thing that made people come out to see her in droves was Danny Gatton, of course," he says. "Jeff Wisor and Danny worked well together, too." Nobody had really settled on a name, so the band did business as Liz Meyer & Friends or the Liz Meyer Band, which Meyer calls "something to put in the newspaper." That arrangement prevailed before Danny joined and stayed in force while he was in the band (though Kennedy remembers their name as Liz Meyer & the Midnight Flyers).

Kennedy credits Emmylou Harris and Meyer as the first local musicians to form country-rock bands. Their sound and style was a revelation to players like himself, especially after seeing Danny. "All of a sudden these guys with their Les Pauls and Marshalls realized they had a lot more wood-shedding to do," he says. "Danny was playing through a tiny little amp with just a Tele and no effects, and he was knocking everybody's socks off."

Out-of-towners soon got the message—like Little Feat, for whom the Meyer band opened near the end of Danny's tenure. "They used to do this song called 'Black Cat,' and Danny would solo for ten minutes," Kennedy recalls. "After Danny had torn up the place with his really, really aggressive chops, Little Feat sounded a little bit *too* laid back."

Danny had also established himself as a prodigious banjo player, so the gigs started with a showcase of his abilities on that instrument, followed by low-volume electric material. The group soon decided that the presence of an electric guitar required an electric bass, too. Meyer wasn't terribly keen on the idea, since most candidates couldn't play bluegrass. They set-tled on ex–Jim Kweskin Jug Band bassist Bob Siggins, who had learned all sorts of music in the Woodstock folk scene. "He could thump around on my songs, and it wasn't too awful," Meyer says.

Siggins lasted only about five months before hurting his back and leav-ing the band. Needing someone to come in quickly, Meyer called Billy Han-cock, "who ended up staying, 'cause once Danny got his hands on a good bass player, he wasn't going to let him go," she says. Billy was happy to grab the lifeline. He and Danny hadn't been going anywhere particularly fast after abandoning the Web.

Before joining Meyer, Billy and Danny had hooked up with Dave El-liott, who'd been playing with the house band at Hillbilly Heaven in Woodbridge, Virginia. The owner was Earl Dixon, father of actress Donna Dixon; he'd started off with the Pizza King, a more rock 'n' roll–oriented joint, before buying the other club. Business at Hillbilly Heaven was hum-ming along—Elliott recalls working six nights a week—until an auto crash put bandleader Larry Black (not the steel guitarist) out of commission. "Earl asked Billy to fill in for two weeks while Larry was in the hospital," Elliott says. He'd never met Danny, but vividly remembered Billy from a George-town gig in 1969, where the bassist had sported a large pompadour, a blue shirt with white stripes, and red, white, and blue pants.

Soon after he hooked up with Danny, Elliott learned that a style ad-justment was in order. "Danny said, 'You're playing way too much shit, but underneath it all you're laying down a good, solid *two* and *four*, so just play that.'" No longer did Elliott have to worry about filling holes behind er-ratic bassists and guitarists. "[Billy and Danny] knew how to play their in-struments correctly, so all I had to do was play the drums correctly. Wow, this sounds like a song instead of a dogfight!"

A friend was similarly impressed after sitting in for Elliott one night. He was Andy Funt, nephew of *Candid Camera* host Allen Funt, and a "ham-and-egg drummer" by his own admission. Funt was among a bunch of musicians shelling out $20 per week for the privilege of living and partying at Elliott's Haycock Road home, otherwise known as the "Haycock Hilton." One night, Funt got to play behind Danny and his '80s-era cohorts Kennedy and bassist John Previti. "I was figuring, Now we're going to play some stuff that Danny always plays," Funt says. "We didn't. We did two Beatles tunes and a Hendrix song, and I'd never heard him play any of that before, but it was so easy. Believe me, I was not a great drummer, by any means, but you just knew where you were supposed to be and what was coming next." Funt had seen Danny before, playing a free concert in the park at Fort Reno with Liz Meyer & Friends: "[Their sound] was like a never-ending toothpaste tube: it just kept coming at you, and hit you in the chest and surrounded you. There was no escape. It all made sense, he never seemed to make a mistake—and he was going at lightning speed."

Elliott says that Danny's music grew ever more complex in composition and concentration. "It kicked your ass by the end of the night, but you really felt like you'd accomplished something." The band rehearsed in Billy's basement in Alexandria and began working up a repertoire that included familiar instrumentals like Santo & Johnny's "Sleepwalk." Elliott recalls playing "Harlem Nocturne"—Danny's signature showpiece over the years—because people often requested it.

After the band had rehearsed a few times, they started playing at a local pizza chain, the Village Inn. Elliott recalls one gig at a Village Inn parlor in Springfield, Virginia, that drew an overflow crowd. "The parking lot was literally packed with people dancing, and inside people were standing on the tables. The manager fired us because we drew too many people. The guy says, 'Man, I'm trying to sell food here.'"

Heintze wasn't with Danny anymore, having been lured into the first of numerous balls-out Roy Buchanan road bands. Although Danny had no trouble picking up the instrumental slack, his new trio, Fat Chance, wasn't exactly doing gangbuster business, the Springfield night aside. So joining one of Washington's hottest, hardest-working bluegrass and country-rock bands made sense. Elliott was drinking beer at Danny's house when Meyer called to say that drums were fine, so he could join, too. That was the good news; the bad news was that a hung-over Elliott's first gig required him to report to Channel Five's studio at roughly 6 A.M. the next morning. Not only that—they'd have to play live on *Panorama*, then fronted by tabloid talk show host Maury Povich.

"I'd never played with 'em before, and she did all original material," Elliott says. "We had no PA, no monitors, and she stood with her back to me. The [vocal] mike went right up to the control board." The band had to play at low volume, "but somehow we got through it, and it was just fine. To this day, I don't know how I pulled that off." Playing with Danny for a year had paid off, since it required an uncommon degree of concentration. (A good example of this kind of interplay is visible in Danny's second Hot Licks Video, *Strictly Rhythm Guitar*, where the rhythm section looks mostly at him—not the cameras.) "That was one of the things that kept him and I together for so long," Elliott believes. "I wasn't a pimple on Danny's butt, as far as a musician goes, but we had this ESP thing going, this mental telepathy. Sometimes we'd pull off stuff when we were looking in two different directions. It was really a cool thing, especially to do it for 18 years. It was the best job any musician can have."

Meyer says that Elliott's recruitment arose from necessity. "We got rather loud, and at that point you need drums. We had a band within a band, and things got a little strange." The influx of musicians also required more and more compromises to satisfy them. "We had to do some cover material that Billy would sing," she says. "We were doing songs that were kind of a waste of time, like [the Byrds'] 'Mr. Spaceman'—silly stuff."

The band had been starting each night with some acoustic numbers, but in the late spring of 1973, "there was a little coup, because Dave didn't want to sit out the first part of the set," Meyer says. "He wanted to play on everything…[and] he couldn't really play with brushes, so the electric part started to be better than the bluegrass." More tension arose after Danny began stretching solos to 10 and 15 minutes, leaving Wisor "droning two chords," Meyer says. Wisor also didn't get along with Billy or Elliott, so they started to have "the usual band problems."

Still, the results could be hilarious when traditional and nontraditional worlds collided, such as the band's spring 1973 appearance at Berryville, Virginia's Watermelon Park Bluegrass Festival. At first, Meyer ran into resistance over the band's inclusion of drums and electric instruments, which were anathema to bluegrass purists. She recalls saying, "Look, I have a drummer—I can't just send him home without paying him, and if Danny can't go electric, they'll all go home." The compromise involved allowing the band to play acoustically at first, with the drums coming out for "Orange Blossom Special." "I don't think they quite realized what that meant," Meyer says, "because there was nothing loud for the whole festival, and suddenly there was this screaming Telecaster! We were going over gangbusters and played a long electric 'Orange Blossom Special' that just lifted people's scalps."

The local folks took such moments in stride. Meyer and friends had a Monday night residency at Georgetown's Keg, where the crowds apparently didn't mind extreme volume. "We would be so painfully loud in there, I thought my ears would bleed," Meyer says, "and people would be asking us to turn it up!"

The band's most memorable outing occurred in the summer of 1973, when Billy, Danny, Elliott, Meyer, and Morrison went to San Francisco. "This crazy coke dealer flew us out to play his birthday party. We had a whole section of a 747 to ourselves, because they were terribly underbooked in those days, so that was kind of funny," Meyer says. The dealer put them up at a lavish Nob Hill townhouse, from which they were booted out a couple of weeks later and relegated to a bare-bones motel. "Right at the airport, I felt like I was baby-sitting bad little boys," Meyer says. "Dave would be standing in line, 320 pounds, lifting his leg, and making fart noises. Billy could get us thrown out of any restaurant by harassing the waitresses."

Matters got farcical when the dealer booked them into a new club he was opening. "We spent a week playing there for the staff," Meyer says. "It was a ludicrous experience." They next played a warehouse about an hour outside of town, where several members of Hell's Angels showed up. "One of them had a harmonica and wanted to sit in—so we had this guy sitting in all evening, in one key," Meyer laughs. "He had only one harmonica. It was one of those nights."

Bill Heard flew out to ensure that he wouldn't miss the fun, assuring them that one of his best friends was a Grateful Dead roadie, Peter Sheridan. Through her own contacts with the Dead's management, Meyer managed to set up a meeting with Sam Cutler, who'd helped organize the disastrous 1969 Altamont rock festival. The band promptly got invited to meet Jerry Garcia at a bill with Tex-Mex rocker Doug Sahm. During the break, Meyer tried to tell Garcia that she'd brought this wonderful guitar player from the East Coast, and maybe they could jam some time. "He just went, 'Oh, far out!' and walked off," she says. "Danny was terribly insulted, and we left."

The culture clash was further underlined by a visit to the home of mandolinist David Grisman, who would become one of Garcia's major collaborators outside of the Dead. "We played some nice acoustic music for one afternoon, but I think David found Danny a bit overwhelming and strange, musically," Meyer says.

The disasters piled up. One night, after another warehouse gig, Sheridan suggested stopping at his favorite neighborhood bar—which turned out to be home base for the Oakland chapter of Hell's Angels. As the only woman in the joint, Meyer was nervous enough. When she realized that taking a bathroom break involved sidling past numerous pool-playing Angels, she simply returned to the bar, draped a sweatshirt over her lap and vowed to be invisible. Then someone in the band piped up that Sheridan hadn't locked the car that held their instruments. Not to worry, he replied: selected Angels watched the parking lot from the upstairs windows, ready to fire their guns at any intruders.

Just then, Angels leader Sonny Barger entered, "a big, tall, scary-looking guy wearing lots of metal studs and spikes, walking this Great Dane with a big spiked collar," Meyer says. "Peter has to introduce him to all of us, 'cause we've invaded his territory." Heard offered some cocaine to break the ice. Barger whipped out a large Bowie knife to cut the powder. "Bill, with his typical sense of humor, says, 'Hey, man, use my knife'—which has an inch-and-a-half blade!" Barger responded by slamming his big knife into the wall next to Heard's head. A frightened Sheridan scooped up the band and herded them into the car. After several false starts, they managed to drive off as Barger came outside with reinforcements—"so that was Danny Gatton's brush with the Hell's Angels!" Meyer says.

BACK HOME, THE BAND resumed its normal schedule of eight or nine gigs a week, if things were busy; six or seven, if they were slow. Their home base remained the Childe Harold, augmented with bluegrass gigs at lesser-known venues like the Red Fox. "We would play one place in the afternoon and another club at night. We did that all the time," Meyer says. "I'm amazed I can still sing, because there were four sets a night at those clubs in those days."

Kennedy remembers walking past the Childe Harold one night. He had no idea who was playing until he heard a Tele-driven high note, with plenty of vibrato. "I thought, Oh, Danny, must be in there with Liz," he recalls. "I caught myself: I realized I'd heard only one note. That shows someone who's great—all you need to hear is one note, and their style is there."

Beneath the surface, however, there were problems. "Things had reached the point where I could sing a beautiful heartbreak ballad, a confessional ballad, and we would have a 15-minute guitar solo in the middle," Meyer says. Patrons got little relief from the amp that Danny kept parked on his chair, four feet from their heads, turned up loud. Billy was also cranking up the volume, aggravating Meyer's dilemma of how to be heard with only a Shure microphone taped to her acoustic guitar.

An uneasy four-to-three majority prevailed until Wisor quit to work with Eddie Adcock. "Danny had always been a fan of mine, long before I met him, as the banjo player with the Country Gentlemen," Eddie says.

"I was his favorite banjo player till the day he died, as far as I know. The first time he ever jammed with me was the clincher, but he said he'd always admired my style." Adcock and Gatton had spent a night getting acquainted musically on the Alexandria side of the Potomac River, off Mount Vernon Highway. "We just jammed acoustically that night," Adcock says. "Our music was in our heads. It didn't matter what instrument we were holding—it was going to be just as weird and strange if Danny was playing a banjo as if he was playing a guitar."

The freewheeling nature of Danny's style appealed to Adcock. "He had a style, but he *didn't* have a style—it's like everything that you could get, in the Danny Gatton way," he says. "He could do anything. But no matter where I heard him, I always knew it was him. That's the way it is with all the great players."

After Wisor's departure, "we were just plain outnumbered," says Meyer. One of the final straws occurred when banjoist Bill Keith came to town. He'd devised a fingering style that enabled players to delve into jazz, as opposed to the more traditional "Scruggs style," and he often visited the Washington area, where he played at the major showcase club, the Cellar Door. "When his two sets were done, he would come and see our last one," Meyer says, adding that he'd sometimes join the band onstage.

One night, Keith showed up early at the Childe Harold, where he set up his pedal steel guitar for sitting in. "It ended up being one of the worst nights of my life, because Roy Buchanan's manager showed up, apparently to eyeball Danny," she says. "Or at least Danny thought there was some opportunity for him there." When Meyer returned for her second set, she realized that Danny was telegraphing his displeasure the old-fashioned way. "He cranked up twice as loud as the band or Bill Keith. Billy would get about eight bars into a solo, and the guitar would just come running over him. It was not nice, and really embarrassing."

Matters further deteriorated when the band took a break. "Danny came up to me, just livid: 'Roy Buchanan's manager is here, and I've got to do my best and show him my stuff, and I'm not having that pedal steel player sit in the next set.'" If Keith didn't leave, Danny promised to beat him out the door. "As a mature person, I would have said, 'Fine,' and probably quit that night, too," Meyer says. "In any case, I had the humiliating job of asking Bill not to play with us for the second set. He was, needless to say, rather insulted."

Meyer puts the incident down to Gatton's unpredictability. The band might be having a good time onstage while Danny would be getting flustered about something no one else had noticed. "On a good night, we had a lot of fun," she says. "He'd laugh and drink tons of beer—maybe, I think, to pull that off. Looking back, he was probably kind of manic depressive. I didn't know it was called that at the time. It was just 'moody' to me."

By Christmas 1973, Danny, Billy, and Dave Elliott had given notice of their intent to secede. Elliott maintains that there were disagreements about the terms of a record deal. "It was a damn shame, because the timing was perfect," he says. "With Danny Gatton as the head of the ship, it couldn't get any better than that. We had lots of offers from major record labels, and Liz turned them all down because she thought she was worth twice the money they were offering."

Meyer says that the labels wanted her, not the band—which she couldn't tell them, least of all Danny. "The same thing happened to Emmylou, and she left her band." But Meyer had no desire to follow Harris's example, even if it meant a reversal of her own fortunes.

Billy says the Meyer band was a good learning experience that he abandoned for purely musical reasons. "I'd never played bluegrass music before, but if you're a bass player, the last thing you want to be is the bass player in a bluegrass band. *One* and *three* is it, pal!"

In any case, Danny had created a buzz based on his talent. "Liz did a lot for getting him noticed by more upscale clubs," says Ed Eastridge, "but he was starting to get well known, anyway. It would have happened, because he was so good—he would have pretty much taken over D.C."

Danny's new group, dubbed the Fat Boys, could make more money as a trio and still give the local crowds what they wanted to see: Danny's guitar playing. "He really liked Liz Meyer, appreciated what she did and all, but he had more in common with Dave Elliott and Billy Hancock," Jack Jensen says. "Danny didn't like to front and couldn't sing."

From the start, it was clear that Danny, Billy, and Dave had been an instrumental band within a band, putting them at odds with Meyer's country-rock orientation, since the genre is vocal-oriented. "Guitar fanatics were going to hear the guitar stuff," Pete Kennedy says. "Liz, justifiably, didn't want to make the gig all about long guitar solos with her singing a little bit in between." Kennedy believes that Meyer deserves credit for giving Danny the chance to escape from the Prince George's County honky-tonk circuit. "Then [the Fat Boys] could go off on their own and play the clubs where the hippie rock-music fans were going," he says. "Lowell George [of Little Feat] would never even have heard Danny if it wasn't for Liz putting Danny in front of that type of audience."

Eddie Adcock puts the departure from Liz down to Danny's innate refusal to settle in one place for too long. "Danny Gatton was a restless musician. He would not conform to anybody, or anything, and once you played all the tunes about 175 times, everything started sounding the same to him. He'd get extremely bored. He wouldn't stay with anybody very long. Danny never had any business doing bands with anybody; he was so strong by himself." His wife adds, "Danny's talent was much, much too big for one field of music."

Although the year had been difficult, Meyer came to regard it as an educational experience of what to tolerate—or not—as a bandleader. "I was just barely 20, so it was a lot to deal with," she says. Not surprisingly, the band's burgeoning local popularity made its demise all the more difficult to swallow, because there was no shortage of work available. "We parted company on reasonably amicable terms, and that was the end of the band. I had a backlash at that point and said, 'I just want to play with mediocre musicians.' I couldn't deal with the superstars. But that didn't work, either: mediocre musicians are not interesting to me."

Meyer recalls having to resolve one last piece of business involving Danny, which turned out to be characteristically messy. She maintains that the band divvied up its earnings equally, and Danny took home $25 to $35 per gig "which was okay in those days." The problem surfaced in 1974 when Meyer was doing her taxes. "I don't remember what each of us made that year, but it was probably $7,000 or $8,000. It wasn't tons of money," she says. Since she didn't have receipts from Danny, Meyer had to call him—a task she never relished, especially if Jan happened to pick up. "If I was calling to say we had a rehearsal or gig, she would hang up on me!" Meyer recalls. Just as Meyer dreaded, Jan wouldn't let her talk to Danny. "She asked how much it was and said, 'No way! He never made more than $10 or $15 [per night]!'"

Only then did Meyer discover what had apparently been happening: Danny was taking home $25 to $35 per night but reporting lower sums to his wife. "His wife was paying the bills, and the little money he had to play with, he used to buy guitars, strings, amps, and parts for cars. He was a child, on that level. Jan worked, and he was gone [at night]. She was at home by herself, so she had lots of legitimate gripes and good reasons for being unhappy. Unfortunately, I was the enemy."

Jan acknowledges that she disliked Meyer, but says it was because of the way the band treated the Gattons' new home in Alexandria. "They'd come and rehearse, and squash cigarette butts all over the floor. Liz's big St. Bernard tore up all my flowers one afternoon, and I never liked her after that," she says. "He had never played with a woman before, and I was probably pretty jealous, too," Jan adds, although she says she was never worried about his faithfulness. "My father was a ladies' man, and it tore my family apart. I never, ever saw that in Dan. That was one thing I really respected about him: he was very honorable."

Jan doesn't recall the phone conversation about taxes and questions the premise of Meyer's story. "I can't say that it didn't happen, but he would never have to hide money—because he never made that much." Nor does Jan recall trying to manage her husband's spending habits. "He always bought whatever he wanted. He never asked me, and I never said, 'No, you can't.' "

Jan and Danny's stay in Alexandria lasted only about a year. "We had to move from there, because one of the people he knew in somebody's band had a brawl in the street with his wife!" Jan says. "It was always something like that—it wasn't Danny. He certainly couldn't help that, but some of the people [involved] weren't very stable, I guess."

The couple moved to Camp Springs, where they ran through two rental homes. They vacated the first after only one day. "We thought the house was haunted—I found a dead frog in the refrigerator," Jan laughs. "We moved out the next day." Through Danny's dentist, they managed to find a one-story brick rambler on Linda Lane, where they stayed for a year. Even there, things were a little strange. Danny was doing guitar repairs in the basement, and "he said it made him nervous down there," Jan says. "He just got a funny feeling, so he put up mirrors so he could see behind him!"

*D*anny's drive to "build a better mousetrap" had been a driving force since his preteen days, and it's worth examining separately at this point. Now that he wasn't cutting up sheet metal—or slugging it out on the road, squeezed into a tux—Danny could pursue his obsessions with function, sound, and tone. Phil Zavarella believes that Danny's effort to harness those qualities in service of his guitar stemmed from a feeling of being "bored to death with his instrument—so he sought to re-make it."

Phil should know: he sold Danny the '53 Tele that he made famous and watched him spend countless hours bent over a tiny workbench at Zavarella's Music, knocking that guitar into shape. He estimates that Danny spent about six months at that workbench—which was allowed, as long as it didn't disrupt business—sharing elbowroom with six full-time employees, including Phil and his father.

Tony Zavarella had often warned his son: "Do not ever fool with these professional musicians, because you can never satisfy them." He would also chide the musicians constantly: "Have you ever looked at those people you're playing for? Do you think they care what your horn, guitar, or amplifier sounds like?" Phil agrees. "He was absolutely right, 'cause they don't. They're there to get drunk or pick up a chick, or both." But he also understands why musicians of Danny's caliber fret constantly about their gear. "When these guys play at the level that they play at, first of all, they have nothing to do all day, so they're just bored out of their minds. So they start looking for 'the sound,' and that's a curse."

Not surprisingly, Danny burned through numerous guitars in his search for the ultimate instrument. "Danny ruined this great '52 Tele that he had," Phil recalls. "He decided one day that his guitar was going to be all black—neck, body, everything—him and Robbie Weaver. And he was going to inlay 'Danny Gatton' on the fingerboard. They were going to make this a work of art, and all they did was fool with it for a couple of days and then throw it under the bench."

A similar fate befell a 1955 Les Paul that Phil bought for $80. The customer claimed that the Dakota red color was a factory refinish, but Phil was skeptical. "Most guys would strip the finish off or put decals on it," he says, "but they wouldn't put the guitar in a box and send it back to the factory." Phil took the guitar home for a closer look, and to his surprise he found "an unbelievable finish—it was perfect. It could only have been done by the factory. And then I said, 'I wonder if that gold is under there?'" Suitably motivated, Phil got out a bottle of Dupont #2 rubbing compound, removed the pickguard and scraped away. "The red went away, some gray appeared and guess what? The gold was there! So, a blister on every finger and eight hours later, it was a gold-top again."

Phil called Danny to report his discovery. "He came over and said, 'I *have* to have it.' I said, 'Danny, this guitar is no good. It doesn't even have a Tune-o-matic bridge on it.' He said, 'Oh, it doesn't matter!' 'Well, yes, it does—this guitar won't play in tune. You've had a million of these things, and so have I—they're awful.' 'No, man, this is the shit, this guitar is cool.'"

Danny had the reborn gold-top under his arm when he left, and Phil knew it wouldn't stay unmolested for long. "I probably sold it to him for $80, what I paid for it," he says. "He took that guitar home, hacked it out, made a swimming pool in it, and put three white-coil Patent Applied For humbucking pickups on it." (These classic pickups are known for their smooth tone and sustain.)

The guitar suffered a terrible gouging in the process. "He had to glue the [pickguard] screws—there was nothing for them to grab onto," Phil says. "He butchered this '55 Les Paul. It just broke my heart. And then he said, 'Listen to it, it's a piece of shit. It won't play.' I said, 'Danny, I told you that. Why'd you think this one was going to be any different?'"

Then Danny hatched an idea: why not sell the guitar to Aerosmith, who happened to be playing at the Capitol Centre? Surely the band's lead guitarist, Joe Perry, would be an appreciative customer. "So we get back in the bowels of that place, and here comes Joe Perry," Phil says. "He knows Danny. 'Look at this—it's so cool, this guitar.'" Phil remembers that Danny asked $1,800 for the gold-top, which was an astronomical sum in the mid-'70s. "Joe Perry goes like this [makes hand motion]. This guy comes over, wearing a suit and tie; 'click, click' with the attaché case full of cash: eighteen $100 bills. Danny gave me half of 'em, he kept the other half, and off we went."

Both stories summarize the difference in their attitudes: Phil considered the guitars he bought as treasures while Danny treated them like the tools in his garage. Danny had a similar approach to cars. "He bought a '32 Ford one time—finally got his '32 Ford," Phil says. "Paid $5,000 for it; his wife borrowed the money to pay for it. He drove it home—an original, unmolested '32 Ford—and he calls me up. I told him, 'Leave this car alone. There's none of these left. This is so cool, just like this.' The next day, at 6 A.M., my phone rings. He's taken the car completely apart and sawed off the roof. 'What'll I do?' he says. He did that to everything."

THE '53 TELECASTER THAT loomed so large in Danny's playing history surfaced almost by accident. "I acquired that Tele from a guy I'd never met before," says Phil Zavarella. "He said he was from Florida. He came in, opened the case, and there was this guitar. I put on my game face, poker face—whatever you want to call it—and said, 'What can I do for you?' He said, 'I want a Mini-Moog.'"

Phil was more than happy to oblige, having bought a Mini-Moog from a customer who couldn't figure out how to play the synthesizer. "I said, 'There it is.' He said, 'I don't have any money.' I said, 'You don't need any money. We're going to trade.'"

Danny visited the store not long after he'd wrecked his '52 Tele. "He says, 'Phil, I want to buy that Tele from you, but I don't have any money. That's why I brought Jan, so she can promise that she'll pay you for the guitar.' I said, 'Fine, the guitar is $600'—which was about $2,000 less than it was worth at that time. Sure enough, every now and then a check would come in the mail, and pretty soon she'd paid me for the guitar. It took a little while, but it wasn't a ridiculous amount of time."

The deal had some stipulations, however. "I told him that the only thing with that guitar was you could not alter it, other than change the electronics—couldn't dig any holes in it, put any extra pickups or bigger pickups in it. He totally respected that," Phil says. "He never did. He just wore out that guitar. I never saw anybody wear out a guitar like that." Also, if Danny ever got rid of the guitar, he had to sell it back to Phil for $600. "Well, that part of the deal he didn't keep. He traded it for a '34 Ford, but I didn't mind. I did remind him of the deal, and he just looked at me. He didn't even comment on it. But that's okay."

Danny's new-found devotion to Telecasters represented a sea change from his previous guitar preference, when people had nicknamed him Danny "Les Paul" Gatton. "That's all he would play," Phil says. "He hated Fender guitars. He wouldn't even look at one twice." Phil has a simple way of dating the switch: "I was driving a '73 Buick, and I bought that new."

Joe Tass asserts that Danny's incentive to get "Tele'ed up" stemmed from his interactions with Billy Hancock and writer Bob Berman, who'd done the first major Roy Buchanan interview for *Guitar Player*'s March 1972 issue. "Hancock had probably brought a Telecaster over, but when Berman met Danny, Danny said, 'Here, look at the Les Paul, look at the inlay.' And Berman said, 'No, no, listen to *this* guitar.'"

The change is significant, because "Danny never played with that tone, never used that approach [before]," Tass adds. "He would play that style, but he would still be playing his jazz licks. And playing a million miles an hour—somehow, it always seemed that more was better to him."

Danny's quest for the ultimate sound earned him another nickname: "Danny Gat-tone." "He got on the tone kick, as all those guys do," Phil says. "And that's when you do the pickup thing, the amp thing—another form of insanity: hundreds and hundreds of wasted hours, changing those pickups, changing those [volume and tone] pots."

When Fender rolled out its Danny Gatton Signature Telecaster some 20 years after Danny and Phil had argued about all that guitar vandalism, the instrument's namesake had only one request: could Phil call when they arrived, so he could adjust every guitar? "He'd kept rejecting the prototypes, [due to] the neck size or the color," Phil recalls. "I said, 'Danny, they're not going to fool with you! They're finally going to say, 'Forget about it.' Just get one of these guitars and say, 'This is fine.'" Just to be safe, though, Phil didn't bother calling Danny when the production models arrived. "I had 'em pre-sold already," he says. "That's the pride thing: 'I want to personally adjust and set every one of my guitars that you get, Phil, and you're the only one ordering 'em, anyway.' And every one I got, I sold before he even got here."

Phil attributes the switch in guitars to Danny seeing Roy Buchanan for the first time. "We used to go and watch him play. They had those duels that only lasted for minutes. Roy would just put down his guitar, get off the stage and sit with me or whoever. You couldn't compete with Gatton. There was no sense in trying to throw notes at him, because he'd throw 19,000 of 'em back at you." When Gatton would show up where a local rock band was playing, Phil says, "as soon as these guys would see him, they would just fold like a wet tissue."

Phil recalls going with Danny to see a Merle Haggard show, because Danny admired Roy Nichols's guitar work so much. They made their way backstage, where "all of us went into this room, closed the door, and they started playing. Within a minute, everybody's guitar was down and just Gatton was playing. You couldn't play with him. If you were a guitar player, all you could do was put down your guitar when you were in his presence."

THE DIFFERENCE BETWEEN A Gibson guitar and a Fender Telecaster is simple, as many players have noted: a Tele makes for harder work. "They're two completely different animals," Phil says. "A Les Paul is a Rolls Royce, and a Fender is a Ford or a Chevy. You've got to drive it, or it might drive you. That was a challenge to Danny, so it was a good thing."

Tom Wheeler says, "The Tele gave him the same thing it gives everybody else—that blistering, high-end twang. If you know how to play those guitars without being screechy or too top-endy, you get a wonderful, round, ringing twang that nothing else'll give you. He heard that and made it his own." Danny himself summarized the difference succinctly to *Maryland Musician*; where the Tele allowed him to play whatever styles he wished, Gibson Les Pauls were too much of a good thing: "Too many volume knobs, too many tone knobs; there's too much crap to try to work. Plus you can't bend strings behind the nut."

Joe Barden—who'd win acclaim for his pickup and amp work with Danny—enjoyed bouncing ideas off Dan Senior, whose role was being "sort of a real good *ad hoc* machinist and sheet-metal-tool guy." "He made the first stainless steel bridge for Danny's '52 [Tele] that was later transferred to the '53 device that held the Magic Dingus Boxes," Barden says. (The Magic Dingus Box was a homemade effects device that Gatton used; more about that later.) "He made the jigs that Danny used to make the early Charlie Christian [pickup] replicas."

Dan Senior would offer questions and suggestions that helped to spark Barden's mind in new directions. "We'd be drawing something out, and I'd want to put a screw here or there, and he'd say, 'Well, why don't you put it in with a bracket from this other angle here, and you can hold this part down, that part down, and get the adjustment you want.' I'd be like, 'Oh, okay, wow, cool, never thought of that.'" Dan Senior intimately understood the workings of guitars, which helped immensely.

Danny was always looking to get more from his Telecaster, and "that was the guitar that was going to be played—no ifs, ands, or buts about it," Barden says. "If the pickups were wimpy, and the thing hummed, so be it. But that was the guitar that made the roots music we liked, everything from Muddy Waters to Merle Haggard." Barden considers the Tele "the world's hardest guitar to play, because it's the most unforgiving one around. If you can master it, you can get sounds you can't get out of any other instrument and develop an individual sound you can't get with any other instrument. Look at the '70s and '80s: how many people with Les Pauls sound the same? Look at the '90s: how many people with Strats sound the same?"

Danny in his repair shop in Accokeek, Maryland, in the late '70s. Danny's garage became a focal point for anyone who wanted a repair job—and to learn a lick or two in the process.

A Tele is highly sensitive. "If you do something good on a Tele, it sounds like no other guitar," Barden says. "If you do something bad, everybody's aware of it for miles around. You just can't hide; you're totally exposed. And my pickups accentuate this quality times ten. I have had people pick up Teles with my pickups, plugged into loud amplifiers, and they just play a couple of notes and walk away: 'I can't control that.' It's like driving a Ferrari for the first time—they leap over the curb and embarrass themselves."

Barden says a Fender amp was also part of the Gatton formula. "The whole thing revolved around Fender. Obviously, he played a lot of different kinds of music, but the taproot for all of this was the basic Fender sound, the Telecaster, and blackfaced amp. That's the religion. Some people are Catholics, some people are Jews, some people are Muslims; that was our religion, that blackfaced sound."

Early Fenders amps are divided into three distinct eras, named after their exterior appearance. The tweeds ended in 1960; brown-and-whites ran from 1960 to '63; and blackfaces were prominent between 1963 and '67. Each generation refined the sound of its predecessors. "Danny used tweed amps for a while, but they just didn't have the clean headroom,"

Barden says. "The blackface was definitely the most refined of all those amps, in terms of the circuitry." Barden says they were the ideal amps for creating the sounds produced by Danny, as well as Don Rich, Roy Nichols, and Jimmy Bryant—"all the cats that were seriously important Telecaster guys. And Roy, not to forget him."

By the early '70s, Danny's notoriety was confined largely to local guitar buffs and like-minded gearheads, but he made an indelible impression on the better-known players who entered his world—as Commander Cody & the Lost Planet Airmen's guitarist Bill Kirchen did in 1972 or '73. The Cody band was playing on a bill with NRBQ, and Kirchen mentioned to NRBQ guitarist Al Anderson that his Tele needed refretting. Anderson told him: "Go see Danny Gatton. He'll take care of you."

Kirchen took his Tele to Danny's guitar shop, with bassist Bruce Barlow tagging along. "He made me a brass nut and refretted my neck," Kirchen says. "And then he said, 'You've got a great old Tele, you should have old parts on it.' He gave me a different pickguard, knobs, and string tree." (Kirchen still has the guitar with the parts Gatton supplied.) After refretting Barlow's instrument, Danny asked Kirchen if he wanted to jam. "I remember thinking, I'm sure this friendly repairman will enjoy learning a lick or two from me," Kirchen laughs. "Of course, you hear him, and it's like, Jesus Christ! Never heard anything like it in my life. I didn't see him again, but I stayed in touch, though, 'cause he knocked me out."

TOM PRINCIPATO SAYS HE first encountered Danny at a Liz Meyer & Friends gig at the Childe Harold in 1973 or '74. "I had always been into a really eclectic mix of music: Les Paul, blues, and Chet Atkins," he says. "Danny was the first guy I had ever met, up to that point, that was into all of that and could play it. And Charlie Christian, too. I was blown away by that, so I went up and introduced myself."

Principato found Danny "a little bit shy," but still friendly and approachable. "We struck up a guitar friendship, and I started hanging out with him. A lot of people gravitated to Danny, because he was just so great." Principato never witnessed the Les Paul phase; like Kennedy, he observed Danny using the '53 Tele, 4×10 Bassman, and a gray tube Echoplex. "The amazing thing was that once he picked up the Les Paul again [on *Redneck Jazz*], he could make it sound like a Tele," says Principato. "That's a pretty difficult thing to do, because the guitars are so different."

Danny could also do the reverse. "He could make a Tele sound like a Gibson, too," says Principato. "A Tele has single-coil pickups, which are very bright and twangy—that's the whole trademark sound. A Gibson has humbucking pickups that are double the size and electronic output of Fender single-coil pickups, so they're very dark, not trebly but beefy and fat. The Tele is sort of like bright and thin, so they're opposites, in a way."

Principato says that, regardless of the guitar he was using, Danny was "master of everything—he played jazz, he played rockabilly, he played blues, he played rock 'n' roll...[and] he put them together in a personal way. He just had this raw, God-given talent, and there was not really a lot of education involved—just a lot of know-how." Principato says that when the two guitarists were collaborating on the *Blazing Telecasters* album, Danny asked the name of a chord that Principato had played. "I said, 'That was an *A11*.' He thought for a minute and said, 'Is it the same thing as an *A7*?' Just to ask that question, I think, is very telling. Danny didn't have a lot of knowledge, but he had a lot of know-how. He knew what sounded good, and he knew how to get it."

Earth, Wind & Fire guitarist Al McKay was another peer who became a solid convert. Danny remembered their first encounter positively—although he mangled the band's name as "Earth, Fire & Water" in a 1974 *Unicorn Times* interview. McKay laughs when reminded of the malapropism. "Danny could have been kidding me on that one, you know! He was quite a guy, quite a player." McKay is hazy about where he first saw Danny. "He was playing a club somewhere in the Washington area. In fact, one of my roadies turned me on to him: 'You've got to go *hear* this guy!' We were going to stay for only a set, but he blew me away."

Bobby Hancock remembers the introduction coming from a guitarist he didn't know at the time: Virginian Pat Moore, whom he'd meet on a cruise ship in 2002. "This guy said his claim to fame was that he was the only white guy in an all-black soul band," Bobby recalls. In the early '70s, Moore had played with Joe Quaterman's Sir Joe & the Free Soul Band, an outfit from southeast D.C. that toured the East Coast and opened for numerous national acts, including Ray Charles, James Brown, the O'Jays, and Wilson Pickett, as well as EWF. "When they opened for Earth, Wind & Fire, he got to know Al McKay," Bobby says. "After the gig one night, McKay says, 'I want you to take me out and show me the baddest guitar player in Washington.' Pat says, 'No problem.'"

Moore took McKay to the Childe Harold, where Danny was playing with Liz Meyer & Friends. "I'll never forget it, because when we walked in it was wall-to-wall people, and Danny was tearing it up on the banjo," Moore says. "When they took a break, Danny saw me and came over, and I introduced him to Al McKay. They went on to be friends, and I think Danny did some sessions with him. When the *Redneck Jazz* album came out, I was really thrilled to see a quote from Al on the liner notes, as I knew that I was responsible for their meeting. I guess that's my claim to fame."

McKay stuck around, surprised to have run across someone with such a firm grasp of so many idioms. "He played *everything*—from R&B to jazz to rockabilly to whatever. He was just a phenomenal player. Other players had given me the idea Danny was supposed to be a country player, but he played so many different styles. It was just unreal to hear all that coming out of him. And it was all clean—very seldom did Danny ever miss." McKay, who had grown up on country music, retains fond memories of Danny doing "Hot Rod Lincoln." "It was a tune I grew up with, too. It had that Tele, really low country pickin', but it was super-fast and I just dug it."

To McKay, what happened onstage seemed even more unreal when the two players compared digits afterwards. "I thought I had short fingers, but Danny had *short* fingers! I had at least a quarter of an inch [in finger length], but he could roll through the guitar, man, especially the Tele." Danny also showed McKay some of the stylistic tricks he'd picked up from Buchanan. "He showed me how to do the 'cry' with the volume control—just [moving the knob] up and down, bending the note so you get that 'cry' thing. He had dexterity in both hands. He could do just about anything."

McKay was especially struck by Danny's typical onstage reserve. "The things that were flying off his fingers [with] no [apparent] emotion! It was like, 'I do this all the time, all day, you're hearing it, and I'm just kind of bored with it, but here it is.'"

*B*illy had a better idea for his future than pumping out quarter-notes on bluegrass tunes. He planned to jump-start the dormant Aladdin label—known for the output of R&B shouter Amos Milburn, a longtime Hancock favorite—and fill out the paperwork for a business license. Billy, Danny, and Elliott would pay for studio time, control the master tapes, and remain free agents to seek national distribution. If everything worked, they'd split the income three ways; if not, they'd at least have a calling card for the next release.

The sessions started on Valentine's Day 1974 at Track Recorders in Silver Spring, Maryland, where the trio convened at seven o'clock to lay down tracks for what became their Aladdin debut single: "American Music" b/w "Harlem Nocturne." Billy hired local doo-wop group the Memories for the A-side's backing vocals (although the album version would feature their better-known '50s counterparts, the Clovers). But it was the B-side that captured listeners' attention and would become Danny's signature tune. Although he'd re-record it for *Cruisin' Deuces* (1993), the original version is considered the definitive effort.

The engineer felt strongly about the sounds he was capturing on tape. Obie O'Brien had grown up outside Philadelphia with guitarists like Lance Quinn and Rick Vito ("the hot player in my neighborhood"). He and Quinn had played in Maryland and Virginia as teenagers, before O'Brien decided to mothball his drumming for an engineering career.

O'Brien found *American Music* to be an inauspicious debut for his engineering skills. "Oh, it's just a *rotten-sounding* record. I had no idea what to do," he says. "I didn't understand balances, all the ancillary gear, all those vintage compressors. I wasn't very good at turning the equalizers back down." Even so, the album's tracks are pretty fair baby pictures: any band boasting Danny, Billy, Elliott, and Dick Heintze was bound to hit some high notes. "After Hours" and "TV Mama" let their bluesy side hang out, while a crisp "Ubangi Stomp" kept rockabilly in the equation, too. Hancock's resigned expression of love gone wrong, "Move On Down the Line," is notable as Danny's only documented stab at reggae. There were also strategic pauses for R&B ("Memphis Disco Funk") and nods to the jazz and swing that Danny played so supremely well.

The studio atmosphere was pretty lively, according to bassist Steve Wolf, who'd play with Danny's late-'70s Redneck Jazz Explosion ensemble. Tenor saxophonist Teddy Efantis blew hot and heavy on Fats Waller's "Honeysuckle Rose" and an original by Billy, "A Tribute to Amos Milburn." The first takes weren't fierce enough for Billy, though, Wolf recalls: "He's going, 'Teddy, just burn it, man! That wasn't quite it.' So Teddy goes, 'Gotcha.' He pulls out these wraparound shades, walks up to the microphone, and just honks off this devastating solo."

According to Billy, *American Music* took roughly a year to assemble, for economic reasons "and [also because] Danny and Dave had a love/hate relationship—always. Danny would get mad: 'That's it, fire that fat MF!' And we'd do it. Finally, I said, 'Danny, here's the telephone—you know the number.' He'd get good drummers, but they wouldn't fit the style as good as Dave. That's why there's so many drummers on there." One of them was Robbie Magruder, who'd played with Roger McDuffie at Gus & John's and later turned up in Roy Buchanan's band.

Obie O'Brien chipped in some piano, and a number of other musicians contributed, including Joe Barden's father, Charlie, who played vibraphone on "Honeysuckle Rose" and "A Tribute to Amos Milburn," and Scott Taylor, later of the Redneck Jazz Explosion. Elliott felt the extended cast watered down their tight interplay. "I still don't know why Billy kept bringing in all these other people," he says. "But I know a lot of people who like that album better than anything else we ever did. It's a matter of opinion."

Guitarist Joe Kogok played on "TV Mama" and Horace Silver's "Opus de Funk"—which would become a Redneck Jazz Explosion standard—although his contributions remained unheard until the NRG reissue appeared in 1997. (The CD reissue adds about 10 minutes to the original 40-minute album.) Kogok doesn't believe the album expressed what the Fat Boys were really about. "If you've only heard the Fat Boys on the *American Music* album, you haven't heard all of what they did," he says. Kogok, who later joined the band for six months, says, "They were absolutely terrific as a trio—you wouldn't believe how much music they could put out. I thought that Danny did his best in that situation."

Recording quality aside, *American Music* is important for two reasons. The album laid out a template for the Danny Gatton style to come—bebop, country, jazz, rockabilly, and swing filtered through his thrill-a-minute guitar figures, lightning-fast arpeggiated runs, and impeccable rhythmic comping. More important, the contents signaled a different stylistic approach than the disco and Top 40 fodder then dominating the AM airwaves; roots music lovers could heartily salute the bumptious '50s-style title track's sentiments as bellowed out by Billy: "Never could I find such good American music, and it's mine."

Five years before bands like the Blasters drew their own conclusions (as their 1980 album *American Music* indicates), Danny and his compadres already knew the secret. The album galvanized players like Pete Kennedy, who'd long admired The Band's explorations of American musical history. "Danny & the Fat Boys were like a version of The Band in my hometown," he says. He started collecting similar records, assisted by friends like Billy Hancock and Tom Principato.

DANNY GATTON'S FLAIR FOR experimentation also extended to his instruments, as rockabilly singer-guitarist Tex Rubinowitz discovered on meeting him in 1974. "He had put an original Charlie Christian pickup in his guitar," he says. "I looked at that and said, 'Now that is just the coolest thing.'" With Brent's help, Danny and Rubinowitz built more of the single-coil Christian pickups—and even made some into belt buckles. The work was time consuming, according to Rubinowitz: "I would take a humbucking [pickup] frame, cut and glue a piece of black plastic across, and cut a hole out. We didn't have any machinery. It was all done by hand."

In August 1974, the amateur pickup makers secured an unlikely endorsement from one of Danny's longtime musical heroes: Merle Haggard's lead guitarist, Roy Nichols. Danny, Dan Senior, Rubinowitz, and his girlfriend, Joan Dubit, had gone to a show at a theatre-in-the-round in Shady Grove, Maryland, and made their way backstage. "Roy asked if we could give him a Charlie Christian pickup," Rubinowitz says. "He said, 'Can you come and put it in the guitar tomorrow? We practice here.' I was so excited. I knew that Danny was impressed with Roy."

By the next afternoon, they'd rebuilt the guitar and made a little plaque for it, Rubinowitz says. When Danny gave the guitar back to Nichols, he pulled out his own instrument and jump-started a jam. "They played 'Honeysuckle Rose' so bloody fast, it sounded like they were playing it on a Theremin or something," Rubinowitz laughs. "Danny had to lead the whole way, but Roy never let him get away. It's a damn dirty shame we didn't have a tape recorder."

Danny's next round of experiments would soon eclipse these casual efforts. It all began when Virginian Joe Barden—a longtime aficionado of roots music himself—experienced an epiphany on January 5, 1975, at the Keg. He happened to walk in and see Danny playing "Good Enough to Keep" to an empty house. "It was a transcendental moment for me, because I'd been into guitar since I was eight years old," Barden says. "I'd studied classical guitar, and I'm standing there watching this redneck from outer space. He's got a classical left hand, which is absolutely bizarre."

Danny was also picking with his little finger, "which is totally unusual for anyone playing anything other than classical—it never occurs. Banjo players do it. I knew from looking at him that he hadn't been taught by anybody. It just flipped me out completely: he was playing the passing runs, the solo, the whole thing." At the same time, Danny's style proved "totally comprehensible," Barden says. "I've taken people to see [jazz-rock guitarists] Mike Stern or Allan Holdsworth, and they're like, 'It's nonsense, what is this?' What Danny was playing was a composite of everything you've ever heard, and everything you felt like you wanted to hear. You had that constant feeling of going, 'Oh yeah, that, too.'"

Although Barden wouldn't start winding pickups for Danny until April 1980, "it increasingly got to the point where I couldn't justify coming to see him night after night without doing something," he says. "The pickup thing seemed like something technical to latch onto. Clearly, they didn't know what they were doing." And Danny wanted to stretch beyond the limits of his current guitar and amp configuration. "I was the only person who was readily available and interested in pushing this envelope," Barden says. At that time, "everybody from Martin to Fender to Gibson was making the worst imaginable junk. Where I came from in northern Virginia, Telecasters were considered unfinished guitars. If you couldn't get anything better, you wound up with a Fender—but you ultimately hoped to get the 'finished' guitar, the cool guitar, which was a Gibson that had the binding and the trim."

Two questions arose: How could a Tele be boosted to compete with its Gibson cousins, without ruining the sound? And could anyone get rid of the never-ending hum without destroying the output and tone? "All of it had to fit in the guitar with no modifications, so that was a pretty tall order," Barden says.

Danny had some good instincts for the task at hand, but Barden wasn't impressed by the quick-and-dirty repairs he had done for his buddies. "Danny was doing bang-up jobs, slamming in nuts with a ball-peen hammer, cutting a nut any way he could. I don't want to be unkind here, but the quality was not particularly good."

Unlike Rubinowitz, who was content to make a few Charlie Christian pickups for friends, Barden wanted to get into manufacturing. "I was looking to step up production and start selling these things to people," he says. "Clearly, Seymour Duncan had some grasp of [the sound issue], because his whole pickup line was out—him and DiMarzio. But there was no parts industry like there is now."

DANNY'S UNIQUE APPROACH GOT surprising support from the industry trade magazine *Billboard*, whose January 10, 1976, issue featured *American Music* among its Top Album Picks. *Billboard*'s writer praised the album as a "superlative effort," calling its music "an amazingly good blend of '50s rock 'n' roll, country, swing, jazz, blues, soul, and even reggae." "Gatton is backed by very competent musicians and the soulful vocals of Bill Hancock," the review noted, which singled out "Good Enough to Keep," "Ubangi Stomp," and "Memphis Disco Funk" as the highlights. Such unexpected praise offered the first glint of hope that Danny might yet transcend the local scene.

Like many people around town, Bobby Hancock loved the stripped-down format of the new band: "Out of all the things Danny did, I think he was at his very best in a trio of guitar, bass, and drums." Jack Jensen also appreciated the no-frills approach. "Dave was by no means a Gene Krupa," he says, "but he didn't need to be, and Danny didn't want him to be. And Billy Hancock would just lay it down and play the tune."

Joe Barden feels that, in some ways, the Fat Boys era represented one of Danny's most consistently satisfying musical peaks. "I know Danny loved the studio, but my feeling is that he was one of those people who should have released nothing but live albums. It should have been just Fat Boys albums and gigs."

Local musicians who caught the Fat Boys' elemental roots-music alchemy never forgot it. Guitarist Jimmy Thackeray—whose blues-rockin' Nighthawks were known as the "Kings of the Far End" after the D.C. club where they'd snagged a residency—says that people kept telling him he should hear a band called Fat Chance. (According to Elliott, this was the Fat Boys' original name, until another outfit "raised a stink" about it.) "Here's Billy Hancock up there, singing every song known to man, Danny playing all the guitar, and Dave playing this very unorthodox drum part," Thackeray says. "We were completely blown away, and we felt our little cruddy gig was probably in serious jeopardy."

Dave Chappell ran across Danny in 1975, when he accompanied a friend who needed his guitar refinished. The work was being done at Danny's ill-fated guitar shop in College Park, which he ran with partner

Mike Faour. "The guy at the counter said, 'You see that guy in the back? He's one of the best players in the country,'" Chappell recalls. He found out the reason when he caught the Fat Boys at the Psyche Delly a couple weeks later. "Danny came in last, huffing and puffing, with a Fender Bassman. I thought, Hey, that's the guy! They just started playing, and it was a mind-blowing experience. All the trios up to that time either modeled themselves after Jimi Hendrix or Cream, and that's what you were expecting. These guys were doing rockabilly—'Mystery Train' and things like that."

As gratifying as this kind of recognition was, Elliott recalls some confusion greeting the album's release. "A lot of people thought we were an oldies band, until they came to hear us live," he says. "It was different, mainly because of Danny's playing—it wasn't Harvey & the Hubcaps!" The band celebrated *American Music*'s October 1975 release with a gig at a Rainbow Tree record store, but Elliott had mixed feelings about the album. "I was still excited about being on my first album, but when Billy brought it over to my house I didn't even like it. It didn't sound like us, and I was disappointed."

NORMA GATTON DOESN'T RECALL any specific conversations about whether Danny hoped to learn a living playing music. "He was so engrossed in it, I just surmised that's what he wanted to do," she says. "My husband knew he had talent, and I knew he had talent. We both encouraged him. We didn't hold back." Both parents made a point of seeing Danny play whenever possible; "we'd try to go Saturday night or Sunday afternoon, where he'd be playing these little two-bit jobs," Norma says. "We would go and let him know we were there, backing him. We were engrossed. We knew the musicians. They befriended us, and we befriended them."

Dan Senior was so committed that "he used to walk around and hand out cassettes of Danny on a hot night," Tom Principato says. "I've still got a couple. He was just a proud father." Those who were really close to the family received the belt buckles fashioned from pickups; Eddie Adcock was among those who got one, complete with an inscription on the back: "To my good friend Eddie Adcock, the best banjo player I've ever heard. Danny Gatton, Sr., July 24, 1979."

Danny also distinguished himself through loyalty to his friends, whether they played with him or not, according to Norma. "And the men he worked with were all nice people; to this day, they're all nice people. They were devoted to him, and their camaraderie was nice—no backbiting or criticizing each other, anything like that. They were all together for each other."

Norma worked hard after *American Music*'s release to complement Al-addin's slender promotional efforts, which amounted to little more than some blue-and-white stickers made to push the album. Norma's own favorite gambit followed the release of "Harlem Nocturne" as a single. "I advertised him on the radio at lunch time. I said, 'The people'll have to hear you, 'cause they're eating their lunch,' and it worked."

Norma had no shortage of ideas about what her son's next move should be, which she expressed in a simple declarative statement: "I like it when Danny does the blues." According to Principato, "She always thought her favorite thing about Danny and the music ought to be what should be perpetuated. I don't think Danny always agreed with her." Though she sometimes came off as "a very strong-willed, almost domineering person, I've never seen Norma as more than anything except a mom who cared a lot, just a basically great person," he adds. And she didn't mind taking care of the business end—arranging the bookings and counting the door money—so Danny could play the guitar and not be hassled.

Billy Hancock had an abundance of ideas himself, which included the taping of a live album at Bethesda's Psyche Delly. Lou Sordo had opened the club in 1975 across the street from WHFS, the maverick station generally considered the most supportive of local music. Fans received their advance invitations in July, as Brawner Smoot recalled in his liner notes for NRG's *American Music* reissue. The August 7, 1976, gig started with a set by the Nighthawks, whose harp player, Mark Wenner, joined the Fat Boys on several numbers. WHFS broadcast the proceedings live, but the promised album never happened, although some tracks crept out on an album that Billy released in 1989 as *Fat Boys: Vintage Masters*. "That's a little bit of it, but they still held back all the good stuff, I think," Joe Kogok says.

Kogok says that the Fat Boys would sometimes do gigs that became "stump the band" competitions, where the crowd called out songs for them to play. "Billy Hancock was a bottomless pit of old tunes. There wasn't anything he didn't know, and Danny fit right in with what Billy knew," Kogok says. "It was just unbelievable. They were so tight and so polished, I don't know why that band didn't make it."

Kogok was among the local legions that followed Danny around with a tape recorder, capturing the gigs on cheap cassettes—until he'd learned whatever tricks he needed to know, anyway. Then he'd wipe the last show to record the next one, a practice he regrets today. "I kind of took it for granted, because I recorded that band all the time. Had I known, I would have saved every one of them." One night, Danny asked Kogok if he had his guitar with him. "I said, 'I can pick it up real quick.' So I sat in with him, and that's when he asked me to join the band. I was in heaven. I learned more by following him around with a tape recorder, but the experience of playing with him was something else."

Twin lead guitars were a popular feature then, thanks to the popularity of Southern rockers like the Allman Brothers and Lynyrd Skynyrd. The Fat Boys' jazzier imperatives helped to distinguish them from their heavier brethren, although Danny sometimes fretted over how Kogok perceived his musical role. "We were talking one time, and he said, 'Do you think the reason I have you in the band is so I can blow you away every night and look good?'" Kogok recalls. "I said, 'Yeah, isn't that the reason?' 'No, that's not it at all!'"

Danny's unusual timing set him apart from other guitar players, and it made a twin-lead version of "Stumblin'" especially challenging for Kogok. "He'd start comping chords on this timing, and you'd get lost listening to him. It was just the rhythm that he had. I mean, a real good jazz player wouldn't get lost, but somebody like me, listening to that—I'd get lost in it, because it sounded so cool. It sounded better than anything I was doing."

Exciting as the twin-lead setup may have sounded, Danny soon tired of it. "After a while, Danny figured he didn't need another guitar player playing lead," Kogok says. "It was Bobby Hancock [on rhythm guitar] after that." Kogok retains one keepsake from his life as a Fat Boy: Danny's '59 Les Paul. "He took the covers off the humbucking pickups—they had magnets in 'em from a Hofner bass; made 'em just a little bit stronger," he says.

OUTSIDE OF THE D.C. AREA, promotion remained an uphill task. There were only a few big corporate labels, and getting their attention required a track record or the kind of grassroots following that had made Roy Buchanan's Crossroads days legendary. Indie labels were beginning to make noise nationally, but lack of cash flow limited their reach. Budgets were smaller, which wasn't necessarily a bad thing: numerous blues, punk, and rockabilly bands were showing how to make compelling records for mere fractions of the six-figure budgets spent by the majors.

The indies ran on small margins, and financial concerns often interfered with "doing the right thing." Judgment lapses by a label owner or failure to pay on time by a key distributor could torpedo the best-laid plans. There were no video or Internet outlets to spread the word, so bands had to hustle whatever clubs, record stores, and promoters they could to establish a sympathetic support network. Stores largely operated on a consignment basis—meaning that nobody got paid until somebody *bought* those albums or singles they'd been persuaded to stock.

Night Life, by Tom Principato's band Powerhouse, became the next Aladdin release after *American Music*. Billy Hancock had gone to see the band and "he was into Amos Milburn and all that stuff," says Principato. "We blew Billy away, just because we were probably the only band he'd seen, other than his own, that attempted jump blues."

Top 40 cover bands tended to dominate the club scene, which meant a great degree of hustle was needed to survive. For a time, though, Aladdin's potpourri of releases—the Fat Boys, the Nighthawks, Powerhouse, Bobby Radcliffe—managed to generate some local excitement. "Being in a roots music band—for a lack of a better term—you sort of operated on the fringes, or more in the suburbs," Principato says. "Danny used to moonlight in a lot of redneck country bands, in dives around La Plata [Maryland]. I never experienced very much of that, but I know about it."

There were major distinctions between music audiences only a few miles apart, according to Joe Barden: "Virginia people, a lot of times, didn't come to Maryland, and Maryland people didn't come to Virginia. Plus, there were very few places to play in Virginia—there were more in Maryland and D.C. So when Danny came to Virginia, it was always a pretty big deal. It just didn't happen very often." Local quirks affected the live music scene, too: for example, the city fathers of Fairfax, Virginia, didn't allow dancing, which crimped any club's chance of success. "Virginia just wasn't happening," says Barden.

WHFS remained the most relevant local music outlet, with college stations like Georgetown University's WGTV and Catholic University's WAMU providing reinforcement. "That made an enormous difference, and it was especially evident after they stopped doing it, because everything fell off," Principato says.

The *Unicorn Times* was another crucial bastion of support, which is how Brawner Smoot got to know Danny. He remembers being stunned by the fluency and strength Danny had shown during the Liz Meyer days. "Like a lot of D.C. people, I'd been a big Roy fan and thought Roy wrote the book," he says. "When I started seeing Danny, it just blew me away that he could do everything Roy did, and better." Smoot got to know Danny at the Childe Harold. Between sets one night, he and Danny were talking about an article about Charlie Christian called "What the Hell Are We Playing B For?" Danny asked Smoot if he'd seen it, "and I said, 'Well, I wrote it!' We kind of became instant friends at that point. He was sporting his Charlie Christian belt buckle and had the Charlie Christian pickup in his Tele."

Although not inclined to be a frontman, Danny never had any trouble getting attention. He radiated an unspoken charisma that made the sloppiest beer drinker pay attention, even during elementary tasks like tuning up. "All eyes would go to Danny," Norma says. "Everybody's waiting for him to start doing something. We'd all be watching him, seeing what he was going to do next. He was like a monkey." Even on casual family outings, people would stare at him, which would move Danny to ask, "Why's everybody looking at me?" Norma recalls. He was uncomfortable with all the attention. "He used to say, 'I never wanted to be a star; I just wanted to be a guitar player,'" Bobby Hancock says.

Danny's self-effacing nature expressed itself in surprising ways. One night, he sat in at a Nighthawks gig and had a ball playing Elvis Presley and rockabilly numbers. "At the end of the night, we handed him 200 bucks—and that was flabbergasting to him," Jimmy Thackeray recalls. "'What's this?' 'You played the gig; this is what you get. Sorry it's not more.' I don't think he was used to that kind of treatment."

Some of Danny's encounters with other local musicians have become local folklore. Cold Steel Benders bassist Terry Benton remembers the comedy of errors that plagued his second meeting with Danny, at a bill in Manassas, Virginia. "It was some kind of festival thing. All I remember is, we were up there playing, and Danny & the Fat Boys were all sitting in the first row, looking at us with big goo-goo eyes, and the drummer blows the whole thing! We were all nervous. There we were, playing for Danny Gatton."

Benders guitarist Tommy Gros says that watching Danny play was a study in frustration. "Most guitar players, you'd go and pick up something: 'I could do that.' But you'd sit there through a whole night of watching Danny—you'd be inundated with all this stuff, and you couldn't remember a damn thing. You just couldn't keep track of it all."

When he wasn't stumping the local guitarists, Danny had his ever-restless fingers wrapped around some vintage instrument or other. Bassist Johnny Castle learned as much when Danny called him in 1975 or '76 to boast: "I got the best bass that Fender ever made." "I kind of laughed and said, 'Well, I'll believe that when I see it,'" Castle says. "He said, 'I'll bring it over.'" At first glance, the bass didn't seem that promising. "It was ugly to look at—just a sunburst bass, pretty worn, and all the finish on the neck was gone. It'd definitely been played. But it had the fastest neck I'd ever seen on a Precision. It was just real comfy and had a wonderful, warm tone." Castle promptly offered $500 for it, which Danny accepted.

Thereafter, Danny would ask, "How's Marvin?" The question puzzled Johnny, until he learned the bass had belonged to Marvin Carroll, who'd worked with singer Jimmy Dean (of "Big Bad John" fame). "He had gotten this bass somehow—I guess from the Carroll family—and wanted it to go to a good home, so he thought of me," Castle says. "I'm really glad he did, because I still have it."

Guitarist Pat Moore recalls another transaction. "I told him if he ever came across an old Telecaster, I would buy it if he wanted to sell it," Moore says. "One day, the phone rang and it was Danny. He said, 'I have your guitar if you want it. It's $800.' That was a lot of money back in those days, but I bought it—and today it's worth thousands. Years later, he autographed it inside the body and the neck. It's a '53 Telecaster, which I still own to this day. Danny always said that this particular guitar had the fattest neck that he had ever played. He had short fingers, and it was too fat for him."

AMERICAN MUSIC DID FAIRLY well locally, since people had long wanted a true Danny Gatton album—"but I didn't think Danny was mixed well on it," Principato says. "And Danny said that it was kind of a hodge-podge. It's really not what the Fat Boys were—a power trio with Billy out front on vocals. It wasn't what you saw at the Childe Harold or the Psyche Delly."

There were other problems, too. Although Aladdin had managed an impressive roster of local releases in a short period, the label was starting to run out of steam. "They were trying, but they really didn't have the money or the expertise to pull it off," Principato says. The major factor, however, was Danny's frustration with Billy's handling of the business, many associates say. There's the oft-told "rock story," which goes something like this: At the last gig Danny did with the Fat Boys, they were playing somewhere in Maryland where there was a door deal and a huge crowd. Billy felt nervous about carrying around the large sum that he'd collected, so he put it under a rock. When he came back to retrieve the money, it was gone. The minute that Billy told him, Danny packed up his guitar and left without saying a word.

Elliott says that Billy's behavior crossed the line from unpredictable to undependable as time passed, which manifested itself in "playing the wrong song on purpose, looking around the room, and being late onstage. He couldn't possibly get bored with what Danny was playing—but he just wasn't paying attention anymore."

Billy asserts the problems stemmed from finances: American Music proved less successful than Aladdin's albums by the Nighthawks and Powerhouse. "I remember this: when I ended up paying these people that weren't members of the band to come in and play on these tracks, and paid for my tape and my studio time, I had $5,000 in that. I'd pressed an initial run of 5,000. When the album first came out, I didn't meet the nut, so I didn't pick up the option to press more. I just shoved it back in the can for later use." Billy had always intended to release the Psyche Delly gig, but then the band broke up. "I had lost interest in it. I wanted to play more jazz and swing—that was my thing, anyway."

There was also the issue of temperament, Bobby Hancock believes. If someone had told Billy that he could become famous by "wearing a pink jockstrap and playing punk rock, he'd have done it in a minute," he says. "He just wanted to be the center of attention. He's a very talented guy, but he's also a legend in his own mind." Danny simply wanted to play guitar and leave the business hustle and bustle to others—but if someone crossed the line, there was hell to pay. "Danny just got upset with Billy, I guess, and that was the end. Dave and I waited about a week to talk to Danny."

Kennedy didn't know the principals well enough at the time to say what happened, but he suspects that Danny's restlessness had an impact. "On a musical level, Danny might have wanted to play more jazz—that's why, after he got to know John Previti, he wanted to work with John more. And Billy might have felt like Liz: that he didn't want his vocals to be the punctuation between guitar solos."

There was another problem, according to Tex Rubinowitz (who'd release a single on Aladdin and wind up on another local indie, Ripsaw Records, which would release his best-known song, "Hot Rod Man"). "They'd walk up to Billy and call him 'Danny,' because Billy sang—and the singer is always the leader of the band, right? It always bothered Billy a lot. I tried to tell Billy: 'They don't know! It's not like they're trying to insult you.'"

"I think Danny began to consider Billy off the wall," Jan recalls, "but they seemed to get along well when they weren't onstage together. I think Billy had aspirations that were far beyond what Billy could bring off, and I guess what Danny wanted was something different. That was a horrible time for Dan. I guess it was rewarding in one way, but in another way it wasn't. He was distraught about some of the situations that were created onstage."

Richard Harrington believes that the Fat Boys' implosion left the same taste in Danny's mouth as his Liz Meyer days: "Neither of them were tremendously rewarding outside of the pure experience level. He didn't really benefit from either of them, outside of his reputation. It just strikes me that all these things contributed to his negative expectations of the business—and his wariness."

Whatever the reason, the Fat Boys were done—although they never went away completely. Through the years, the original trio would regroup periodically for anyone who cared to book them. They might be the Fat Boys again for two or three gigs "and stick together for a couple of months—it wasn't like once it ended, it ended," according to Jack Jensen. Whenever they did those gigs, Elliott jokes, they'd immediately realize why the band couldn't become a full-time proposition again.

Redneck Jazz
(1977–1978)

Another era was happening, as fate would have it: the first of many Danny Gatton Bands. "We got Tiny McCloud—who was a really good guitar player—to play bass, and we regrouped as the Danny Gatton Band," Bobby Hancock says. "It was basically the same thing as the Fat Boys without Billy Hancock, really. We did a wide variety of stuff."

The revamped band "hid out" at Sam's Crab House in Clinton, Maryland. "Nobody really knew we were there, and that's where we just kind of put it together," Bobby says. "Then Tiny McCloud realized, after a few weeks, that he wanted to play guitar again." (The group worked for all of December 1976 as the New Danny Gatton Band, according to *Capitol Rock*.) McCloud "didn't get it," in Elliott's lexicon (perhaps because frustrated guitarists don't make the best bass players).

Because Danny's name was out front, when Bobby collected the money it only seemed fair to pay Danny a little more than everyone else. If they got $500, he'd give Danny $150 or $200, with the boys splitting the rest. When Danny raised the point, Bobby said, "These people ain't coming to see us, they're coming to see you! Take you out, and we're just another band." He remembers Danny describing the arrangement to Jan, "like he was proud of it—he deserved it."

Bobby was now running a music store, Discount Guitar Center, in Clinton, which gave Danny ample reason to hang out. So did John Previti, who'd end up playing with him for nearly 20 years. "He was a friend of a guy that was teaching guitar for me, and I think John also did some bass teaching for me," Bobby says. "Of course, Danny would come around and start playing a little bit, so John had the chance to play with him. When Tiny McCloud left, I asked Danny: 'What do you think about John?' To make a long story short, he came to play with us, until Danny left to go to the West Coast."

Previti's recruitment was typically low-key. He'd spent his teen years playing rock 'n' roll before turning to jazz after graduating from Surrattsville High School in 1972, according to Opsasnick. Previti didn't meet Danny until July 1976, at Bobby's guitar shop. "During the course of the evening Bob introduced us and we talked a little bit, and Robbie Weaver was there, and we all plugged into one Magnatone amp and we jammed for a few hours," Previti told Opsasnick. "It was all I could do just to hold on, but Danny thought I played good." Five months later, he added, Danny called him to the shop and asked, "How'd you like to play in an old redneck band?"

Previti recalls his debut gig as December 27, 1976, at the Crazy Horse. (Besides Danny and himself, Previti said, the lineup also included Elliott, Bobby Hancock, and vocalist Tommy Branch.) He would prove a rock-solid, reassuring presence while extending the band's musical vocabulary in ways that had been unimaginable during the Fat Boys era. He was also quick to grasp the range of Gatton's talent. "What doesn't get talked about much is, when we played any particular tune, Danny covered all the parts," Previti told this author in an interview for *Vintage Guitar*. "He could phrase like a horn player or an organist. I got used to that very quickly."

The next significant change came with the arrival of singer-guitarist Evan Johns, who'd left the turmoil of his McLean, Virginia, home at 14 to strike out on his own as a musician. He dropped out of high school during tenth grade, but made up for the lost time by taking a year-and-a-half of classes in one semester at the Emerson Institute. "[My parents] couldn't bitch, because I was paying my way," Johns says. "So I was up at Dupont Circle every day, hanging out with the hippies after school—and there's the Childe Harold, and down the street was My Mother's Place."

By 18, Johns had already traveled extensively across the United States and was fully immersed in the local music scene. He'd first seen Danny during the Fat Boys era ("I went up and introduced myself") and had begun to make a name for himself with the Cold Steel Benders. However, Johns is quick to correct stories of him being responsible for the Benders' creation: "It was not my band. I got the gig because of the songs. I was underage, but I was so damn big, it didn't matter."

Johns would end up bringing two songs from that band to the *Redneck Jazz* table, including its witty title track and the out-and-out belly laugh of "Ugly Man." "It was just truck-drivin' country music and Elvis," Johns said. "If I had a band like that right now, I could work all over D.C." In fact, "every band up there did Elvis, no matter what genre—you couldn't get the South out of 'em." (The same can be said for Danny's famed medley of Sun-era Elvis classics—"Mystery Train," "My Baby Left Me," and "That's All Right, Mama"—which didn't get an official release until 1993's *Cruisin' Deuces* yet stretched back two decades, to when Danny cut an unreleased version with vocalist Tommy Branch, according to Elliott.)

The King's imprint is only one measure of what Johns regards as the area's contrarian touch. "The first oldies station in the world was in D.C.," he says. "It was a direct backlash against the British Invasion. They're listening to the Beatles doing Chuck Berry songs—they weren't buying into it. They were pissed off, because this is like walking all over the U.S.A.!" For that reason, Washington remained a reliable stop for '50s rockabilly pioneers like Carl Perkins—who could still draw there, long after passing his chart prime—and a factor that kept bands from getting too trendy for their own good. "Locally, the bands were so good that you didn't get led astray by fads," Johns says. "You'd get shot down from out of the sky if you showed up copping something. Roy took heat for that from being in the British Walkers."

John Previti's recruitment marked a departure of sorts, for he came from outside the "usual suspects" cadre of local musicians. "John was there when I showed up [in 1976]—he popped onto the scene out of a clear blue sky," Johns says. "He wasn't one of the guys that had been in 30 bands, but, boy, he could sure play the bass." Elliott remembers the initial transition as bumpy, with Previti quitting and then returning to replace McCloud. "I don't think he 'got it,' at first," Elliott believes; needless to say, once he did, his massive upright bass became as crucial a voice as Danny's trusty '52 and '53 Teles.

The Benders had supported the Danny Gatton Band at the University of Maryland. The memory of that experience came in handy one night in La Plata, where Danny—most unusually—went home with the flu. To salvage the night, Danny suggested Johns as a sub. "He came down, and it went good," Elliott says. "We had a ball."

"He knew that I had been so many places and been through so many things," Johns says. "He respected me. I was a little guy, 11 years younger, but I had so much strength and faith and fortitude, and it all worked. I did what I said, and that was all he needed." Johns's decision left the Benders adrift without their colorful frontman and essentially killed the band, according to Benton. (The news wasn't all bad for Benton. He and drummer Brooks Tegler—who'd strike a unique two-sessions-for-two-tracks bartering arrangement with Danny in the '80s—wound up playing together for 20 years.)

One of Johns's next gigs with Danny found him at the Childe Harold, where he got a vivid glimpse of the local color. The band had just finished

Evan Johns (left) and Danny cut loose at Childe Harold in D.C., 1978. Danny wields what became his guitar of choice, the '53 Fender Telecaster.

a tune when some scraggly looking character approached Johns: "Hey, you! You're the new singer, aren't you? You're pretty good!"

"He put his foot through a chair and walked back into the crowd with the chair around his leg," Johns says. "Danny, Dave, and the others were all laughing, and then it came to me: 'Oh, they must know this guy!'" When he asked about the stranger's identity, his new bandmates told him: "That's Bill Heard, the clubowner!"

Danny had less affection for Desperado's owner Rich Vendig, whom he sardonically christened "Rich Vindictive"; Johns took a more straight-forward view of their relationship ("I'm playing his nightclub; I want to get paid and come back"). Such pragmatism didn't stop Danny from having a run-in one night over a trivial issue. Johns had sung only five or six tunes with the Benders, so necessity dictated the inclusion of covers like "Six Days on the Road" and "Big Boss Man," and "because I wasn't a lead singer," Johns says, "the plan was to do 'em again in the last set." To take off some of the pressure, Danny decided to stretch out instrumentally during the second set, which culminated in a 45-minute "Linus and Lucy." Vendig confronted him during the break, shouting "This is a lyrical club!"—meaning one where people expected to hear a singer. "Danny said, 'Whose name's out front?'" Johns recalls. "And Vendig said, 'The Danny Gatton Band.' And Danny said, 'Well, they don't have any problem with Danny Gatton not singing, do they?'"

Johns describes their musical relationship as an implicit one, with precious little worked out in advance. "The dude was so hip, he let me run wild—he knew to tell me what to do would be wrong." Danny would take most of the leads, but Johns would solo on the songs he sung, and they'd even play the odd dual-guitar line. "Most of it was just kind of winging it."

They hit upon an entertaining shtick along the way, with Johns and Danny making up song lyrics about local figures. Everybody got a line or two: "The sun came out, and it was a mighty ray; I heard a rumble, and it was Link Wray!" Danny would then play an appropriate guitar figure that matched the person being sent up—or celebrated—as the mood dictated. Danny's rival couldn't escape a name-check in these hijinks, of course. Johns reeled off the appropriate allusion to Buchanan ("There was a mighty racket, and it was ragin'; it was Roy, the Cajun!"), "and Danny would start clicking his teeth, like he was on the cocaine thing," Johns says. "We knew this dude; he used to grind his teeth." Johns himself didn't get off unscathed: "Then the next thing we knew, it got a little worse; holy mackerel, Evan Johns got the curse!" As Johns sang these lines, "Danny would retune the guitar, make it all out of tune, and play horrible," Johns says, laughing.

Danny found other ways of stretching his wings, too. The turn of 1976–77 saw him making trips to Nashville, where he struck an alliance with the pedal steel player who'd become an integral part of his next band, the Redneck Jazz Explosion: Buddy Emmons. Norma remembers seeing the two players throw down "at this nightclub in Nashville…and we had a ball. Emmons has always been fantastic; he was fantastic even then."

Danny made regular trips to Nashville during the early '80s, until the Pickin' Parlor closed. "He liked that place," says Eddie Adcock, "because it was a bluegrass place that would let him play. All the greatest jazz players in town would come to see him. He'd have four or five of 'em get up onstage at one time, and give 'em their turns at taking solos. Most of them loved him, although they didn't want to take a break after he was done." Their reluctance was understandable. "Danny only respected people he couldn't blow away," Eddie says.

The locals took notice, as an April 5, 1977, *Music City News* review showed. Significantly, Bill Littleton said that his interest didn't center only on Danny's speed: "I simply mean he plays more approaches to the instrument and better than anyone I've ever heard." Going a step further, Littleton added: "Gatton avoids cutesy tricks and dazzling gymnastics; he just picks—and does he *ever* pick!"

The great country guitar pioneer Chet Atkins also took notice of the hot young newcomer. He was doing A&R (Artist & Repertoire) and production work for RCA, so he came by to see what Danny could do. Spike Ostmann, who was with Danny on that trip, says that "Danny played well…[and] Chet put on his glasses to watch him play."

They also encountered Canadian fingerstyle jazz master Lenny Breau, whom Ostmann recalls meeting at a "crummy apartment on Music Row.

The door opens, and this little guy comes out, looking kind of disheveled, and Danny says, 'Hey, Lenny!' He looked very forlorn." Like Danny, Breau would be the object of hero worship that didn't stretch far beyond guitar circles; unlike Danny, he'd be periodically sidelined by troubles with drugs. (He died under mysterious circumstances in Los Angeles on May 12, 1984.)

Ironically, Atkins showed more interest in Breau, which led to a couple of albums on RCA. Breau wound up playing the Cellar Door with Danny on April 25, 1979; a tape of that night remains in circulation among diehard collectors of both men's music. When asked how they influenced each other, Ostmann says, "Lenny was a master of closed harmonics—and, of course, Danny became a master, too."

Danny also picked up another useful quality from Breau's style: an affinity for piano triad–type chords, typically spaced five or six frets apart, according to Johns. "What is fluid to some is so uncomfortable that it looks like your hand is webbed like a duck's foot, know what I mean?" But Danny could play those chords, using the same determination that had enabled him to absorb other players' styles. "He knew all the Sugarfoot Garland and Chet Atkins stuff," Johns says. "Danny figured, 'I'm going to learn this stuff right, and I'm going to get it from the top.'"

"I'm sure he absolutely scared Chet to death—I'm sure he did," Eddie Adcock says. "He's got a few scales he can run, with some fast fingerpicking, [but] he's not what Danny was." Jan thinks that Danny would have loved any interaction with Atkins, whether he was offering assistance or not. Unfortunately, the only time came after Danny called to express condolences after Breau's death. Jan recalls the conversation as brief and frosty, with Atkins wondering how Danny had gotten his number. (He'd gotten it from Breau, as it turned out.)

Danny didn't do much better the first time he met his musical inspiration, Les Paul. According to Tex Rubinowitz, he and Danny were in Rockville, Maryland, where the guitar pioneer was interrupting his retirement long enough to play for the opening of a music store, backed by his son on drums. "I chatted him up real good; I knew the right things to say," Rubinowitz says. "Finally, Danny said to Les, and he sort of said it looking down: 'Isn't it a shame that you can't play what you want to play?'" If Danny was seeking empathy, the master wasn't in an empathetic mood. "Les explodes: 'Wait a minute! Where's my son? Get my son over here!' When his son's there, he says, 'I want both of you guys to hear this: When that drunk at the end of the bar leaves, I want him to be whistling the tune you just played.' Danny didn't like that at all—he went, 'Oh, fuck.' He didn't say it, but, boy, I tell you, it was written all over his face."

Their second encounter, at My Friend's House in Langley Park, Virginia, was more positive. "Les Paul came to see us there," Elliott says. "He sat right in front and stayed there the whole damn night—it was way cool!" They got an idea of how special the night had been from Paul's girlfriend, who said that he never stuck around for a whole set. (Elliott later backed up Paul at another store opening in Landover, Maryland, "and Danny was in the audience, giving me signals," he says.)

Danny signed the headstock of Paul's guitar with a screwdriver; Paul, in turn, entrusted his serial number 002 guitar to Danny's care. The night had seemed to glow with promise; Elliott recalls Paul saying, "I'm going to put you guys on the map so fast, it'll make your heads spin." There was even talk of Danny doing an album for Paul's Outrageous label, but nothing happened—the terms, which included doing all-original material, were too restrictive or too vague, according to a 1977 article by Brawner Smoot in *Unicorn Times*.

"I gathered that no offer was ever made," Jan says, "or if it was, it was not very definite. It was just all about Les, in my opinion, and I don't think he was ready to give up his crown."

Ostmann heard about the whole business from Danny. "He had told Danny, 'I'm going to take you under my wing. I'm going to make you a star.' Of course, Danny was in seventh heaven. Les backed off; I don't know why. I called Les myself several times, on Danny's behalf." Ostmann learned during those conversations that Paul's former wife and vocal partner, Mary Ford, was gravely ill. "She was in real bad shape, and poor Les was distraught. When I called him up, he was very nice, but he was just talking about Mary."

THE DANNY GATTON BAND was well received, but the Elliott-Johns-Previti grouping lasted only about six months. Elliott attributes the band's demise to problems with Johns. "He got a big head real fast. He would step all over Danny's solos. It was weird, 'cause when he first started playing with us, it was fine."

Johns scoffs at this comment, saying that he understood the unspoken rule of not getting in Danny's way. They'd worked out that issue soon after he'd joined. "It was funny, because I couldn't tell when he was done [with a solo]," he says. "He'd have to go around and do another chorus, and if I missed that one, then he'd have to take it up another notch. I was totally new to this stuff. Eventually I had to say to him, 'Danny, I can't tell when you're done.'" He suggests that Danny's eternally restless nature may have also played a role. "I wasn't in that band long enough to know the undercurrents that were dictating the flow."

Bobby Hancock returned for the band's next incarnation. "Once again, Danny wanted one of his buddies in the band," Elliott says, "so Bobby played rhythm guitar with us—as if we needed one. It was a treat to have him in the band, and he was a great guy, too. He didn't get in the way, and he laid down a nice rhythm."

From Bobby's perspective, stamina was an important aspect of the Danny Gatton experience. "I'm disappointed they never got his true version of 'Orange Blossom Special,' because it was phenomenal. Traditionally, it was done at a brisk tempo, then—at the very end—played much faster. But we started off at the faster tempo and went to the ozone with it! Danny's speed was just unbelievable."

Bobby had to remain alert to Danny's mood—"Sometimes he played a whole lot, and a lot of times he played very little"—and be content to take the backseat. "Other than my flat-top picking, when I'd take a solo on a bluegrass tune, nobody had any idea that I could really play."

Working with Danny was always a learning experience, as Joe Kogok explains: "He showed me this unique way of playing octaves. He used to just blow me away, because he'd play octave 16th-notes. He would do this, and I couldn't figure out what the heck he was doing! He called them 'octave fake notes.' He said, 'These notes are inferred, and they're not really there, but it all goes by so fast, your ear thinks that it heard them.'" Kogok also picked up on Danny's way of playing fast triplets. "You only pluck the string once, but you move your fingers over three frets." Danny's use of octave pull-offs also made an indelible impression on Kogok. "That's where you play the octave, and pull your fingers off the strings. To this day, I've never seen anybody else do these things."

When other players broke those tricks down for themselves, it didn't do any good—because Danny always had something different up his sleeve. "People would copy [these techniques] and build styles off these things that he did," Kogok says, "but he would just do these things for a short period of time and then move on."

Local excitement about the band remained unabated, as a September 19, 1977, article in the University of Maryland's *Diamondback* newspaper made clear. The writer, Slaton White, opened his review by posing a simple proposition: imagine Les Paul doing the surf classic "Walk, Don't Run," Charlie Byrd doing "Orange Blossom Special," and Jeff Beck tackling Mantovani—and the breadth of Danny's stylistic bag would become apparent. "Gatton is all this," he wrote. "His style is a tumultuous blend of funk, rockabilly, schmaltz, and assorted odds and ends garnered from years of playing around town." He noted a pre-gig comment he'd overhead in the Student Union lobby before the gig: "He doesn't move an inch. Man, he just plays and plays."

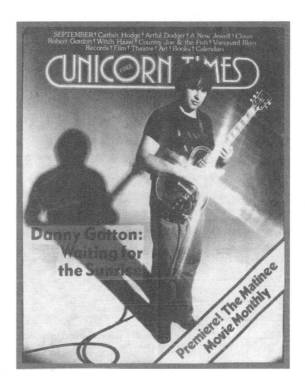

SEPTEMBER† Catfish Hodge † Artful Dodger † A New Jewell † Clown
Robert Gordon † Witch Hazel † Country Joe & the Fish † Vanguard Blues
Records † Film † Theatre † Art † Books † Calendars

UNICORN TIMES

Danny Gatton:
Waiting for
the Sunrise

Premiere! The Matinee
Movie Monthly

*The September 1977
Unicorn Times cover
featuring Danny. Writer
Brawner Smoot quickly
progressed from awed
acolyte to manager during
the Redneck Jazz era.*

"He hypnotizes an audience with his blinding speed," White continued. "He has a dazzling array of special effects that he coaxes from his guitar." White was impressed by Danny's use of the Echoplex, which he said made his guitar sound like a Wurlitzer organ on T-Bone Walker's "Stormy Monday." Other highlights included a makeover of "That's All Right, Mama" into bluegrass, before segueing into "Orange Blossom Special," and then back to boogie. "The crowd ooed and ahed at each display of his technical facility," White wrote.

That same month, the *Unicorn Times* splashed Danny on its cover for Smoot's first-ever paid article (he'd previously received albums and movie tickets). "Waiting for the Sunrise: Brawner Smoot Explains Why Our Best Guitarist Is Not a Star" was the first major overview of Danny's career, spread over five newspaper pages. (Ironically, some readers initially thought Richard Harrington had written the story, because he was known to use various pseudonyms.) Smoot's article was illustrated with photos of Danny's guitar collection, the Magic Dingus Box (his homemade multi-effects setup), and the five-piece Danny Gatton Band assembled before a '30s-era roadster. And fans could ponder Danny's ambivalence about the road he'd taken so far: "I give it up every other day. I'm either real happy or real depressed. I'm not looking to be a millionaire, but I'd like to get as far as, say, Little Feat."

Danny went on to say: "I don't want to play in beer joints, I'm sick of that.... Music is a business; it's not fun and games at my age anyway." In some respects, Smoot's story amounted to a plea for the world to realize what it had been missing. "Will the next John Hammond please step up and take this man where he deserves to go," he wrote.

Vocals remained a nettlesome issue, as Smoot's article made clear. Tommy Branch had just left the band, having lasted only weeks, so the band enlisted rhythm guitarist Chuck Tilley, who'd also sung on Roy Buchanan's first three Polydor albums. He appeared in the *Unicorn Times* photo beside Bobby, Danny, Elliott, and Previti. Some partisans found singing a distraction from what they'd come to hear—Danny's guitar work—while the man himself endorsed it as a way of reaching a wider audience. "What we're going to be doing with Chuck is for damn sure a lot more commercial," Danny told Smoot. "A lot more people can relate to it than what we've been doing all along. We're not going to drop some of the things we've been doing.... I'm not going Top 40 or anything by any means...but there's going to be a lot more material."

Danny would spend much of his artistic life trying to figure out how to straddle that divide. The conflicts didn't surprise Johns, who'd sing three of his songs on *Redneck Jazz*. "Nobody wanted to be the frontman—[that was] very uncool," he says. "That was the geek job of any act."

Danny with car and band, as pictured in the Unicorn Times *article. From left to right: Bobby Hancock, John Previti, Chuck Tilley, Danny, and Dave Elliott (note his Danny Gatton Band T-shirt!).*

Tilley sang one of his songs on the B-side of the single that preceded *Redneck Jazz*, "Ugly Man" b/w "Love Is What You Need," while Johns handled the vocals on his A-side tune. Johns also took the first guitar break, followed by Danny, which marked one of the few times that Gatton ever gave that honor to someone else. For Johns's money, Danny's solo sounded a bit too similar to the one he'd played on the rockabilly classic "Good Rockin' Tonight." "I was so new in the band, I didn't want to make waves," Johns recalls. "I said, 'Hey, man, sure you want to do that solo? You did it on *American Music*.' He said, 'Yeah, but nobody heard that record.'"

"Ugly Man" got an excellent response when WHFS played the song. Elliott and Johns heard it while driving to a gig at the University of Maryland. "That's a good feeling, the first time you're hearing yourself on the radio: 'Man, this is fuckin' making it. Hey, we're doing it, that's a good record,'" Johns says.

The enthusiasm carried over to the sessions for *Redneck Jazz* at Bias Recording, in Springfield, Virginia. "We would go in the studio and the clock's running," Bobby Hancock says. "We didn't know exactly what we were going to do, and Danny would go over these guitar tracks. [The engineer] would say, 'That was good, Danny. Play it like that.' He'd say, 'Okay, play the tape back to me, so I can learn it.' He hadn't a clue what he did. It was always off the top of his head! The guy could go all night long and never play the same lick twice, I'd repeat the same lick three times in the same set. He just had such a command of his instrument— I've always said, 'He didn't play it, he played with it.' He could do whatever crossed his mind."

Danny's all-consuming perfectionism could be a curse, though. "It was like working on cars—he'd just go, go, go," Elliott says. "He was always picking apart his guitar work, which was good and bad. I wish there would have been somebody around who could have cut him off at certain times— he was overwhelming himself. There's no sense wasting 24 hours to come up with a kazillion ideas: just pick one!"

For all of Danny's obsessiveness, however, the mood still tended to be easy-going. "We were laughing as much we were trying to make it perfect," Elliott says. "There were never any tempers flaring or anything like that— which is pretty remarkable in itself, as tense as any studio situation can be."

Terry Benton has similar recollections. He and Syd Bandle, Tim Dunn, and Jeanne Parker were recruited to sing backup vocals; the newly dubbed Gattones finished their parts in one night. The whoop that popped up during "Ugly Man" was actually a mistake made by Dunn, who hadn't been sure when to come in. "They decided to leave it," Benton says. "I thought it fit pretty well."

IN LATE 1977, DANNY opted to try his luck on the West Coast and see what he might accomplish there as a sideman or studio musician. Evan Johns remembers Danny explaining the implications to the band, though he didn't dwell on them too long: "The Good Humor Band hired me, and I had a job before I untied my shoes."

The Gatton family had just moved into a rented farmhouse at 15939 Livingston Road in Accokeek, where there's little to divert the visitor except a couple of churches and a post office about a half mile down the street from where Link Wray grew up. Now that he was in the country, Danny could crank up to his heart's content. One of his neighbors was curious about the racket. "He heard music at four or five in the morning, but it wasn't a complaint," Jan recalls. "I said, 'He's a musician, and he plays at night out in the garage,' and the guy was just impressed."

Jan says she never saw Danny practice much. "But he listened a lot. He had so many tapes, CDs, and records. When we began to pack up things for the [estate] auction, there were just hundreds and hundreds. That's what he did: he listened to everybody. He had something inside that just sucked all that in."

Danny's initial reason for going west was to join a country-rock band fronted by vocalist Larry Hosford, who'd supposedly been promised an opening slot on an upcoming tour by George Harrison. However, the ex-Beatle—who'd played slide guitar on Hosford's Shelter Records album, *Cross Words* (1976)—hadn't visited America since his critically panned 1974 solo tour and apparently wasn't about to break his streak. So those plans fell through, Danny informed the *Unicorn Times*.

"He was out there for a while," recalls Jan, who was pregnant with their only child, Holly, at the time. "We didn't have a lot of money, and my dad brought me big boxes of food so I could survive." They couldn't afford to call, so Danny wrote instead. His letters were brief but affectionate, and he'd always tell Jan not to worry—success was just around the corner.

Jan guesses that Danny didn't stay for more than six months. "We were both in foreign territory. I didn't understand totally about his music, and he didn't understand totally about my need for family around me, because I'd always had such a big family. But we loved each other, and that's what we were trying to do: be supportive. He was down in the dumps, but he did not write about that."

Smoot would later document some of those feelings in a July 1978 *Unicorn Times* article called "Gatton Hits the Road in Search of New Lease on Playing Life." At the time it appeared, Danny was mulling a move to Nashville, where he could look for session work. He'd hardly gotten unpacked from the California trip, but he was getting ready to join yet another country tour as Sonny James's banjoist and guitarist.

The California experience had been a convoluted affair. When the Hosford alliance evaporated, Danny did sessions for Commander Cody and Al McKay, who'd sought him for an album he was producing for Earth, Wind & Fire's ARC label. Danny found the Cody experience to be a big letdown, with his guitar relegated to the background while the hottest parts went to other players. He played on two tracks ("He's in Love, He's in Trouble" and "Vampira"), but the results aren't revelatory. "You can't really tell that it's Danny," Smoot says.

Roger McDuffie remembers receiving a telegram from Danny during the Cody sessions, which he still has. "It says, 'Urgent: Roger. Don't miss the chance of a lifetime. I'm with this band, they need a sax player, I told them all about you, we're going to coincide it, and I want you to call me.'" Roger called the phone number that Danny provided, which happened to be for Cody's manager. "I already had a nice house gig at a Holiday Inn, of all places, but it paid real good. It was steady; I'd been there for four years." Needless to say, Roger declined.

Al McKay's project wound up being a lot more fun, as far as the playing went. According to McKay, ARC was created through Earth, Wind & Fire's Columbia deal as a vehicle for its members' side projects. Danny laid down five-string banjo and guitar on several tracks for the Curtis Brothers, though McKay remembers just one title ("Youngblood"). "He just did some strumming or some fingerpicking—we didn't have too many places for guitar solos," McKay says. "I just wanted to play with him. I wanted to have him on the tape."

McKay says that "he just came in and did Danny Gatton. That's all I wanted him to do. He was happy, I was happy; we went along and had a drink after that. We were cool." But morale soured when Columbia wouldn't release the album—"There was a real letdown," McKay says.

In 1988, Danny told *Maryland Musician* that he had mixed emotions about putting his imprint on "really black hardcore disco music." "They'd never heard that before. It was really weird...[and] it never came out." Other than rekindling his relationship with Lowell George, being in Los Angeles held no charms for Danny. The musicians who invited him to sessions didn't have many gigs, and when they did, "they had to drive 50 miles to make 25 bucks," he told Richard Harrington.

Danny abandoned L.A. for Santa Cruz, up the coast. He was all but ready to go home when he received an invitation to appear at the Fender Exposition in Costa Mesa—where he'd be playing for music business professionals.

He did a recorded set with guitarist Lee Ritenour's band, and the enthusiasm generated by that appearance led to talk of an endorsement deal with Fender, according to Smoot's article. The Expo gig demonstrated that "Gatton's guitar mastery is adaptable to any genre—in this case, jazz fusion—replete with chicken-picking and string bending!" Smoot wrote.

While Danny experienced his share of disappointments, he found some value in the trip. "I couldn't say I learned any new licks, but I learned a different way to put a lot of that stuff together," he told Smoot. "I started thinking more melodically rather than relying on clichés."

Liz Meyer remembers being impressed by the Expo tape, which she copied from Heintze (and later lost when the basement where it was stored was flooded). She felt differently on hearing another tape of Danny rehearsing with studio musicians. "Studio players can play by ear, but they can also read and write music. They can read charts, and they know the names of all the chords, and they know music theory inside-out. These were L.A. jazz musicians, and he was out of his league. They'd say, 'Oh, what's that chord there?' And the poor guy would say, 'That was a *B*-fourth something or other.' He didn't have a clue, and he was so humiliated. You could just feel it on the tape."

In Meyer's opinion, the West Coast "was a bit of a nightmare for him— meeting guys who could play as well as he did, who could play on his level, but were also musically educated. It was a very painful experience, and he couldn't wait to scuttle home with his tail between his legs."

Shannon Ford, who started seeing more of Danny after his return, has a different impression. He remembers hearing him talk with excitement about the chance of working with Lowell George. The notion made sense, as Danny was a major fan of both George and Little Feat, but George's drug use was a major stumbling block. "That disturbed him a lot," Ford says. "I mean, Danny just wasn't a drug user—he drank beer, that was it."

Ford didn't ask many questions about Danny's West Coast experiences, because their relationship was too new. "I was more concerned whether we were going to do anything or not with *Redneck Jazz*—I didn't ask a whole lot of questions. I didn't really know anything other than what he shared with me."

Jan doesn't recall much discussion either. "It was just a negative kind of deal—it didn't turn out to be what he thought it was going to be. It's so ironic, because he was so good and yet that was always how it went. It isn't as if he didn't try."

Redneck Jazz Explosion
Goes Supernova
(1978–1979)

D anny's return signaled a radically different agenda: the Redneck Jazz Explosion. As its name implied, the group's approach drew on the collision between jazz and country—which stemmed from the players and the supercharged level of improvisation they brought to the table.

But first there was a false start: Rockabilly Avalanche, which merged the guitar front line of Danny and Evan Johns with the former Fat Boys rhythm section of Billy Hancock and Dave Elliott. "Billy, who never gets enough credit, was Danny's right-hand man—he was turning people on to all this rockabilly material," Pete Kennedy says. "I'm sure [Stray Cats guitarist] Brian Setzer must have heard those guys at some point."

Billy, with his encyclopedic roots-music knowledge, and Danny, who could summon an entire vocabulary from his fingertips, had made an ideal team during the Fat Boys era. Their knowledge and enthusiasm trickled down to younger players like Kennedy, who began hunting down Bullmoose Jackson and Amos Milburn records. "Billy always knew where the songs came from and what label they were on," Kennedy says.

But Rockabilly Avalanche sputtered to a halt after barely six weeks. "It was the worst conglomeration that we ever had," Elliott says. "Too many personalities clashing." Johns adds: "Billy had his own rockabilly records coming out, thought all these people were coming to see him, and he was going on to fame and fortune—or some such bullshit."

Things were further complicated by oddball gigs at places like the Annandale, Virginia, fire station. "By ten o'clock, the place was closed down," Johns says. "There'd always be a fight—and the police station was right next door! The hall would say, 'You're out of here!' It wasn't the band's fault. The same people would come back and do it again in four months."

Many pundits regard the *Redneck Jazz* era as Danny's most creative period. Tom Principato agrees. "Even though I think he always played great, I don't think he ever played better, and a lot of times not as well as he did then.... A lot of ingredients came together that he needed: the group, the enthusiasm, his age, the time. And the presence of certain important people who were an emotional support for him: his dad, his mom, and later Billy Windsor and Dick Heintze." Kennedy, Principato's guitar partner of the time, believes a happy confluence of interests enabled Danny to reach a musical peak in the mid-'70s. "He had the ultimate classic Tele tone... [and] he had the right influences for audiences that were just discovering Buddy Holly and Merle Haggard."

Bobby Hancock considers the Explosion's birth a sign of Danny's desire to reach a higher level of virtuosity than his other bands had achieved. "Danny finally got to the point that he started associating himself with musicians who were [more] on his level than the rest of us were—John Previti being one, Shannon Ford being one," he says.

The signature sound of this era had already arrived on *Redneck Jazz* with a specially designed effects-control device built by Danny and his father: the Magic Dingus Box. Twenty years before guitarists got blasé about having multiple effects at their disposal, Danny was already scrutinizing the banks of foot pedals in vogue among his peers and thinking there had to be a better way.

Few aspects of Danny's craft are so lionized, yet so little understood. The principles were simple enough, according to another Maryland resident who sweated with Danny to bring the Dingus Box to life: Robbie Weaver (or "Robbie Reverb," as Danny called him). "Danny wanted to be able to control his echo, volume, and repeats right on his guitar," he says. "Danny never did use reverb, 'cause he always had the old 4×10 Bassmans and tweed Bandmasters that didn't have reverb. He used an Echoplex, but got tired of having to reach behind him to adjust the stuff."

Weaver had first seen Danny during the Liz Meyer era, and it had made a seismic impact on his 20-year-old mind. "The guy played at the speed of heat—I didn't know you could do that with a Telecaster. I had a Telecaster, and I couldn't do that with my Telecaster!" Those revelations certainly were more exciting than the routine at Weaver's job of the time: working in a tobacco shop off Branch Avenue.

Weaver, who was still living with his parents, got in Danny's good graces by riding his motorcycle from Hillcrest Heights to Danny's Linda Lane home to give him a Fender volume pot. "I left it sitting on the door handle to his truck. I guess I called the next day to make sure the raccoons didn't eat it or something, so that's kind of where we started."

Weaver knew where Danny lived because he'd taken a Gibson L6S over to his house for setup work. He'd bought the guitar from Zavarella's Music, but the frets were too high. "So I took it to Danny, had the frets filed and polished, and tried my damnedest to get lessons from him. Of course, you couldn't nail Danny down to a time or a place, but it just evolved from there."

Weaver saw Danny play every chance he got. They became better acquainted after Danny opened up a guitar-repair shop in the College Park-Brentwood area in 1974. He later opened a second shop on Silver Hill Road, in Silver Hill, Maryland. "That was probably in '75," says Weaver, "and it was very close to my house. I started hanging around there, quit the tobacco shop, and went to work for him."

Danny was running the shop with a partner, Mike Faour, whom he'd sardonically christened "Mike Failure." Weaver says, "The less said [about Faour], the better. I never got paid—I just kept accruing back wages. Since I lived closest, I'd get there first and open the shop. If a shipment came in COD and I had money, I'd pay for it. If not, I'd put it on the bill."

One day, Weaver arrived to find the shop almost empty. "All the guitars and amps were gone. Mike Faour had taken them all up to his house. I didn't know if Danny knew about this or not, but I called him and he said, 'Well, get the rest of it.'" Faour then compounded the absurdity by calling and asking if Weaver would switch loyalties "basically for free." Instead, Weaver took the remaining equipment—a bandsaw, drill press, and workbench ("the total sum of wages I ever made working with Danny") — and put them in storage at a friend's house.

Weaver then started a shop in his neighborhood, Sounds Better, with a new partner, Tom Noeman. "I did all the crafty stuff with the guitars, and he did the electronic repairs." Danny liked the situation: he could bring repair jobs there "or arrange to meet people so he'd be working out of a shop, if that's what people wanted to see. I made some money, he made some money, and it worked just fine."

In 1976, Les Paul came to the area to play at the Cellar Door in Georgetown. "Danny bought everybody in the shop tickets," Weaver says. "We all went down, and it turns out that Les's amp broke and his guitar popped a fret or something." Weaver took the amp to Noeman, while Danny refretted the guitar overnight. "We just walked up to this place with Les Paul's Les Paul," he laughs, which led to them being invited to stay for the show. Weaver ended up chatting with the master's son Bobby, who was his drummer.

"After his gigs, Danny would come down to the Cellar Door to jam after hours," Weaver says. "At one point, he was playing two of Les's lines at the same time—as he was known to do, before he learned about multi-tracking. The only thing for Les Paul to do was stand there and play his own third harmony part!"

Paul had come armed with his guitar-mounted effects device, the Les Paulverizer, which made several different sound modifications. That got Danny thinking. "He got this humongous cable, pulled a bunch of wires through it, and brought the wires for the volume control and his Echoplex up to his guitar," Weaver says. "Okay, that's cool, but you've still got three or four wires through this cable—so he pulls more through, and then you got another one to control the tremolo, on and off." They then rigged a motor to operate the echo control.

They soldered a nut to the back of the treble mechanism in the Echoplex and ran a piece of thread through it. They followed with mounting posts to go on either end, ground down the threads, and added springs and washers. "You would run off the nut—it wouldn't jam—then you'd reverse direction of the spring rotation, to get the nut started again," Weaver says. "We fiddled with that thing for days to make it work." When they were done, the Echoplex could be operated by controls on the guitar.

Johns had witnessed some of this activity during his Danny Gatton Band days. What seemed like "a concerted effort at farting around," as he called the work, carried a surprising degree of purpose. "He had a Fender pickup-selector switch that would go only one way or the other way, and it would move [controls on] the head. It was funny as shit to watch him do that."

Danny's Fender amp was mounted in a Leslie organ-speaker unit. The modified Echoplex unit—now equipped with its motor-driven controls—sat on top. It required another set of switches to run the Leslie. "What controls that is a 110-volt AC [alternating current] relay," Weaver says. "Well, you don't want 110 volts in your guitar—it's a bad idea." Weaver and Danny hit upon using a 12-volt relay to trigger the 110-volt relay, added the necessary circuitry, "and put the Leslie control up on the guitar. And everything had LEDs [light-emitting diodes] to show status."

The finished control unit—dubbed the Magic Dingus Box—slid onto the bridge plate, which meant that Danny didn't need to alter his guitars. ("That's where Dan Senior came in handy," Johns says. "With sheet metal, he could make a bracket out of stainless steel.") With the Dingus Box in place, Danny could control the Echoplex and Leslie right from his guitar. There were four optional functions to hook up whatever he wished, be they garage door openers, smoke bombs, or sirens, Danny later told Brawner Smoot.

Not everyone understood the need for the Magic Dingus Box or the oft-cited inspiration behind it, according to Weaver. "For some reason, he didn't feel he could use a foot pedal. He didn't like foot pedals." Only a handful of the devices were built, as they weren't practical to manufacture. (Weaver built a similar box for himself with everything mounted in his guitar's control cavity rather than on the top, as Danny preferred.)

The Magic Dingus Box gave Danny mastery over as many as 13 options, he told Smoot: "It basically controls echo, reverb, Leslie, and playback, if you want to play along with it, and it also has provisions for pre-recorded tapes and things to play with.... It's worth its weight in gold to me." In his mind, such tinkering was a natural extension of his playing: "That's why I built all this stuff, so I wouldn't be in such a rut. And now I've gotten used to that, and I've got to do something else."

LIKE MOST OF DANNY'S BANDS, the Explosion was fated to remain a local affair, although there were occasional road trips to Atlanta, Boston, Nashville, and New York. According to Smoot, the group played its earliest shows as the Danny Gatton Jazz Explosion, which marked a big departure from past practice, according to bassist Steve Wolf. "Danny and the Fat Boys was every bit as much Billy Hancock's band," he says, "no matter what anybody says." The Danny Gatton Band had been a stride toward full independence, but it still relied heavily on Evan Johns to front it. "The Redneck Jazz Explosion is where Danny stepped out and said, 'This is the Danny Gatton thing, Danny Gatton is the leader.' And he wasn't relying on anything but his own ability as a guitar player. So it was a major step for him personally, in his career."

Wolf had long been interested in jazz, which he'd studied in 1970–71 at Prince George's Community College. "I was there one year ahead of John Previti, so I've known him since all the way back then. I don't have a degree, though—I pretty much got my music degree on the bandstand." Wolf had met Danny in 1972 at a demo session for "some never-to-be-heard-from-again" country singer whose name he doesn't remember. It was at the Old Brickskeller, off P Street, near Rock Creek Park in Washington. Dick Heintze was also on the session.

In 1974–75, Wolf played in a band with Bill Holland (who would become *Billboard*'s bureau chief) and future Redneck Jazz Explosion drummer Scott Taylor. They got a gig at Ernie's, also on P Street. "There was a topless place downstairs and this other club upstairs," he says. Wolf worked there five nights a week, and the Fat Boys were also regulars. One night, Danny and Billy asked if Wolf wanted to take over on bass so Billy could concentrate on his singing. Wolf was familiar with Danny's ability, but rejected the offer. "I was being totally practical: Bill Holland is working a lot, I'm a working musician, I need to make a living. And if the Fat Boys get on hard times, Billy Hancock is a bass player and I'm out. Today I go, 'You idiot!' but back then, I was being totally pragmatic."

Wolf's next encounter with Danny came in 1975, after he'd asked Ernie's management to add a jazz gig on its only off night, Monday. He invited Danny to play, knowing how much he loved jazz; Heintze followed, because he'd sat in all along with Wolf's band. "Heintze had called me up to do some gigs with him, because he knew I could play rock 'n' roll and jazz, too," Wolf says. "I might not have been as good a jazz musician as a lot of the guys they could've gotten, but I had versatility and could get around the wide range of music they knew how to do."

Wolf eventually decided that he needed to study music more seriously, so he moved to Boston. The city boasts one of the nation's most renowned music schools in Berklee, although Wolf never actually enrolled there. "By then, I'd had a lot of professional experience and was way ahead of most of the guys in school." Instead, he studied privately and filled in for ensemble classes at Berklee whenever they needed a bass player.

Wolf had met his wife-to-be, Nancy, and become heavily involved in the Boston jazz scene when Danny called in late 1977, wanting to know if he'd join his new band. "I was playing in various jazz ensembles and a reggae band, none of which was terribly inspiring, but at least it was paying the bills. I said, 'Danny, I'm getting married in one month, and I'm going to have my honeymoon in New Hampshire. I'll come down after that.'"

The Wolfs returned to the D.C. area after getting married in January 1978. The first Explosion gigs occurred in late winter at an Alexandria restaurant, the Lobster Shed. Wolf remembers playing there with Danny, Heintze, and drummer Rick Davies; Tom Principato appeared as a guest soloist, and Ronnie MacDonald sang a song or two. "The shows were loose, but it was like a concert. There are tapes of that floating around; it was fun stuff. Dick was still in good form, although he was not doing well and was using a cane. He was in the early stages [of ALS], but he could still play and, boy, could he play."

Danny also guested with the Good Humor Band when his schedule allowed. One such appearance is preserved on the band's 2001 compilation disc, recorded on June 3, 1978, at Desperado's. Danny's searing slide guitar gets plenty of slash-and-burn room on "DWI," an Evan Johns–sung country-rock ode to the perils of drunken driving.

Danny's place in the Good Humor saga has become a point of contention among his old musical compadres, who consider it a footnote to their work with him. Johns maintains that Danny didn't play more than ten gigs with the "Humoroids," as the Richmond-based band was called. Guitarist Jim Stephanson—who often saw Danny in the '80s and later took lessons from him—scoffs at wider involvement: "Gatton worked one show in *50* with the Good Humor Band." On the other side, Good Humor guitarist Mike McAdam asserts that Danny appeared at one out of every five gigs, although his image doesn't appear on their compilation disc. "The cover is a collage of old photos and posters, and one of them had Danny's face," he says. "We took it off for that reason."

Principato says he didn't catch many Good Humor shows, "but one in five sounds too often and one in 50 sounds too seldom. If I remember right, he would usually just fill in for a weekend somewhere when he had a hole in his schedule. Redneck Jazz [Explosion] was definitely off and on, too, because Buddy [Emmons] wasn't always available."

Regardless of how many gigs Danny played with the band, everyone agrees that the experience proved fruitful when he got involved. McAdam had formed the band in 1974 with vocalist Jimmy Morgan and drummer Mark Corvino. The arrival of keyboardist Greg Wetzel two years later provided some stability, as did bassist Drake Leonard and steel guitarist Bruce Bouton (later replaced by Bucky Baxter). Shunning the notion of set lists, the Humoroids quickly became known for an omnivorous musical sensibility—something that undoubtedly appealed to Danny.

Danny's guitar hot-rodding inspired McAdam to put a Stratocaster pickup in the middle of his Telecaster. "It's kind of what everybody does now," he says. "It gives you the capabilities of a Strat sound and a Tele sound [together]; Fender makes production models that have that now. I did it over at Robbie Weaver's shop—he helped me cut the pickguard." He adds: "I did everything that Danny did to his guitar, at one time or another. He always used brass bridge saddles, because that's what was on the original '50s models and he thought they sounded better. I think they do, too."

McAdam never ceased to be surprised by Danny's melodic invention. "He could work the melody of any cartoon or TV theme into a solo, somewhere," he laughs. "By the time you figured out, 'Oh, that was the *Flintstones* [theme],' you were on to something else. That was one of the cool things about his playing: there was often an element of humor in it." (There was also no trick that Danny hadn't learned. If he wasn't sure about his tuning, there was always the telephone. "The dial tone's an *F*," McAdam says, "and from that, he'd tune his *A* string, a third above the *F*, and then tune the rest from that.")

The Humoroids' material consisted of "pretty basic" rock 'n' roll and country, with the odd blues or swing number; Danny brought "Harlem Nocturne" and some other instrumentals that he taught the band. "It was obvious that he loved all the different styles in music," McAdam says. "He wasn't a guy that happened to learn jazz because he had to, or because it was a technique thing."

REDNECK JAZZ CREATED A ground swell of local excitement on its release at the end of July 1978. Sales reached 2,000 copies within six weeks, but peaked at 8,000 because the album's availability outside the D.C. area was limited to mail order, according to a 1988 report in *Maryland Musician*.

The release coincided with a triumphant two-night stand on July 28–29, 1978, at Randy's Old Time Pickin' Parlor in Nashville, where the band was joined by Buddy Emmons, who'd barnstormed with Danny to such devastating effect on "Rock Candy." Fiddler Buddy Spicher and session guitarist Bucky Barrett also helped out, and Dave Palamar was established as the new drummer (although he'd soon be supplanted by Scott Taylor). "That show wasn't really well attended," says Steve Wolf, "but the music was great, and everybody had a great time."

Paul Tester shared credit for the *Redneck Jazz* cover design with Danny, Smoot, and Charlie de Limur. The cover showed Danny wearing a brightly patterned shirt and cradling the '61 Les Paul Custom that was featured so prominently on the album. The large letters of the album title covered Danny's face. The concept was an homage to Wes Montgomery's *Full House* album cover, where his face was also obscured, Smoot says. (Two framed copies of the cover art hang side-by-side at his Arlington home, with and without Danny's name painted across the guitar's fretboard.)

Danny's parents personally dropped off copies to the stores, with tireless help from Smoot. "If it wasn't for Brawner, I don't think we'd have made it, 'cause he worked his legs off going to all these little independent record stores, trying to get 'em to take Danny's record and sell it," Norma says.

Ostmann had helped the Gattons set up their NRG label, for which his girlfriend, Pam Fox, designed the logo. Norma wasn't really thinking about starting an independent label, though. "She just wanted to set up a company to put out her son's records," Ostmann says, "because he wasn't getting anywhere. He wasn't getting signed, and everybody knew that if you had a record, it gave you a certain prestige." The Gattons also underwrote the recording expenses, seeing that the musicians got union scale, according to Wolf.

Mike Haney, an assistant warehouse manager for the local Penguin Feather chain, told the *Washington Star* about Danny's amazing popularity in the area. He reported that *Redneck Jazz* had outsold the Rolling Stones' *Some Girls* within two weeks of its release and was a top-five seller at the chain's four Washington stores. "It's just one of those albums that everybody wants," Haney told the paper. "Danny's got such a reputation around town, and a lot of people have been following him for a long time."

One key factor in *Redneck Jazz*'s success, according to Danny, was his rediscovery of playing clean, unaltered guitar: his gold-top '61 Les Paul Custom plugged straight into a Twin Reverb. "I'm kind of getting back to the roots of playing guitar straight," he'd told Smoot in August. "I really had fun just playing straight out of that Twin. It sounded like three years ago, pickin' a Tele through a 4×10 Bassman."

The *Unicorn Times* felt the album's strength lay in its instrumentals. "Rock Candy" struck reviewer Charles D. Young as similar to early Dave Brubeck "or the Miles Davis tune Gatton and his rhythm section performed years ago as members of the Liz Meyer Band. Sweet indeed." Young likened "Sax Fifth Avenue" to the Lovin' Spoonful's "Coconut Grove" or Anton Karas's "Third Man Theme"; early proof, if anybody needed it, of Danny's ability to evoke different responses with his genre-hopping. Heintze's keyboards also came in for praise on that track and the epic "Comin' Home Baby," which Young likened to "I'm a Man" and Van Morrison's "Moondance." He added: "Let's hope Gatton records more of these instrumental gems in the tradition of his certifiable masterpiece, 'Harlem Nocturne.'"

Ostmann has fond memories of "Sax Fifth Avenue," which he had heard at the Bayou one night. "Danny said, 'Man, you've got to hear this.' He had a four-track TEAC, and he had recorded 'Sax Fifth Avenue.' It was just incredible. I still think that's one of the most amazing things he ever did. I just love that song." (Danny eventually redid the track with Bob Dawson of Springfield, Virginia's Bias Recorders.)

Smoot nominates "Rock Candy" as his favorite track. It wasn't even going to appear on the album, until he persuaded Norma and Dan Senior to make the 14-hour drive to Nashville, where they bought the tapes from Audie Ashworth. "Danny and Buddy [Emmons] were like minds in musical approach," Smoot says, "and when they were trading fours, one could have been the other." (Elliott remembers the session well. "We did this stuff real early in the morning, and we were hung over as hell. My high-hat kept sliding away. My left leg was straight out, trying to keep it from sliding. Those two idiots starting trading fours towards the end of the song, and I didn't think we were ever going to stop.")

Of the vocal tracks, "Ugly Man" and "Love Is What You Need" got the *Times*'s highest marks. But Young had mixed feelings; he asserted that they "fall into a sameness which the instrumentals somehow avoid," since he believed they pushed Danny's guitar too far into the background. The album, he wrote, "occasionally buries the star of the show by attempting to present the public with a more accessible product."

The cover of Baltimore's Sun Magazine, July 1, 1979. The local newspaper's extensive look at Danny's career to date maintained a buzz that began with his 1976 Guitar Player *poll showings.*

Unreserved praise held true elsewhere, as Smoot later noted in an NRG newsletter. *Guitar Player*'s May 1979 issue declared: "Everything about this record is hot, from Gatton's searing chops to the fire-engine red vinyl they were pressed on." Tom Wheeler had joined the *Guitar Player* staff in August 1977, so he hadn't been around for the 1976 reader's poll, where Danny tallied votes in several categories. "He was still very much an underground buzz," Wheeler recalls. "There were several players that were famous for not being famous, and Danny Gatton was linked to these guys in many ways—the obvious one being Roy Buchanan."

"Danny Gatton was one of the guys that we all heard about before we heard him play," Wheeler continues. "But *Redneck Jazz*, for anybody who could get their hands on it, was a piece of solid gold. I mean, it was a mind-blower." Wheeler and his colleagues spent a lot of time pondering the nature of fame "and why he wasn't more highly regarded in the guitar community by the population at large."

The *Washington Post*'s "Recordings" section also heaped superlatives on the album's three instrumentals. "The praise pours in from all quarters, yet Danny Gatton remains unsigned," wrote Smoot in the *Unicorn Times*. "Hopefully that will all change soon."

As might have been expected, the album's title caused a fair degree of debate. Shannon Ford (one of the four drummers on the album) found the title a clever inversion of how some listeners might perceive jazz, "which was seen as music played by African-Americans. And, of course, putting the term 'redneck' with that stirred up a whole lot of stuff. I applaud him for that, because sometimes I think jazz takes itself a little too seriously." Few fans realized it, he says, but Danny "approached jazz, especially, with a lot of humility—he never thought he was that great a jazz player. Which, as we all know, wasn't true. But he had this view that he didn't measure up sometimes."

AN EXPECTANT AIR SURROUNDED the band's September 22–24 weekend run at the Cellar Door. Their name was now certified as Redneck Jazz Explosion, and everyone was clad in colorful red T-shirts specially made for the occasion. The *Washington Star*'s pre-gig write-up posed an oft-raised question: with all the glowing endorsements, why wasn't Danny playing larger venues like the Capital Centre? Like many of his peers, writer Mark Kernis hailed *Redneck Jazz*, citing "Sax Fifth Avenue," "Comin' Home, Baby," and "Rock Candy" as the album's highlights. The last track, in particular, was noteworthy for its deft use of the featured players: "The combination of Emmons and Gatton is combustible," Kernis pronounced. "Comin' Home, Baby," on the other hand, was noteworthy for letting Danny express his more sensitive side.

But Kernis also felt *Redneck Jazz* suffered from "some of the flaws that have held Gatton back all along": he thought Johns and Tilley were weak vocalists and found the rhythm section to be merely adequate. "It's too bad that Emmons is featured on only one track, because it's obvious that he brings out the best in Gatton, and the best in Gatton can be awesome."

Another problem plagued the album's prospects: the lineup pictured on the back cover (Elliott, Bobby Hancock, Heintze, Johns, and Previti) had already broken up. Tilley set those events in motion by quitting on the day of the album's completion, Elliott recalls. "He started drinking Southern Comfort and cussing out Danny's parents in the studio. He went out of his mind thinking that we were trying to steal his songs from him."

Johns was disheartened when the reality of the situation sunk in. "Danny wasn't going to take this band on the road. He didn't want to do that, and that was the bottom line." He, too, had expected great things. "This would have been a real springboard for him—then and there—to go to the next point." He vowed to head off future disappointment by working only for himself. "I'd been in two bands with Danny, and Danny had pulled the plug for the second time. I said, 'I will never work for anybody again in my life, except myself. Nobody will ever do this to me again.'"

The *Star* reviewed the Friday night gig. Although Heintze was present, he "regrettably showed only a sample of the tasteful, thoughtful playing of which he is capable," Tim Warren decided. The set reached a number of triumphant peaks, he thought; he was especially taken by a frenetic medley of "Orange Blossom Special," "Foggy Mountain Breakdown," and a Duane Eddy–style boogie that ending by revisiting the first tune's bluegrass frenzy.

Emmons and Spicher "sparked on the country songs and filled in quite nicely on the jazzier numbers," Warren wrote, while the Palamar-Wolf rhythm section kept the proceedings reasonably tight. But the night's looseness and informality cut both ways. The musicians' comfort with each other seemed obvious, yet a lack of familiarity also held them back, he felt. "Most of their numbers were either country tunes or 'safe' mainstream jazz songs which did not truly test the considerable talent available"—but it seemed safe to assume the group wouldn't take long to get hotter once they'd played together more often, Warren concluded.

After the gig, Danny's parents asked Smoot to take on the management and booking duties, supplanting John Doniphan. One thing struck him right away: "Anytime Danny did a jazz gig, a special segment of his audience came out, because you just didn't hear him play jazz that often and he did it so well." Smoot sought to capitalize on that by restricting Danny's local gigs to multi-night runs at the Cellar Door or Blues Alley, where he played in a trio format. This strategy immediately boosted the band's take-home pay to $2,500, with Danny pocketing $1,000—"a good pay raise, and he liked it," Smoot says. "Everybody was getting paid pretty well." If Danny wanted more work, Smoot would book "hideaway" gigs at Charlie's West Side with Steve Wolf and Shannon Ford.

Despite its good reception, the Explosion was not a stable unit. Buddy Spicher decided not to stick around. "Buddy wasn't really digging it, because it was really loud, and he was getting buried," Wolf says. "We would back off, but Danny—his sound was big." The other Buddy, Emmons, remained in the lineup when his schedule allowed; "they were fire together," Wolf says. "Danny has done a lot of his best work against a foil of another really great musician—like *Relentless*, with Joey DeFrancesco. Those two, they obviously had stuff going on."

Heintze didn't last long in the band, having been diagnosed with the amyotrophic lateral sclerosis that would kill him at age 42 on January 20, 1981. "We watched Dick go from when he just had it, to when he couldn't walk very well but could still play his ass off, to when he couldn't even walk," Bobby Hancock says. "I used to go visit him in the hospital; it was heart-wrenching. A friend of my parents died of the same thing, so I knew what was coming. That's a very cruel disease."

Family and friends did their best to make Heintze comfortable. "One time, they had a surprise party for Dick in the entertainment room at some big apartment complex—he was in a wheelchair," Bobby says. "Everybody was in there, and when they opened the door, Danny and a bunch of guys started playing."

"It's hard to talk about it, 'cause he was a really good guy," Wolf says. "The guy could play like Bud Powell with his right hand, and then double it with his left hand. Plus, he had incredible soul; he was just all soul. He was always really encouraging to me and teaching me stuff. I tried to be the same for him when he was in ill health."

There was a temporary improvement after Heintze's nurse put him on a vegetarian diet, but the outcome was never in doubt. Bobby got the bad news at the Gorospes' house, as he and Ernie were getting ready to pay Dick another visit. "My first thought was, I've got to go see Danny," Bobby says. "Danny was playing an afternoon gig at Gus & John's in Clinton. We went over there, and Danny knew about it. But his way of dealing with it was playing." Danny later told Richard Harrington: "When he died, a big piece of me went with him. We never got to do what we wanted to do."

"I think it made a difference in Danny's life," Tom Principato says.

"Danny always had somebody in his groups that was a close friend who went way back—their presence seemed to make a difference. In a way, it was sort of like security. When he lost Dick, that was the first big blow." The emotional fallout may not have been apparent right off, "because he appeared to be so easygoing—but I think he took it really hard."

THE LOCAL SCENE WAS still enjoying a healthy period, led by favorites like the Redneck Jazz Explosion and the Nighthawks, in a phenomenon that moved critic Mark Winter to call them "Blue Wave"— Washington-based bands that were blues-and-roots oriented. That state of affairs would hold true until the early '80s, when local music would no longer find a welcoming format on stations like WHFS and the mechanized throb of disco and its emphasis on the DJ/mixmaster would prove irresistibly cheaper than hiring live bands. Crackdowns on drunken driving further cut into club attendance. "Musicians used to talk about it: the cops would hang out, and all they had to do was wait for the bar to close and start picking off people," Ed Eastridge says. "It was like shooting fish in a barrel."

Bluesman "Steady Rollin'" Bob Margolin recalls jamming with Danny at the Psyche Delly during this period. "He was friendly and just outrageous onstage. When we sat in with the Nighthawks, he asked me to play 'Honky Tonk' as close as I could to the original, while he threw in a second guitar part that I can't imagine anyone else could have conceived or played." From Margolin's standpoint, "Danny's guitar chops and mastery of the instrument put him in a different class from other guitar players. I enjoyed that, as well as the humor in his playing."

Few lineups could push Danny as hard as the Explosion, whose December 31, 1978, Cellar Door gig has assumed legendary proportions for its place in Gatton history. Swearing that you were there has become akin to saying you saw the Beatles at the Cavern Club or caught the Yardbirds' hot, sweaty nights at the Marquee. "Danny had huge success at the Cellar Door," Principato says. "It was a great venue to present the group—it was small, it sold out quickly, and it had great sound and great atmosphere. It was Washington's best club."

That night, engineer Bob Dawson was parked outside the club in a mobile truck to record the music. According to Eastridge, local public-TV station WEPA provided the truck; "I think it was a 16-track," he says.

A grainy black-and-white video was also shot; on it, Danny announces: "We're here to make an album." A brisk rendition of Horace Silver's "Opus de Funk" gets the night off to a flying start: the interplay between Danny, Emmons, and Wolf is far more assertive than on the *American Music* version. The ride gets wilder with "Song of India" and "Raisin' the Dickens," as Emmons drops in glistening fills on steel guitar. The band then dips back into its jazz bag with the Benny Golson standard "Killer Joe," where Danny and Emmons swap statements over a gliding Wolf bass line.

Matters don't stay moody for long, as the band kicks into "Rock Candy," taken at a faster tempo than its *Redneck Jazz* cousin, followed by a crisp run through Chuck Mangione's "Land of Make Believe." The band shifts to a gentle swing feel for a seven-minute exploration of Count Basie's "Little Darling," and then Danny ratchets up the energy with a feverish "Comin' Home, Baby," where Wolf emerges as a crucial soloing voice. Brief renditions of "Famous Blue Raincoat" and a classical showpiece, "The Nutcracker," round out a night of inspired eclecticism.

Nearly 20 years later, Norma worked with Wolf to reissue the performance as *Redneck Jazz Explosion Live!* (1995), which he calls "just a sample of what was going on—I mean, it really got hot and heavy." There are also scratchy, hiss-infested bootleg tapes in circulation, as well as the reference video, which runs for nearly four hours.

The matching T-shirts might have been the performance's oddest feature, given Danny's well-documented disdain for such contrivances. They're not flashy, with no decoration except the players' names on the front. Principato doesn't recall who dreamed up the shirts. "I have to admit, it's a little exaggerated on these guys—there's some beer bellies going on there," he laughs.

In hindsight, Danny's reluctance to engage in showmanship became a weakness, especially as the rock 'n' roll circuit got increasingly theatrical. The minimalist approach favored by Danny played well to people who loved his musicality, "but for the man on the street," Joe Barden says, "it was like: 'Nothing's happening, why should I care that this guy plays great guitar?'"

The band's Cellar Door gigs never failed to sell out, and they were sometimes extended to five- and six-night runs. To these, Smoot added road trips to selected venues. Thus, Emmons was aboard for another big gig at New York's Lone Star Café; the venue was a country-themed bar that provided roots-based acts with an inviting home-away-from-home. Ford wouldn't experience its charms until joining the band in April, but retains fond recollections. "I loved that place," he says. "It was a small, narrow bar, and it just had a ton of energy, especially when we played there with Robert Gordon. It would be packed with people; they'd be hanging from the rafters and excited about seeing Robert—and Danny. There were a lot of Danny fans, too."

Smoot was trying to get major-label recognition—"that's why we went to New York as much as possible," he says. Danny wasn't crazy about the Big Apple, though, and as the skyline drew closer he would parody the city's famous TV commercial, singing, "I...hate New York."

The February 1979 Lone Star gig was especially memorable for its coverage by John Rockwell of the *New York Times*. "The notion of 'redneck jazz' may seem a little cutesy, but actually jazzish improvisation with country roots goes back long before the Allman Brothers," Rockwell wrote in a piece entitled "Jazz: Danny Gatton's Guitar Plays 'Redneck' Style." The review, which Smoot included in the band's promo package, said that "Mr. Gatton...plays with remarkable speed and agility, no question about it." Rockwell noted Danny's absorption with "a device that transformed his notes and chords into something like those of a Hammond organ"—which could only refer to the Magic Dingus Box. Danny's combination of technique and guitar-craft wizardry recalled that of Les Paul, according to the critic, as did the accompanying danger of confusing flash with musicality. "But on this slightly superficial level, Mr. Gatton is pretty impressive," Rockwell concluded.

The band returned to the Lone Star for a well-received stand on April 4–5, 1979, with Ford replacing Taylor, who'd moved to Richmond. "The Explosion once again had heads turning and jaws dropping as Danny led the band through their repertoire of mainstream jazz, Gatton trademark tunes, and of course, the Heineken bottle blues," Smoot wrote in the NRG newsletter. (The last comment referred to Danny's trick of playing slide guitar with a beer bottle.)

A&R representatives from record companies were present for that gig, and the most solid interest seemed to come from Atlantic Records. An offer was apparently made, but Danny let it slide for reasons unknown. "He would have had [famed label head] Ahmet Ertegun behind him, and the power of that record label—at that time, they were one of the prominent labels for rhythm & blues," Wolf says. Ostmann says he made a call to Atlantic on Danny's behalf, trying to follow up, but nothing happened. "I was

Danny at the Lone Star in New York City, 1979. A rootsy booking policy and atmosphere made the club a welcome stop for artists like Danny who didn't fit the mainstream. Note the Magic Dingus Box on his Les Paul Custom.

calling somebody in A&R," he says. "I might have gotten a guy once, and he just said, 'Well, let me get back to you.'" Needless to say, nobody did.

The band also made forays to venues like Atlanta's Great American Music Theatre (whose $500 check bounced) and the Exit Inn, a Nashville club that held about 200 people. "There were chairs and tables—it was kind of upscale," Ford says. "It was a concert venue."

Ford quickly discovered that the Explosion's all-out approach wasn't like the easy-going music he'd played with his friends. "It required a jazz touch, but it also required a lot of power and stamina. And the ability to pace yourself to play a lot of choruses and not blow your wad during the first two or three, because Danny would just go and go and go forever. You had to be willing to go from 'Foggy Mountain Breakdown' to 'Round Midnight' convincingly, musically, and in an entertaining manner." Ford also got some drumming tips from Danny: "He actually taught me, physically, how to play a shuffle on the drums. I'll never forget that."

The band's bedrock repertoire consisted of '50s and '60s bop, jazz, and rhythm & blues tunes that any player would know, like "In the Midnight Hour." "You'd just have to be familiar with that stuff," Ford says. "Everybody knows 'Mustang Sally,' 'I Got You,' stuff like that. And, of course, 'Linus and Lucy' was one of his famous things." Vince Guaraldi's celebrated *Peanuts* theme actually had a longer shelf life than most listeners ever realized, according to Bobby Hancock, who remembers seeing Danny work out the changes at his Marlowe Heights apartment years before. The song quickly became one of Danny's showpieces, as well as a vehicle for unlikely medleys. Although he attempted numerous studio versions, not one ever clicked.

Bobby says that during his days in the Danny Gatton Band "that song would encompass one whole set—it'd start off with 'Linus and Lucy' and then it would go into whatever crossed Danny's mind at the moment" before eventually reprising the theme. "Previti and Dave Elliott and I—we never knew where Danny was going to go. You had to be on your toes to switch gears like that." Most of the transitions worked by eye contact. "Danny would throw you a little hint," Bobby says. "If he'd never done it before and was going to change keys, he would let John and I see his hands on the guitar, [to see] what key we were going to."

The best moments sometimes involved blasts from the past, such as the theme from the *Looney Tunes* TV show, Ford says. "Who doesn't know that? That was what was fun about it—because even if it was the first time you'd ever played it, you knew it. There was always this playful nature, even in the more serious tunes." Ironically, Danny's sense of humor sometimes put off the jazz purists. "I would hear criticisms of Danny's thing, in that regard—that it was a little silly sometimes. Even the term 'redneck jazz' turned off some people."

Danny & Lowell's 20 Million Things (1979–1980)

8

*B*obby Hancock wasn't surprised to see the Cellar Door tapes languish in some kind of out-take limbo, because Danny approached cars and music in such painstaking fashion. If someone said, "Man, that's killer," Danny would respond, "Nah, there's one teeny little thing." Many projects languished in the can because Danny couldn't bring himself to finish them.

The struggle to realize a creative concept became more important than the work itself. Bobby recalls one Sunday afternoon when he and Danny started working on a stock vintage model they were going to convert into the ultimate street rod. "We stripped that car to a pile of parts," he says. "Everything that came loose, we took it off. When we got done, it was a chassis and four wheels." Nothing else happened, and the car sat on Danny's property for several years.

Finally, Danny installed a motor and drive train, "and it sat again for a couple of years, and then he finally sold it. Always had the goal he was going to get it on the road, but obviously he didn't much care about that. He'd get halfway through one project and start another one. That was just how he was—if he'd bought an electric razor, he'd have had to modify it somehow, probably."

Someone like Brawner Smoot wasn't going to push Danny too hard for fear of ruffling his feathers, in Tom Principato's view. "I don't think anybody ever wanted to take a firm hand and try to direct him," he says. "I think that was damaging." Some guidance might have been useful, "because he was, in so many ways, directionless." He'd wait for nearly 15 years for a major-label deal, when Ellis Duncan finally got him signed to Elektra. "Ellis was the first guy that really stepped in and was a pushy asshole who could get somewhere, and it worked."

THE BAND CONTINUED to garner its share of musical high points. One of Shannon Ford's favorite nights was April 25, 1979, when he and Danny jammed with Lenny Breau and Buddy Emmons at the Cellar Door. Judging from the bootleg of that night, the musicians were having a ball. There are frequent bouts of laughter between songs, which range from the Explosion's trademark high-flying ensemble outings to lesser-known choices like "Once I Had a Secret Love," which Breau introduces as a cut from one of his Flying Fish albums.

In Ford's view, the group's eclecticism was its secret weapon. "I would pull out the brushes, and we'd play 'Secret Love' with Lenny Breau—real low-key—and then we'd play this monster version of 'Mustang Sally,' with the amps turned up to 10," he says. "There weren't many boundaries or restrictions, musically, on that gig. I was in way over my head at times, which is exactly what you need when you're 21 years old."

The Explosion worked in spurts throughout the spring. Danny didn't have to worry, since he could fall back on Jan's income, while his colleagues had to find other projects to pay their bills. In Wolf's case, that meant going with the Kennedy-Principato guitar duo. "I would always call and get them on the bill. I'd have them working when I was with Danny, so they wouldn't be mad at me for not being available," he says.

Jack Jensen was doing well with the Crazy Horse, and he hit upon the idea of showcasing Danny there at Beneath It All. He didn't create the room for him, he says; "it was an afterthought after I got there, to do that." Keith John—who'd anchor the drums for Evan Johns's first cast of H-Bombs—was the doorman. John had logged considerable mileage in the club wars; he'd been in various bands since 1972 and booked plenty more during the summer of 1979–80, which is how he met Danny. (According to John, the Beneath It All arrangement involved shares of 10 percent apiece for himself and Danny, with Jensen taking the rest. Jensen just says, "Well, I worked out an arrangement with him on the door—put it that way.")

Being the doorman required dealing with all manner of people, whether they had social graces or not. Beneath It All's normal cover charge was $2 to $4, but it was $5 for Danny, which sometimes caused complaints. John would simply say, "But the greatest guitarist in the world is playing here tonight: Danny Gatton." Most customers promptly paid up after hearing Danny's name. For those without a clue, he would take their money and say, "If this guy isn't the greatest guitar player you've ever heard, I'll give your money back." John gave that guarantee thousands of times, and only two people wanted refunds. "I got upset, cussed them out, told them they were liars and said, 'Here, take your money, don't ever come back.'"

Although Danny's responsibilities required little more than three sets a night for one or two nights per week, the arrangement lasted only three or four months. "He didn't really want regular stuff," Jensen says. "That was not Danny. Even knowing that he had a piece, *per se*, of the bottom line, he still lost interest after a while."

Danny essentially got bored and wanted to move on, which was fine with Jensen. "It had been a business move—a move to try and help Dan, and help myself, too," he says. "It was just good fun, and it gave us an excuse to drink beer together. That's basically what it boiled down to." Jensen converted Beneath It All to a disco format, followed by thrash metal bands.

DANNY HAD YET ANOTHER brush with fame that was cut off by the death of Lowell George on June 29, 1979. Or so the story goes. George had allegedly been flustered by Warner Brothers' rejection of *Redneck Jazz*, so he was going to show the tastemakers what they'd been missing by hiring Danny as a sideman. What better way to showcase his favorite guitarist?

The story has become ingrained D.C. folklore, though it sounds suspiciously similar to whispers of Buchanan's almost-recruitment by the Rolling Stones. Both stories share elements of a music-business morality play: the humble player who shuns involvement with certified somebodies who presumably embody some kind of commercial entrapment, and escapes with integrity unscathed.

George had been working on a new album with Little Feat, but the band's status was in question and he was touring behind his willfully absurdist solo album, *Thanks, I'll Eat It Here*. The tour brought him to Washington's Lisner Auditorium, and he invited Danny to the show.

Phil Zavarella says that Danny came by on the day of the gig. "He said, 'Man, this guy's pretty cool. You've got to come down—free beer, y'know?' So down to Lisner we go." He says George seemed tickled to see Danny again, after they were ushered to his dressing room backstage. "He had a Mason jar full of white powder," Phil says, "and he immediately opened that up. He had one of those hippie wooden dishes that you used to clean your pot in—to get the seeds out—and he filled it up and handed us a tablespoon: 'Here you go, guys.' And we're like, 'That's okay.'"

Phil, who acknowledges smoking marijuana at the time, says he hadn't been around hard drugs before. Eventually, the telltale knock summoned George to the stage, "so he takes this Mason jar—I'll never forget this—and he fills this thing up again, says, 'Damn, I've got to go do this,' and walks right onto the stage. He's got it right in his hand, puts it on his Super Reverb, takes a spoon [makes a sniffing noise], turns around, and starts playing. I was like, 'Man!'"

George remained in high spirits afterwards. He told Danny that his doctor had prescribed the drug he'd been consuming so giddily. "I really was ignorant of drugs—and still am—but he was sniffing heroin," Danny told Richard Harrington. "He said, 'I want you want to finish out the tour with me; I'll call you tomorrow.'"

Danny wanted to hit a nearby party, but Phil begged off. "It was late already, and I had to work the next day," he says. "I get up the next morning, turn around: 'Lowell George died last night.' 'Huh? I just saw him a couple of hours ago!'"

The official findings showed that George died of a heart attack in his sleep; the general consensus was that it had been brought on by the additives he'd been putting into his system, forever scuttling the "20 million things to do" he'd sung about on his solo album. If those plans had included a second guitarist, Phil certainly didn't know about them, and Danny offered little comment beyond, "He was a cool guy."

"Danny really didn't react to his death," Phil says. "It was just like, 'Oh, wow, that's too bad,' and that was about it." Holly and Jan don't know much more themselves, except for acknowledging Danny's discomfort about the drugs involved. Norma takes a more philosophical stance: "That was a blow. It wasn't meant to be, was it? It just seemed like everything was uphill."

Little Feat guitarist Paul Barrere can't confirm the rumors about the proposed hiring. "At that time, the band was once again in a state of break-up," he wrote in an e-mail, "as Lowell and [keyboardist] Billy [Payne] were at odds again, and Billy and I were trying to start our own band. I know that Lowell loved the way Danny played, even back when we were all together doing *Feats Don't Fail Me Now* in Maryland."

Guitarist Fred Tackett, who played on *Eat It Here* and tours with the reunited Little Feat, says he remembers hearing that "Lowell had called Danny and asked him to join the band the next day in Richmond, but Lowell didn't say anything to anybody in the band about it. He might have been talking about sitting in with the band in Richmond, so he was talking about the solo tour, not Little Feat."

Tom Principato doubts that Danny would have kept such a story to himself, and he dismisses it as "embellished Washington lore." "To tell you the truth, seeing as how I was seeing him pretty regularly in those years," he says, "I would have thought he would have mentioned it to me, 'cause that would have been a big thing for him to talk about."

Steve Wolf swears there was some foundation to the whole business. He remembers Danny urging, "Prepare a demo tape, something really cool is going to happen. Lowell George is leaving Little Feat, and he's starting his own band. He's asked me to be the guitar player; I want you guys to be the rhythm section." Wolf says that when George was in town, he did a radio interview on WHFS. "Danny was in the studio and on the interview with Weasel, one of the main DJs at the time. He hung out for a couple hours with Lowell afterwards. I guess, in part, they talked about the future of the band they were going to have together."

Elliott says he's not surprised that Danny would have kept the potential good fortune of working with George under wraps, because he'd been let down so often. "Danny wasn't the type to get all hyped up about anything like that. All he wanted was to make enough money to make a living. It wasn't a party; it was a job. Danny was too normal to be in that business. He liked his home and normal things, like playing with his cars and stuff like that."

Smoot acknowledges George's patronage of *Redneck Jazz*: "Lowell was pretty big on it—this was what floated back. I understand that Lowell really pushed it." As for George's last night, he feels the stories involving Danny have some basis. "Some of his missed opportunities were self-imposed, but I think he was ready to go with that one."

Principato wonders if Danny's well-documented distaste for touring would have scotched such an opportunity, in any case, since he was a "super-homing pigeon" capable of driving back after gigs in Nashville and New York City. "I think Jan used to pressure him, too, to be home, and have a home life. He liked to hang around home and tinker with his cars."

Johns dismisses the stories as myth-making. "Danny didn't like that 'booger sugar' scene. I know people that were there that night, and Lowell George was doing lines a foot long," he says. "Danny left because he didn't like that stuff. He would turn and walk right out of the room." And then there's the logistics. "People don't hire people in the middle of a tour," he scoffs.

DESPITE THE POSSIBLE MISSED opportunity with George, Danny was still riding high in the local scene—until he cut his hand at his Accokeek home, effectively derailing whatever progress the band was making. According to Norma, the accident occurred when Danny put his hand through a glass pane of a side door. "He thought the door was unlocked, and it wasn't," she says. "When he pushed his hand up against the glass to open the door, the door didn't give and the glass did."

Jan sensed something darker. "He just had a fit of anger, because of his mother. When I came home that night and found his hand all bandaged, he said: 'Now she won't be able to...'" Asked what Danny meant,

Jan responds: "Whatever she was doing—trying to push him out on the road, I guess." She contends that Norma's financing of *Redneck Jazz*—which Johns estimates as $10,000—was being used as a club to accomplish those goals.

Jan was horrified, because she'd never seen Danny so angry. She didn't understand why he didn't just tell his mother to back off. But the business of Danny's injury took precedence, because he'd sliced through the tendons of his hand, giving rise to fears that he wouldn't play again.

Even then, Danny's restless nature meant he couldn't let the healing process run its course. "He got his stitches put in, but he didn't wait 'cause he wanted to make sure he had movement in his hand," Norma says. "He took the bandages off sooner than he was supposed to, but it didn't hurt him. I guess he did the right thing, although we thought he was crazy at the time. He said, 'That's all right. If I hadn't done it, I'd be stiff and wouldn't be able to play again.' "

After the accident, Danny often said that he'd never played better, and Jan doesn't disagree with that statement. Neither does Robbie Weaver, who recalls seeing Danny with his hand bandaged up at his August 1979 wedding. "He was concerned that he wouldn't have the dexterity to do the banjo rolls. Obviously, he did." Weaver says Danny soon regained the finger strength that was an integral part of his ability. "He could have played bailing wire and bent it two-and-a-half frets. He was bending strings four and five frets—it takes a lot of pressure to do that, 'cause the more you bend it, the harder it is to bend that next fractional amount."

Smoot regarded the accident with frustration and resignation. "The next thing I know, he was playing $50 bar gigs again," he says. "You always come back to Danny being the homebody." This mindset accounted for those long, grueling drives back home, because Danny usually talked the band into canceling their motel reservations. "One time, Steve Wolf woke up in Nashville, in the back of the van, and said, 'Oh my God, we're on our way home!' " Smoot laughs.

Shannon Ford had already taken up with Vision, a group started by some old friends who'd tried their luck on Arista Records as a progressive-rock band called Happy the Man. "I used to jam with them, because they lived in northern Virginia, near where I lived," he says. "When Happy the Man broke up, I joined Vision, which was more like what Genesis was doing at that time—early '70s Genesis." Danny wasn't doing many gigs, so he simply followed his friends to New York.

Wolf read the injury as a sign of Danny's love-hate relationship with his career. "That was his excuse for stopping playing for a while," he says. "During that time, his best friend in the world, Dick Heintze, who was one of his musical mentors, degraded badly and quickly—so badly, I almost couldn't go over there." Wolf had little trouble imagining how Danny felt, although he didn't hear about it directly. "Danny was not somebody who could deal with things up front and directly. He didn't talk about [his feelings]; he internalized them. Something like that, he'd kind of keep to himself."

Ford doesn't think that Danny deliberately injured himself, but he does tend to support Wolf's reasoning, "because Danny was always cynical about the business end of music, and the career end of his music.... But I don't think his letdowns were any more profound, or any more numerous, than anybody else's, certainly not mine—or anybody else I know in the music business."

The injury didn't stop Danny from working on his hot rods, which reflected another long-running conflict. "The people who played music with him, me included, found it very frustrating sometimes—because we were hungry to play music with the guy and hear his music," Ford observes. "So we probably were kind of hard on him when we had to deal with the fact that his passions were divided."

"There was a part of him that needed the centeredness of living in Maryland and being with his family," Harrington says. "His desires on that level played out against his need to do better [as a musician], so I think there was an inherent tension." Yet Danny was never less than accommodating, Harrington remembers, even to the fellow musicians who approached him while they were doing an interview: would he lay down some licks for such and such session at 2 A.M.? "Sure, just give me $50," Danny responded.

Principato often heard Danny threaten to quit the game altogether, but even that vow was more complicated than it appeared. "Knowing about that love-hate affair—even without threatening to do it, there'd be these periods where he'd disappear for a while and just work on cars. He wouldn't really announce it, but he wouldn't be out there, either." When that happened, Danny would sometimes moonlight with country bands in the La Plata area but avoid the D.C. scene, which made getting back in touch more difficult.

One of those subterranean groups was Front Porch Swing, a band that held a six-month Wednesday-night residency at the Birchmere in 1980, Pete Kennedy says. Danny played bass in this western swing-style band. "We knew he would enjoy it, 'cause there wouldn't be any pressure on him. Of course, he ended up playing lead anyway, on the bass; he could still play 'Orange Blossom Special' faster than anybody. We did it for fun. We weren't intending to make a record or anything like that. It was just getting together and playing some songs that we all really liked."

If Kennedy had any control over the situation, he'd arrange gigs where Danny could just play music for its own sake. "We played for weddings and stuff, and did gigs at fire halls—those were the most fun, 'cause there was nobody there but the firemen and their wives, and they didn't care about guitar, so he could just play. Those are a lot of my best memories of playing with Danny, that kind of gig."

There were also one-off projects. Keith John remembers working with Danny at Aldi, Virginia's Solar Sounds on a version of "Song of India" in 1980–81. "It was an astounding piece," he says. "At the time, disco was still happening, so I played a 16th-note 'Smoke on the Water' disco high-hat." Danny also played bass on the track, "which was rockabilly, rock 'n' roll and Les Paul styles all wrapped up in one. It was unbelievable in its sound."

Danny was using a Les Paulverizer, which he'd gotten from the man himself, but he cast it aside. "He took this black box—just threw it on the floor and said, 'I don't need this piece of crap,'" John says. "He continued playing, and it *still* sounded like 100 guitars. That's when I knew this guy is something else."

Principato remembers Danny's periodic threats to quit playing and work on cars. "I think he was naïve enough to wish that he could just—all of a sudden—be king of the guitar world, without having to go through any of the crap that went with it." Although he might have been able to pull it off. Principato recalls seeing a gig where Danny claimed not to have played in six months, "and his chops were incredible," he says. "I remember saying to whoever was there with me: 'God, he said he hasn't played guitar in weeks, and he's still got the same chops!' In that way, it was astounding. There appeared to be no rust at all. I don't know if he was just perpetuating some of his own folklore, or if it was really true. I'm 50-50 on that; I could believe either way."

Ostmann says the ambivalence amounted to "a love of the music and a hate of the business." And the business side, as Danny knew, wasn't often fair. "Bobby Hancock used to say: 'Danny, if you could play golf the way you play the guitar, you'd be a millionaire.' Because that's a pure meritocracy: for a golfer or a tennis player, if you're that good and you stick with it, you're going to the top. But music is serendipitous."

When asked if Danny feared success, Robbie Weaver responds: "I don't think it was fear, I think it was distaste." Danny didn't suffer from stage fright, but his intensely private nature separated him from his peers. "I would be reluctant to say he was engaged with the audience. He didn't like bantering with them. I think he'd have been a lot happier if they'd just drug him behind a curtain, shot a spotlight on the curtain when it was time for him to play, and turned it off when he was done."

This desire for anonymity had hilarious consequences at times. In 1975—when Danny had the first guitar shop—he and Weaver were sinking all their money into the business, which meant having to play Friday and Saturday night pickup gigs. One night, someone called looking for a bass player, and Danny took the job under the name "Dick Wood." "He had a great time, because guys would come up to him and start talking about this guitar player, Danny Gatton, and how good friends they were with him: 'Oh, we go to Pope's Creek and have crabs all the time.' He thought it was hilarious. He had a marvelous time doing that. That was a totally new experience for him, and we talked about it for a long time afterwards."

STEVE WOLF HAD ONE more go-round with Danny after the Explosion ended: they regrouped with Elliott and Johns for another band that gigged mostly at Beneath It All. It didn't last very long. "He was still friends with Jack on a personal level, but he didn't want to deal with it anymore," Wolf says. (Wolf has no recollection of the name, but thinks they worked under the Danny Gatton Band banner.) He viewed Danny's on-again, off-again tactics with a "been there, done that" feeling. "After maybe six or eight months, he'd get bored just working on cars. If you go through his career, it was always like that—start, stop." Evan Johns recalls the band playing from March through August 1979 as the Maximum Brothers. The lineup paired Danny and Johns with Elliott and bassist Michael Maye. Most of their gigs were at Beneath It All. "Then me and Michael started our band, Evan Johns & the H-Bombs, and Steve Wolf joined up with Danny for jazz gigs," Johns says. "Then Danny had to quit playing just to get out of the obligation of having a nightclub."

Wolf decided not to wait around and joined Catfish Hodge's band. "I wanted to not be poor when I was old; I wanted to have some assets. John Previti wasn't married, so he could deal with it. That's why John was able to stay with him in those latter years for so long. He would say, 'Danny, I'm there,' but it wasn't without a price."

Weaver understood that price. As much he enjoyed doing the odd gig with Danny, he felt increasingly called to get a real life. He began taking college classes, which gradually curtailed his presence on the local scene. In September 1983, he closed Sounds Better and became a federal employee. (He managed to get out debt-free: "I didn't earn any money, but didn't lose any money.") "At one point, Danny said, 'Robbie, you could be the best unheard guitar player in D.C.,'" Weaver says. "I thought, What's that mean— $75 a night and cirrhosis of the liver when you're 50?"

The Magic Dingus Box was another casualty of this era, although Danny wouldn't retire it completely until the early '80s. (Mike McAdam recalls last seeing him use it in 1980 or 1981, while Jay Monterose fixes the retirement date at 1982.) The minute people confused Danny's effects and his playing ability, he had no desire to use it—especially after hearing himself derided in some quarters as "Danny Gadget."

As Evan Johns points out, D.C. musicians had no more empathy for '60s psychedelia—and the genre's most visible symbol, the ubiquitous wah-wah pedal—than they had for the British Invasion. "Why hook yourself up to all these pedals and make yourself sound worse? They couldn't tell if they were in tune or not." He was sorry to see the Magic Dingus Box go, though, after all the thrills it had provided. "That shivered my timbers, but he didn't pursue it—it was too heavy, he owed money on it, whatever."

Weaver attributes the "Danny Gadget" slurs to "sheer, unadulterated jealousy," coming from players who couldn't approach Danny's ability. "If you went up against him, as opposed to playing with him—thinking you were hot shit—you were in for a very, very rude surprise." Even so, Danny felt it prudent to retire the box, if only to prove that he still had the fingers to do whatever he wanted. "When people ask me about the sounds I get and my equipment, I tell them it's 90 percent operator and 10 percent devices," he told Frank Joseph in the September 1983 *Guitar Player*.

Danny with Holly in 1983. Behind the "World's Greatest Unknown Guitar Player" persona lay a devoted family man who liked staying close to home.
• •

Amid these professional frustrations came a welcome distraction: the birth of Danny's only child, Holly Anne, in October 1979. She'd been conceived at the family's rented farmhouse in Accokeek. "He loved his little girl, I'll tell you that," Bobby Hancock says. "He really thought the world of her. They had tried for a long time to have children, and Jan was at least in her late thirties when Holly was born."

When they were ready to take the plunge, the Gattons bought a small white home—seen on the cover of *Unfinished Business*—at 1201 Accokeek Road. They'd stay there nearly ten years, until they moved further south in February 1988 to Newburg, Maryland. "Basically, he bought the garage. It happened to have a house, too, so he kind of stumbled into it," Wolf says. "He was more interested in a place to do his cars than concerned about what kind of shape the house was in."

Getting to the house involves a pleasant, winding drive off Maryland Route 210 (Indianhead Highway), through the small towns of Waldorf and La Plata. There's no shortage of rural greenery to enjoy along the way, as well as the usual array of strategically positioned motels and take-out joints. You know you're getting close once you hit the twin sets of lights; from there, it's a right turn and ten more miles to reach the house that's now owned by Steve Wolf and his wife, Nancy.

They proudly point out the features that Danny added over the years, including the barn built to house his car projects, such as the Model T roadster fated to sit on blocks perpetually. "I never actually saw any of them finished, but he always had a lot of them going on," Steve laughs. "He enjoyed the work of doing it more than the completion. He'd get far along, and then he'd find some other car [to work on]."

The garage was the epicenter of Danny's life whenever he wasn't playing. It was the place where his buddies came to hang out, and it was the appointed spot for most rehearsals and jam sessions. The garage door's inner side also served as Danny's phone book, which is how names like Joe Barden, Billy Hancock, and Dick Heintze wound up being scrawled next to those of former manager Ellis Duncan and Roger Miller bandleader "Thumbs" Carllile.

"He had an antique refrigerator with a compressor on top, where he kept the beers cold," Steve says. "They would watch ballgames by putting the TV on the hood. They'd sit in the car and watch through the windshield." (Not for nothing did Bobby Hancock's wife, Liz, like to joke: "Danny wished that it was 1955 all the time.")

Steve says the house had been crammed with antiques when the Gattons lived there. "That thing was just packed. Every square inch of wall space was covered with antique furniture they'd collected. It was way too small for the stuff they had." The situation didn't change much when Steve and Nancy bought the house. Jan never finished moving everything out; then Danny died and Brent asked if he could reclaim the antiques. "His brother didn't get around to it for another six years. Finally, he came over with a friend of his and started hauling stuff."

Remnants of Danny's life still lie scattered around the backyard, like the old acetylene tank now being reclaimed by the bushes. A doghouse and fenced-in coop, complete with its own nesting boxes, were once part of the scenery. When Steve came to visit, he always observed some type of fowl running around, including ducks, geese, and guinea hens. At one point, some goats briefly joined the birds, acquired for their alleged lawn-maintenance prowess. Danny got them because he hated mowing the grass and thought the animals would relieve him of that chore, according to Steve. "He found out they were very selective, so he ended up going to the John Deere dealer in La Plata and getting himself a small lawn tractor."

Holly doesn't remember seeing her father very often "because he was almost entirely nocturnal, due to his job," she says. "I remember that he would hang a 'Do Not Disturb' sign on the bedroom door during the day, because he was trying to sleep. When I did see him, we had a lot of fun together." Father and daughter "would go on nature walks in the local park in Fort Washington, hunt for arrowheads in freshly plowed fields, go for rides in his old cars or on his tractor, identify constellations, collect bugs and other critters, philosophize about our place in the universe, and listen to music. He was my best friend during my childhood and taught me to love and respect all things in the natural world."

Holly says the relationship worked for one simple reason: "He never treated me like a child, always like an adult. He taught me to take pride in my intelligence, which is probably how I ended up with nicknames like 'Human Encyclopedia' at school." And, as had been true of Danny's childhood, "music was always around in our house.… He used to play a record by Les Paul & Mary Ford called 'Johnny Is the Boy for Me,' and I used to dance around to it. I thought the guitar was so beautiful in that song."

Holly heard plenty of her father's music, too. "Whenever he made a new record, he would come home and play the demo tapes for me, even if it was at four or five in the morning and I had school in a few hours. I was excited to hear it. He truly valued my opinion about the mixes and would ask me what I thought." Danny would also play his guitar for her; she remembers him doing songs like "Teddy Bears' Picnic," as well as themes from TV shows like *The Twilight Zone*. "We used to watch a lot of old TV shows in our house, and consequently I was raised on '50s culture, not '80s. We loved the Three Stooges and Laurel & Hardy and the Little Rascals. We also liked to watch cheesy old sci-fi movies like *The Creature from the Black Lagoon*."

She adds: "Dad really didn't spend much time practicing guitar, though. When we were together, I really had to beg him to play for me. He never taught me to play guitar, either—absolutely refused. He was afraid I'd get into music and not go to college."

SHANNON FORD KNEW THAT Danny had begun playing full time again in September 1980 when he got a call about playing with singer-songwriter Roger Miller (of "King of the Road" fame). Ford's not sure how Danny got the gig, though a number of sources—including guitar tech Jay Monterose—have named Carllile as the connection. Ford says, "That was a hell of a lineup, man: 'Thumbs' Carllile and Danny Gatton together."

Ford promptly flew out to join Miller's band in Las Vegas, where they did two shows per night for seven weeks. "It was the first time I'd ever worked in Vegas, first time I'd done any kind of gig with a major artist like that. Danny and I had an amazing time, and it was one of the best times of my life—in spite of the fact that we stayed up one night and gambled both of our $650 weekly paychecks on a dollar slot machine." They ended up "trolling for nickels"—scooping up loose change that other people had dropped, which they duly crammed into the one-armed bandits.

The whole exercise ran until 6 A.M., when the pair had finally exhausted their cash and retired to the bar for the standard reward of free beers. What happened next was enough to put Ford off casino gambling for a long time. "Boy, were we hot," he says. "We'd been up all night, drinking beer, and lost both of our paychecks—and then we watched somebody else win the money."

The Humbler
(1980–1982)

*T*he well-worn aphorism "have guitar, will travel" seemed appropriate as Danny began the '80s, since he was now holding down three jobs. He'd already been augmenting his doings on the D.C. circuit by joining Roger Miller, mostly for gigs in Las Vegas and Reno. And then he tapped his beloved well of rockabilly by enlisting with Robert Gordon, who'd known Danny since the late '60s and had emerged from the late-'70s New York punk scene as a force to watch.

Gordon had fronted the Tuff Darts before signing to Private Stock as a solo artist in 1977. He joined a roster that included Blondie, New York's flashiest New Wavers, and Four Seasons vocalist Frankie Valli (then embarking on a solo career). Gordon's new sound, however, owed little to the noise being generated in clubs like CBGB's and Max's Kansas City, as affirmed by his collaboration with '50s guitar pioneer Link Wray (*Robert Gordon with Link Wray,* 1977). *Fresh Fish Special* (1978) further boosted Gordon's profile, thanks to his rendition of Bruce Springsteen's "Fire," with The Boss himself making a cameo appearance on piano. (The Pointer Sisters later made the song a No. 2 U.S. hit.) The momentum helped Gordon land a deal with RCA Records, and he sold out clubs and colleges wherever he played.

He continued to show impeccable taste in guitarists, working with British ace Chris Spedding on *Rockabilly Boogie* (1979) and *Bad Boy* (1980), and then hooking up with Danny on *Are You Gonna Be the One?* (1981), which rockabilly aficionados consider his finest hour. The hot supporting cast also included the likes of upright bassist Tony Garnier, fiddler Buddy Spicher, late-night TV bandleader Paul Shaffer, and guitarist-coproducer Lance Quinn. Shannon Ford was in the band, too, at Danny's behest. "I showed up at a rehearsal hall in Queens and did a bunch of dates with them," he says. "That was fun—we played some really wild rock 'n' roll."

Ford found the recording a bit restrained, though. "I thought Danny was a bit held back on that particular record—it had nothing to do with the live gigs. The live gigs were really the fun thing to do." However, he did enjoy working with Marshall Crenshaw, whose four songwriting contributions marked his first national exposure. One of them, "Someday, Someway," had been widely touted as Gordon's first big pop hit, but the song flatlined at No. 76 U.S., spending just four weeks on the *Billboard* charts in mid-1981. Even worse, "Drivin' Wheel"—a tough rockabilly number co-written by T-Bone Burnette and Billy Swan—failed to chart for Gordon, while Emmylou Harris's version shot right into the Top 10.

Gordon and his group, dubbed the Wildcats, worked hard to promote the album throughout the summer and fall of 1981. The gigs ranged from small clubs to larger venues like Chicago's Park West and New York's Lone Star Café. And the band's visit to Berkeley, California's Berkeley Square nightclub provided the setting for an accidental album that became a cornerstone of Danny's underground legend.

The set might have run longer if fire marshals hadn't been so adamant about shutting it down, because the club's 120-seat capacity had swelled to 300 people, according to producer Glenn Holley's liner notes. On hearing they'd get to do one more song, the band responded with "Red Hot." It was an appropriate choice to close the night, with Danny's trebly, piercing lead work racing all over the fretboard.

Nobody knew they were being taped on what was the second gig of the tour, according to Ford, who was preoccupied with the crazy happenings in the audience. "It was the first time I'd seen a bunch of guys doing the 'mosh pit' thing," he says. "You'd get all these punk rockabilly guys dancing around, diving off the stage. I wasn't used to really wild, raucous, rock 'n' roll crowds. This was more punk than I'd ever seen. It was cool; it was great."

The punks had plenty of good old-fashioned showmanship to engage them, too, such as when Danny and Quinn would cross hands and play on each other's guitar necks. "My studio experience helped, because I could always find a part to play that was not competitive with Danny's," Quinn says. "He could play three harmony parts at a time. It was just amazing what he was doing to make me look good, but it was nothing for him."

The tour was enjoyable for Quinn, whose pilot's license freed him from lengthy bus rides. Danny, on the other hand, would say, "I'd rather be home playing the Cellar Door than doing this." Ever the diplomat, Quinn responded, "Well, everyone likes different things." Quinn also welcomed a chance to get away from the disciplined life of a studio musician. "On the road, I was totally out of control," he laughs. "I would bring hookers to the room. Danny was so embarrassed, he'd hide in the bathroom till the hookers left."

THE BOOTLEG RECORDING FINALLY got an official release when Norma put out *Robert Gordon with Danny Gatton: The Humbler* in 1996. The mood is fast and furious, with 14 songs flying by in 48 minutes. Part of that stemmed from Gordon's dislike of long shows: 35 to 40 minutes was the norm, Quinn says.

The *Humbler* tape acquired legendary status among guitar buffs, who would say to each other: "Think you're hot? Well, listen to *this!*" (Guitarist Amos Garrett is credited with dreaming up the title after procuring a copy.) Although he's technically a sideman, it's hard to miss Danny's lickety-split picking on the hard-rocking likes of "Cruisin'" and "You Got Heart Like a Rock"; at other times, he confines himself to taut fills that accent the mood of fatalistic weepers like "There Stands the Glass."

Are You Gonna Be the One? may well have been aimed beyond the rock-abilly crowd, but the live shows were an altogether different beast. And Jan believes Gordon knew that it was rare to share the stage with a talent like Danny. "He did allow Dan a lot of freedom," she says. "It was almost like he understood that 'I should let the audience see this.' That was one of the best times for him."

Robert Gordon and Danny at Berkeley Square in 1982. Although Danny often complained about how his sound fared on Gordon's albums, "he always said that Robert allowed him so much latitude and he was grateful for that," Jan says.

Back home in Virginia, the ever-industrious Joe Barden drew a different lesson from the original *Humbler* tape while striving to wind a better pickup. He scoured shops around the area to get the wire needed for his experiments and bought new Fender pickups from Phil Zavarella—"so I'd have relatively new parts to use, as opposed to really, really used parts." Getting those parts remained a largely hit-or-miss process, though, until Barden went to a machine shop one day because he needed somebody to shear blades for a single-coil pickup.

On the back wall stood a row of large green books, which turned out to be the *Thomas Register*, an industrial catalog for nearly any commodity manufactured in the U.S. Barden couldn't believe his eyes. "Holy shit, there's 400 pages of metal-shearing shops; there's 200 pages of shoe-eyelet companies that also sell miniature eyelets like Fender used to connect the wire on their pickups; there's 40 or 50 pages of magnet-wire suppliers. God, there's no secrets! All this shit is readily available."

Armed with this knowledge, Barden had the source material he needed to build better pickups. "My single-coil pickups still didn't really sound that good," he says, "but in terms of the quality of their manufacture, they just kept getting better. The engineering was just getting better and better."

The Humbler proved a watershed in the trial and error that led to Barden's discovery of double-bladed pickups in 1983, which Danny then started putting in his guitars. "Everyone had been telling me: 'What you're doing is great, but these things hum worse than ever because they have so much output.' And I couldn't argue that point—listen to some of those *Humbler* tapes with Lance Quinn. For the first part of that tour, there was no string ground in [Quinn's] Telecaster. The only time there wasn't mind-blowing hum was when his hand happened to be touching the control knob. The rest of the time, it was a completely ungrounded guitar with high-output single-coil pickups. It was absurd—really, really bad."

Barden estimates that he went through roughly ten generations before developing a double-coil pickup that had the snap and twang of a single-coil. Literally hundreds of prototypes went into his or Danny's guitars. "A lot of this, I could do on my own," he says. "I was a decent enough player and had a decent enough ear to where I could rule out some nonsense." But to really determine if a pickup was good or bad, it went into Danny's guitar—though "bad" was a relative term: to Barden, it just meant one that didn't fit his mandate of sounding like a Tele. He strove to be "rabidly consistent" and found most of the pickups sounded too dark, heavy, or thick. Eventually, Barden realized it took only 100 turns either way to make an audible difference.

Barden kept tabs on his prototypes with a DC multimeter, "which is a pretty crude way to measure a pickup," he says. "All it really does is tell you the length of wire that's been wound around the pickup. If you're winding a wire, you'd go around a corner and it's real tight; stretch the wire and it's going to get skinnier. Skinnier wire has a different resistance value."

The meter revealed subtle differences of 15 to 20 percent between the prototype pickups. "They were different enough to be an entirely new model, were I to want that. I was like, Holy shit, with my pickup, it's going to have to be perfect—or nothing—because these pickups clearly are revealing much more than the stock Fender pickups.'"

Many refinements were needed to realize the final version. "I didn't know what my pickups sounded like until the first time I heard them, in the same way that Leo Fender did not know what a Telecaster sounded like until the first time he heard it," Barden says. "Nobody went, 'Okay, we need twang and the top snap harmonics on the G string.' People don't understand that this whole concept of tone, this quest for tone, was absolutely foreign to the pioneers of this industry."

In short, pioneers like Fender weren't looking for a sound—they were just trying to build a reliable product that would promise what it delivered, according to Barden. "Likewise, with a hum-canceling, high-output, side-by-side pickup for a solidbody electric guitar—no one had done that before me, that I know of," he says. When he showed his double-coil pickup to Seth Lover, who had invented the Gibson humbucking pickup in 1957, Lover said, "I was always going to do this, but I never got around to it!"

FOR SHANNON FORD, *The Humbler* brought back the frustration he had felt, as a 12-year-old aspiring drummer, upon seeing Buddy Rich. "I would have thought if you were a guitar player and you went to see Danny Gatton, you'd have some thoughts about continuing." Danny's eagerness to draw on horn and keyboard players also made him think about his instrument, Ford says. "Not just drawing from drummers all the time for your influence, but singers, horn players, piano players, percussionists."

Ford says that, ironically, "we hardly ever listened to guitar players—I can count on one hand when we were checking out a guy's guitar playing. It was always another instrument; most of the time, it was an organ player." Ford regards Heintze as the obvious inspiration for that, although they never got to play together. "I came on the Redneck Jazz thing when Dick was really ill. At that point he wasn't playing anymore, but I heard a lot of recordings, cassette stuff from rehearsals and gigs. It was pretty amazing."

Nothing exemplifies Danny's hot dog side more than *The Humbler* CD's single bonus track: a soundcheck of Roy Clark's signature instrumental,

"Fingers on Fire," that features only Danny and Ford. They start quietly and hotfoot to a frenetic middle before cooling off the tempo—as if to show how much they can flex their creative muscles. Danny's speedy, echo-drenched picking is a delight, even if the track is just a mono recording from one channel of the house system (according to Glenn Holley's liner notes).

Guitar purists have long drooled at the nimbleness Danny exhibits during the two minutes it takes for the tune to flash by, but Ford says his initial reaction was: "Oh shit, you taped the soundcheck? I don't want to hear that…okay, that's all right, but let's not listen to that again." Ford didn't hear the whole *Humbler* tape until years later, but he's glad to see something still survives from that era. "I was very impressed with how cool it was. I didn't think I could play that well back then, and it was a revelation to hear how good the band was." (Bassist Tony Garnier adds: "Once Danny knew the songs, he just caught on fire. It was incredible!")

"I think [*The Humbler*] showcased his rockabilly playing better than anything," Ford says, "but—as we all know—the rockabilly thing was just a portion of what he did. You don't hear a whole lot of blues playing; you don't hear his jazz thing; you don't hear the country thing in that band. You hear some hardcore rockabilly with smokin' guitar. There was probably some night somewhere down in southern Maryland, where he's sitting in with some country band—that would have been his best country night. It's all wherever you dropped him in."

LOCAL FANS MIGHT HAVE been excused for wondering where Danny had gone while he was on the road. They got an answer, of sorts, in a February 26, 1982, *Prince William County Journal* article. Writer Nick Adde found Danny in an expansive mood but still determined to do things his way. Danny revealed that he'd spent most of January playing with Roger Miller at the MGM Grand Hotel in Reno, but didn't have much else to say about the experience. His silence about it goes a long way toward explaining how he felt about the gig.

The article asserted that Danny was keeping a low profile locally; not surprisingly, a late-January reunion with the Fat Boys at Desperado's received the biggest mention. Danny also mentioned another gig he'd been doing five nights a week in Waldorf. "Nobody knew who I was, nobody clapped, and nobody cared," he said. "I loved it." Citing the approach of his 37th birthday in September, Danny stated a desire to reform the Redneck Jazz Explosion; otherwise, he'd end up going back to sheet-metal work.

Danny insisted that three or four gigs per week were enough for him. Ideally, he'd tour for three months, record for another three, and spend the remaining half-year working on his vehicles, which now included two

1934 Ford panel trucks, a 1932 Ford panel truck, and a Model T roadster. "I'd give up guitar in a minute if I could just work on cars," Danny confessed. He signed off by asking if anybody could track down the Offbeats' 1962 single that featured him, since he didn't have a copy.

Danny appeared on the next Robert Gordon record, *Too Fast to Live, Too Young to Die* (1982), which featured a wider array of talent than the previous albums. This time around, the troika of Lance Quinn, Scott Litt, and ex-'60s girl-group man Richard Gottehrer shared production credits with Gordon. Danny got a co-writing credit on the title track and shared the guitar responsibilities with Spedding and Wray. Nearly two dozen names crowded the credits, including Elvis Presley's backup vocalists, the Jordanaires, guitarist Billy Cross, and bassist-pianist Rob Stoner, who'd worked with Bob Dylan. "I'm not on the whole record; I think I'm on one or two tracks," Ford says, "Anton Fig's on that record playing drums somewhere, 'cause Anton took over after I left."

As the credits indicated, a different band was emerging. Spedding reclaimed the lead guitar spot, and Fig moved behind the drum kit, followed in turn by Billy Idol's drummer, Tommy Price. "He started going with, in my opinion, more straight-rock guys than rockabilly guys," Ford says. "I consider Chris Spedding a great musician, but he's more of a rock player than a rockabilly guitarist. It just kind of changed direction, and Danny started doing his own thing again." Ford, who joined up with the Gatlin Brothers, wouldn't see much of Danny for a long time after that. "The Gatlin thing was great, because I was able to buy a house. It was cool for seven years, although I went nuts after about five, because we were on the road so much," he says.

Jan doesn't know why the lineup changed. "I know that towards the end there was some kind of friction, maybe with Robert's lifestyle. I do remember some dissatisfaction on Dan's part—but he always said that Robert allowed him so much latitude and he was grateful for that."

Danny wasn't idle for long. He began another notable professional association in November 1981, when he recorded his first tracks for Billy Poore, a rockabilly collector and raconteur extraordinaire. Poore was looking for an appropriate vehicle for Johnny Seaton, who'd attracted attention as a hot rockabilly singer and Elvis impersonator. The relationship would yield 49 days of studio time and 183 gigs through August 1987, according to *Runnin' Wild* (2001), the sprawling four-CD box set of Danny's work with Seaton and Poore's other main artist, LesLee "Bird" Anderson.

Poore first met Danny at Desperado's in the spring of 1979, where the Fat Boys were doing one of their many reunion gigs. He was already booking dates for rockabilly wildman Charlie Feathers, and he knew Billy

Hancock. While he'd heard of Danny, guitar players made little impression on someone who'd sung lead as a teenager in doo-wop groups. "The guitarist had a job to do, he got paid to do it, and that was it," Poore says. "They didn't sell the records. There were exceptions, like Duane Eddy, of which Danny laughed: 'I learned all that stuff in five minutes!'"

Danny's feverish work on "Mystery Train" convinced Poore that he'd heard someone surpass Scotty Moore's playing on the original, but his rock 'n' roll classicist streak didn't cotton to long instrumental breaks. "A song better be damn good, if it's over two-and-a-half or three minutes, to hold your attention," he says. "Danny would get into these ten-minute things on the guitar, and that wasn't my thing at all."

However, both men discovered plenty of common ground when they talked after the Fat Boys gig. "He was neat to hang out with and loved to smoke cigarettes and drink beer—so, at the time, he was my kind of person!" Poore cracks. Danny also loved hearing Poore reel off stories about getting drunk with rockabilly icons like Gene Vincent. "I don't think it really hit him till he came over to my trailer in Laurel, and saw the gobs and gobs of pictures of me with all these people."

The two men spoke by phone several times in 1980, but nothing suggested they'd be working together. Jan doesn't believe the friendship was mutual. "Dan tolerated him, but I don't think there was any great closeness on Dan's part. Billy says they were great friends, but I don't think Dan viewed it that way." Poore avers that if their relationship wasn't widely acknowledged, it's because he never capitalized on it. "Danny's mother said I was the best-kept secret of all, for years. He had closer friends than me, but we had a bond of closeness to each other."

In the fall of 1981, Poore called Danny with a proposition. He was looking to help Seaton, whom he'd met in 1978. The singer had trekked to California, but no big break had come, so he was returning home by Christmas. "Me and my wife were there [to help out], and we just thought he had a whole lot of talent and could get somewhere," Poore says.

Poore had decided that a good record was needed, and Danny's years of know-how would be just the thing to make the project successful. Seaton had already cut a Feathers-produced unreleased single in July 1980, but the results hadn't impressed Poore. "I was telling Danny, 'I want it played just like the way they played it, but cleaner,' because Charlie cut it on his old eight-track and it was kind of muddied up." (Ironically, the two unreleased songs were among the only tapes to survive a disastrous electrical fire that gutted Poore's Tennessee home. He lost 17 years of master tapes of work with Danny and other artists, 30,000 vintage albums, and 40,000 photographs. As a result, Poore had to rely on his daughter Stacy's vinyl albums and cassette copies of unreleased tracks to produce *Runnin' Wild*. "That's what killed me on this fire," he says. "I lost the earliest stuff me and Danny did together.")

Poore wanted to marry the energy of '50s rockabilly with '80s playing and production techniques. Danny expressed interest, but asked if he and Poore could do some jamming first. They booked a four-hour session in November 1981 at Kensington, Maryland's Omega Studios, where Danny startled Poore by asking him if he could sing. "I said, 'Back when I was 18, it was a lot easier. I was smoking one cigarette a day, not 100, you know?' 'Never mind,' Danny said, 'just have fun.'" They ran through five songs, including "Shake, Rattle & Roll," instrumental versions of "Runaway" and "Sleepwalk" for Poore's wife ("'cause she liked that stuff"), and "Cold, Cold Baby," which Poore had written as a 17-year-old. When they parted, Danny asked Poore to let him know when his protégé would be back in Maryland.

Danny didn't charge Poore for that get-acquainted session, or for his first session with Seaton on February 23, 1982, at Reel Time Studios in Silver Spring, Maryland. That day, Poore oversaw the recording of four songs that were distilled into the "Uptown" b/w "Git with It" single on Renegade Records. (Poore says he named his label for the teenage gang in a cheesy '50s horror flick, *The Ghost of Dragstrip Hollow*.)

Danny and Evan Johns handled the guitar and bass work, respectively, while John Britton doubled as drummer and engineer. It was Danny who'd suggested keeping the participants to a minimum — for pragmatic reasons, as well as for capturing the bare-bones rockabilly feel that Poore desired. "The less people we got around, the less mouths we have to listen to," Danny told him.

Poore was surprised by how long it took to get the right sound. "We went in about one-thirty, two o'clock in the afternoon," he says. "We didn't come out of there until seven o'clock the next morning. That was because of Danny. Evan got mad, but Danny wanted to get those parts right. That's the thing I liked about Danny all through the years: he was so meticulous, but he'd give me a [flat] rate, whether it was $250 or $200. It went down as time went on."

Johns found the session unusual, because Britton had prerecorded the drums. "This guy had rolls from when you went from the chorus into the bridge, so me and Danny were playing to that." He was also struggling to play the big acoustic bass. "Danny knew I could play upright," he says, "or he thought I could." Poore says, "Evan wasn't used to playing upright bass. He could play it, slap it, but his hands weren't ready for it. Danny would make him do it over, but Evan did a good job, too."

The single appeared on May 1, 1982. Just over a month later—following another marathon session—they had 11 tracks for an album, also titled *Uptown*. (Poore limited album runs to 500–1,000 LPs and 200 cassettes.) They then took the show on the road, with live gigs on July 25–26, 1982, at the Chancery in Washington.

Danny had lost his regular Waldorf gig in March, after his singer got into a fight with the owner of the Mousetrap. That led to an ultimatum: "Sing, or get fired." Danny retorted, "Well, give me my 40 bucks and I'm out of here." In the CD booklet for *Runnin' Wild*, Poore wrote: "Me and Evan and Danny all really laughed when he said that. Evan and I both said right there and then that we'd both pay whatever to hear Danny sing anything."

Dave Chappell had been among the regulars trooping out to hear a heavily bearded Danny at "this little funky place," even if he was just churning out Top 40 hits. Between his gigs with Roger Miller, Danny was playing in the Naturals, a band that included his old friends Ronnie Mac-Donald and Roger McDuffie. ("I don't know that they had a bass player," Chappell says. "I think Roger played keyboard bass." MacDonald left to front his own band, Nightwatch, before briefly rejoining forces with Danny in 1985.) Chappell and his future wife hit the Mousetrap at least once a week. "At one point, I got the nerve to tell Danny how much I admired his style, and he was very friendly. He was playing great. It didn't matter what the material was—he could still make something great happen with it." Better yet, Danny asked Chappell to play for him. "I kind of shyly did. 'Well, that was all right, that was cool.' He was like a god to us."

While they were working on Seaton's album, Danny had suggested cutting an instrumental album. Poore initially begged off, because he wanted to finish *Uptown*—which was requiring a lot of overtime at the Park Service to help finance the sessions. He also didn't want to immortalize what had least impressed him at Desperado's. "It won't be any of that blues that's eight minutes long, right? 'No, no,' Danny said, 'I'll be writing that hot rod stuff you like.'"

Poore felt that was worth doing and wanted Danny to sign a simple contract. Instead, Danny proposed an alternative: "Just pay for the studio time and [cutting the] record, and always give me records to sell." Poore demurred. Poore says that Danny then talked it over with Evan Johns. "He said, 'Christ, Danny, there's nothing in that contract—there's more for you than there is for Billy. He has some tapes, and he'll be willing to sell 'em back to you for whatever he's got in 'em.' They were not bad contracts. So Danny signed, and he cut some instrumentals." (Jan says that Danny never actually signed with Poore, although she did not oppose the release of *Runnin' Wild*.)

Poore recalls them cutting three instrumentals around August 5–6, and four more later that month. "I was cringing at the thought, but I was having him do stuff in the vein of 'Honky Tonk,'" he says. "I was trying to choose songs that he'd brighten up when he found one that he liked. I was trying to make a list of instrumentals that I liked, that he wanted to do."

Danny wasn't present for the September 1982 local triumph that fueled Poore's belief in Seaton's future. Seaton bested 45 of his peers—including Evan Johns & the H-Bombs—in a battle of the bands. Ironically, Danny had refused to have anything to do with the affair, which had to be billed under the Johnny Seaton Band banner for them to enter, Poore said. The band included Jay Monterose (lead guitar), Pete Folota (rhythm guitar), Mike Damron (bass), and Billy Bogus (drums). "You had all these bands with half a million dollars' worth of equipment and things flying off the stage," Poore says. "It proved to me that if you have raw energy and work your ass off for a crowd, it'll work almost every time." He also thought the event showed something to Danny, too: "You need a front singer, a young guy, somebody with charisma."

Monterose quit the band a month after the victory. Chappell, who had gone to California, learned of Monterose's defection after calling back home. He'd played a couple gigs with Seaton before heading west and was interested in the job. "Rockabilly was a happening thing," he says. "It was starting to trail off a little bit, but it was still going—they were working 25 days a month. It was a full-time band, and I had played three gigs since I'd been in Hollywood."

Chappell auditioned and got the job, joining Bogus, Damron, and Seaton. They'd indicated Danny would join them whenever he was in town and they could afford him, which happened at Baltimore's 8×10 club a couple weeks after Chappell's return. "A guy walks in with a red jacket and slicked-back hair: it's Danny, and he's on the gig," Chappell says. "It was like crawling from the wreckage and getting into a brand-new car. One minute, I'm out in California and starving. The next thing you know, I'm in a full-time band and Danny Gatton's coming to sit in with us."

Danny played at high volume, "which isn't a bad thing, in my book," Chappell says. "He was just very intense, and played with this deliberate force that would knock you up against a wall. The authority that he played with was unbelievable: 'I think it goes like *this*.'" The hapless soundman objected to the volume level, telling Danny to turn down. "He said, 'Well, I've heard that before, I'll hear that again. I'm going to get a beer—what're you doing?'"

Danny maintained his gigs with Robert Gordon and Roger Miller throughout the year, "but when he'd come back to town, Billy Poore would have a wad of money for him," Chappell says. They'd often play Oliver's, a small club in Fairfax, Virginia. "Being around him, you had to get your game up—just to try to save face. Every once in a while, I'd think I did something okay, and he'd play a fill that would just knock you up against the wall. It was good for you, but you got a royal ass-kicking in front of everybody."

Chappell knew something had changed when Danny praised his playing on a Carl Perkins song. "He goes, 'That solo you took was really good.' That was the first time he'd really paid me a compliment. Before that, he wouldn't insult you, but he wasn't going to tell you that you were doing something good if you weren't doing anything to get his attention."

Uptown generated positive attention on its December 1982 release. "It got reviewed in *Billboard* as 'recommended,' stuff like that," Poore says. He even heard a belated apology from RCA's A&R man, who'd signed the Rockats even though Seaton had made a better impression. (Poore had made a trek to the label's New York offices in the spring, where he'd had to get past "10,000 cops" during the St. Patrick's Day parade to drop off a demo.)

The full-color cover—inspired by a key lyric on "Get with It" ("I'm just a bellhop")—also didn't hurt. Poore had suggested putting Seaton in a bellhop's outfit, standing next to an attractive woman. Both album and single got airplay on WHFS, Poore's favorite station of the time. "I took it right over, and they just started playing it," he says. He does recall some snide comments from people who suggested that Seaton's vocals were okay for a former Elvis impersonator. "Man, that used to tick us off so bad, you wouldn't believe it. They'd just have to get that little dig in there, no matter what."

THE WAX MUSEUM hosted yet another Fat Boys reunion in December, with McDuffie aboard (though the December 26, 1982, *Washington Post* review identified him as "Ralph Duffy"). "Gatton may not show much emotion or even movement on stage, but his guitar smokes," Mike Joyce wrote. "Notes were bent, slid, choked, or simply popped into place in a number of pieces designed to showcase his dazzling speed and dexterity."

Danny's apparent detachment from audiences was hardly accidental, according to his brother. "He loved to play what he wanted to play and liked for people to hear it," Brent says. "He didn't care if they saw him or not." Danny's expressionless demeanor and stock-still posture were a marked contrast to the frenetic stage movements and visceral grimaces so often associated with his instrument. But Danny would never provide fodder for parodists with those clichés: the essence of his performance style emphasized intent listening over onstage histrionics. As he often told Brent, "You can't play if you're jumping around."

Joyce also had praise for Billy Hancock, whose performance on songs like "Mystery Train" proved him "one of the few rockabilly singers working today whose delivery is free of affectation." The reviewer praised Elliott's work on R&B classics like "Don't Let Go," and he felt that McDuffie's playing "gave the ballads a lyrical lift" while lending the right degree of emotional heft to standards like "The House of Blue Lights."

Danny's ties to Roger Miller continued after the Gordon experience ran its course. Although neither gig was artistically fulfilling or demanding, they'd at least given him a steady income and exposure outside of his local stomping grounds. Whether he could show the necessary deference that a sideman's role demanded was an altogether different question—as anyone can plainly see on a videotape of Miller's January 24, 1983, performance on PBS-TV's *Austin City Limits* concert show. (The first broadcast was in March or April, according to producer Terry Lickona.)

Danny was featured fairly prominently and even got to solo on three songs. The most notable moment occurs on Miller's "England Swings," which Danny gooses up with a ringing, rockabilly-tinged solo—followed by a bemused facial expression that suggests, "Am I in tune here?" The rest of the show trundles along in agreeable fashion, capped off by an old-fashioned hoedown on fiddle and guitar, respectively, featuring Miller and special guest Willie Nelson.

"He knew exactly what he was doing, especially on that dumb little solo," Shannon Ford says. "We would all lay for when he'd get to do 'Orange Blossom Special,' and sometimes Roger would whip out some of the old stuff that he wrote for Ray Price and some of the old western swing things—and we would really get to cut loose. Danny would shine on that stuff." Other times, "he'd just do the hits, and it was all business."

The gig didn't require a lot of time on the road: Miller would fly in the band for a one-nighter or a week in Las Vegas. According to Ford, "his line was that he'd never believed in the forced busing of musicians." Nor was it grueling work. "It's always fun showing up at those gigs, because there wasn't a lot at stake. The band was a great bunch of guys, and we always had so much fun."

One time, the band got marooned in Omaha. "It was the dead of winter, and we were doing one show a night at some gymnasium—it was a bullshit gig," Ford recalls. "There was absolutely nothing to do. After the show, everything was closed down." Stuck at the motel, the musicians filled their idle hours as best as they could. "We constructed a 'fart tape'— it was mostly Danny's farts, but we all contributed. It was a complete A- and B-side of a 90-minute cassette that Danny composed with his Recording Walkman, which, in the early '80s, was still kind of a novelty. We thought we were pretty high-tech." The musicians played back "a symphony of these farts," Ford laughs. "Back to back, just nonstop—different pitches, different lengths."

The boys saluted New Year's Eve as "New Year's Heave," while "Jingle Bells" turned into "Jingle Belch." "He would play guitar, and there'd be a fart at the end of every phrase," Ford says. Danny developed a routine of going through airport security with the Walkman in his bag, turned up full blast. "As it was going through the X-ray thing, you'd have this farting bag. We thought that was the funniest thing we'd ever seen," Ford says. "You'd have these security guys looking at each other: 'What's with the farting bag?'"

Such hilarity aside, Ford says that "you had to be on your toes with Roger, because he had an unusual sense of phrasing. He would drop beats on you and forget arrangements—just stop in the middle of tunes, things like that. And he had this habit of blaming it on the band." Miller's gentle admonitions didn't sit well with Danny. "He would screw up and then turn around: 'C'mon, boys, stay with me.' That used to infuriate Danny. It really would piss him off, because he was of the school that you should completely respect your fellow musicians onstage. We were pretty much the buffoons in those situations, and he didn't like that at all."

Danny with the Roger Miller Band, circa 1983. The two men parted on an abrupt and acrimonious note in the Nevada desert.

"Roger had a warped sense of what was funny," Jan says. "I went to see them in Florida, and he was a very nasty person. Holly went up to him, and she was maybe three years old. He said, 'I know your daddy'—and she thought he said, 'I'm your daddy.' She picked up a handful of sand, threw it right in his face and screamed, 'You're not my daddy!' And he was *very* angry. I thought, 'Well, that's not right.'"

Jan saw few of the Miller shows, because she didn't have a baby-sitter for Holly. One time when she was in attendance "he looked right at me and thanked all of the women who supported their men," she says. "He did give Dan a chance. I did hear him introduce Dan with a lot of accolades, but I guess they just butted heads."

Brent Gatton recalls hearing a story—Danny never mentioned the locale—that began with the ever-mercurial Miller telling the band to learn three new tunes for the show. That night, he said to the audience, "I'm going to do a new one for you. Danny, do you want to kick it off?" But Miller hadn't told Danny which song to play, so there was a long pause. "Finally, Roger said the name of the song, and they did it," Brent says. "After the show, Danny said they almost came to blows. I think that's when he quit."

Ford says, "He got in a big fight with him onstage, somewhere in Vegas—maybe the Sahara." He was hardly surprised, because he knew that showing mutual respect onstage was important to Danny. "He wasn't one of those guys that could be the punch line." Brent adds: "I don't think he ever really liked being a sideman for anybody—that isn't what he wanted to do. He wanted to do his thing." He summarizes his brother's view of the sideman's lot as: "You're not even a hired gun, you're just the hired help!" (Miller obviously had mixed feelings about losing his star guitarist. Billy Poore remembers introducing himself to the singer years later as a friend of his former employee, which provoked a memorable outburst: "You tell that Danny Gatton I'll offer him so much money, he'll have to come back so I can fire him again!")

Eddie Adcock maintains that Danny liked the Miller band experience "because Roger would actually let him play and wouldn't lean on him like he's the boss. Everybody else was: 'greatest guitar player I've ever heard, Danny, you're a monster guitar player—now here's your 12 notes.'" Of the Robert Gordon gig, Eddie says he'd often hear Danny grouse: "I can't understand why they tell me I'm such a goddamn great guitar player, and then they tell me I got 8 or 10 notes I can play and I can't play no more. What the hell do they need me for? Any dumbass can play that many notes!"

In a January 1989 *Guitar World* profile, Danny said: "I never played anything on anybody else's records where I really got to do anything. I would go to a session with Robert, and they'd say, 'Hey, forget everything you know. Play like you're 12 years old. Don't do anything flashy. Just play real dumb.'" If that's what the producers wanted, so be it—but the future promised to be radically different. "I'm 43 years old. I figure I deserve to say what I have to."

Evan Johns says that Danny's duty with Sonny James had elicited another blistering condemnation of the sideman's lot. "I said, 'What's it like?' He said, 'Oh, man, you got to press your trousers and all this shit! You've got dress-code rules, and you're playing for old fuddy duds.'" The final straw apparently came when Danny decided not to let his employer win a mock banjo duel. "He said, 'Well, I don't think he's going to be inviting me back anytime soon.'"

Tom Principato says, "I remember him remarking to me that, musically, those gigs were enormously frustrating. He couldn't really stretch out, and stretching out was what his whole deal was based on. He was doing it for the money, basically."

Danny reached one conclusion after all the ups and downs of working with Gordon and Miller. "The sideman route was a definite dead end," Richard Harrington says. "It might just be a way to make some cash—but he would still use the opportunity to do the best job he could to best serve whoever was giving him the paycheck. That's more than a lot of folks do. But, ultimately, Danny's talent couldn't be confined to sideman status."

Jack Jensen saw a different problem: Danny hated routines. "He never really wanted a steady job is the way that I looked at it, basically. That was the problem when he played with Roger Miller: too routine, no creativeness." Jensen had marked the start of the '80s by opening a new club in Fort Washington, Maryland, called Billy Jack's. Billy Windsor became a partner and helped to run the place, which got him back into singing when Danny showed up. The loose atmosphere was perfect for Danny, Jensen says. "He could come and go—play what you want to play, drink beer, and bullshit with the people. There wasn't a ton of crowds, but it was a real low-key, fun thing."

Into the '80s
(1982–1985)

10

F or anyone looking in from the outside, Danny's life appeared to be rolling along as usual. But a different reality revealed itself when Danny pressed a .22-caliber rifle against his forehead in the garage of his home on Accokeek Road. Holly was only 18 months old when Jan struggled to wrest the gun from her husband's grip. After the horror seemed to have passed, she called Dan Senior. "His father came right over, had a talk with him, and took the rifle home," Jan says. "When Norma left for Georgia, she gave him that rifle back, and it's the one he used [to kill himself] in Newburg."

After the incident, Jan suggested that Danny quit the music business and start his own enterprise, such as restoring antique cars. "Steve Wolf said—in this whisper, but loud enough so I could hear it—that I was what was wrong with Dan," Jan says. "I never spoke to him again, until Dan's funeral. I was so angry that he could think I was the one who was at fault."

The whole situation seemed like a terrifying rerun of an incident that had happened shortly after *Redneck Jazz*'s release—only that time it had involved a handgun that, somehow, Jan had managed to pull away from Danny. "I was surprised I was able to do that, because he was like a bear— a pretty strong guy," she says. "It was real scary, and he said, 'Make her stop, make her stop!'"

Jan had then called Danny's parents to the farmhouse, but found their response not quite what she'd expected. "They didn't say this, but this is what I inferred: 'If you had not cut him off from all his friends and family...'" Her voice trails off. "I said, 'No, no, he doesn't want to be pushed into this music business like this.'"

Dan Senior's presence seemed to exert a calming influence on his son, something that Jan and Holly felt forced to revisit when they found an undated note after Danny's death that read: "Holly: You'll never know how much I miss my father." Jan says, "Holly was furious. She said, 'I suppose he didn't know how much I'll miss *my* father.' She was really angry about finding that. We found it in the box where his father presented him with the Heineken beer bottle, the velvet-lined box he presented at one of the gigs—Danny was so proud of that."

Jan felt bound to protect Danny, but was unable to get between him and his mother, because he'd get upset. "I figured, until that gun incident, he could take care of himself," she says. "That wasn't the case. She was stronger than either Dan or his father. She was the power in the house."

Just how powerful became clear after Danny and Jan returned from their Seattle misadventure and lived with his parents for a brief period. "She would say things to her husband that were absolutely beyond belief," Jan recalls. "And she would say them in front of everybody: 'I could have married a doctor. I was dating this doctor, but I married a sheet-metal worker.' One time, her husband spoke up. We were coming back from a gig, and he said, 'Well, why didn't you, then?' And there was this total silence."

Jan was at a loss to understand what was happening, because she felt "on the outside looking in." "That's how he made me feel about [Norma]. When he would do such terrible things, and say that these things happened because of her, that's all I could think—that she was a very bad character to push him in this way. I didn't just pull that out of the air."

Jan doesn't dismiss the sacrifices that Norma made on Danny's behalf, and how "she loved him totally, more than she loved her husband, I'm sure—she told me that. But there had to be something very, very wrong with that relationship for him to not be able to say, 'Butt out of this,' and have to find another way to get out of it. That's my take on it."

How much other factors may have played a role is speculative, but Danny's maternal great-grandfather had also committed suicide—which Jan only heard from Norma after her husband's death. Ultimately, though, she doesn't attribute his death to genetics. "If he could have just done what he felt he should do—as far as his family—then maybe things would have been all right," Jan says.

The intra-familial divide inevitably looms over any discussion of the issue. Norma doesn't discuss her feelings toward Jan. Brent didn't speak to Jan and Holly for years, after voicing his disapproval of how they'd handled his late brother's property and belongings. He maintains that family tensions had existed for a long time, with Jan often at the center. And, like his mother, he believes that Jan never took any great interest in Danny's music.

One question naturally arises: why didn't Danny see a psychiatrist or at least get some kind of counseling? "I didn't think the problem was his," Jan says. "I know that sounds nuts, but I didn't think that he had a problem. I thought *she* had a problem. I thought he had trouble with their relation-ship as far as saying, 'No, no more.' I just could not understand why he could not say no, unless he depended on her financially to do these [al-bums]. How else are you going to feel if you can't pay that person back or somehow make retribution for a great sacrifice?"

Looking back, Jan feels she should have gotten help for her husband. "When I got married, my father and my mother were both so unhappy, but if I had listened to them and not said, 'No, I'm doing this,' Holly would not be here. And I would not have had 28 years with somebody I loved very deeply." Ultimately, Jan didn't think that Danny would actually fol-low through on any impulses to harm himself, since he didn't appear con-sumed by such feelings. "Anyway, I didn't do anything. I just thought it was over; he was just so much better. I thought when Mr. Gatton spoke to him that everything had been resolved."

DANNY'S PEERS CONTINUED TRYING to lure him back from hibernation. Pete Kennedy remembers getting a call from John Previti around the turn of 1982–83. The bassist had talked Danny into doing a few nights at the Gen-try on 8th Street in Washington—would Kennedy play rhythm guitar and sing? Dave Elliott would also be involved.

Kennedy agreed, and they spent six to eight months gigging around the Baltimore-Washington area. One of his favorite compliments followed a gig at the Gentry, where one of the regulars said, "I've seen Danny with a lot of rhythm-guitar players—you're not as good as him, but you don't care." Kennedy didn't mind such an appraisal. "It was no competition whatsoever, 'cause I didn't have any notion that I was going to 'smoke' Danny," he says. In his mind, the right rhythm guitarist needed the same appreciation of guitar history that Danny carried at his fingertips. "That made it fun. If he did a Scotty Moore thing, I did a Scotty Moore thing— it would make him feel comfortable, and we'd just take it from there. It was a [musical] conversation back and forth, and I knew where he was com-ing from, in terms of the references."

Danny appreciated that kind of support, because it made him play a little harder, according to Kennedy. Other times, the musicians would dou-ble up in laughter, unable to play, and the song would lurch to a halt. "That's my main memory of Danny—he joked around, made funny voices. He made the guitar talk in funny voices. That was his favorite kind of gig, really, not being treated as a serious guy who's going to change the world."

The repertoire was typically eclectic. Kennedy recalls Danny playing a few originals, like "Sky King" and "Defeat on the Beach" (later recorded as "Puddin' & Pie" on *Cruisin' Deuces*), along with *Redneck Jazz* standbys like "Rock Candy." The theme from the TV show *Perry Mason* also began popping up. Sets started at 9 P.M. and ran for 90 minutes non-stop before the first break. "I like to play that way, too—and we'd pretty much cover everything from Buddy Holly to modal jazz, all in that one medley, but make it work, lead logically from one thing to the other," Kennedy says. They also did some "unplugged" gigs as a trio, with Danny and Kennedy on acoustic guitars and Previti on his upright bass.

Kennedy left after getting hired for a theatre pit orchestra. Whereas Danny's gigs were on weekends, Kennedy could play every night with the pit orchestra, and he really needed the money. "I called up Danny, and he said, 'Oh, sure,' 'cause he was a working musician and he really understood that. We continued to be friends. It didn't matter whether we were playing in the same band or not; we were just guitar-playing buddies."

Danny also started spending more time at Billy Jack's. "It appeared to be moderately successful, but ended up, like so many of them, not really staying [in business] very long," Bobby Jones recalls. "He was very busy," Jan says. "He didn't make an enormous amount of money, but it was comfortable and steady. He was home, and that made him happy. He loved southern Maryland and the people of southern Maryland."

LANCE QUINN HAD BROUGHT Danny to New York for assorted sessions like Cindy Bullens's *Desire Wire* (1978), as well as the Robert Gordon albums. The tour that yielded *The Humbler* had marked Quinn's only real road trip, because he'd been so busy working at New York's Power Station studio.

Their most profitable relationship involved Danny's work on several instrumental albums by the trombonist Meco Monardo, who went by his first name. According to Quinn, Danny didn't play on the extended disco suites of *Star Wars & Other Galactic Funk* (1977), the thumping album that established Meco as a writer and producer. However, Danny did contribute to *Pop Goes the Movies* (1982) and *Hooked on Instrumentals* (1986), which solidified his studio credentials. Roger McDuffie was aboard for these projects; he remembers working at the Power Station on the same day that Chic and Kiss were there. "I didn't recognize Gene Simmons. I didn't even really know who Kiss was," Roger says. Once Roger made the connection, he and Danny agreed on one thing right away: facially speaking, Kiss's bassmeister sorely needed his makeup.

The pair also worked on an obscure soundtrack for Meco, *Highway 44*, as well as an unreleased version of the theme for the TV detective show *Simon & Simon* for *Hooked on Instrumentals*. Meco recorded it as a single, but it never came out. The B-side was a Danny Gatton original. "It was really good—I would pay anything to have a copy of that," McDuffie says.

One of their most inspired one-off projects was the single "Love Them Hogs" b/w "Redskin Fever," saluting the Washington Redskins' Super Bowl victory. Billy Hancock had already done his own tribute to the NFL franchise, "Redskin Rock," so it seemed logical for Roger to do likewise. The A-side centered around an uptempo, barrelhouse-style piano riff. "I was almost embarrassed by the way it sounded," McDuffie says, "because I just did it on a little tape recorder—and, at the time, I didn't play the piano that well. I gave it to Danny, and he said, 'That's it! We'll make a hit out of that.' It went on to be No. 1 in D.C." They worked at Law Studios in Virginia; McDuffie played piano while Danny handled the bass and guitar parts. "I told him, 'I want a Les Paul & Mary Ford solo,' and he said, 'I already know what I'm going to play for you, Roger.' He played that in one take."

For as many sessions as Danny did, Quinn doesn't think he could have made a career of the studio musician's art, where less is often more. He says he once took Danny along to a disco session, which inspired him to comment, "'Man, you didn't play anything!' I said, 'I know, but the guy loved it.' You just had to stick in your part, stay there, and leave room for everyone else to shine. He didn't like that."

IN JANUARY 1983, JOE BARDEN quit the auto-parts job that had allowed him to hunt down items that Danny needed. "I was making pretty good money, and I was heading towards managing the wholesale side of the auto-parts store," he says. "I definitely would have had a pretty fat career." But Barden had different ideas, which he had freedom to explore after getting a job house-sitting the northern Virginia home of a United Airlines pilot and his wife, Les and Helen Hewitt. "I knew them because their daughter Denise had been my sister Amy's college roommate," Barden says.

Les was being posted to the West Coast for 18 months. He and his wife didn't want to rent their home, since they planned to come back—which is how Barden wound up living rent-free in a fully furnished home and driving the couple's luxury car. All he had to do was pay the utility bills. "I had a year and a half to woodshed and experiment without having to worry. All I had to do was sell enough pickups to eat sandwiches and just sort of get by. That was an absolute godsend."

Barden set up shop in the basement, where he could refine his ideas about pickups. He wanted to solve the hum problem while increasing the output and keeping the single-coil sound. Other manufacturers had wrestled with these problems. "Seymour Duncan had his stacks out, and DiMarzio had a stack copy," Barden says. "Those things fit in the guitar, but they sucked—they had less output than a stock Tele pickup and no tone, and they weren't available for the neck position, because that pickup is so small."

Barden was amazed, then, to develop a neck pickup "that would bolt right in and was every bit as powerful as a bridge pickup. Danny was just as dumbfounded as I was. I was stunned: 'Holy shit, this is really happening, it's working.'"

His next major breakthrough was the double-bladed pickup. The first one he made was a Strat pickup, but within weeks he'd made a couple of Tele pickups for Danny to try out. "We both naturally understood that the Telecaster had to be maintained as a Telecaster," Barden says. "We couldn't change the good things about a Telecaster, but we could change the bad things."

In other words, if Barden had made a set of pickups "where my neck pickup was as wimpy compared to my bridge pickup as the Fender was, that would have been pointless," he says. Once Barden realized that the hum-canceling proposition would work in both positions on a Tele and sound good doing it, "you've got a world-class product," he says. "I knew that instantly. All of a sudden, you've completely opened the voice of the Tele to where you'd get the twang that you'd normally get with a stock pickup—plus all this other fidelity and incredible sensitivity."

Ironically, these developments didn't excite vintage guitar fanatics. "They didn't want anything to do with me, and they didn't particularly have any respect for Dan's sound," Barden says. "Who would dare to say they could go beyond vintage? And that lingers to this day." Barden has only one problem with such reasoning: "The people making 'vintage' pickups—what a joke. All they're doing is making replicas of other people's work. What kind of an innovation is that?"

Local players formed Barden's initial constituency, but he soon began attracting believers from rock's higher echelons: in 1983, he sold pickups to Bonnie Raitt, former Rolling Stones guitarist Mick Taylor, and Steve Ferris (of Eddie Money and Mister Mister). Barden's discoveries "opened the bandwidth on the guitar completely, so you were able to get all the Fender stuff plus all this other stuff, and all this incredible horsepower that was not in every other person's pickup," he says. "If you had horsepower, that ruined the tone; in my pickup, you had horsepower *and* tone. It was almost too much to believe."

Progress also continued on the recording front. In March 1983, Billy Poore began talking with Boston's Rounder Records, who called back on the day after receiving a copy of *Uptown*. "They'd got 47 rockabilly-type records," he says. "They were very interested in Johnny Seaton, because he was the only one that didn't sound like the Stray Cats!" (That October, he'd license *Uptown* to a Dutch label, Rockhouse Records.)

Danny, Dave Elliott, and bassist Jim Cavanaugh would record five tracks that November for Rounder's consideration, including "The Wheels Start Turnin'," "Like a Baby," and "'59 Phantom," which appear on *Runnin' Wild*.

Bookings had picked up following Seaton's battle of the bands victory, and Danny was by now an integral part of the show, which often featured him instrumentally (as shown by his eight-minute exploration of "Sleepwalk" taped on February 25, 1984, at Baltimore's Marble Bar). Poore felt sufficiently encouraged by these developments to organize a "Three Generations of Rockabilly Tour" that ran June 9–21, 1983.

Besides Seaton, the lineup included Charlie Feathers, Evan Johns, Bob Margolin, and Tex Rubinowitz. The gigs ranged from a five-night stand in Richmond to clubs like the Wax Museum and the Lone Star in New York, and even a biker bar in Edgewater, Virginia, that paid $1,500—"which was a lot of money for the time," Poore says. He had to put in a lot of work to pull off the shows, "because everybody told me they'd help with things, and then they'd get drunk. It was something I got nice memories about now, but I wouldn't do it again in a million years."

Danny also continued to burn tape on sessions when the mood suited him—and not just with Poore. In 1983, Lance Quinn and Obie O'Brien opened the Warehouse, a large studio in Philadelphia that boasted "a giant live room," according to O'Brien. "Bands that weren't working there used to come and hang out. It was a great place," he says. Suitably inspired, he started inviting Danny to sessions. "It was so amazing. You'd start pulling tapes out: 'I've got this great rhythm track, just play on this, no vocal or nothing on it, just play.' He was always way into it."

Danny taking a solo at the Wax Museum nightclub, Washington, D.C., June 16, 1983.

O'Brien still has four of those tracks in his archive. "This is the way that I approached the work with him: you didn't try to confine him. You couldn't say, 'I want the same guitar lick in the B-section every time.' If you have ten tracks, put 'em down, and make what you want out of those ten; don't tell him he has to be confined, because that's not what he was about. He was a creative, spur-of-the-moment guy."

Their mutual interest in cars helped the relationship. "We were both hot rod guys—at one point, my wife and I had a bunch of E-type Jaguars," O'Brien says. "So, of course, I had a garage full of parts, because that's what you need to have when you own those cars. When I got rid of them, Danny bought all my Jag rears to put in hot rods—back then, that was the cool independent suspension to put in. I always dug it, because I could always talk about hot rods with him."

For Holly, the '80s started on a difficult note. "I remember being a nobody when we moved," she says. "I was in the third grade at my new school, and kids picked on me for having naturally rosy cheeks—they thought I was wearing blush and would take me in the bathroom and scrub my cheeks till they were raw. But my fourth-grade teacher knew who my father was and played his album *Unfinished Business* for the class. Suddenly, people were a lot nicer."

Jealousy would be a constant underlying theme throughout Holly's school years. "One time I wore a Danny Gatton jacket, and one girl said I was just wearing it to get attention. But I just really liked the coat. So I guess I was the most indirectly famous kid in school right up through high school—the only one in *Rolling Stone* twice, I know!" (Stranger still, Dick Heintze's sister Anna-Mae was Holly's elementary-school art teacher.)

Joe Sheets witnessed another classic studio encounter during his mid-'80s engineering days at Richmond's Alpha Audio, where the region's biggest Tele buff happened to be cutting jingles for Gibson. Sheets wasted little time pointing out Danny's virtuosity to assistant engineer Paul Bruski. "When Danny opened up his guitar case, there wasn't a lick of finish on the neck," Sheets says. "I said, 'Look, Paul, he plays all the notes, all the time,' and Paul was just amazed." Asked if he needed anything, Danny responded, "Just a little bit of compression and a clam filter." Once assured of those commodities—the compression, anyway—Danny got down to work with Velpo Robertson, the other guitarist on the session.

"The session was interesting, because we put 'em both in the studio and said, 'This is a duel to the death!' Obviously, nobody got injured—they were best friends by the end of the session. Both men just stood their ground and played their asses off," Sheets says. Sadly, no evidence of this encounter survives. "When we left Alpha Audio in '90, we took nothing with us but our butts and our elbows. The company has been closed. I went in there a few years back and looked for those old tapes. There were some tapes in the basement, but they weren't his."

Ed Eastridge—who logged more studio time than anyone with Danny—says he "used to get angry quite often working with him, because he would completely disregard anybody else's problems with time." Those problems typically arose after an oft-heard request for "one more time." For that reason, whenever they'd start a session, Ed made a point of saying, "Okay, I've got another session starting at seven o'clock." Workdays that started at ten A.M. were supposed to end by six, so Eastridge could set up for his next session.

But Danny didn't care much for schedules. "If I had a nickel for every time I heard 'One more time,' I'd be rich," Eastridge ruefully jokes. More often than not, 12- and 14-hour sessions punctuated by short breaks were the norm. He remembers one occasion when his next clients had arrived punctually at seven, with Danny still saying "One more time." The other clients were sent away for something to eat so Eastridge could finish up with Danny. Upset, Eastridge stormed out of the mobile recording truck. "There were steel stairs that led to the back of the truck," he says. "I managed to pick them up and throw them against these steel shelving units that were right against the wall."

He paused to catch his breath, and then walked home. His wife asked what was wrong; he explained what had happened. Having calmed down, he returned to the studio, where another session was already underway. "The next day was just like nothing had happened," Eastridge says.

The first Gatton-Eastridge collaboration was the NRG single "Diggin' the Dirt" b/w "Honky Tonkin' Country Girl," which appeared in 1985. The A-side was done at Eastridge's studio; the B-side at Bias. The other musicians included John Previti and Jim Cavanaugh on bass and Dave Elliott on drums, but this single was Danny's and Billy Windsor's show all the way. The A-side was intended to cash in on tractor pulls, apparently, and it even opens with the rumbling sound of one of those farm machines. "It was real weird—just a hideously awful song," Eastridge laughs. "'Diggin' that dirt and pull it.' It was almost like 'The Ballad of Jed Clampett'; it had a big banjo thing in it." The B-side, on the other hand, expressed its disaffection with that honky tonkin' woman in a suitably wobbly Windsor vocal. (The tune would enjoy a second wind on October 24, 1991, when Danny appeared on the PBS-TV program *Austin City Limits*—where he enlivened the admittedly slight song with his beer-bottle slide treatment.)

Payment arrangements could be tricky, with Eastridge always trying to hammer out specifics. "Danny didn't want to deal with business, but his heart was in the right place," Eastridge says. Looking back, the only truly upsetting experience was not getting paid for the demos that laid the groundwork for the Elektra deal. "They ended up being the demos that were all redone, and it was totally pointless—some of 'em ended up sounding better, but some of 'em ended up sounding worse," he says.

He puts the problem down to a combination of the record-business mindset and a hefty dose of uncertainty. "We've got to go to a big, expensive studio and get the songs to sound that way." Naturally, he felt upset about not getting paid for those sessions, although he got some satisfaction from Danny's push for his involvement on the second Elektra album, *Cruisin' Deuces*.

"It used to hurt my feelings sometimes to have other people's names show up as producers, when, really, it was me," Eastridge says. "The main thing, after a while, was that I just told myself: 'Well, if I got paid, I should be thankful for that.' And it was still a privilege to work with the guy. You've got to look at the up and down sides of it. It was definitely an interesting trip."

During his time out of the spotlight, Danny often graced Baltimore's 8×10 club. This January 1983 Evan Johns and the H-Bombs gig featured (left to right) Johns, Gatton, Ivan Brown (bass), Jim Dougherty (drums), and Mark Korpi (guitar).

Not surprisingly, the guitarist who could spend hours on a solo had no problem revisiting a song with a completely different cast of musicians. A good example is "Gold Rush," off the odds-and-sods compilation *Untouchable* (1998) and Rhino's *Hot Rod Guitar* (1999) anthology. Eastridge helped assemble the latter affair, which he feels is the better take of a song he got to know by heart. "We did that song for years and years. We must have done it ten times with different bands, different sidemen. He wasn't totally satisfied with the one that's on the Rhino [compilation], but that was the best of 'em."

That same perfectionism extended to other people's tracks. "He drove everybody hard, himself more than anybody," Eastridge says. "There was never anybody who had the authority to tell him that [a track was finished], not even record executives. Even when I was paying him to do something, I couldn't tell him!" Then again, not every moment of creation lends itself to being frozen on tape, which is why Eastridge never got a definitive studio take of "Linus and Lucy." "We could never get that to work—it's so spontaneous, I don't think it can work in the studio."

The *Untouchable* album could almost be taken as a road map of live and studio pit stops. "Deep Purple" is an out-take from the Redneck Jazz Explosion's Cellar Door gigs, while the slow, funked-up "Sweet Georgia Brown"

At the 8×10 club, Evan Johns (left) wields a '52 Fender Broadcaster while Danny concentrates on his '53 Telecaster. Note Danny's Charlie Christian pickup belt buckle.

came from a fan's live cassette, according to Eastridge. "Stand by My Side" and "Ain't That Peculiar" are Gatton-Windsor songs that had actually been intended for a Windsor album; the latter is feisty, barnstorming R&B belted out by keyboardist Tommy Lepson. "One for Lenny" salutes the troubled genius Breau, while "Poinciana" hails from a '70s-era Bias Studios session, Eastridge says.

One of the highlights is Danny's reworking of the theme for the *Untouchables* TV show, with a feedback-driven solo tracked at yet another grueling session, according to Eastridge. The winning combination turned out to be a Tele and a Fender Deluxe; Danny had to sit in the isolation booth with the amp to get the requisite feedback. Eastridge estimates that Danny sat on the floor for four or five hours straight, with his feet up against the amp. "When he came out of there, the toes were pointing up like elf shoes, and his hair was all messed up—I mean, he looked like he'd totally been through the wringer! Billy and I just cracked up laughing."

Although Danny could suffer to get what he wanted on tape, he knew how to have fun, too. Guitarist Mark Korpi learned as much while playing a handful of gigs with Danny in late 1983 and early 1984. Korpi—who played in one of the final H-Bombs lineups—had first seen Danny in 1975, in his hometown of Manassas, Virginia. Aware of Danny's reputation as a Telecaster disciple, he was surprised to see him using a Les Paul. "He got pretty much the same sound that he got out of a Telecaster," Korpi says.

Later on, Danny used his familiar Tele on their gigs. "It was strung up like a jazz or country player would have it, but the way he played that made sense," Korpi says. "A lot of the quicker stuff that he did, he'd have been hard-pressed to do that with action as high as most guitar players have it."

Korpi says the gigs he played with Danny were all "pretty similar," such as the affair at Baltimore's 8×10 club on January 23, 1984. Evan Johns has a tape of the gig in his private archive. Johns contributed Vox-style organ runs, leaving Danny and Korpi plenty of room for their spindly lead lines on the tape's highlight, "Can This Really Be Real?" (an unreleased mid-tempo Johns song). "Danny was a real professional," Korpi says. "He showed up every night and played his ass off."

Danny also kept playing with Cavanaugh and Elliott, who joined the Seaton lineup by March 1984, according to Poore. Although Elliott appeared on the singer's 1986 Rounder album, *Reaction*, "I didn't use Dave in the studio that much—I can't remember why," Poore says. "I used him all the time for live gigs. Danny liked having Dave, 'cause they worked so well together."

Elliott's first show with Seaton was one of the oddest: a spring-break gig at the singer's alma mater, High Point High School in Beltsville, Maryland.

"Talk about weird," says Poore. "We had five shows: 7, 8, 9, 10, and 11 A.M. We had to be onstage playing at 7 A.M." Setup started at 5 A.M., so the band could play separate assemblies for grades 9–12. "It was 40 [minutes] on, 20 off—it was just weird, because you had to go out the back, get a cigarette and be back when the next group came in," Poore says. "But it was good money." The band made $1,500, which wasn't bad pay for waking up at such an unmusicianly hour.

The new year also saw Danny join a new band with Tom Principato, with whom he'd had little contact since the *Redneck Jazz* era. Principato had been a sideman until he'd hatched the idea of doing a solo project and adding Danny as a special guest, which is how the *Blazing Telecasters* album came about. "There was more to it, musically, than that, because Danny and I got together and rehearsed a lot," Principato says. "But because it's just a board tape [of a live gig], and it's really not the ultimate mix, it's hard to tell sometimes that there are a lot of twin guitar leads on there—but there are. We'd worked out a lot of stuff. It wasn't just a throw-together."

The cover—which featured both guitarists clowning for the camera, with Danny clutching a Heineken bottle—was meant to underline that point, according to Principato. He recalls telling Danny: "Well, it's really great to have you playing again. The response to this group so far has been great, and I think we could really do something, if you want to."

"Well, that's why I'm here," Danny responded. "He indicated that— just the fact that he had showed up for the photo session, he thought we could have a group for a while," Principato says. And they did. The band lasted for most of 1984, mainly playing the D.C.-area circuit with the odd foray to Richmond and the colorfully named Mineshaft club in Charlottesville, West Virginia. "We were working pretty often, but not all the time with Danny," Principato says. "We'd book a couple of weekends a month with Danny—maybe five or six gigs. And there'd be a while where we didn't play with him, because we needed enough money to pay Danny. Not all my gigs were paying enough to do that." Danny expected $100 to $150 "to come out of the house at that point," he adds.

Blazing Telecasters was taped on April 27, 1984, under the most somber of circumstances, according to Principato. The band was doing a two-night gig at the Washington club Adam's Rib, which was only a few blocks from the White House on Pennsylvania Avenue. Rich Vendig had opened the new venue after losing the lease for his former club, Desperado's. As it happened, Adam's Rib lasted only for a year—but it played an important role in Danny's story.

Tom Principato cutting up with Danny during the Blazing Telecasters *taping, April 1984.*

"A couple of days before the gig, Danny's father died," Principato says. "I'm thinking, I wouldn't blame Danny if he didn't even show up. And what turned out was, Danny went from his dad's funeral to play the gig that became the *Blazing Telecasters* album—no one knows that." Actually, at least one person did: Bobby Hancock, who was as amazed as Principato. "Knowing Danny the way I did—his way of coping with that, same way when Dick [Heintze] died, was to crank it up and play his ass off," he says. "Jan told me, that's what his words were: 'I'm going to play better tonight than I've ever played in my life.'"

Principato's blues-based background forced Danny to vary his approach, and his playing had an extra edge on the night of the recording. "Danny played differently when he was in my company—just slightly—but I think he was a little more reined in, a little more controlled," Principato says. "He played the most stunningly great 'Harlem Nocturne' that night. And, of course, the damn tape ran out in the middle of the song." Principato still has the original recording, which cuts off on one cassette and picks up on another.

The album contains material that most people wouldn't associate with either guitarist, particularly the riveting 11-minute version of Bob Dylan's

"Don't Think Twice, It's All Right." Principato holds the Dylan cover dearer than his own material, which he dismisses as too fusion-oriented at the time. "That was my first endeavor at writing songs," he says.

The *Blazing Telecasters* album has gained a second wind on eBay, with bids escalating to $25 and beyond, depending on how desperately people want it. Principato finds this amazing, because he still sells it at his gigs and through his website. "There was some kind of rumor circulating for a while that the album was listed as being 'deleted,' as 'not available'—and that has never been true," he says. One enterprising eBay seller claimed that the album was pulled because Danny didn't like how he appeared on the cover, which Principato dismisses. "You know what? He did remark to me that the only thing he didn't like about the album was his photo on the cover. But he never indicated to me that he wanted to stop selling it."

Matters were interrupted when Principato got a gig with Billy Price in May, which required a move to Pittsburgh. "It was only temporary, but this was a full-time thing, and I stopped playing with my band—and stopped doing gigs with Danny." Principato says the project remains one of the most gratifying of his career. "The biggest compliment that I've ever gotten is, 'Man, you can't tell the difference between you and Danny sometimes.'"

THE SUMMER OF 1984 found Poore overseeing one of Danny's oddest sessions, the recording of Steve Simonds's "I've Got a Lot to Say (But That's OK)" and "My Baby Gives Me Too Much to Eat." Simonds was willing to finance the session to satisfy his singing aspirations. "Danny called: 'Well, I don't know,' and I said, 'No, the guy can sing, but he's going to need a lot of help,'" Poore says. "I felt like I was part of it, 'cause he was using the Johnny Seaton band." Simonds even sought a management deal with Poore, who rejected the proposal. "I said, 'No, every time you sing anything, Steve, you sound exactly like Elvis—the older Elvis.'"

Listeners can judge for themselves by listening to *Runnin' Wild*. The songs aren't terribly remarkable, with Danny's guitar and Simonds's loose but untutored vocal style being the most noteworthy elements. The sessions were in June or July, with Cavanaugh and Elliott joining Danny at Glass Wing Studios, Poore's favorite place to work between 1984 and '88. "I always liked going back to Hyattsville, my old stomping grounds," he says. The bargain rates had some bearing on Poore's choice, too, since he'd gone to high school with the older brother of engineer Richard Sales.

Seaton's biggest break came in July, when he won the lead in an off-Broadway musical that seemed tailor-made for his previous specialty: "Elvis Mania: Three Decades of Gold," which ran from July 29 to October 14, 1984. Poore came along as research historian, but Danny declined the gig because he didn't want to live in New York, even for a few months. Also, "he didn't want to play the same 30–35 songs six nights a week," Poore wrote in the *Runnin' Wild* booklet.

Seaton signed a one-album deal with Rounder in September. "That's when Rounder decided to get off their butt and put Seaton in the studio to do the album, so we had to rush right in and rehearse the songs," Poore says. "We went over to Danny's garage in Accokeek, and we spent a bunch of nights over there." Most of the material came from the 100 or so songs that Poore had written since the '60s. The record company also suggested some covers. "Rounder submitted about four or five that we—for the most part—hated," Poore says.

Principato had regrouped his band after returning to the D.C. area in August, but his work with Danny was tapering off because John Previti wasn't in the lineup. They did join forces on October 20, 1984, for a *Unicorn Times* benefit on the Washington Monument grounds, at the Sylvan Theatre, followed by a November 3rd gig at the Psyche Delly. Principato even did the odd guest spot with Seaton: "I was just added on and got some money. I think Danny arranged that."

Principato says the band "petered out" after Danny missed a gig on December 15 at the Brick House in Pasadena, Maryland. "It was sort of an icy night, but it wasn't too icy for the rest of us to make it there, and I always felt that Danny was using it like an excuse," he says. When he called the next day to ask what happened, Danny responded: "I couldn't get out of my driveway." Jan's not sure why the band died. "It wasn't explained to me really well, but Dan seemed to resent or not like the music on that record. I don't know what was wrong; I just know there was some discord there."

Principato feels that he couldn't have worked much longer with Danny, anyway. "In '85, I started to get in full swing with my own band, and I was traveling a lot, so I saw him less than when I used to hang around town," he says. Principato continued to see Danny every now and then. Sometimes, it was for small guitar-repair jobs; other times, they'd hang out, eat crabs, and play. "He was a little bit more outgoing if it was one-on-one, especially if it was on his turf. I think he usually felt comfortable around me, anyway. He knew that we liked a lot of the same stuff."

Danny's relationships "seemed to revolve around guitars or cars—that was pretty much it," Principato adds. "He didn't seem to have any old school-buddy friends, unless they were guys he'd been in bands with, like Ron MacDonald or Billy." The relationships tended to be segregated. Principato says he never met any of Danny's "car buddies," and there were different types of "guitar buddies," too. "He had this whole slew of people that sort of followed him around, but they were never invited over to his house. There were guys that would come around, carry his amp for him. And then there were other people like myself and Steve Wolf, who did go to some of the family events. I went out to dinner a few times with the whole Gatton family, to the crab house. They liked to do that—take a crowd of people out to the crab house. We'd do that, hang out at Danny's house, play guitars, and tinker. If you wanted to tinker, he always had something that could be tinkered on."

Danny finished the year with a four-day session at Glass Wing on December 3–8, 1984, hashing out the 12 tracks they wanted for *Reaction*. Dave Chappell wasn't involved, because "Danny was going to do most of the guitar, anyway," he says. "Danny wound up, I think, dictating to everybody: 'Here's what you're supposed to play.'"

Taking lessons at Danny's house was a different affair. Chappell still has three or four cassettes from those times, which show two guys just kicking back and having fun running up and down their fretboards. At one point, Chappell asks, "Can you help me with that basic thing you just did, maybe show me some ideas that you've been thinking about?" Danny says, "Well, give me a cigarette, and I'll show you everything I know in five minutes!" The memory still brings a smile to Chappell's face. "That was Danny's wit out of nowhere—and I was totally stupefied, because I had just smoked my last cigarette."

Other tapes show Danny breaking down his soloing approach over simple chord changes like "Crazy Arms," pulling out melodies that Chappell hadn't heard before. "To lift you up and go, 'Here's a golden opportunity to sit with me, I'm going to be very giving of myself, this is what I'm doing'—it was incredible."

The Glass Wing sessions included Poore-penned songs like "Rockin' Man," "Big City Baby," and "You'll Never Change Me." Besides Danny, the core personnel included Cavanaugh, Elliott, keyboardist Mitch Collins, and saxophonist Ralph McDuffie. According to Poore's records, the quintet reconvened for the actual album sessions on February 11–15, 1985, at Bias Studios, with Rounder promising to release the results that summer. Elliott recalls the recording as a pleasant experience. "It's some of the hottest and tastiest playing that Danny ever did, mainly because he wanted to get the hell out of there. They were knocked out that we did it so damn fast."

Elliott says that Danny made a wry post-session comment: "You know, that damn thing sounds pretty good. We shouldn't have wasted it on him—we should have saved it for our own stuff." "I thought that was funny, but I don't think he realized why that was so cool, because he just wanted to get in there and get the fuck out," Elliott laughs.

As word of Danny's reputation spread, artists continued to seek his talents. The most tantalizing story involves John Fogerty, who called one day while Danny was out working in his garage. According to Elliott, Creedence Clearwater Revival's former singer-guitarist was assembling a touring band for *Centerfield*, the rootsy solo album that he released in 1985. The proposition would surely have been satisfying to hardcore Danny fans: finally, people outside the D.C. area would see what they had been missing. Elliott was looking forward to being involved, too, but there was a hitch: Danny forgot to call Fogerty back.

Poore remembers the issue popping up during a rehearsal break at the Accokeek house. Elliott asked, "Did you call Fogerty's people back yet?" No, Danny responded; he'd forgotten, because he'd been too busy working on one of his cars. He repeated the same statement to Poore, adding, "I got too many things to do around here. I can't be gone that long." Joe Kogok was incredulous when he heard the story. "I thought, 'Man, you let that get away from you? C'mon!' Same thing all over again: he's missing his breaks." (Joe Tass questioned the premise of the whole story, asserting that it didn't make Danny out as nonchalant as he wanted to appear.)

Danny's next band proved short-lived: the Drapes, a rockabilly-style outfit that didn't play more than ten gigs in 1985, according to Elliott. (The name comes from a '50s slang term for clothing. The band had special jackets made; Holly still has one.) Steve Wolf was asked to join but declined; he was firmly established with the Tom Principato Band, now creating a buzz as Washington's hottest rhythm & blues act. "We had a huge draw at the Roxy; our record was being played on the radio; we were getting invited to go play in Europe," he says. "The band was popping, I was making good money, and I could smell a house coming up. I knew that Danny was an off-again, on-again [proposition]—I figured that the Drapes would be another six-month-to-a-year project. Danny never had his business sense together."

Guitarist Jim Stephanson says that he watched the short-lived band evolve into something else. He'd first seen Danny at Beneath It All and developed a relationship with him through Jensen's late son, Jack Junior. The two got closer at Billy Jack's. "Danny was there every Wednesday," he says. "At the beginning of the summer, it was Ronnie MacDonald [on vocals]; at the end of the summer, it was Billy [Windsor]." Windsor's entry into the ranks marked the transition to Funhouse, which would soon spin off into two groups: a hardcore jazz band—with up to four horns—and a straight-ahead rockabilly outfit.

As he was expanding his musical options, Danny wanted more options for his gear, too. Cohorts like Robbie Weaver watched him move from Bandmasters and Bassmans to blackfaced Twins. "Oh God, he had more amps than the law *allowed*," he laughs. By 1985, people had started to wonder how the standard equipment configurations could be improved, even if they didn't always know how to get there, according to Joe Barden. "Mesa Boogie was out with their multi-function 'Swiss Army knife' amps," he says. "And the whole hair-band thing had started—people were still playing really, really loud Marshall amps left over from the Jeff Beck and Led Zeppelin days, but starting to add lots of neat little functions to them. What we were doing [with vintage gear] was kind of a lost art, restricted to just a small coterie of people that were really into this thing."

There was another problem. "Nobody knew how to fix these amps—there was all this bizarre misinformation about how they worked," Barden says. "Nobody really understood, and nobody really gave a shit. Nobody was really getting into the tone of amplifiers." Although there was no shortage of people doing amp repairs, "most of them were doing hip modifications that they'd dreamed up on their own—and there were no parts available. Once again, there's no industry supporting any of this."

Players with vintage amps had two options: get replacement parts from Fender or get by with substitutes from electronics stores. "People were looking at the schematics [that Fender had printed]: 'Well, if the part's broken, we can replace it'—your basic appliance repair-type thing." There was plenty of room for improvement, but Barden didn't know where that search might lead. He had no desire to branch out into amps, and he didn't even know how to read a schematic. The schematics he'd looked at "were just arcane nonsense to me. I knew some people who did [understand them], but I don't think they were very well-versed in how they related to the sound of the amp."

Every now and then, he says, "this really, really good amp would turn up, and it would last for a couple of months and then it would, quote, 'go bad.' Danny would say, 'Oh, it blew up.' No one really knew what to do about that."

Suitably fed up, Barden worked from a simple premise: if Roy Nichols had played such amps when they were new, why couldn't anybody get that sound now? "I used to take my blackfaced amps to guys: 'Hey, man, make this thing sound like Roy Nichols, 1966.' And they'd look at me and say, 'Who's Roy Nichols?' And I'd go, 'See ya.' If you don't know who he is, and you don't understand what he is, then you don't understand where I'm going, and you don't understand what I want. I don't need my amp fixed—I need my amp *right*. It's not a toaster."

Barden had been hanging around with someone who worked on amps in Falls Church, where they'd eat dinner and watch movies. "Oddly enough, I never learned anything from him, in terms of how amps worked. I would watch him work, but we hung out more as friends. I sort of understood, Okay, this is a capacitor, this is a resistor—but he didn't give me any lessons or anything. I didn't really probe." He sought out his friend with instructions to get the '66-era Nichols sound. The amp came back extensively modified. "It had all kinds of 'genius' shit that he thought was cool to put in a Fender amp that bore no relation to any of my instructions."

Now Barden understood the problem. "This guy is the smartest guy I know about amps, and he simply made what he thought was cool, not what I was trying to do at all. It can't be that difficult, because we've already done it brand-new in 1964 and '65 and '66." So Barden sat down and set about the dreary business of mastering schematics, aided by an amp, a layout diagram, "and a chart that showed the color code of resistors and stuff. Over a period of a couple weeks, I just laboriously broke the code."

Barden eventually sought additional advice from "one of the most incredible fiddle players I've ever seen, bar none": Dave Dan Blackmon, of Athens, Georgia, who also happened to play guitar and repair amps. Blackmon was able to explain the basics and cement Barden's circuit-reading skills. Not content to quit there, he followed up by calling Ken Fisher of Train Wreck Circuits, in Colonia, New Jersey, who'd worked in nearby Linden as a design tech for Ampeg. "I realized pretty quickly that this was a guy that everybody and their brother pumped for information. He could basically fix amps over the phone. He had worked at Ampeg for a long time. He was a serious guy."

Barden continues, "I'd call him up and go, 'I just smoked a transformer, because I thought I should have done this, what do you think?' And he'd go, 'Well, learned your lesson, didn't you?'" He credits their relationship with raising issues nobody else had even broached, such as what really produces tone in an amp. "Ken was already into the quality of carbon-comp resistors versus metal-film—the balancing of power supplies, stuff that Fender and Marshall weren't into at all. That was an enormous leap forward that Ken was making, but nobody else was. I mean, people were starting to—whereas, Ken was just happily sitting there, smiling. He knew it all."

Barden was also spending time deliberately causing key components to fail, "just going through every possible permutation, to see what I could do," he says. "Again, the goal was really to optimize these blackfaced amplifiers." Barden wanted to streamline the process and make it a more scientific affair than it had been previously. "Fender was just going by rote: 'put these resistors here,' willy-nilly, and they never really stopped to balance out the voltages. And then there's a bunch of parts that need to be replaced, because these amps are 20 or 30 years old, and the parts are no good anymore—so I started to figure this out."

What emerged was "a thoroughly optimized Fender amplifier, so that your Vibrolux Reverb was the best Vibrolux Reverb it was going to be. It was really cool. I was able to call up Danny, 'All you need to do is find me a Fender with two working transformers,' and the rest of it—a piece of cake." He estimates the whole process took a couple of months, but the big pay-off wouldn't arrive until Danny started recording *Unfinished Business*. "He came over to my house, and he's looking at my workbench littered with all this amp stuff. 'Why don't we check it out?' So he starts playing my Super Reverb, and he's playing it and playing it. The next thing I realized, he's not playing it. I hear this lumbering coming down my basement steps; he's gone out to the truck and got his Super. He proceeds to unplug mine, lift it out of the way, put his where mine was and plug it in. He goes, 'Well, you can have your amp back when mine sounds as good as yours.'"

Barden had to laugh at the audacity of such a move. "I go, 'Okay, so my amp just got hijacked.' And off he went to do *Unfinished Business*—most of that was done with my amp and the Vibraverb that was in [Eastridge's] studio, a blackfaced Vibraverb." Barden worked on that amp quite a bit, as well as Danny's Super Reverb. "In the end, his amp came out sounding better than mine. It was just by nature a stronger amp."

He remembers telling Danny "how lousy metal-film resistors sounded in these amps, versus these other types that were cheaper—so I would put in a metal-film and a carbon-comp in each location. And on the other side, I'd put in an alligator clip. I'd clip to the metal-film, and he'd play: 'Okay, sounds good.' And then I'd clip to the carbon-comp—exact same value, different material—and he'd go, 'Whoa, listen to that.'" Thereafter, "basically every amp that he got came over to my house," Barden says.

11

Unfinished Business
(1985–1989)

The Johnny Seaton gigs continued at clubs like the Marble Bar, which became one of Poore's favorite pit stops and also provided him with another artist for his roster in the form of LesLee "Bird" Anderson. Poore had come across the club during a search for places to book Charlie Feathers. "We never made money there," he says, "but we drank until six o'clock in the morning."

LesLee's nickname was derived from a hairdo that puffed up over her head like the crest of a cockatoo, as a photo of her and Danny in the *Runnin' Wild* booklet confirms. She and her husband, Roger, ran the Baltimore club and lived in the back. Poore found them a different breed from most other clubowners: they booked only acts they liked, be they surf (the Ventures) blues (John Lee Hooker), or selected punk and New Wave (Huey Lewis & the News, before they broke). The Andersons could even have hosted a young, hungry Police for $500, but Roger had passed after hearing their tape. "He said, 'That's terrible! I wouldn't pay 'em nothin'!'" Poore reports.

Punk and rockabilly enthusiasts alike enjoyed the Gatton-Seaton combination. "Even though it was rockabilly, you'd see slam dancers," Poore says. "It was a wild scene, but they'd all be into the same kind of music. And Danny? There'd be eight or ten people to see him, and he'd always do an instrumental set. But everybody more or less liked what Seaton did." The $100 to $150 guarantee went to Danny, with Poore paying everyone else from his pocket.

Roger had his own musical outlet, a comic band called the Alcoholics that remained confined to the bar. Sadly, a massive heart attack felled him at the age of 37 in April 1984, and LesLee found the bar too difficult to run alone, so she shut its doors in June 1985. By then, however, Poore had gotten an inkling of what LesLee could do when she'd sung at his birthday party in February—perhaps this untutored talent had something to offer. Poore made plans to work with LesLee when she returned that fall from California, where she'd gone after Roger's death.

There were always one-off sessions to pick up with Seaton, too, like a rollicking send-up of Bruce Springsteen, whose *Born in the U.S.A.* album had yielded the career breakthrough that his champions had always anticipated. With the album all over the radio, even a backhanded salute to Bruce would arouse some interest, Poore recalls telling Danny—especially if it targeted *Backstreets*, the official fanzine of all things Springsteen.

"He's the Boss" was cut at a September 22, 1985, session at Track, where Danny led a "usual suspects" cast of his musician friends—including Cavanaugh, Collins, Elliott, and Roger McDuffie—in a credible takeoff on the E Street Band's no-holds-barred roadhouse style. Poore coupled the song with a track from 1984, "Take a Chance on rock 'n' roll"; the credit went to the Big Boss Band.

A month after cutting the Springsteen parody, Seaton put his formidable energy to work singing Poore's "Lonely Lady," which had been among a batch of songs he'd submitted to Glen Campbell's Nashville publisher. Poore would return several times to this tune, which he first recorded on October 25, 1985, with Seaton on vocals, Danny on guitars and bass, and Teasley on drums. Danny had heard only *a cappella* versions from Seaton and Poore, which didn't stop him from knocking out the basic tracks while Poore went on a beer run. Poore says he was motivated to record the song after hearing from Campbell's publishing company. "They told me, 'Make sure when you write anything for Glen that they are definitely hit songs.' I got mad: 'Huh, I'll write a hit—I'll show them.'"

MOST OF 1986 WAS spent promoting *Reaction*, which Rounder had finally released in May. Danny played most of the shows, with Elliott—as ever—on drums. By that point, Danny was well into production of his next album, *Unfinished Business*, which was threatening to live up to its title until it made its appearance in 1987. *Unfinished Business* came at a propitious time for Ed Eastridge, who'd just finished assembling a mobile recording unit. "Danny was looking for some cheap studio time," he says. "We bumped into each other, and he knew I was working on that [truck]. He said, 'Well, maybe I'll come over and check it out.' It was as simple as that."

Sessions proceeded in the basement of the American Guitar Center in Wheaton, Maryland, with Ed's truck parked outside. Ed and Danny joked that "all the boxes and spare guitar parts were scientifically placed for the perfect acoustic [balance]." (Eastridge eventually set up his "Big Mo" studio—named in honor of the truck—in Kensington, Maryland. He says it was "a little more advanced: we had a nice grand piano, a B-3, and isolation booths. Danny started to work in there a lot.")

The lack of a recording budget made the recording experience an unusual one. The work stretched out over 18 months, as money became available or—more often than not—Danny bartered for studio time. "It was pieced together over a long period of time with a small amount of money," Eastridge says. "He spent basically nothing with me, so he could go and blow his money on mixing it."

Eastridge didn't mind the drawn-out process, though. "As long as there's somebody like Danny, who's working with a vision of what he wants, it's going to work," he says. Nor did he worry about matching tones from different takes. "Everybody gets so hung up on continuity. Who cares? I never cared about that. I just want everything to sound good." Roger McDuffie remembers recording his sax solo on "Sky King" a good two years before the album appeared. "I did it way before I went on the road," he says. "Danny went to Zavarella's: 'Give Roger a sax so he can blow on my album.' When I was up in Michigan, some guy said, 'Roger, I got Danny Gatton's new album, *Unfinished Business*—you're on it.' I was amazed."

Eastridge says he recorded Gatton's guitar on two or three tracks, using two amplifiers and a direct signal. "One [amp] would sustain longer than the other, and the sound moves around in the stereo image," he says. "I really like that about the guitar sound on Danny's stuff, and he only seemed to like the guitar sound I got." He remains especially fond of the ballads, which included a glistening remake of Santo & Johnny's steel guitar–oriented weeper, "Sleepwalk," and "Melancholy Serenade," otherwise known as the theme from the classic '50s-era TV sitcom *The Honeymooners*. Danny played it as a chord-melody piece. "The hot licks, I don't think, were much of a challenge for him," Eastridge says. "The ballads were the real demanding stuff."

Eastridge makes it clear that it was Danny who called the shots on the album. "He produced that stuff himself. Nothing was going to happen without his final say-so, no matter what anybody said." And just one hot day in the studio might yield a lot of material, Tom Principato confirms. "He was definitely one of those 'live in the studio' kind of guys, although he loved to work at overdubs. If he was on, you could let the tape roll, and if he didn't stop you, you'd have some great stuff."

AS MUCH AS DANNY seemed to enjoy working on the album, there was another side that sometimes emerged. Johnny Castle remembers an idle remark made as they were getting ready for a corporate gig near Dulles Airport. "It was a beautiful spring day. There was a nice little pond in front of us with geese and stuff, and we're getting free food," Castle says. "You never knew about Danny, but he usually had a twinkle in his eye. He said, 'Don't you just hate this shit?'"

Castle replied that he didn't hate anything, and the subject was quickly forgotten. Only after Danny's death did the comment slip back into his mind, because it seemed to signal a certain restlessness. "He could never be happy with what he was doing: 'Oh, damn, I wish I wasn't here at this gig. I wish I was home, working on my old coupe,'" Castle says. "You could tell that in his playing."

Bill Kirchen recalls a similar remark. He hadn't had much contact with Danny for a while, but that changed when he moved to Washington in 1986. They got reacquainted at Gallagher's Restaurant on Pennsylvania Avenue, where Danny would invite Kirchen to sit in, and they played a few gigs together—maybe a half dozen. "It was for about a month, and then he got back with his old buddy, Billy [Windsor]," Kirchen says. "People would say, 'Aren't you intimidated [to share the stage with him]?' I'd say, 'No! He's Danny, and nobody does what he does, so there's nothing to worry about.'"

Kirchen shared a variety of different experiences with Danny, including dates at the Flood Zone in Richmond, Virginia, as well as the Lone Star Café and Les Paul's 75th birthday party at the Hard Rock Café, also in New York City. But it was at a private party on the St. Mary's River when Danny looked at him and asked: "Don't you just hate these gigs?" Kirchen was taken aback by what he'd heard. "I thought he was kidding, 'cause I was thinking, Shit, this as good as it gets. Or maybe he was just saying that I thought it was beneath my dignity or something. I don't know."

Danny's comment passed without further conversation. In hindsight, though, Kirchen thinks Danny was "playing stuff that maybe he thought he ought to play, rather than stuff he wanted to play. I didn't know him well enough for him to take me into his confidence—it's just an impression I got."

The easygoing exterior tended to conceal such matters, "but I think there was a lot of stuff that did bother him," Principato says. He remembers an incident from the *Redneck Jazz* era, in which an otherwise positive opening-night review included a cutting remark about Danny's haircut. The next day in the Cellar Door's dressing room, someone asked Danny if he'd seen the comment. Danny denied it, but Principato thinks differently. For Danny, dealing with acceptance and rejection was a never-ending preoccupation. "He was an extremely sensitive guy," Principato says.

Another occasion involved a silly stage trick that went awry, in an eerie echo of Danny's decision to retire his beloved Magic Dingus Box to stifle the cries of "Danny Gadget." The scenario involved Danny's Echoplex unit. "The old ones had playback, and you'd hear 15 seconds of what you just played," Elliott says. "I'd hand him a drumstick in the middle of a song, and he'd start playing guitar with one hand and drums with the other. Then I'd slip over and take his guitar off him and turn my back to the audience, and he'd slide behind my drums. The audience would say, 'Wow! Gatton plays drums!'"

One time it didn't work right. Danny hit the Echoplex, Elliott went through all the stereotypical rock-star gyrations and the crowd went wild— "the guitar was playing its ass off," he laughs. When the set ended, people practically mobbed Elliott, saying, "Goddamn! We didn't know you could play guitar!" "This is the kind of audiences we have in the Washington area," he sighs, clearly exasperated by the memory. "It was just mind-boggling, and it hurt Danny's feelings." They tried the trick three or four more times before dropping it altogether. "It was supposed to be funny, but it ended up being a heartbreaker," Elliott says.

AT LEAST THE MUSIC could take Danny's mind off such matters, if only temporarily. Trumpeter Chris Battistone entered the picture in 1985 or '86, marking another transition back into playing pure jazz for its own sake. Battistone remembers getting a call from Previti. "He called me up to do this gig: 'Danny Gatton's going to be playing guitar.' I'd heard Danny's name—I'd been in school in Texas for years and then came back to the area—but at that point, I don't think Danny was playing out that much." Battistone doesn't recall hearing many explanations, other than the oft-told story about how Danny had injured his hand.

The resulting Columbia, Maryland, gig was one of the first signs of Danny's gradual re-emergence. A band quickly coalesced around Battistone, Previti, and drummer Barry Hart. "It wasn't advertised as 'Danny Gatton,'" Battistone says. "It was just one of those generic quasi-jazz gigs where you're keeping it quiet during the dinner set, and you may be able to stretch out and play a few more things later—with volume always a concern of the management. That sort of thing."

According to Battistone, the set consisted of "very standard standards" like "Days of Wine and Roses," "Georgia," and "There Will Never Be Another You." What sticks out most in his mind is the effect Danny had on the crowd. "It wasn't the volume. I just noticed, in pretty short order, how everybody around the dinner tables was quiet and was watching." He found it all the more amazing, because "I'm not sure how many people, on that night, knew who he was." Such an ability, he says, transcends technique. "When you hear a musician who has that ability, you know it. He just had that power to captivate."

As usual, Danny said little before the gig, let alone on the bandstand. "I remember him seeming to be in a really good mood," Battistone says.

"He seemed to be kind of pleased and excited about the fact he had a nice night out just playing jazz tunes in a nice atmosphere." By early 1986, Previti was booking the band into local venues like C'est La Vie, which was off 20th and L Streets. The band had a low-key weekly gig there; "in the summertime, we'd do these outdoor jobs in the courtyard," Battistone says. "Same sort of thing: we'd play as a quartet, and we'd play jazz."

Battistone doesn't recall the billing for these gigs, but he's positive that they led into the hardcore jazz of Funhouse. The band would begin taking shape in 1987 on Thursdays at Gallagher's Restaurant, where they'd play a residency that lasted from a year to 18 months. "That was when word of mouth really got out," Battistone says. "At that point, it was being advertised with Danny's name; I know for sure, at Gallagher's, it was [called] 'Danny Gatton & Funhouse.'"

The Gallagher's run also came to include tenor saxophonist Bruce Swaim, but Swaim couldn't always make it "because his schedule would get crazy, especially in the summer," according to Battistone. Whenever Swaim's schedule got too crowded, the band would play with another tenor saxophonist, Phil Berlin. One time, "both guys were there—and I remember Danny saying, 'There's so many people coming in here, we ought to get a raise, get enough money to have another horn.' And I remember Phil sort of smiling and saying, 'Yeah, the two tenors sounded good.' Which they did—it was a nice sound. Danny said, 'Yeah, that's it—let's just do that,' which is how it became the three horns."

Ironically, the increased traffic almost led to Funhouse losing the gig, because the waitresses couldn't keep up—or so the management said. "Can you imagine that?" Elliott marvels. "Danny Gatton drew too many people. Half the time, we couldn't get enough to pay the rent—I don't get it!" The club's management solved the problem by hiring more help.

The band also maintained a regular Sunday gig at the Tyson's Corner Holiday Inn in Falls Church, which became one of Eastridge's favorite spots to hear them. "That was a phenomenal lineup," he says. "They did a lot of straight-ahead jazz."

The two-, three-, and eventually four-person horn sections adapted to whatever scenario played out, Battistone says. "All of the players had pretty good ears, so if we decided to play background on the blues, we'd all grab a note and play a harmony. We fell into arrangements on the spot." Every now and then, they'd work out songs on the way to a gig, "but most of it was off the cuff," Elliott says. "If they missed it the first time around, by the second time, they had it. It wasn't like, 'If we don't have a chart, we can't play this gig.'"

Battistone would sometimes sketch out parts, which usually proved unnecessary after they'd played the song a few times. Rehearsals were equally rare; one of the few times was at Windsor's Clinton, Maryland, home to run down songs for recording purposes. By the end of the Gallagher's run, Danny was doing more country and rockabilly tunes, which boosted Windsor's involvement. "That was sort of like the changeover—for a while, we had the band at Gallagher's and we'd do some other jobs," Battistone says. The "other jobs" included gigs at venues like the Spanish Ballroom, in Glen Echo Park, Maryland, where they played with Asleep at the Wheel.

The lineups fluctuated in the two bands that became known as Funhouse I and Funhouse II. Elliott got back into the picture "because they'd done all that [non-jazz] material for years and years, I guess, with the Fat Boys," Battistone says. When Danny began playing larger clubs like the Birchmere, two more horn players showed up: John Jensen, the Navy Commodores' lead trombonist, and baritone saxophonist Don Stapleton, "a guy that kind of grew up with Previti and had played with Danny Gatton & the Drapes," Battistone says. "When we did things in the studio and recorded, it was [Stapleton's] bari, trumpet, and two tenors. On some of the stuff, Phil would play alto, so we'd have trumpet, alto, tenor, and bari." Battistone also recalls Stapleton being present "when we did a few places in New York and Boston on a little Northeast tour—a mini-tour. We also went out to the NAMM show in Chicago and played at the Cubby Bear, I think. That would have been in '89."

WHILE THE FUNHOUSE BANDS played, work continued on *Unfinished Business*, which remains Norma's favorite album for its choice of music. She recalls her son's penchant for nonstop work on the project: "He'd stay in the studio all day and all night. He practically drove Eddie [Eastridge] crazy, 'cause Danny knew what he wanted to hear. He had a keen ear; he knew what was right and what was wrong. It had to be just right, or he wasn't happy."

Dan Senior had displayed a similar temperament. "My husband was one of the neatest mechanics you ever saw," Norma says. "Anything he did was right; there was no wishy-washy bit about the quality of his work. They didn't come any better than my husband when it came to tools—and Danny took after his father in that respect."

Nobody could accuse Danny of approaching his work half-heartedly—less was never an option, as Eastridge already knew from his previous work with him. By now, the effort of post-production was getting as important as the recording process, starting with the physical snipping of assorted bits of tape. "It's weird to cut out a measure, because you've got an odd number of measures," Eastridge says. "He wasn't averse to cutting out a whole chorus or a whole verse if he didn't like it, or he thought it was too long."

Eastridge reserved the most extensive editing for Danny's guitar solos. They'd listen for several hours and then winnow the highlights into a composite master. If everything didn't fit together quite right, Danny was always willing to punch in and overdub the existing tracks—a prospect that frightened Eastridge, especially if they'd just spent eight hours assembling one solo. On the bright side, the effort required to pull off such feats helped to improve his engineering skills. "It's like putting the finishing touches on a piece of woodwork: one slip of the blade and you're starting from scratch," he says. When the sessions were finished, Danny had to mix the tapes at Bias Recorders, because Eastridge's studio wasn't really geared for the task.

The recording work was a welcome distraction following the final implosion of the Seaton relationship—which, according to Poore, had been on shaky ground since Seaton landed his "Elvis Mania" role and became less willing to take direction in the studio. "I always figured if I ever got him to the point where he could make a million dollars, he wouldn't want some crumb bum like me around," Poore says. "Me and Danny, that's why we got along: we were both in the blue-collar range. He loved working on cars, and I loved driving 'em."

The relationship disintegrated further after Seaton locked up another Elvis role in a short-lived TV show, "Good Rockin' Tonight," for which a meeting had been arranged with the King's wife, Priscilla. But Seaton overslept—"He was laid up with some girl," Poore claims—and missed the affair, only to land on his feet next to Donny Osmond in the popular Broadway musical *Joseph & the Amazing Technicolor Dreamcoat*. Poore's contract with Seaton expired on May 5, 1988—ending the relationship just as the singer's star finally appeared to be ascendant.

"I had $300,000 invested, and that was 20 years ago," Poore says. "It did a lot of head trips on me. Danny was the good guy. He was always trying to calm me down, telling me to forget it. I'd say, 'It's easy for you to say. It wasn't your money.'" In hindsight, Poore believes that he spread himself too thin booking and managing both Seaton and LesLee, who'd returned to the area that summer and was logging a great deal of studio time. (She cut 29 tracks between December 1985 and March 1988; Danny appeared on 16 of them, according to the *Runnin' Wild* notes.) Poore was also involved with the affairs of Billy Hancock and another Ripsaw artist, Bobby Smith.

By the end of 1986, however, Poore decided his policy of "havin' to pay musicians a whole lot of extra money when we didn't make enough at live shows to go around had to come a halt," as he wrote in *Rockabilly: A*

Forty-Year Journey. Danny had also begun working with his old buddy Windsor, whom he likely considered a more congenial—if not more honest—partner than Seaton.

In the end, money proved the decisive wedge in fracturing the Poore-Seaton relationship beyond repair, especially after Poore found the singer had pocketed more than his share from two 1986 gigs. Poore refused to continue handling the money for that reason, though he still booked the shows. "I said, 'I'm going to collect the money, take my ten percent, and give you the rest. I'd been putting all this money out. If somebody was screamin' and hollerin' and bitchin', I would give 'em the money: 'Shut up and leave me alone.'"

Danny, on the other hand, never hassled much about money. Poore recalls a time when he owed the guitarist $100, which led Danny to comment: "Don't keep calling me up and telling me you're going to send it. I like little surprises in the mailbox. I'll get it when I get it." Other sources recall seeing Danny tearing up checks he'd receive from NRG, because he just couldn't take money from his mother. "If I was hurtin' for money, he would trust me," Poore says. "Nobody would trust Johnny, and when he started handling the money, that's when things fell apart. I should have quit when Danny did, because Danny refused to work with him after that."

Problems arose after New York and Baltimore gigs in January and February, when Cavanaugh, Elliott, Danny and soundman Jimmy Barnett—who'd also handled lights and sound during the "Elvis Mania" run—didn't get paid, according to Poore's account in the *Runnin' Wild* booklet. Seaton promised to make good after a gig at the Roxy on April 18, 1987. "Dave made sure he got his $400 owed for those three shows," wrote Poore. "[Seaton] owed Danny three times that much and didn't have it to give to him and wanted to borrow money from me again. No way!" Ironically, the set had included "Lonely Lady," the song on which Poore had pinned his commercial hopes; Danny had logged his final studio work with Seaton on March 30, 1987, when they sought to give the song a suitable arrangement. (Danny tried it yet again in December 1989, in a Latin version with vocalist Todd Monroe that never saw an official release. The public wouldn't get to compare all the different versions until the *Runnin' Wild* package appeared; Danny was on record as saying that he liked the first version best.)

Danny ran into his nemesis once more, purely by accident, when he was playing the Lone Star in the summer of 1990. He spied Seaton during the load-out process, which moved him to jump in front of the singer. With typical directness, Danny demanded: "Gimme all that fucking dough you owe me." Not satisfied with the response, Danny dug a hand into Seaton's wallet, extracting what he could. "When Danny told me this story

I laughed my butt off," Poore wrote. "I asked him how much was in Johnny's wallet. Danny said, 'Almost three hundred dollars. That wasn't what he owed me, but it's more than I ever thought I'd see from the punk.'" Danny never saw him again.

In his book, Poore recounted Seaton's take on their relationship: "His version is, when he won the battle of the bands, he took all the money, produced the *Uptown* album, got the Rounder deal, and became famous." Seaton also allegedly told fans that "me and my wife were just people that he let come backstage at his shows in the early years," Poore added.

Poore consoled himself by turning his attention to Anderson, with whom he'd done sessions on December 2, 1985 ("Pink Slip"), April 14, 1986 ("Burn That Candle"), and January 5, 1987 ("It Only Rains on Me"). His new plan centered on "Runnin' Wild," which Poore brought to Danny's attention in late 1987. "I had it by Les Paul, on a Capitol 45. He never even knew Les Paul did the song." Poore, who had picked up the record for a nickel, told Danny: "I'm looking for one song that's just out of the ordinary, and this is out of the ordinary, and I think this is right down your track." Poore suggested featuring it on an Anderson album that mixed rockabilly, country, and ballads.

Working with LesLee proved to be a painstaking exercise, simply because she was such a raw, unpolished talent. They'd normally just lay down a scratch vocal, so they could take the time to cut a "real" one later. Danny didn't mind, because he could use the extra time to sort out his parts, according to Poore. "She needed a lot more [coaxing], but was easier to work with than Johnny Seaton, 'cause Johnny thought he knew more than me."

Whereas Seaton wanted to be a star, LesLee was reticent about the spotlight. "She had the drive, she could work, but she was very insecure, nervous about going onstage, about her appearance, about her weight, what she looked like," Poore says. Seaton could nail a vocal in a couple of takes, but LesLee rarely did less than eight or ten. They did 50 takes on "Pink Slip," the chugging rocker that became her signature tune. "I told her I'd use the first take, 'cause she was one of those [artists who says], 'I could do it better, I could do it better,'" he says.

Anderson cut "Runnin' Wild" on March 3, 1988, at Glass Wing, recording it with 14 tracks of Danny's frenetic guitar and bass supporting her urgent vocal. "That song didn't throw LesLee off hardly at all," Poore says. "When her back was up against the wall, and she knew Danny wanted to get the final track, she got it. Danny took that song seriously. He really wanted to make that into one of his best songs."

"It's the Les Paul [sound] with the high-speed guitars and everything," Evan Johns says. "Danny finished this track, did the mixes, called Les Paul up, and played it for him. Les said, 'Who's the singer?' So, apparently, Danny was pissed, but what do you expect? It would be frustrating for him to spend all this time on the track and find out, 'Well, all for naught.' I think he was finding out that imitation was not going to take him farther than it already had."

On this point, Brent and Jan agree: Danny's relationships with high-powered peers like the Wizard of Waukesha often had an element of tension. The year before his death, Danny went to New York, ostensibly to have lunch with Eric Clapton. "His manager came, but he didn't," Brent reports. Similarly, when Danny traveled to England, "Jeff Beck was supposed to do this thing with him, but he backed out—these guys didn't want to get onstage with him."

On the other hand, Eddie Van Halen responded positively when Danny played Les Paul's 75th birthday party in New York. Aerosmith was the headliner, and Danny opened the show. Danny didn't get to talk with Van Halen, because there were so many people around, "but when he came offstage, Eddie gave him a thumbs-up—[his wife] Valerie [Bertinelli] was with him, and I think they even had their kid [Wolfgang] with them," Brent says. Danny wasn't into Van Halen's incendiary hard rock, but he did appreciate Eddie's style and finesse. "He liked Eddie, and he told me more than once that he would have loved to have done something with him," Brent says. "He had a lot of respect for Eddie, because of Eddie being the innovator of what he did."

UNFINISHED BUSINESS WAS finally a done deal, and rapturous reviews poured in from all corners. The *Washington Post*'s December 20, 1987, critique ("Danny Gatton: Pickin' a Mood") focused on how Danny's guitar style extended, yet also differed from, the work of the masters who'd influenced him. "You'd expect *Unfinished Business* to be a guitarist's guitar album—and it's that, all right," wrote Mike Joyce, who found "Cherokee" and "Homage to Charlie Christian" to be its strongest performances. But he added: "It's likely that even listeners who can't tell a Fender from a Gibson are likely to find something appealing here."

Guitar Player's March 1988 issue noted that the ten-year gap between *Redneck Jazz* and *Unfinished Business* made the release of the album akin to the Second Coming, at least for guitar players. "Sure, the playing is excessive—that's the point," Dan Forte conceded. "It's also at times awesome, always musical, and tons of fun."

The March 25, 1988, issue of *CMJ New Music Report* also focused on the dexterity and virtuosity on display. Jeff Tamarkin's "American Stars & Bars" column noted that listeners might be surprised at Danny's mastery of so many different musical idioms. "One of the songs is called 'Fingers on Fire' on this vocal-void LP, and that is as accurate a description of Gatton's playing style as any," he wrote. "Guitar freaks, don't miss this."

Rolling Stone ran a brief but ecstatic review in its "Hot Issue" (May 19, 1988): "Danny Gatton sounds like every great guitarist you've ever heard. The incredible thing is that he sounds like all of them playing at once." The review singled out several highlights, including "Cherokee" ("climbs all over the fretboard like a trio of Les Pauls"), "Homage to Charlie Christian," and Santo & Johnny's "Sleepwalk" ("with Telecaster howls and growls that would make Jeff Beck's jaw drop"). It was obvious that Danny "can riff away at ungodly speeds," but his incorporation of "so many classic styles into a rhythmically and harmonically assured attack" deserved consideration, too. The verdict? "*Unfinished Business* proves that Danny Gatton is the business," *Rolling Stone* decided.

Runnin' Wild had less of an impact when it was released in July 1988, possibly because of its eclecticism, Poore says. "Record labels hate 'em—they don't know how to market 'em—but I don't have any offense if some guy throws in a western swing and does a blues tune, if he can do it well." The quest for offbeat sounds extended to Danny playing viola on "The Birds & the Bees." "I wanted every mix to be different—in a way—at that time," Poore says. "'Allright, Goodbye,' I wanted to give that a '50s feel. And I wanted more modern stuff, like 'Pink Slip.' I was really getting into mixes at the time."

It wasn't long before Danny began to cut more material, and the four-horn lineup was present for a live recording on July 10–11, 1988, at the Birchmere, with Buddy Emmons guesting. Eastridge worked hard to capture something useful from the night, drawing on his lengthy experience with remote recordings. "We did them every weekend, so it was no big deal—especially there," he says. "We would just pull up, and I knew where the power was." The band could plug in, do a soundcheck, and get something to eat; everything would be ready to go at showtime. Eastridge remembers that recording effort for one other reason: "I got paid in cash that night. I was shocked! Danny was notorious for putting me off on studio bills, but he came to me with a big wad of cash and paid me off. It was amazing."

Danny eventually decided against releasing the shows, a decision that Eastridge supported with some disappointment. ("I couldn't believe we couldn't get anything [to release], 'cause some of it sounded burning to me," he says.) Gatton continued to try to capture his live lightning in a bottle, most notably at Washington's Roxy on March 2, 1990, where five cameras were trained on Danny and his backing quartet of Elliott, Previti, Swaim, and Windsor. The pregnant silence that explodes into Danny's intro lick for "Harlem Nocturne" alone is worth the trouble of searching for this video. The set included country weepers ("Heartaches by the Number"), the Windsor-sung Elvis medley ("Mystery Train," "My Baby Left Me," "That's All Right, Mama"), Charlie Christian's "Seven Come Eleven," and an exuberant country-rock version of "Linus and Lucy," which Danny used as a launch pad for some truly heart-stopping displays of speed on "Orange Blossom Special." (The latter three songs can be heard on the *Portraits* compilation.)

The Roxy video would be the only live recording that ever satisfied Danny. He and Eastridge mixed the results onto 24-track for editing into a planned commercial video release. If guitar diehards would follow Danny around live, then why wouldn't they pay $20 or $25 for a permanent snapshot of that experience? Unfortunately, only one complication was needed to sink the project, as Eastridge quickly discovered.

"I investigated how much it was going to cost to license all those songs for a video—outrageous!" Eastridge says. "To license it for a CD, it's $600 or $700 per song. For this, each license was going to be thousands of dollars, which is a whole other can of worms." Upsetting as the decision was, they let the project die after Eastridge told Danny, "Look, we're talking about 20 or 30 grand to get this thing produced."

Locally, life remained very much a case of "business as usual," as Mike Joyce suggested in his February 20, 1989, *Washington Post* review of a Funhouse gig at the Twist & Shout. The band played two sets that roamed from Duke Ellington to the usual TV themes ("The Untouchables") and R&B chestnuts ("Mustang Sally"). "Actually, calling Gatton's repertoire varied is akin to calling the Grand Canyon a gulch," Joyce decided. His praise concluded with one concession to commercial reality: "No doubt much of this was far more interesting to guitar devotees than to your average listener, but as bassist John Previti and other musicians in the band demonstrated, Gatton is not exactly surrounded by lightweights."

New York Newsday noted likewise in a February 26, 1989, interview with Danny. The article was previewing a jam session that night at Riverside Church with ex–Jefferson Airplane bassist Jack Casady and guitarist Jorma Kaukonen, two former Washingtonians. Just two weeks earlier, the paper had caught a Funhouse gig at New York City's Cat Club, where the show had segued from "Linus and Lucy" to the bluegrass frenzy of "Orange Blossom Special," as well as polishing off several TV themes, including themes for *Perry Mason* and *The Untouchables*. Writer Steve Bloom called the set "a remarkable display of eclecticism from the man who would be guitar king." Danny described his mission in typically straightforward terms. "Pop music has gotten pretty stale. It's time for something different," he declared. "A little entertainment, a little humor, a little bit serious." Not for the last time, he added: "Yeah, my style's pretty much everything."

Bloom posed what would become a standard question over the years: if Danny was so great, why hadn't somebody discovered him before? Where had he been all those years, exactly? Danny did his best to answer. After seeing how much it would cost to renovate his new home, "I decided I better pursue that musical career I always wanted—before I got too old," he said. "I always wanted to be successful at it, but when I was younger I was rather lackadaisical about the whole thing." He freely admitted that he'd hoped for someone to come along and discover him during his younger days; "unfortunately, that doesn't happen much if you just play around D.C." The proposed remedies included a new album that would incorporate his version of "The Untouchables," as well as an Elvis Presley medley—and he had hired the first real manager of his career (Ellis Duncan, whom he didn't name).

Outside Washington, guitar fanatics were getting acquainted with Danny through the March 1989 *Guitar Player* cover story. They got an added bonus from the five-minute "Nit Pickin'" Soundpage recording—intended as a snapshot of the different styles that he played. Although there were a few overdubs, "Nit Pickin'" largely featured Danny straight-up, on one guitar. Eastridge worked with him on the recording. "It was a mishmash of a bunch of things—he tried to just mix up a bunch of different styles," he says.

Guitar Player's *March 1989 cover played a big part in extending Danny's reach to a national audience. The cover shot made a visual reference to Danny's celebrated "near misses" with fame.*

From a public relations standpoint, Dan Forte's *GP* story was an un-qualified success. Danny got to lay out his approach to the instrument in ten pages, recounting his life's ups and downs in the engaging, low-key manner of a veteran who knows exactly what he's doing. Danny's story was genuinely refreshing in an age of overexposed superstars: how did someone so talented stay under the radar so long?

The cover shot featured Danny peeking from behind a tragedian's mask, while the opener showed him smiling, holding the mask above his head. Then–*GP* editor Tom Wheeler says the concept was chosen to illus-trate Danny's brushes with fame. "He did not strike me as the tortured-artist type at all—completely a regular guy, upbeat. Obviously, there was a side to him that I never did see."

New York guitarist Arlen Roth had heard of Danny long before they struck up a friendship. He'd toured with the likes of singer-songwriter Paul Simon, and then settled into session work that owed much to Danny's aware-ness of him. "I used to get recording sessions in New York, thanks to him: 'I need you to play some country guitar, and Danny Gatton recommended you.' He was throwing me work before I even met him. That was the beau-tiful thing about him, and that's why our friendship grew so quickly."

The two finally met after the Riverside Church gig. Danny was pleased that Roth shared his fascination with cars. "I was a big Buick nut, whereas he was more of a Ford guy," Roth says. "Danny said, 'I got this great set of wire wheels for you, I'm going to bring 'em up to New York. Danny came up in a pickup truck, in a blizzard. He's not thinking of the gig—he's think-ing about getting the wheels to me." Roth, who likens Danny's playing style to "the finish on a Cadillac," got his wire wheels for $200, which helped to cement their friendship.

WHEREVER HE PLAYED, Danny's virtuosity was trumpeted in the advertising. When the seven-piece Funhouse appeared on May 14, 1989, in the Charles-ton, West Virginia's "Mountain Stage" series, the ad declared: "You may not have heard of Danny Gatton, but you'll hear him in a big way on this Mountain Stage." Audiences were asked to imagine a guitarist who'd start with a Charlie Parker standard before moving to rhythm & blues, ballads, and "Foggy Mountain Breakdown." "Imagine someone who can do all of that with virtuosity, sensitivity, and style. That's Danny Gatton."

Dave Elliott found the night exciting—for a different reason. "That was totally scary, because it was live and on the radio, and I couldn't hear the rest of the band. They had me in a booth, with headphones on, but nothing was coming through. Danny went '1, 2 , 3, 4' and the headphones didn't come on till '4'!"

Danny does his thing for another rapt audience in Clubland, U.S.A., 1989. The guitarist's bandmates noticed crowds picking up after Guitar Player *featured him on the cover.*

Stories continued to swirl around in the local newspapers that summer, and Richard Harrington's "On the Beat" column of May 3, 1989, repeated suggestions of an imminent deal with CBS. Nothing came of the speculation, which left Danny fuming when *Newsday's* John Anderson raised the subject for his August 10 profile ("Whaddya Mean He Doesn't Practice?: Danny Gatton, the Guitar Man"). "We got jacked around by CBS," Danny said. "They swore to God they were going to sign us, said it was okay to say it on TV and all that. And I knew I should never have said anything. I should never have said it, 'cause sure as hell if I do it won't come true." Poore says, "Danny had announced onstage, at Club Soda, that it was CBS—that they had cut the deal, it was finalized. I don't know what happened to that deal."

In his article, Anderson marveled at the simplicity of Danny's setup: a '53 Fender Telecaster plugged into a '63 Fender Super Reverb amp. Such economy of equipment seemed all the more remarkable when you considered the techniques and sounds that Danny had so inarguably made his own—the deft comping of B-3–style chords, imitations of pedal steel and banjo sounds, simultaneous execution of lead and rhythm lines.

Danny pooh-poohed the whole "world's greatest" idea. Once a player had attained a certain level of ability, he said, "you're just dealing with opinion about who's the greatest. It doesn't mean anything. I've still got a long way to go to learn about playing."

Could he get better? Anderson wondered. Probably, Danny responded, but he didn't play much outside of gigs. He had practiced intensely between the ages of 9 and 16; thereafter, he'd do it only when he needed to learn a new style. "I'm pretty much a one-track-mind kind of person," Danny conceded. "If I'm into the music or the cars, my blinders are on." (Danny liked to maintain that he didn't really practice, but Eastridge says: "I know when I was on the road with him, he would practice a lot. He always had the guitar out in his hotel room—constantly.")

IN THE ANDERSON ARTICLE, as in other interviews of the time, Danny indicated that one of the potential pitfalls of a major record deal was that it would surely impinge on the relatively laid-back pace of his home life. The family was now firmly ensconced in Newburg, which had been "completely" Danny's idea, according to Holly. "We did not want to go down there," she says, "but he wanted to get out of P.G. [Prince George's] County, 'cause it was growing and getting so crowded. He made up his mind, and we did it—and it was the worst thing he could have done. There was nothing left in that house that was original."

The Newburg house had to be gutted to make it livable, and the family lived there during all the improvements, which Danny spent the rest of his life overseeing. "That was a big impetus for him to get his career going," Holly says, "because up until that point, he'd just been farting around."

Although NRG now had the makings of a profitable business, Danny saw no point in going that route again. "The stuff we did is very commercial, and I'd hate to see it wasted on a 10,000-seller when it could be a 500,000-seller," he told Anderson.

A mention of his gigs with Gordon moved Danny to lament the death of the clubs that they'd torn up so frequently, including the Lone Star, the Ritz, and U.S. Blues. "I just hope it's not going to be a trend happening there like it was here," he said. "It's damn near impossible to make a living as a musician in Washington anymore."

Danny also revealed his preparation for a rather uncharacteristic assignment: taping an episode of the soap opera *The Guiding Light* the following week, for airing on August 21. He'd agreed after the show's head writer had invited him. "I don't know what to think," he groused. "I still don't understand it." The episode is easily one of the most unusual moments in an unusual career. The band was hired to play in a bar scene, nattily attired in shirts and ties. They functioned primarily as a musical backdrop, although Danny got solo time beside country-pop diva Reba McEntire. "We got there at six o'clock in the morning, and they took Danny away to learn lines," Elliott laughs. "He's going, 'Lines! What? What?' Every time there was a bar scene in the show, you could hear us playing in the background. It was neat."

Danny took pains to shrug off an accident he'd suffered the week before. The wheel of a circular sander had flown off and struck his eye, just missing the cornea. Although he expected to regain his sight, the lesson wasn't lost on him. "Every time I get hurt it's from messing with cars," he said. "Unlike other people in the business I'm in, I have to go out and physically work on things."

JOE BARDEN WAS WORKING on things, too. He'd reached the point of having to make more pickups, yet could no longer spend the time needed to produce the individual metal and plastic pieces he needed. Another review of the *Thomas Register* provided the answer: laser cutting. "I started drawing up some simple blueprints and getting my parts cut by laser. You could get a box of 500 parts, and they were as consistent as mine. That was a major innovation."

Under the old regime, Barden estimates that he could produce about eight pickups in a ten-hour day, if he wasn't interrupted. His discovery of the laser-cutting technique freed him to concentrate on retail packaging for his business, now centered in Vienna, Virginia. He was still working out of his basement, although he'd added two employees to help him out. "It wasn't all gravy. I had to get a job as a courier for a while, to keep everything afloat," he says.

Barden made a major connection in 1987 with New York guitar repairman and builder Roger Sadowsky, who'd worked on everything from vintage Martins to modern Fenders for stars like Paul Simon and the Rolling Stones. Sadowsky was also making his own line of guitars, which is how the connection arose. "He wanted to use my pickups in his guitars, which was an incredible compliment," Barden says. "I might have sold odd lots here and there to a music store, but I really didn't have a concept of a wholesale price." Sadowsky was manufacturing and selling both instruments and preamps, "so he knew a lot about this, and he knew all the people in the industry. I was clueless. I was in Vienna, where there is no industry. And I was not undercapitalized—I was *uncapitalized*."

Meanwhile, Danny was continuing to help with other projects. During the recording of *Unfinished Business*, he'd gotten drummer Brooks Tegler to contribute some big band–style stickwork to "Cherokee" and "Homage to Charlie Christian"; in return, Danny played guitar on two tracks of Tegler's album *Hot Jazz...And Not Only That* (1995), without any money changing hands.

Tegler had recruited a slew of local musicians, who recorded 47 tracks (with some appearing on *Keep 'Em Flying* (1994), which came out before *Hot Jazz*). Battistone, Previti, and Swaim represented the Funhouse contingent, while Tegler's old rhythm partner, Terry Benton, also lent a hand. Recording proceeded in the basement studio at Washington's Catholic University. Danny played on "Lullaby of Birdland," which was intended to revive the small-group swing sound. "It was just a matter of professionals doing their job, doing it right, doing it quickly, and bam!" Tegler says.

Danny's appearance on the title track proved a bit more involved, Benton recalls: "He was like, 'I don't know what the fuck to play.' It was kind of amazing—he was half kidding and half serious." Danny ran down his part again and again. "We'd all be standing there, going, 'God, that was great! That was marvelous!'" Tegler says. "And Danny would go, 'Can I do this again?'"

Tegler also hit on the idea of pairing Danny with another hot guitarist, Steve Abshire from the Navy Commodores band. They did two takes of the Thelonious Monk standard "Well You Needn't." During one of the takes, Danny came up behind Abshire and began playing his guitar for him. "Everybody was always laughing, having a good time," Tegler says. But he decided against releasing the Monk takes, which would have broken the two tunes–for two tunes barter deal. "I never would go, 'Cool! I've got Danny Gatton on tape! I'm going to seize the day!'—which a lot of people would have done," Tegler asserts.

But bigger things were afoot, and Poore found it impossible not to get caught up in the excitement when he stopped in to see Danny at Club Soda. "It was after I went to the Bayou to see a couple of rockabilly bands," he says. "It was still early, about 12 or 12:30 A.M." He ended up hanging around until 4:30 A.M. Danny was whiling away his after-hours time drinking with Billy Windsor, and the atmosphere fueled a vortex of small talk. Danny jabbed at Poore's impending move to Nashville: "Nah, you don't want to go down there. All that's down there is creeps and liars and thieves!"

"I know he didn't like it [in Nashville]," Poore says. "The only relationship he kept up down there was with Buddy Emmons. When an interviewer would bring it up, he would say, 'Well, I couldn't be just another player down there, 'cause they'd tell me what they wanted.'"

His feelings about Nashville aside, Danny appeared to be brimming with confidence that night. *Unfinished Business* had racked up near-unanimous critical hosannas; media interest had never been higher; and he was now working steadily around the area. "He told me that night, things were going to bust loose so big—he had this big record deal, he was getting two million dollars." All that was needed, it seemed, was a career-making song that could introduce Danny to the masses without any overt compromise.

Amid the euphoria, one question lurked in the back of Poore's mind: would Danny's need for independence be a problem for a major label? He only had to remember what had happened in the wake of *Reaction*, after Rounder approached Danny to do his own record for them. "Rounder could have had him in 1986 for $30,000—lock, stock, and barrel." Danny had set the price as a minimum benchmark for any advance, along with insisting on creative control and final approval of the finished product.

"They just thought he was crazy—it was way too much money," Poore says. "They called me about it. They were almost scared to ask him, so they had me ask him. They said, 'Well, we have to have a representative there.' I said, 'All he wants is a representative to deliver his check.'" The talks collapsed, but one insight became obvious to Poore: "I'm thinking, 'All the money that Elektra paid him only a short time later—Rounder would have had an album.'"

88 Elmira St.
(1989–1992)

12

llis Duncan swore that he'd help Danny, if he ever got the chance, because he loved his artistry as well as his personality. Such pledges are
fairly standard among committed fans of a particular artist. What made
this one unusual was that it came from a '70s-era teenager sitting in the
backseat of a '48 Chevrolet as Danny and his bandmates began the night's
drinking. "We thought that was a nice thing to say," Elliott says. "Some
years later, that's exactly what he did. The bottom line is, he put Danny on
the map almost single-handedly."

The evidence of Duncan's success includes a 168-person guest list from
a gig at U.S. Blues, where top session drummer Jim Keltner and his counterpart from Weather Report, Omar Hakim, paid their respects. Elliott also
recalls the late billionaire Malcolm Forbes turning up at another New York
gig—because Danny was his favorite guitar player. "He came in the dressing room and was shooting the shit with us, like a regular guy," Elliott says.
"He had his arm around Danny, and Danny had his thumb in his side, saying, 'Gimme all your money, Malcolm!'"

The cousin of blues-rock guitarist Tinsley Ellis, Duncan seemed like a
strange choice as a manager, as he had no music industry track record. He had
worked in the real estate business, helping New York City's Hard Rock Café
with its expansion project. To Elliott, Duncan's background didn't really matter; he knew they needed help, citing the unlikely forums in which Danny
had appeared during the turn of 1989–90, like the *Guiding Light* episode and
MTV's *This Week in Rock*, where Kurt Loder introduced the Funhouse-era
lineup playing the theme for TV's *Perry Mason*. (Ed Eastridge shudders when
recalling the MTV experience. "That was a nightmare! I had to set up all this
shit that didn't even show up till noon, and the band didn't get there till
three," he says. "I was about to have a heart attack. I'm not a real technical
guy; I'm a musician that happens to know how to engineer.")

The Loder piece attracted the attention of Howard Thompson, head of Elektra's A&R department. "It wasn't long until I got a call from Ellis Duncan, who requested a meeting with me," Thompson says. "I went and saw Danny a number of times before deciding to sign him. I probably had some of the same reservations many people had initially, but in the end his great talent could not be denied."

Thompson also got a nudge from the owner of the New York club Tramps. "Steve Weitzman was a big fan and promoter of Danny. He has very good taste, so when he suggests you look at someone, you do." The deciding moment came on June, 15, 1990, at Les Paul's 75th birthday party at the Hard Rock Café, "where he played a stunning set," Thompson says. "It was so good, I just thought, Fuck it, this guy's too good to be without a record deal."

Danny signed on August 16, 1990, according to information provided by Elektra's Todd Giblin. Holly recalls her father being "very excited about the prospect that he would be able to make four or five albums and retire after that." The deal didn't yield any dramatic changes in their lifestyle, although she did get a jacket with the Elektra Records logo.

FOR SOME WHO KNEW Danny well, hiring Duncan seemed to signal a desire to find out what lay beyond the comforts of home. "That was a big move for Danny," Tom Principato says. "He had always surrounded himself with familiarity." Elliott thought that such a move was long overdue, because Danny had never had an established manager—or, barring that, at least someone with a more business-like outlook. "Billy Windsor just booked the gigs, collected the money, and served as the go-between," he says. "When we signed to Elektra, he dropped out of the picture—he wasn't up to dealing with the New York folks."

Others around Danny were less convinced. Joe Barden recalls lobbying for the better-connected Tom Carrico, who he thought was likely to make a stronger impression on Elektra than an outsider like Duncan. "He was going to make calls, and they weren't going to be returned, because no one knows who Ellis Duncan is." It was painful, Barden says, to see "Danny's thing go into the tank, basically, and watch [Carrico client] Mary Chapin Carpenter turn into a superstar."

But things were looking up with the Elektra deal, and Danny's burgeoning national reputation helped him to land a deal with Fender for production of his own signature-model Telecaster. In a *Musician* magazine interview, Danny matter-of-factly enumerated its qualities like a lawyer outlining his case. All of them had been included at his recommendation, including a larger neck, zirconium position markers, and a specially designed stainless steel bridge. There was also a toggle switch bent just enough to stay within reach without bumping the volume knob (which was larger than usual). The pickups came from Joe Barden, of course.

The appearance of the signature model spelled the end of Danny's '53 Tele, which he traded to Jack Jensen for a 1934 Ford. The guitar made its last appearance in Arlen Roth's *Telemaster* video. His disbelieving friend still can't quite believe that Danny got rid of the '53 Tele. "I said, 'You're nuts!' reports Roth. "And he said, 'Well, I like the car more than I could ever like that guitar.' He said he could always buy it back, but that never happened."

Washington's alternative *City Paper* reported that the Gatton signature model was selling for $1,499 at Chuck Levin's Washington Music Center in Wheaton, Maryland—although the salespeople had their own idea about how to reproduce those golden tones. According to writer Dave McKenna, they were "telling people who ask about it to just buy a '52 reissue Telecaster and throw some Bardens in there themselves. That'll save them hundreds of dollars, and they'll still get the same sound."

Barden's fame, McKenna mused, seemed to be following the same path as his guitar-playing friend's: why wasn't he better known outside the area? Danny had a ready answer: "He's had big people come to him and offer him money to license his name. Joe could be rich right now. But he didn't think they'd be able to maintain the quality, so he's turned them down."

The two men would spend a fair amount of time discussing this new level of interest in them—Danny, with his Elektra deal and signature guitar, and Barden, with his growing client list and expanding business. "We were sitting at my kitchen table one night," Barden says, "and we looked at each other: 'What are you going to do?' We were both scared to death. I was like, 'I don't know how to work a business,' and he's saying, 'I don't know how to be a rock star.' What are we going to do now?"

Elliott wasn't scared—he thought that better days were just ahead for the whole band. "Me being naïve, I figured, We're rolling along, we got a record deal," he says. But it wouldn't be that simple. He knew that things had changed when the band played a party in Oyster Bay, New York, to celebrate the signing. "These people that came to this party—the women had spike heels on, in a park! The guys are dressed in the hippest, latest styles, and it's 90 degrees outside. And they just mobbed Danny. I got pissed off, went to the RV and took a nap. We couldn't even talk to our friend."

BILL HOLLOMAN HAD CROSSED paths with Danny in the '80s. Holloman first heard his name while playing sax and keyboards in B. Willie Smith, a popular Northeast club band whose guitarist also happened to be a Gatton freak. Opening for Robert Gordon in 1982 should have been the ideal way to experience Danny's six-string magic, but Holloman was too preoccupied by his own set. "It was one of those things where we did the show, went downstairs and drank beer. I caught part of it, but I really wasn't paying that much attention." He had no clue that a casual conversation with Danny that night might prove important.

In fact, Holloman didn't realize the extent of Danny's fascination until much later. "He'd come up to the Hartford area, where I was living most of the time, and ask people: 'Do you know where this guy is?' He'd remembered me all the while, from that night."

Inevitably, Holloman's band ran its course. At their "last bash," someone asked Holloman if he recalled meeting Danny Gatton—because Danny remembered him. "Well, if that's true, send him this tape," Holloman said. He promptly forgot the conversation. Six months later, Holloman got a Sunday morning call from someone identifying himself as Danny's manager. "Ellis [Duncan] called me and asked, 'Is John there? John Holloman?' 'Well, no, this is *Bill* Holloman.'" Once they got that straightened out, Duncan said to Holloman, "Danny got your tape about a week ago, and he's done nothing but talk about it ever since." He then told Holloman that a deal with Elektra was imminent. Did he want to play with Danny? "I said, 'Let me think about it...*yes!*'"

Shannon Ford was finishing up work with the Gatlin Brothers, who were ready to stop touring and build their own theatre. Their road calendar still had 18 months to go, but Ford had already found a new gig, drumming for the revamped *Hee Haw* TV show, when Danny called. He needed little prompting to head for New York City.

Holloman also came to New York after the deal was confirmed. He met with Danny in Duncan's apartment. "We played, just the two of us," he says. "It was one of those immediate things where it just clicked." The bond between them, in Holloman's mind, was that "we weren't particularly 'musician types.' We were more normal guys that happened to play music. We found a lot of the same things funny, and we generally had a great time."

Holloman soon found out that playing with Danny was unlike his previous musical experiences. "Danny was never one for rehearsal: just get up and play," he says. "I had not come from that world. I just assumed, not knowing Danny, it was going to be a tight show that I was going to somehow try to fit myself into."

Holloman was invited to help finish the demos for the upcoming record. Danny had planned to do them at Eastridge's Big Mo, "but he got some kind of a tooth infection," Holloman says. "He called: 'Bill, my mouth blowed up real good, can't do this today, so we're going to have to do it at Bearsville.'"

Danny looking dapper and debonair for his Elektra Records publicity shot. However, he would recall his tenure with the label as riddled with conflict about musical direction—and about money.

No one was more surprised than Eastridge. "We did the whole album and presented it as a demo to Elektra," he says. "He got signed, and then they sent him to Bearsville to redo almost the whole thing. They ended up keeping a couple of our original tracks." (Danny's Latin-swing reworking of Martin Denny's "Quiet Village" was one; Eastridge doesn't recall the other.)

Eastridge felt strongly enough about the superiority of the Big Mo demos to include the original "Pretty Blue" on his *Portraits* compilation. "It's got a much better groove, and it's much more soulful," he says. "It's just a better take—it's got magic." Eastridge says Danny lifted the theme from the '50s TV show *Superman*. "That's where the melody line came from—I busted him on that. I said, 'Danny, did "Pretty Blue" come from *Superman*?' I hummed the melody and then he said, 'Oh, yeah!'"

Howard Thompson has little patience for suggestions that he exerted an influence on the *88 Elmira St.* material. "I've never signed a group or artist and then tried to change them," he asserts. "If the artist is smart, they realize the problems and make their own changes. Those are the people I prefer to work with." He also doesn't recall any suggestion that Danny should recut the demos at Bearsville. "I may have requested certain songs that I might have heard live that weren't on the tapes that were kicking around. Certainly, I asked him to record 'The Simpsons' [theme song], and I think 'In My Room' was an idea that came in late from Billy

Windsor, possibly others, too.... [But] I defy you to find better versions of songs from this album on any tapes that were already recorded." As additional evidence, he cites the following letter that he received from Danny before he signed the contract with Elektra:

Howard:

I apologize for the quality of this tape. I have better versions of some of these things but I can't find them at this time. Please bear with me because the best ones are still in my mind and I am very excited about recording them once and for all. Like I told you at Bearsville, I am easy to work with and I always do my best to accommodate everyone. I think the idea of doing *The Simpsons* theme could be a *real* challenge! I will continue to search for other contemporary things that I can do my way. Bill Holloman also has some original material that I will be hearing soon. There are some other tunes that I love that I would like to do, like "I Only Have Eyes for You" very lush and angelic, but I don't have the records of them anymore. You *know* I can do the killer guitar album everybody has been waiting for even if some of them don't know it yet. It is a privilege for me to be associated with you and Elektra.

Thank you so much,
Danny Gatton

LOCATED IN UPSTATE NEW YORK, Bearsville had landed on the recording map through Todd Rundgren's productions for his original band, Utopia, his solo albums, and his work with such heavyweight clients as Badfinger, Shaun Cassidy, and XTC—among many, many others. "I thought it was really cool when Dad told me that REM talked to him when he was recording," Holly says. "I was like, 'Holy shit—REM!' He's like, 'Who are these guys?'"

Holloman was "secretly thrilled" to find himself working there. When he arrived, two or three tracks were already done, including "Funky Mama," which gets *88 Elmira St.* off to such a strong, decisive start. Holloman spent his time laying down horn parts and doing whatever else needed doing.

Danny soon called to tell Holloman that the deal was signed and sealed. The first task was a track for the compilation record Elektra was releasing to celebrate its 40th anniversary; it was a collection of new versions of songs that Elektra artists had done. Danny chose Rhinoceros's "Apricot Brandy," which soon became a staple of the live show. Windsor wasn't needed, since the tune was an instrumental. "I don't think he was even at the studio," Holloman says. "We'd rehearse in the barn and cut it the next day. That was the first time we'd all played together as a band. In fact, that was the first day I ever saw Shannon."

BACK ON THE LOCAL FRONT, storm clouds were brewing. The absence of Elliott, Swaim, and Windsor from the sessions had fans questioning why such longtime colleagues were being left out. "Bruce is a world-class player—what's wrong with that?" Dave Chappell says. "I remember him telling me [after Holloman was hired] that he went for a long walk around Manhattan. 'Either I've had it wrong all these years, or…' " (Swaim declined to be interviewed for this book.)

Elliott puts his departure down to someone's behind-the-scenes notion that Danny's new music demanded a funkier drummer than him. But he didn't blame Danny. "He said it was Elektra that did it, and that was good enough for me. Nobody could re-create what me and Danny and John had."

Holloman doesn't think there's any mystery: the wheel just turned in another drummer's favor. If anyone from Elektra was interfering, Holloman didn't notice, and he was made to understand that the *Elmira St.* lineup amounted to Danny's dream band. "Danny, to the end, always talked about what a good shuffle player Dave was, but there were other things that Danny wanted to do that just weren't Dave's bag—that's all," Holloman says.

No other horns were needed, because Holloman could cover all the parts. "I played full horn sections on 'Funky Mama' and stuff like that, so he'd seen that in action," Holloman says. "He knew, recording-wise, that was the way to go. When we did 'Apricot Brandy,' it featured a big horn section, which was all me."

As far as Ford was concerned, the Bearsville demos and rehearsals suggested a reasonable framework: tight but loose, instead of jamming for its own sake. Ford had come to feel that the hometown crowd didn't consider the bigger picture, and that Danny was "capable of so much more." Such comments might seem treasonous, especially in light of Ford's Redneck Jazz Explosion history. "That's how I came to know him and appreciate him, and that's how many people did," he acknowledges. "But I still maintain we would have been better off exploring some of the stuff we started to do in Bearsville."

The band followed its compilation assignment with a gig at the Cat Club. Then it was back to Bearsville for the album sessions, with Holloman driving in from Connecticut while everyone else arrived in the large RV that Windsor had dubbed "the muthaship." The joke inspired an *Elmira St.* song title.

Recording went fast, as *Elmira St.*'s CD booklet details: the whole affair ran from September 24 to October 10, 1990. Mixing started on October 29, and the album was finished on November 17. Time was at a premium, because the Gatlins still needed Ford, who spent a week laying down rhythm tracks with Previti. Then it was Holloman's turn to spend two weeks with Danny.

They received help from studio manager Ian Kimmet, who served as Thompson's liaison. (Kimmet would get an executive producer credit for his role.) "They seemed to work very well together, and they were always joking around," Thompson says. "Shannon was always goofing around, and Danny Gatton enjoyed a joke or three. John Previti was more reserved, at least in my presence, but everybody treated me kindly, and I tried to make it as easy as possible for them to enjoy the process. I never saw any arguments. In fact, watching them overdub was amazing."

Holloman says he "didn't feel like there was a solid game plan, really; Danny just had a number of tunes that he wanted to do." But he did his part to keep the project moving. He was still playing with a wedding band, which required him to commute between those gigs and the recording sessions. He'd work up the horn charts from rough session tapes while lying in bed every morning.

He says that most of the tracks had been demoed numerous times, though some surprises unfolded during the sessions. It was Windsor who suggested interpreting the Beach Boys' "In My Room." Thompson rates it as his favorite cut; "it was sort of my idea to mix it in a way that suggested David Lynch's arranger, co-producer, and composer, Angelo Badalamenti," he says, noting that he was a fan of Badalamenti's work on the *Blue Velvet* soundtrack.

"In My Room" is also Ford's favorite *Elmira St.* moment. "I was starting to come up with ideas for drum tracks that weren't all that conventional, especially considering what Danny had recorded before. I had some influences outside of what he was used to listening to, and I started bringing those in." He especially enjoyed overdubbing assorted percussion instruments; on "In My Room" he created a "wall-of-sound drum sound and kind of an unconventional groove," he says. (After Danny's death, Jan found an autographed picture of Brian Wilson, with a note hailing her late husband's version of his song. True to form, Danny had never mentioned the photo.)

Ford thinks Windsor's presence sparked Danny to do things that wouldn't have happened otherwise; if he couldn't sing, he'd be the sounding board for his friend's ideas. "He was somebody that Danny trusted more than anybody, more than me or Bill Holloman or John Previti," Ford says. "He seemed to trust Billy and depend on his support and input. And he had good ideas. I think it was valuable to have him there, just for Danny's sake."

Thompson suggested that the album be instrumentally oriented, to play up Danny's strengths, and he minimizes Windsor's role. "I won't speak ill of the dead," he says, "and Billy was a lovely guy. Clearly, he had some effect on Danny's career. He was Danny's compadre, and Danny needed someone around all the time that he could trust implicitly."

Many of the artists that Elektra signed during this period—Billy Bragg, The Cure, Metallica, The Pixies, Sisters of Mercy—enjoyed little radio support, but they boasted a distinct image that helped in nurturing a fan base. Once that base had been built, sales followed—and then the radio stations got onboard. "I had hoped Danny would get out on the road, amaze people across the country, and become the 'people's guitarist,'" Thompson says. "He could play any style brilliantly and had a charming personality, so it was really just a question of getting him out there and letting him be seen."

Holloman shared arranging credits with Danny, sometimes prodding him to develop different guitar parts, as he did on the sultry after-hours groove of "Blues Newburg." "I kept after him: 'Danny, this has to have a melody. You've got to have something the kids can play on guitar,'" he says. "Finally, he relented and came up with that nice melody." The live performances were a different beast: "a lot of times we never bothered with the melody, or he'd play the first three bars and that'd be the end of it," Holloman says.

Thompson's suggested reworking of the "Simpsons" theme was *Elmira St.*'s most unexpected or unwelcome surprise, depending on the viewpoint. Although Danny disliked it, "we actually played it quite a lot," Holloman recalls. Thompson suggested doing the track as "something contemporary that people might recognize," he says. "The Danny Elfman tune is very intricate, and I wanted to challenge Danny a bit. I don't think, in retrospect, it was such a good idea. Or maybe it was, but not given a very good reading. If it had turned out better, I might have hoped Matt Groening would use it on the show, but I wasn't really thinking about it as a single or anything."

Music magazines were rapturous in their views of *Elmira St.* (even if *Musician* misspelled it as "Elmyra"). *Musician*'s Gene Santoro wanted to know the secret to Danny's endlessly inventive style. "Basically, it's options," Danny told him. "At every turn there are maybe 10 or 15 different possibilities.... A lot of rockabilly and blues and rock guitarists think in riffs. I don't. That's because of a jazz background; improvisation makes you do that." He cited "Funky Mama" as an example, having taken pains to include a banjo section, a pedal steel part, a jazzy part, and the long, frantic runs that distinguish the tune. For the rock-meets-Dixieland feel of "Fandingus," he placed a fan by his amp to mimic a Leslie cabinet's revolving-horn sound.

88 Elmira St. split the D.C. crowd. Elliott thought it too slick, while Principato believed it offered a fresher take on Danny's style. "I remember Dave saying, 'Me and Danny used to just make it up as we went along,' which, in a lot of ways, was true," he says, "but it was sort of making up different ways to work within the same Gatton vehicles they'd been doing for years." *Elmira St.*, on the other hand, "had some of those vehicles—but they were in a much newer and fresher context."

Steve Wolf appreciated the album's display of studio mastery, but preferred the organic charm of the Redneck Jazz Explosion or *The Humbler*, "because he's just playing, and he's at his best," he says. "He's just blowing, and it's not overly edited. A lot of those other records are edited and edited and edited."

In Pete Kennedy's view, Danny's guitar sound was obscured by the production. "A lot of Danny's thing was tone; it wasn't just chops," he says. "And to really hear the tone, you want to hear one guitar—not five parts overdubbed playing in harmony, speeded up and slowed down, with Leslies and stuff like that. Just a Tele screaming out of a tweed amp was Danny's real genius, but he didn't think that was enough in the studio, for some reason." Danny shone live, where retakes weren't allowed. "That's why I always tell people you had to be there to hear that," he says.

Joe Barden maintains that the whole Elektra period was "very, very stressful for Danny and his family," and he felt let down by the resulting albums. "All of a sudden, you've got a circus: 'The World's Greatest Unknown Guitar Player,' 'The World's Fastest Guitar Player,' 'that wacky guy with that wacky beer bottle.' It didn't make any sense. It wasn't what Danny was [about]. I know Danny loved the studio, but my feeling is, he was one of those artists who should have released nothing but live albums."

Holloman says the band had virtually no rehearsals. "We'd talk it over on the bus," he says. "And maybe John would get his bass out while we were going down the road: 'Okay, let's play that.'" Otherwise, the opportunities came in soundchecks, which is how Holloman wound up singing Jackie Wilson's "Reet Petite." Ford ran it down while they were setting up, and "we were playing it for the rest of the time I was in the band," Holloman says.

Holloman says there was a practical reason for Danny's no-rehearsal policy. "He had a limited song reference. Most of it was songs he had already been playing for 20 or 30 years, so I had to sort of learn it by myself. Of course, that was mostly done on the bandstand." The classic example is the "Linus and Lucy" medley, which could roam for 20 minutes from Guaraldi's melody to "Apache/Surf Medley" to the fret-busting acrobatics of "Foggy Mountain Breakdown." "The same songs would show up, but you never knew in what order; it was whatever came into Danny's mind at that moment."

John Previti "would follow him like clockwork, 'cause they had been doing it for 20 years," Holloman adds. "Finally, I'd heard the songs enough, and played them enough, that I would know what the next one was going to be. But that took a year, probably, at least!" If two sets were required, the band just went unplugged, with Danny and John and "maybe Billy—when he was there—strumming along [on acoustic guitar]," Holloman says. "It was really nice. John knew all the songs that Danny was going to play, and where he was going."

Although Danny wasn't pushy, "it was clear that he was in charge. It was his band, and he would let you know that," Holloman says. "He got the band on and off stage, and he did the stuff that a road manager or music director would do." Danny also made up the set lists, which was a big break from his previous make-it-up-as-you-go-along approach. Holloman and Ford both say some structure was needed—at least tight beginnings and endings—so that "average people could get ahold of it, instead of just the guitar players and their reluctant girlfriends," Holloman jokes.

He recalls the first set lists being made in the fall of 1991, after a string of gigs supporting the Radiators—no strangers themselves to flying without nets. "We were pretty well received, although it wasn't exactly our crowd," Ford says. "They were kind of a Grateful Dead thing, a precursor to the [jam-oriented] Phish thing. Danny was able to pull off the free-flowing jam thing most of the time, better than most people I've played with. The band could have continued to do that and nothing else, and it would have pleased all the D.C. fans. I just felt we were capable of much more."

Ford maintains that he wasn't terribly concerned "about record sales, or getting on MTV, or any of that. I just wanted it to be a great band that lived up to its potential, and I think we did not live up to our potential by following Danny around in a jam."

The first steps toward a more structured show took place after a night at Toad's Place in New Haven, Connecticut. Ever unpredictable, Danny had played a set of straight-ahead jazz. Afterwards, "we said, 'Danny, we can't do that. We're trying to make something of your record,'" Holloman reports. "He said, 'I thought it was a jazz club.'"

"It was a drag. It was not cohesive at all," Ford says. "It felt embarrassing—we just didn't live up to our potential that night. No, it wasn't a jazz club, and so what if it was? Let's do our thing. We're not a jazz group." After that, the band convinced Danny to start writing out set lists.

DANNY'S *AUSTIN CITY LIMITS* performance on October 24, 1991, remains his most widely circulated clip among collectors. Producer Terry Lickona wasn't all that familiar with Danny, until he recalled the 1983 Roger Miller appearance. "Believe me, he stood out [in that show]. All of a sudden, the focus shifted to him and his guitar," Lickona says. "I got curious, and checked out a couple of CDs that he'd done. I was blown away by his talent and decided that he certainly could carry a show of his own, so I booked him."

The band played for an hour and 45 minutes, which was edited into a half-hour show that zigzagged from a fiery "Funky Mama" to "Red Label," the Elvis-inspired "Sun Medley," and an upbeat rampage through Danny and Billy Windsor's throwaway number, "Honky Tonkin' Country Girl." Danny pulled out all the crowd-pleasing stops, using his Heineken bottle as a slide—and keeping up the thrill-a-minute picking even when he put a towel over the guitar neck to wipe away the beer.

Ford came right from his *Hee Haw* gig to do the show. He'd missed six gigs in the South, for which Brian Alpert had filled in on drums. (The band had started off on October 18, opening for the Kentucky Headhunters at Northwest Louisiana State University, followed by a show with Lou Ann Barton in Arlington, Texas. They hooked up with the Headhunters again on October 22, in McAllen, Texas, and October 23, in Austin.) "I walked back into the band after not playing with 'em for two weeks—and it felt great," Ford says. "There's some nice stuff on the show. I was kind of a fresh horse coming in on that."

Holloman thoroughly enjoyed the show. "They give the audience free beer," he laughs. "They don't make a big deal out of it. There's a keg in front, with glasses around it; if you want a beer, you grab a beer." After they'd finished, the band watched the whole show from inside a screening room. "That's the only time I ever saw it," Holloman said. "There was a great version of 'Blues Newburg' that never got on there."

One of the edited version's most memorable images is that of Holloman puffing out his cheeks, Dizzy Gillespie–style, as he blasts a squawking tenor sax solo on "Funky Mama." Ford reprised the old trick of coming from behind the drums and climbing Previti's bass without missing a beat—just as Elliott had done on the Roxy videotape.

Not everybody in the band enjoyed the show. "It was interesting watching Billy's expressions when he would see himself on camera and hear himself sing," Ford says. "Shortly after that, he left the band. I think seeing himself, and how he fit in, was really an interesting moment. Danny told me afterwards that Billy was really bummed out, seeing what was really happening with him in the band. I watched him as we watched the playback, and you could tell that it was a little embarrassing. Nice guy, but I think we were outgrowing whatever contribution he could make."

Tom Principato says, "He never really had a great vocalist in his band. He was torn—what he really should do is an album of great guitar playing, but then there were some politics of having a band with a singer. How could you make an album without having your singer in it?" In hindsight, some of those pressures went with the music business's emphasis on hits, from which no guitar genius was immune, he points out, not even Jeff Beck. Joe Tass felt the problem lay in the approach, not the personnel. On bumping into Danny at Club Soda, he once joked: "Do you ever find you need to send out a fuckin' search party for the melody line?" (He doesn't remember how Danny responded.)

Danny's peers recognized him on November 10, 1991, with no less than nine Washington Area Music Association ("Wammie") awards at D.C.'s Bayou club. His haul included trophies for Best Blues, Country, and Rock/Pop Instrumentalist; Best Blues and Jazz Recording; and Best Musician.

The band shared a New Year's Eve bill with Asleep at the Wheel at a Hyatt hotel in Crystal City. On the surface, "a heavy, intense listening band was not people's idea of New Year's Eve," Holloman says, but it worked out fine. "Danny and I came up and played 'Auld Lang Syne' with Asleep at the Wheel, just the two of us. I remember that being a good gig."

In January 1992, the band appeared at the National Association of Music Merchants trade show in Anaheim, California. "We killed 'em at the NAMM show," Holloman says. "Then I walked around the floor the next day. To have all these musicians come up and say, 'You were great last night'—I really enjoyed that." Musicians were the perfect audience, "because that's who Danny's fans were. Most of the regular people didn't get it." An informal poll of 20 people would have found that "one out of 20 who would just go crazy when you mentioned his name—and the other 19 would not have a clue who he was."

One of those musicians was James Burton, best known for his licks on Ricky Nelson's '50s hits and as musical director for Elvis Presley's touring band. "I had him autograph my guitar," Danny told *Guitar Player*'s Chris Gill. "We consumed many beers and had a great time. I've gotten more stuff off of him than a lot of other players. For some reason or another I've neglected to admit that." Jan says, "He talked about James Burton as being the most sincere person. He told me how much of a down-to-earth person he really was. I think he was really, really happy that there was that compatibility with James Burton."

THE BAND SPENT most of the winter in the Washington area. "We didn't work enough for me to make a living," Holloman says. "I had to do other stuff." Ford had the same problem, which was why he'd stuck with the

Hee Haw gig—"it was a pretty silly thing to do, unless you're broke," he says. "But we weren't working, and nobody was handing out free rent at that time."

Right from the start, it was apparent that large-scale touring wasn't on the agenda. "That's when Danny and I weren't seeing eye-to-eye on things, and it was a real drag," Ford says. "When we were sidemen together, we were the best of friends. We were on more of an even keel, as far as our relationship went. But all that changed when I started disagreeing with his philosophy of what the band should be."

Joe Barden recalls an odd complaint from Norma when they chatted about her son's prospects: "I don't know what the point of this whole Elektra deal is—they haven't gotten Danny any gigs at all." That didn't make sense to Barden. "I remember thinking, Record labels don't get you gigs—they just sell records. One of the fundamental problems was that Danny was 'The World's Greatest Unknown Guitar Player' and the farthest thing from an insider in the music business." Those problems were worse for someone who stayed in the D.C. area, Barden believes. "It's quicksand for anyone with talent, because time's wasting away—the clock continues to tick, you're still playing club gigs, and you aren't learning anything."

Howard Thompson wasn't idle, though. He scouted hard for film, commercial, and TV opportunities, but "there really wasn't any other vehicle, and I suspect had he toured more, he would have sold more records," he says. *88 Elmira St.* sold roughly 100,000 copies, which wasn't bad for someone not hustling on the road—but it might have done much better if that step had been taken. (The album peaked at No. 122 on the *Billboard* charts, while "Elmira Street Boogie" wound up being nominated for a Grammy Award in the Best Rock Instrumental category.)

Ed Eastridge understood how Elektra felt. Danny would end up being the top seller on his Big Mo label, due to the cult-like fervor among his guitar-playing fans. But Danny had no desire to emulate the ethic carved out by Big Mo's second-best seller, Rod Piazza & the Mighty Flyers, who took their bluesy sound on the road 150 to 200 nights per year. "Howard used to beg him to tour. I did, too," he says. "I said, 'Danny, you'll have to get out and support this one, y'know.' It's the only way that somebody who's not already big can sell some records."

Southern Maryland represented a safe harbor that Danny wasn't going to leave long, no matter what career pressures might dictate, Richard Harrington feels. He also suspects that the '90s marketplace wasn't primed for the everything-at-once approach of Danny's art—which could hardly be called "smooth jazz," the category most likely to merit airplay. "The problem with being able to do everything is that you can't do anything," Harrington says.

Danny and Jan during the late '80s.

Danny didn't understand his own appeal. Jan remembers walking through Georgetown and hearing one of her husband's songs being played. "I went in and asked the girl, 'What is that?' She said, 'I've worn out my CD. I had to buy another one.' I went home that night and told him. He went, 'Aw, you can't believe her.'" Another time, Danny asked Jan why she'd bought his album when he could have gotten her a free copy from Elektra. "I said, 'Because it made me feel good.' It was like, 'Oh.' But that's how he was."

Reviewers who mentioned Danny's weight—whether they called him "portly" or "rotund"—could also damage his self-esteem. "He wore black a lot," Holly says. "[Being heavy] really affected his perception of everything." Joe Tass had learned not to push that button after a conversation in which he'd jokingly said, "Now look, Tubby Arbuckle..." "Danny was real self-conscious about his weight," he says. "If you look, the guitar is always in front of his stomach."

As Holly got older, she and her father began to have difficulties over issues ranging from his attempts to limit her involvement in creative pursuits to questions about her musical taste. "He just didn't know what to do with me," she says. "I wasn't a bad kid at all, but I don't think he knew how to treat a teenage girl who was blossoming. It was rather shocking for him." Holly had to hide her liking of Michael Jackson; she also lost a Red Hot Chili Peppers album when her father replaced it with one by Fats Domino. (Jan's John Denver album didn't escape, either—Danny and his buddies used it for target practice. "She was pretty upset about that," Holly says. "It wasn't that she liked John Denver. She just liked one song that happened to be on this album.")

Holly says that she and her father were growing more distant. "He was my best friend until I was about ten. We'd talk about all kind of things, like philosophy and theology. Suddenly, we stopped communicating, because he was afraid of what was going to happen to me. It was very sad—but if he had died when we were that close, I don't know if I would have recovered."

BILL HOLLOMAN'S CALENDAR SHOWS trips in March 1992 to Philadelphia, as well as gigs at the Birchmere and Wheaton, Maryland's Tornado Alley. They then spent April crisscrossing the Midwest. "I drove to Youngstown, Ohio, to meet the bus," Holloman says. They also made stops in Minneapolis and at the Cubby Bear in Chicago ("that was a fun gig"). May saw them return to Big Mo, then make trips to Toledo, Detroit, and Rockville, Maryland. The band did further recording at Big Mo in June, and ventured to Minneapolis and the Milwaukee Summerfest.

A Canadian trip in July was one of Holloman's personal highlights, including an appearance at the Montreal Jazz Festival. "We played three nights—that was really fun," he says. "We were outside, and the streets would fill up with people. They dug it." From there, it was off to another festival in Quebec City, where they played for about 40,000 people. They were playing down the street from a band described as Canada's homegrown answer to Weather Report. "When their show would get over, they'd all come down to see us, and the place was packed. The guitarist—a famous guitarist in Canada—had his own band, and they were on the same bill with us in this Quebec City show. This guy wouldn't go on after Danny, even though he was the star."

Holloman also remembers the Quebec show for another reason. "People ask about monitors—Danny was so loud, I never had him in my monitor wedge, ever. That included this show, which was totally open air—no back of the stage, nothing—and I heard him loud and clear!" The month ended with a flurry of activity at Tornado Alley and the Birchmere, as well as trips to Colorado and Delaware. They also did some sessions at Big Mo on July 26–27.

The band made one of its infrequent European trips that summer, traveling to Switzerland's Montreux Jazz Festival. Ford and Holloman believe that Danny could have done well overseas, where rigid formats and niche-marketing strategies don't play as large a role as in the U.S. But just getting outside the country had been an achievement after Danny had rejected one European tour offer to play "some local thing" instead, according to Ford. "That was hard to take. It was like, 'Damn, play Europe! We'd blow the doors off!' I think that aspect of him playing this uniquely American music would have been extremely successful over there," he says.

Holloman says a simple reason lay behind the paucity of overseas trips: "Danny didn't want to go. He didn't like getting on the planes; he didn't like the passports and dealing with customs." Even on the Canadian trips, "he was terrified that they were going to find something on the bus. I don't really know why—there wasn't anything to find." Ford confirms the notion: "Danny was always really disgruntled to have to open his bags and do the whole customs thing. He just didn't like traveling."

The problem-plagued Montreux gig saw Duncan's exit before a note was played. "Danny, Billy, and Ellis were all there at the same time—bad move," Holloman says. "Billy had been working on Danny for quite a while to get rid of Ellis."

"Ellis always got shit on—I felt bad for him," Eastridge says. "The reason was because he was in the school that thought Billy Windsor needed to go, and Billy won that battle." Nobody in the band was surprised. Windsor had long bridled at being overlooked on the album sessions, which had caused a buildup of resentment—with Duncan as the natural target.

When it came to consider what everyone called the "Billy factor," Ford sided with Howard Thompson, for musical reasons. "I was interested in taking it beyond where it was with Billy. Danny had a great past, but that's pretty much what it was. It didn't apply to what we were capable of doing."

Other forces were at work, according to Holloman. Windsor once called to tell him, "Well, I've almost got the month filled"; the harvest amounted to a grand total of three gigs. "His idea of filling the calendar was to have all the Saturdays filled, 'cause that's all he wanted to do," Holloman says. "He wanted to make a grand on Saturday night, for him and Danny—and I'm thinking, I can't live like that! Fortunately, I had other gigs."

Holloman says that Duncan was "Danny's only true champion, from the get-go. He's the one that got him the record deal. But Danny never saw that." Holloman has no idea what caused the final breakup, "but we all saw it coming. We laughed about it later, because we had this vision that Danny was going to punch out Ellis." As it turned out, "it wasn't that loud"—but Ellis went home. (Duncan declined to be interviewed for this book.)

Amid all this backstage drama, there were onstage problems as well. "We didn't play the main stage," Holloman says. "We played the club, and the equipment broke down." The casualties included Holloman's piano, on which at least half the arrangements depended, forcing him to finish the gig on organ. Bonnie Raitt liked what she heard, but famed producer Quincy Jones didn't. "For some reason, they put him right in front of Danny's amp," Holloman says. "He got up and walked out during the first song, because it was too loud. It was real obvious—he and eight other people got up and left."

Liz Meyer feels that Danny was ungrateful for all that Duncan had done for him. "I think Ellis was very badly hurt by the whole thing. He was certainly out to do the best for Danny—he was not out to make himself a big career. He liked being around the musicians and the music business, but he was not one of the sharks, by any stretch, and he ended up being treated like one."

Howard Thompson says the change was inconsequential. "Ellis wasn't interfacing much with anyone else at the label, and he certainly wasn't getting Danny the big tours, so it didn't make much difference once Ellis had gone, other than that Billy Windsor's influence became stronger."

Jan wasn't convinced about the need for a change, and she even sought to talk Danny out of shedding his manager—which marked one of the few times that she weighed in about a music-related issue. She couldn't fathom how her husband's loyalty to his longtime friend trumped consideration of the long-term picture. "He had a real sense of loyalty, which was admirable, but not wise. He thought he should carry Billy with him, and there was no way that Billy was going to go anywhere."

Holly agrees that the hard-working Duncan got a raw deal, since he walked away with nothing to show financially. Near the end of their relationship, Holly observed an unpleasant incident that crystallized how sharply things had deteriorated. "One time, Ellis was threatening to sue him. Dad told him that he was going to kill himself if he didn't leave him alone. He was just screaming into the phone."

Ford's frustrations were beginning to crystallize. "We had this record deal on Elektra, and I saw it as a major opportunity to do something really special," he asserts. "Bill and I were in agreement most of the time that we were approaching the thing from an amateur standpoint." That's why Ford had supported Holloman's desire for a structured show. "We'd go onstage and do what Danny had done for 20 years, the stream-of-consciousness jam thing. A lot of times, that was lost on our audiences, outside of the guitar heads, who thought he could do no wrong."

Jan believes that Danny always had difficulty reconciling art and entertainment. She recalls a story that he told about one of his trips to Nashville, where a stranger had told him: "You know what you should do? You should dress up in a clown outfit." Jan thought the stranger must have been joking, "but Danny took it to heart. 'No, the guy was serious. That's what I should do in order to attract more attention.' That kind of thing really threw him into a funk—that something more than the music was needed. Danny said, 'I'm not an entertainer, I'm an artist.'"

THE BIAS TOWARD ONE-NIGHTERS continued that summer and fall, ranging from Colorado's Breckinridge Blues Festival (August 8, 1992) to local affairs like the Taste of D.C. festival (October 12, 1992). "We did so many gigs around D.C. We played every joint," Holloman says. "Every little thing that you could think of, we did—also in Lynchburg and Charlottesville [Virginia]. Driving distance to D.C.: that was our range, pretty much."

Holloman says the other Washington-area players shared Danny's distaste for travel. "I used to drive to D.C. all the time, from Connecticut, and it would take me six hours. All the D.C. guys, when they had to come up to New York—you'd have thought they'd driven to California. 'Oh, I'm so beat! I can't believe how far we drove!' I'm like, 'Dude, I come down there every weekend—it's two hours longer!' They were so funny about that, just crying the blues when they had to drive to New York."

Holloman didn't know exactly how well *88 Elmira St.* was doing, "but it was selling a few copies here and there," he says, and was readily available. "I would go to the record stores and look for it, and it was pretty much in every store."

The year climaxed with a project that remains among Ed Eastridge's favorites: *New York Stories*, on Blue Note Records, which placed Danny among top jazz players like French-Algerian pianist Franck Amsallem, bassist Charles Fambrough, trumpeter Roy Hargrove, tenor saxophonist Joshua Redman, and saxophonist Bobby Watson.

Ford didn't play on the album, but he was well aware of how Danny felt going into the project. "He had a lot of insecurities about doing it. He practiced really hard to be able to do that record, because he was in with some real New York jazz players and it was on Blue Note, which is a revered label. He was kind of intimidated by it, but he blew the doors off. I think he's brilliant on that record."

Danny and Watson emerged as the major soloists; five of the album's nine compositions were also theirs, a factor that the *Washington Post* found critical to its success. "Those of us in the D.C. area...are well aware of Gatton's imposing jazz chops," Geoffrey Himes wrote in his October 30, 1992, review, "and he responds so well to the bebop atmosphere that his custom-made Telecaster is the front-cover photo."

On December 2, Danny appeared at Tornado Alley alongside a host of other local favorites—Bill Kirchen's Too Much Fun, Big Joe Maher & the

Dynaflows, Billy Hancock, and Tom Principato—to raise money for Elliott, who was halfway through a double hip-replacement. Everyone had a ball, judging from a video clip that's surfaced of Danny, Hancock, Previti, Windsor, Maher, and Ronnie MacDonald blowing their guts out on a fine version of the R&B chestnut "Shotgun." It's one of the most exciting clips associated with Danny, who embroiders Windsor's frenetic vocals with blistering "answers" from his Tele. "It went great. It was well-attended, and we raised a bunch of money," Principato says. "I thought that Danny was a little more reserved than usual. His eyes were bloodshot, not necessarily from drinking but from being tired. He looked kind of run-down. I remember thinking to myself that the rigors of the road had gotten to him a little bit."

Another era was drawing to a close, as the Eastridges had moved to Vermont for family reasons. Ed would still take his truck down to D.C. for remote work, but that was a far cry from the days (and nights) when Danny could drop in whenever he felt like it.

Danny and Windsor rejoined their American Music Company pals—John Broaddus, Ernie Gorospe, and Jerry Wallmark—for a Christmas party gig at a local American Legion hall. Back problems had forced Wallmark to stop playing drums in 1990, but nothing could keep him away on this night. "That was probably one of the most gratifying jobs that we had," he recalls. "It was absolute fun, and it kicked ass." Broaddus was also thrilled to be playing the oldies again with people he respected. "That was one of the things that made the music business work for us—we were all friends outside of music," he says. "It had nothing to do with Danny being a great player. I still have a car that he and I worked on in the early '60s. We did a lot of that outside of the band over the years, whether we were playing or not."

But Danny had, indeed, come a long way since his Offbeats days, which was confirmed by *Elmira St.*'s Grammy Award nomination (although Texas guitarist Eric Johnson walked away with the trophy). The album's closing track, "Slidin' Home," was even being used at Shea Stadium for New York Mets' games—proof positive that Danny could cross over to larger audiences.

Broaddus couldn't help but wonder if his old friend had thought about what lay ahead. "I don't think he knew how complicated it would be to make it. I think he had a simple idea: 'Well, I play pretty good. I'll work harder and play better, and when I play better than everybody else, everybody's going to flock to see me...' But it doesn't work that way."

Cruisin' Deuces
(1992–1994)

*F*rom a purely commercial standpoint, it's often the second record that de cides if all those dollars amounted to subsidizing misplaced expectations. *88 Elmira St.* had met the minimum benchmark, but the next album involved a dramatic change in the producer's chair. "For some reason, even though the budget was higher, Danny talked Howard into letting him do it himself—with no Ian Kimmet or anybody watching over him," Holloman says.

Danny decided to work at Big Mo. "He never wanted to go to Bearsville in the first place, because he was a homebody," Holloman says. "It's not that he had anything against Bearsville; he just was happy being holed up by himself at Big Mo."

The Big Mo studio was in a garage next to Ed Eastridge's house. The gear was packed into the mobile-recording truck outside the studio. A closed-circuit TV setup provided visual communication—"he could sort of see you, and you could sort of see him," Holloman says. It was odd, "but Danny loved it there. He was very comfortable, and that's what counted."

Danny hurled himself with predictable gusto into the demo process— with Windsor's help. The band earned demo rates for working up the songs; if they became masters, they were paid master rates.

Holloman had doubts about some of the material. Tracks that hadn't survived previous go-rounds were popping up again, like "Honky Tonkin' Country Girl." "They had these country songs with really hokey lyrics," Holloman says. "I knew Howard, and I knew none of this stuff was going to fly with him."

Thompson visited Big Mo only once or twice, according to Holloman. By his reckoning, the recording process dragged on for close to a year. "When we did work on it, it was brutal," he says, "because Danny would try to make every bar so absolutely perfect that he'd get close to sucking the life out of it altogether." Watching the clock was never Danny's strong suit—"left to his own devices, he'd have wanted to make a record every ten years," Evan Johns wryly observes.

Thompson, on the other hand, doesn't recall the recording as taking an inordinately long time. "Danny Gatton and his musicians basically knew what they were going to do before they recorded—for me, anyway," he says. "It may have taken longer in the preparation stage—what songs to do, who's going to sing them—but I always thought his studio work was pretty fast. Danny didn't like to waste *his* money."

Ostmann didn't question Danny's wish to work at Big Mo again. He cites the "Nitpickin'" *Guitar Player* Soundpage, which he reckons captured Danny's guitar tone at its finest, as showing why it was a good idea to work there. He hadn't had much contact with Danny since the Elektra deal was signed, but he gathered that all kinds of possibilities were being floated, judging from a chat they'd had before the *Deuces* sessions began. Danny was mulling a remake of Brenda Lee's "Sweet Nothings," possibly with Carlene Carter on vocals. "I thought, God, that's a great idea: Danny playing the guitar, her singing," Ostmann says. "I don't know what happened to it. That, to me, was the kind of thing that second record should have been."

Sessions were strung around gigs, so if the band was playing Friday and Saturday, "I'd come down on Tuesday and work Tuesday, Wednesday, and Thursday," Holloman says. "But then he'd decide that he wanted to do another song. It was just so weird." Where *Elmira St.*'s brisk schedule had kept everyone moving, the new album's work felt like a slow crawl. If an 11 A.M. session had been booked, the Gatton-Windsor brain trust didn't show up until 2 P.M.

"There was no focusing without Howard or anybody [else] watching 'em," Holloman asserts. "Nobody quite knew what to do." Some improvements occurred when Eastridge insisted on stopping by 7 P.M. every night; even then, there was no way to speed up Danny's micromanagement of every part. As an example, Holloman cites "Rambunctious" (which is on *Portraits*), for which he played an organ part. "Danny was his usual two hours late, but Eddie and I were there [to work on it]. 'Great, that's done.' Of course, Danny didn't keep one bar of it! That was the one I really remember: every four bars, we'd change the pattern."

Danny sat next to his keyboardist "and basically orchestrated the organ part for the whole song, chorus by chorus. 'This chorus, do this.'" This way of working stemmed from how Danny heard music. "When he listened to the 20 or so records that he listened to, he knew every part so well," Holloman says. What's more, every song had to have several parts named after the player who'd popularized the style: "Okay, this is the Billy Butler part; this is the Bill Black part; this is the James Burton part."

Windsor's ever-fluctuating involvement also slowed the momentum, Holloman believes. When the sessions began, "he was all gung-ho; he was the producer with the clipboard. Then, when it started to become clear he wasn't going to get to sing again on this record, he disappeared and quit the band—which he would do on a fairly regular basis." Windsor did manage one vocal appearance, on "Satisfied Mind," which nobody was sure would make the final cut until the record was completed. The other vocals were handled by guest artists Rodney Crowell, Delbert McClinton, and James Lewis, as well as Holloman himself, on "Thirteen Women."

Thompson had devised the vocal cameos to help promote the record. Holloman wasn't even supposed to sing "Thirteen Women"; Thompson had said, "I'm looking for somebody famous to sing this," but when he couldn't find anyone suitable, he decided to keep Holloman's vocal. Danny disliked the song; "we played it once or twice, that was all," Holloman says. "I liked it. It was a great tune and fun to sing."

Ford says, "I think [Thompson] was, at that point, probably getting pressure from Elektra to make this a commercial [success]. You know how this second-record thing goes. It's like, 'Okay, the first record did this many numbers, so find a way to make the second one do more.'"

Lewis's guest spot probably polarized listeners as much as anything Windsor had ever sung. "Beat of the Night" is a lost cause, sunk by an overly frantic vocal and a stiff backing track that tries to mate '60s pop and soul—with greeting-card verses to match. Ford dismisses the track as "really dated" and "ill-conceived." "Danny and Billy said, 'Well, let's just take a little bit of this song and a little bit of that song. It doesn't really matter: let's cop this and let's cop that,'" he says. "I think the track speaks for itself, as far as how effective that concept is." Windsor had actually gotten first crack at the vocal, with everyone rolling their eyes during those attempts, according to Eastridge.

When mixdown time came at Memphis's Ardent Studios, "Danny went by himself the first time—again, just to save money," Holloman says, "because it was coming out of the record budget, his own pocket, to go there." Jack Jensen, ever the pragmatic businessman, recalls having numerous talks about the issue with Windsor, who couldn't understand where the budget was going. "Danny was one of those guys who was dollar-foolish and penny-wise, to a degree," he says. "He was such a perfectionist, it was almost like a disease."

Holloman was allowed to come along on the next trip. They had a top-flight engineer in John Hampton, who'd worked with artists like Stevie Ray Vaughan. "That was a nice experience. John was a good engineer, and we all kind of put our heads together." Their efforts came well before today's digital editing. One time, they were all leaving the studio when Danny spotted an early version of Pro Tools software. Holloman recalls Eastridge saying, "Keep that away from Danny: if he sees that, we'll never get out of here." Holloman found the point well taken, "because Danny, even then, was not averse to cutting actual tape to take out this teeny little piece of a part that wasn't exactly, perfectly in time," he says.

Not every track was fresh. "The 'Sun Medley,' of course, was a big staple of the show," Holloman says. "That was an example of something he had in the can. The drums were redone, but the bass and guitars he'd had in the can for years." The same held true for "Harlem Nocturne," which ended up being divided between two producers: Norma and Tim Olphie of Fastball Productions. The original track predated Holloman's arrival. "It wasn't that old—probably '88 or something like that," he says. "We redid the track, except for the drums; I played B-3 on that."

The recast "Harlem Nocturne" deployed effects and some unusual ideas—in this case, twiddling the tone control to get squealing, spaceship-type sounds. Danny rated this particular version as his finest when he discussed the album with *Guitar Player*'s Chris Gill for an article in the July 1993 issue. On "Thirteen Women," he told Gill, the Tele sound got an assist from an old butter knife, blade cut off, jammed under the second fret. "I play it with a 6L6 tube, a beer bottle, or a couple of old steel guitar bars," he said.

According to Holloman, "Sky King" had started as a demo, and then "we went back and recorded it over again. He already had that in the can; we just redid our parts." Danny confessed in *Guitar Player* that he'd wanted to recut the tune for a better rhythm-guitar sound, but he was happy with the lead work.

The Gatton-Windsor collaboration "So Good" became the set opener, "much to Danny's chagrin, because it was so fast for him to play," Holloman laughs. "But I said, 'Danny, that's our opener—it's got to be.' He liked to open a little more gentle and sort of work into it; I was from the hit-'em-over-the-head school. It worked; people went crazy when we played that song first." The slap bass sound was actually Danny "beating on a fiberglass beer cooler with a pair of brushes or sticks or something."

The song also marked Timm Biery's drum debut. "Shannon was out of town, and Danny didn't want to wait for him," Holloman recalls. "So he got Timm, who'd been bending his ear for a year: 'Try me, try me.'" (Not to be outdone, Danny's friend and guitar tech Jay Monterose also wound up on the track; he's credited with "mournful holler.")

Other noteworthy elements on the album included the extensive use of acoustic rhythm guitars on the rockabilly-oriented tracks, though the

Gibson ES-350 and '53 Tele also saw duty on the "Sun Medley"; according to Danny, "I was trying to get Scotty Moore's exact tone." He also used an alternate-tuned Gibson J-200 for slide guitar on the intro of "It Doesn't Matter Anymore."

As always, Danny was not content to stay in one place too long, musically. "If I do one thing too much, I get tired of it," he told Gill. "My attention span is pretty short. I've always been nervous, and I'm always searching for other things." He didn't want to take a short-cut by overdoing it with effects, though. "I prefer to do it the hard way—with a guitar, a cord, and an amp. If it comes out fine, good. If it doesn't, I'd better go home and woodshed some more."

Holloman's calendar shows that the mixing was finished on January 5, 1993, followed by mastering on January 29. "I wasn't overwhelmed by it, but I thought it was good," he says. "It had good moments." He cites "It Doesn't Matter Anymore" (always the second song live), "Funhouse," "Harlem Nocturne," "Sky King," "So Good," and "Puddin' & Pie"—which had fallen together in the studio and earned him a songwriting credit—as the highlights.

Holloman didn't stick around for the mastering, because he had another commitment. "I'm listed as co-producer but I have to leave, because I have a gig up in Connecticut that night at a racquetball club, with a shitty blues band," he laughs. "I'm thinking, Now there's the music business!" (The gig paid him $100.)

Tom Principato remembers talking to Danny about the mastering—one of the last times he saw him. "He told me that he'd made a phone call, the night before they were going to master it. They had supposedly delivered the album, and it was all set for manufacturing, but there were a couple more things that he wanted to fix on it. And so he called it back and worked on 'em."

In Holloman's view, the finished work reflected "a lot of different forces tugging at each other." There was Danny, "who wanted to keep as much stuff as he already had and try to get as many songs as he could on the record, for monetary purposes." And then there was Thompson, who wanted to pair Danny with well-known guest vocalists "and picked out songs like 'Thirteen Women' that were not hits but could sound like a popular song of the day." Finally, there were the musicians, "who were sort of just trying to get something good on there and work within the parameters."

Not surprisingly, Holloman prefers *88 Elmira St.* "because there's a little more humanness to it—we just kind of came in and did our thing. That was one of the most fun times of my entire musical life, making that record." Having guest vocalists was fine with Holloman; "I just thought some of the song selection could have been better," he says.

Ford demurs. "I don't think it was necessary, although I am proud of being on a record with Delbert McClinton—what's not to like about that?" he says. "Of any of the vocal tracks, I think his worked [best], just because he's Delbert McClinton. Those guys worked together really well."

In the end, Ford says, *Cruisin' Deuces* was "a mish-mash of concepts and ideas. Some of my favorite cuts are on that record, and some of my least favorite cuts are on that record," he laughs. He likes the title cut, "because we're going back to, 'Okay, here we are back at Bearsville'—back in that frame of mind. 'We're a band. Here's my idea, here's your idea, let's make this a band track.'" Ford also enjoys "Thirteen Women" and "Harlem Nocturne," although he considers the *American Music* version of the latter as definitive. "It's just that those guys [who recorded it] had a certain thing."

JANUARY 1993 WAS A slow month, according to Holloman's calendar; the band's outings were confined to Wolf Trap and yet another run to Tornado Alley. February crept by on a similarly uneventful note, except for a couple of gigs at Solomons Island, "near Danny's house—that was about the only show that I ever saw Jan at," according to Holloman. "It was right around the corner from their house." Danny's home was also the departure point for the tour, and "you could see she was particularly thrilled by it all," Holloman says.

Holloman found the *Cruisin' Deuces* tour fun, if grueling. "We were in a tour bus, but it wasn't high-class accommodations," he says. "We did travel the country, and were received well, and the band was playing great. It was just the four of us, with four other guys on the bus—which was no fun!" Jeff McHugh had returned as soundman, and Jay Monterose was onboard as guitar tech. Monterose's friend John Minor "somehow got himself on as monitor engineer, although he'd never seen a monitor board before, I don't think," Holloman laughs.

Such arrangements were typical of Danny's tight-knit circle. "I never saw such a collection of characters in the dressing room," Holloman says. "Guitar players tend to do that, though. These weren't groupies; these were mostly older guys."

Windsor elected to stay home, saying: "I don't want to get beat up for nothing." That suited Elektra. "It was a 'support' tour, so they wanted Danny and Billy not to get paid," Holloman says. "Danny, as the artist, wouldn't get paid anyway, and Howard and the record company didn't care whether Billy went or not."

Not every gig revolved around blasting the Telecaster: Danny thrills his audience with the acoustic at a Solomons Island Holiday Inn In 1993.

To keep things familiar, Danny named Brent as his new road manager. The job's basic chores included plotting travel logistics, unloading the equipment, and collecting the money. Not that anyone had much to take home: most of the gigs paid little more than $500, according to Brent, who found such arrangements typical for such a tour. It's standard insulation against poor turnouts, and the artist is mostly looking for exposure. Besides, there's always a promise of higher guarantees on another tour—if the act gets to do another tour. "The bus driver probably made more money than anybody," Brent says. "A lot of these clubowners are dishonest, greedy people."

As an example, Brent cites a Scottsdale, Arizona, gig, where the band sold out a 350-seat club. The deal promised a guarantee, as well as 80 percent of the door. "There was a break [point] where you actually got into making that extra money. When I went back to get paid, they said, 'Well, you didn't make the cut,' and there was no way I could prove it otherwise. And that happened a lot."

Danny made his feelings about the tour clear, in typical fashion. "The first day we got on the bus, there was a dry-erase board and he wrote on it: 'BAND HELD HOSTAGE, DAY ONE,'" Brent laughs. Ironically, that day marked the start of Danny's first full-fledged U.S. tour since the Gordon era—the only one he'd ever manage, in fact. But Danny would rather have been home. "He loved playing local gigs, especially when they were good-money gigs with good crowds," Brent says. "He loved playing the Birchmere, because they treated us really well."

Danny didn't reveal his feelings when he was working, though. "Whether he hated to be there or he loved to be there, everybody was treated nice," Brent says. "Everybody was treated with respect, too." At the same time, Brent feels that his brother *was* overexposed in the local scene. "I can remember plenty of nights at different clubs where it wasn't packed to capacity, because he was so accessible during that time."

There lay the dilemma: how to break someone so talented out of those confines and give him a shot at major success—without getting entangled in the ugly realities of the music business. Like it or not, touring was part of a musician's job description.

Not surprisingly, Brent's most vivid memories of the tour center on exhaustion. Tight schedules and lengthy trips were commonplace, with band and crew doubled up in some Motel 6's budget accommodations. It was all a bit much for someone who'd never been off the East Coast before. "Every day, it's Saturday night. You're not going to bed till four or five in the morning," Brent says. "One day blends into the next. One town looks like the next, just like the songs say."

The band quickly adopted a rule of thumb: if the next gig was 500 or more miles away, they'd leave right away. "A lot of times, we'd just get a hotel room long enough to take showers or wash clothes. You figure out real quick how to do things," Brent says.

Most of the gigs were in mid-level nightclubs that were "nothing to look at," Holloman says. The schedule also included blues festivals, "and we weren't really a blues act." But winning over audiences wasn't a problem, even in odd settings. Danny could drive himself and his bandmates to reach new peaks every night, although in a somewhat more structured format than what had prevailed before. "The songs would go wherever they went, and I was in favor of that," Holloman says. "I just wasn't in favor of him standing there noodling around, trying to figure out what the next song was going to be."

Ford considers the *Cruisin' Deuces* tour to be the band's peak. "We were down to a quartet, and I thought it was very cool," he says. "It was really streamlined and the best we ever were [musically]."

Principato, who'd moved to Austin, caught a show at Sully's, a little club in Dearborn, Michigan. "I don't think anybody in the band knew that I was there," he says. "It seemed typical. I didn't notice anything good or bad about Danny; he was playing well, and the crowd was a full house, responding well."

Danny unleashes the beer bottle trick at Slim's in 1993. Brent Gatton road-managed his brother's Cruisin' Deuces tour, where long drives and tight schedules were the norm: "One town looks like the next, just like the songs say."

There were offbeat moments to break up the boredom. Brent recalls a venue in Sacramento, California, that resembled an old abandoned warehouse, where the opening act was "a thrash metal head-bangin' band," he says. "When the first band came on, that's what the main crowd was there to see—about half of them left when they finished. But Danny played a two-hour show, and the ones that did stay, he gave 'em their money's worth."

Then there was the steep mountain road that interrupted the band's journey to a Fourth of July festival. The driver "hit the jake brake, and he killed the motor," Brent says. "We were broke down right across the street from a trailer park—I guess it was, 'Wow, we got a band bus broke down on the side of the road.' They brought over a case of beer, and were coming and getting autographs—and they didn't even know who Danny was!"

Eight hours passed before someone could repair the bus, which forced the band to miss the gig. Ironically, Brent says, "it was one we were looking forward to, because we could relax—Eddie Money was the headliner. But by the time we got the bus fixed it was, 'Well, we're out of here—next gig.'"

Brent was dissatisfied with the promotion. "They didn't back him. They didn't do anything to make it fly, that I saw," he says. "We did some store signings and a few radio interviews." The most memorable of those experiences occurred in Chicago, where former *Partridge Family* TV star Danny Bonaduce had carved a niche as a brash, trash-talking DJ.

"Me and Danny and John went to the radio station," Brent says. "That same weekend we played there, the Grateful Dead were there, Sting was there, and I can't remember who else. There were two or three other big-time bands there. And Danny Bonaduce had this running gag: he knew what hotel Sting was staying in, and he knew what name he was registered under." So Bonaduce had Brent call the former Police bassist's hotel, asking for a meet-and-greet. "I got to the desk," he says. "They didn't put the call through to his room. But it was fun. Danny and John played live on the air. It was fine; he treated us very well."

One of the finest shows came at Sheldon Hall in St. Louis, where McClinton reprised his cameo on the "Sun Medley," which was filmed for a potential video. But Elektra dropped Danny before its completion, "which makes sense," Holloman laughs. "They spent money on making the video, then dropped him! They videotaped the entire show and recorded it to ADAT, so it's pretty well recorded. It's really good; in my opinion, it's the best band he had, at the height of his power. We had just finished the summer-long tour, so we were tight as could be." (Holloman was working to release the footage, until economics stifled the project. "I wish I'd had the money to finish it, because it would have been a real tribute to Danny," he says.)

Ford remembers the Sheldon Hall show fondly, too. "There's some amazing, amazing playing on that concert," he says. "It's really us at our best, I think. That's what I'm most proud of, that era of the band."

The band learned how long it takes to drive nonstop across America after their last gig in Eugene, Oregon. The bus left at 4:30 A.M. and continued its relentless path home for 36 hours—with no stops, except for gas and meals. Brent feels that the long grind of the tour did nothing to assuage his brother's distaste for being on the road. "You know, it may have been different, had the money been real good and the living a little better—maybe staying in nicer hotels, not being so frenzied [with the traveling]," he says.

Danny often looked rundown and weary after going on the road, and this time was no exception, Jan says. "He'd put on weight; he would always look like he hadn't slept, had not taken care of himself." They had marked his 48th birthday on the road, but Jan had planned ahead by having Monterose give Danny the present. "He liked raccoons, so I gave him a little figurine of a raccoon."

The tour had been somewhat misleading, Holloman believes; "most of the places were packed, because they weren't that big," he says. "Danny would ask, 'Okay, how many out there got my new record, *Cruisin' Deuces*?' They already had it, so he was preaching to the choir."

Donna, Danny, Norma, and Brent (left to right) relax for the camera. Relations between both sides of the family would grow increasingly strained after Danny's death.

The band didn't have many prospects for further touring, because "there weren't a lot of gigs out there that made financial sense for Danny to do," Holloman says. "The agents that we had were blues agents; they were used to the acts getting $1,000, and Danny didn't really want to do that. He was used to making more than that, especially in D.C."

Outwardly, Danny seemed confident that *Cruisin' Deuces* had finally captured his freewheeling guitar pyrotechnics in the studio. "If we beat them over the head with instrumentals all night, that gets old real fast," he told *Guitar Player*'s Chris Gill. "Playing fast gets old real quick. I'm getting older, I don't care about doing that anymore." He hoped to get into production ("I like working in the studio better than going on the road and playing live") and do some soundtrack work, even as he vowed to gear his next album for modern pop-country radio: "It won't sound like other people's records, either. They're tunes that the average bear can bop to."

Danny's stature at Elektra dipped further after Thompson left the label in August 1993. With nobody left to champion Danny's cause, the loss of his deal by the year's end was no surprise, especially since sales of *Cruisin' Deuces* had peaked around 88,000 copies. However, Thompson figured that the exposure from two major-label albums would give Danny a shot at another deal, and he gave DAT copies of all the Elektra recordings to Norma.

Principato had hoped Danny would do something fresh on the second album, but *Cruisin' Deuces* didn't deliver. "He definitely had his vehicles—he liked those organ shuffles that were like 'Honky Tonk,'" he says. "He did a lot of variations on those. He kept coming up with different versions of what was pretty much the same thing." Where *88 Elmira St.* had radiated a kitschy charm, "it was still Danny in a contemporary context. *Cruisin' Deuces* was: 'Well, there he is in a leather jacket, and does this look comfortable?' And by that time rockabilly was pretty much dead."

SHANNON FORD, FEELING FRUSTRATED, left the band in the fall of 1993, unable to stem increasing doubts over how they were operating. A friend's comment came to mind: "Eventually, you're going to have to betray the master." Ford felt terrible about leaving, since he considered Danny his mentor, "more than any other person that I'd ever been involved with in music—and, in some ways, in life," he says.

"He taught me to be true to my art and to be honest in what I play—and now, as I'm starting to form my own opinions, based on what he's taught me, they don't jibe with what he's doing," Ford says, recalling how he felt at the time. In hindsight, he thinks that the logistics of national touring were too far beyond what Danny and his circle knew. "They were used to playing in D.C.—driving downtown, 40 minutes out of southern Maryland, unpacking the van, doing a four-hour gig, and being home at two in the morning. That's what they were comfortable with."

Ford was long gone before Elektra dropped Danny, but "it wasn't all about the numbers," he says. "It was also about the fact that he wasn't willing to tour. I often wondered if Danny really wanted to be on a major label, anyway."

Jan feels that Danny was worn down by his dealings with the record company. "We were standing out in the garage, and he told me that his heart and soul had been sucked out of him from all that squabbling," she says. Although she wasn't privy to all the contractual machinations, "I know he was frustrated about the money for touring. I know there was some problem about that early on—and maybe when they would do it. He wasn't up to doing big-business records. He wasn't the kind of person who could deal with that—it was foreign to him. I guess we did not see that at the beginning, and he learned it the hard way."

Brent thinks that Danny's versatility ultimately worked against him. "That was the problem with every record company that ever looked at him: his music never fit into one category," he says. "It wasn't jazz, it wasn't rock, it wasn't country, it wasn't blues—in any given song, you might hear it all." Danny's instrumental orientation also posed a problem. "The only thing that could have been done would have been to pigeonhole his music, to concentrate on one type, whatever it was, and hook him up with a really hot singer—which he didn't want to do."

Did Danny resist that notion because of his previous problems with singers? "Basically," Brent says. "I mean, Billy wasn't there [in the band] for that purpose." Many regarded Windsor as more of a business partner for Danny than a musical one; however, Brent's not ready to buy into that viewpoint completely. "Billy was there to do a lot of different things, and they collaborated on a lot of the songs and arrangements. Billy was real smart about that stuff."

Richard Harrington has his doubts that vocals would have helped to get Danny on the radio. Consider *Cruisin' Deuces* guest vocalist Delbert McClinton, he says: "Delbert's never gotten airplay in his *life*." Brawner Smoot lobs the ball back to the label. "I don't think Elektra handled him well," he says. "It's obvious what you do with Danny—he's a guitar virtuoso, and you sell him as such."

Jan regards *Cruisin' Deuces* as a fragmented affair undone by all the different singers. "Dan should have just done it by himself, with his band, no vocals—I wish they could have been daring and done that," she says. Holly believes that if they had to include vocals, Holloman could have sung all the material—but her father wouldn't consider the idea. "He was just way too stubborn. He was like a train, and once he was going you could not stop him. And you could get run over in the process."

Holloman kept trying to raise his concerns about the big picture, even staying behind after a Saturday gig so he could get down to Newburg. There, they could "hang out, drink some beers, and eventually get around to what I wanted to say," he says. Unfortunately, the issues got lost in small talk after Monterose came over. It was an awkward moment, because Holloman considered him "captain of the old school." Monterose's father had been a highly esteemed jazz saxophonist, but that made no difference to his son. "He liked the old Danny thing: guitars, and nothing but guitars," Holloman says. "He was always pushing Danny the other way."

Holloman pressed his point anyway. "He knew I was there for a reason. I mean, I *never* went over to his house to hang out. But he didn't want to listen to what I had to say." Holloman emphasized the importance of writing songs "and what a great opportunity he had with the record label. I remember pointing to his house: 'Think about [Jan and Holly]; let's try to do something good instead of just recycling these old tunes and putting out garbage.'"

Danny appeared attentive, but nothing changed. When Holloman suggested collaborating on some new material, Danny said, "Yeah, that'd be a good idea, but I'm moving furniture in my garage today." Holloman laments, "He'd never get around to it. He had all this stuff in the can that he wanted to get out, because it was sort of free."

Holloman was also having difficulty rationalizing the ever-spiraling drive times—when the band was actually gigging. "We had some other little car tours, when there was no more tour-support money," he says. One such outing began in Virginia, then zigzagged to Pittsburgh, Buffalo, and Ypsilanti, Michigan, before it was time to return home. "It was totally crazy. It was ridiculous, and that's when I was starting to see this wasn't making any sense."

Holly says she sensed "a big letdown" after her father was dropped, "but I don't think he was really worried about it, 'cause he was getting more steady gigs. And he always had his mother's label to fall back on, if all else failed."

Although the last two years of Danny's life were his biggest-earning ones, Jan remained the financial bedrock of the family, which did little to assuage his long-standing guilt. "It wasn't like she could quit her job and everything would be great," Holly says. "He wanted her to retire. He couldn't stand watching her get up at three o'clock in the morning and work so hard all day." Holly emphasizes that her mother never resented this state of affairs. "She wanted to do it for him. She would have sacrificed her life for him, if she could have. She would have been content for him to be out there playing with his cars all day—she didn't care. She loved him."

Danny claimed to feel "totally ecstatic" about being dropped, but Jan questioned the implications on her husband's mindset. "What's this going to mean for him? Will he be depressed? Will he have another chance to put out anything that's creative?" she wondered. "I was making a very good salary, very much above average. I didn't worry about finances. We were doing the house; we were managing. I was worrying more about him."

Danny got another blow on January 5, 1994, when Billy Windsor died of a heart attack. He'd failed to show up for a local TV taping, which was totally unlike him. Windsor had awoken to tell his wife, Donna, "I don't think I can do this today, in terms of going to the TV show." He'd then collapsed and died.

Jan found out when Ernie Gorospe called her at work. "I was scared to tell [Danny]," she says. "I called the TV station, because I didn't want him to hear it from somebody just walking up to him. They said they were still on, and they would have him call when he got off." Still not sure about how to convey the news, Jan asked to speak to everyone but her husband. "I told them, 'Don't tell him,' and somebody said, 'What do you mean, don't tell him? We have to tell him! Somebody *has* to tell him! It's happened!'"

Holly found out when she got home from school and heard an answering-machine message from someone expressing condolences. "I was completely shocked, you know, and ran out there [to the garage]," she says. "He was just—not heaving sobs or anything, just tears in his eyes, drinking a beer, and looking out the window. I grabbed him and hugged him real hard. I felt so bad for him, 'cause I knew that things were never going to be the same after that." Jan got home from work while Danny and his daughter were comforting each other, "and we all stood there in a circle and hugged," she says. "I thought it was going to be okay, but it was just downhill after that."

Ford realized how Danny would feel about losing a friend that he'd so loyally supported. "I was gone by that time, but I knew that it was a huge blow," he says. Principato also knew it was a devastating loss. "His dad, Dick Heintze, and Billy—those were three big blows to Danny. That's what I mean about the sensitive side; I don't think it was instantly apparent because he appeared to be so easygoing."

Danny grew increasingly withdrawn after his close friend's death. Joe Tass saw him for one of the last times at Windsor's funeral, where they stood at a distance from each other. "He looked at me and looked at me, and just went on talking. I was there for 20 minutes, and he never came over to say hello." Jan and Holly say that Danny spent even more time in the garage and ate separately from them, and his consumption of beer and cigarettes began creeping upward.

Knowing how Windsor died, Jan insisted that Danny see his doctor. "She really put the heat on dad to get checked out, and he'd always end up cheating," Holly says. "Dad would say, 'Oh, I feel fine,' and [the doctor] would say, 'Okay, just let him go,' and he never really checked him out the way that he should have. Mom was always nagging him to do it, and he just wouldn't cooperate."

There was financial fallout, too. "All the little local D.C. gigs that Billy used to get went away, because Danny wasn't going to go out and hustle anything," Holloman says. The band did appear at the Birchmere a couple weeks after Windsor's death. "I was very surprised that we played the gig. I thought for sure that Danny would cancel it."

Then again, Danny had always responded to personal tragedy by playing. Only a few days after the passing of his dear friend—on January 12, 1994—he joined Arlen Roth on NBC-TV's *Late Night with Conan O'Brien*.

They'd planned on doing "Tequila," to which Danny had contributed guitar work for Roth's *Toolin' Around* (1994) album. Roth wasn't concerned about the gig—he could cover the parts himself, if necessary—but he was worried about Danny's state of mind after receiving a phone call at home. "He didn't sound like himself," Roth says. "He sounded unbelievably dark and down, like a whole other person. I remember thinking: no way is he going to make this gig."

But Danny did make the gig, and he appeared "all upbeat, joking around, carrying on," Roth says. "The guys in the band were taken aback by how upbeat he was. I'm thinking to myself, Well, this is Danny the performer." Monterose told Roth, "You're the only the person in the world that Danny would do this for."

During makeup, the two friends sat next to author-columnist Jimmy Breslin, whom Roth didn't recognize "because he looked about 100 years old," he cracks. "Danny's going, 'Make me look better than him.'" That night, Danny played the doubleneck guitar he'd just received from the Fender Custom Shop. Unfortunately, the taping turned out to be an anticlimactic affair, due to a missing channel. Roth didn't realize what had happened until he got home and saw the show, after slogging through a blizzard.

Arlen Roth and Danny at the taping of NBC-TV's Late Night with Conan O'Brien, *January 12, 1994. Roth had hardly gotten home in a driving snowstorm when Danny called to complain about the way his sound had been mixed: "Last time I'll ever play on television!" he growled.*

When he listened to the broadcast, Roth says, "all you heard was leakage instead of Danny's part. The phone rings, and Danny says, 'That's it! Last time I'll ever play on television!'" This was his third time on national TV, Danny groused, and he *still* wasn't getting heard. The issue moved Danny to quip, on his *Strictly Rhythm Guitar* Hot Licks video, "Next time when I'm on Conan, turn me up!" (Roth had the Conan O'Brien footage remixed after Danny's death for release on a Hot Licks video compilation and for the *Masters of the Telecasters* video.)

DANNY SIGNED A THREE-ALBUM deal with the Eastridges' Big Mo label, which would offer him an intimacy unimaginable during the Elektra era. He'd already done a session at Big Mo for *Toolin' Around*, where Roth got a taste of Danny's famed studio endurance. "There wasn't a tired bone in his body," he says. "I was like, 'I want to go to sleep,' and he was just pushin', pushin', pushin' to make sure I left with the right mix. He got more and more into it. That was a side of him I hadn't seen before."

Danny's work on Roth's version of "Tequila" was only a warm-up for what would be his last album, *Relentless*—which many fans consider his finest outing. Gone were any thoughts of meeting listeners halfway with the odd vocal cameo; in its place stood the pure jazz trio of Danny, Previti, and Biery, swapping licks with the B-3 organ of 23-year-old phenomenon Joey DeFrancesco. "It was my idea to do a trio album, but he really warmed to it," Ed Eastridge says.

The match proved inspired on several fronts. Danny already knew of DeFrancesco, and when Eastridge called to confirm the session he learned that the keyboardist's brother was "a huge Danny Gatton fan." Not only that—DeFrancesco shared Danny's fascination with vintage cars (as implied in song titles like "Gearheads").

The album was done in a decidedly un-Gattonesque time span of four days—February 22–25, 1994—which Eastridge attributes to DeFrancesco's influence. "When those two guys met, it was like they'd been playing for 100 years—first take, second take, unbelievable," he says. Previously, Eastridge jokes, the situation would have involved "Take 15" for the basic track and "Take 1,000" for the overdubs. "But Joey says, 'No, man, that's beautiful. It is what it is, leave it alone.' I used to whine, but it was, 'Shut up, roll tape.' He steamrolled me. He was definitely the boss."

Eastridge is especially fond of how the featured players negotiated the angular terrain of Thelonious Monk's "Well You Needn't." "If you like it fast, it doesn't get much faster than that. I don't think anybody's ever played that song that fast." He's also partial to the shuffles like Wayne Shorter's "The Chess Players." For "Broadway," he rolled the tape on a whim while the musicians' photos were being snapped. They tried it again later but couldn't duplicate the freshness and feel, so the first take made the album.

Jazz critic Frank-John Hadley called *Relentless* "natural as daybreak." (The CD booklet reprints the review.) Rarely in '90s jazz had there been a collaboration "that provides listeners with the hair-raising thrill of a roller coaster making a 92-foot drop at 65 mph," Hadley wrote. In Danny's work, "the density of the fleet-fingered playing is balanced by an honest propensity for swinging."

Holloman played his last gig with Danny on July 4, 1994, at New Jersey's Liberty State Park. "It was a really odd bill: we played in the afternoon, then Buddy Miles, and then Kool & the Gang. It was really weird." As much as Holloman had enjoyed playing with Danny, the slowdown in activity made it difficult for him to stay on. "I'm looking at my calendar: 'Oh, we got the month filled—two or three gigs.'" He hooked up with Larry Gatlin, who'd written a play and needed musicians. Ironically, Holloman learned of the opening through Ford; before the play's run ended, they'd both secured jobs at the Gatlins' new theatre in Myrtle Beach, South Carolina.

Typically, when Holloman decided to leave, he couldn't reach Danny immediately. "I'd have to call a dozen times before I'd ever get him, and he didn't have an answering machine," he says. "Half the time, he was there and just didn't pick up." Holloman wound up relaying the message through Biery. "I didn't want to do it that way, but I must have called Danny—I couldn't even tell you how many times."

The Danny Gatton Band worked around Holloman's obligations by playing as a trio. That suited Danny, who'd already begun "talking himself into the idea" of regaining his instrumentalist roots, in Holloman's eyes. "I think he loved that, from a musical standpoint."

That summer, Danny made one of his rare European appearances at the Rhythm & Blues Festival in Peer, Belgium. Ray Charles and Ben Harper were the first night's headliners, on July 16; Danny played the next night, sandwiched among the likes of Robert Junior Lockwood, Rod Piazza & the Mighty Flyers, Al Green, and B.B. King, who closed the show.

Gone was the clean-cut, nattily attired look of *88 Elmira St.*'s publicity photos. In its place was a hefty, shaggy guitarist in the ubiquitous Fender T-shirt, peering intently through dark glasses at the fretboard. Holly wonders if the physical transformation reflected something more than a lifetime of poor eating and sleeping habits. "He really started to look sick after Billy died, to look physically ill in his face and his eyes," she says. "His hair went really gray. He didn't look good. I don't know if there was something there that they didn't find."

October 4 &
The Aftermath
(1994–1995)

*A*lthough Danny's commercial track record had been spotty, his future looked brighter than ever. On the Big Mo label, he wouldn't have to worry about fitting a demographic—he could just be himself.

In February 1994, Danny reaffirmed his stance to the *Maryland Independent*'s James Hettinger. Asked why he didn't think a hit record would happen for him, Danny responded: "Just because I don't fit the norm in any way—physically, mentally, musically, attitudinally, I just do not. Never have, never will." A more succinct expression of Danny's philosophy would be hard to find, and he continued to live up to it. The man who'd played the Montreux Jazz Festival could be found "sitting in with singer-songwriter Steve Erwin at a small room in Glen Echo Park, playing world-class guitar for about 75 people," Hettinger marveled.

On the surface, Danny appeared unruffled by the "big fish returns to small pond" angle often used to describe his latest turn of fortune. "I'm as successful as I want to be," he declared to Hettinger. "If I was a failure, I'd be on welfare. I've got my little spot out in the sun. I get to do what I want to do."

Jack Jensen reveals how attached Danny was to that "little spot out in the sun," telling a story about how Danny had turned his back on a possible gig with the *David Letterman* TV show. When Letterman jumped from NBC to CBS, Danny was mentioned as a possibility for the expanded band. The connection was through keyboardist and musical director Paul Shaffer, who loved Danny's style and had played with him on Cindy Bullens's *Desire Wire*. Apparently, Danny decided he wasn't interested in the gig. (The story is unconfirmed, but there's no doubt that Shaffer was a fan.)

There was no place like home, as Billy Windsor's passing had so eloquently reminded him. Losing his best friend since the age of 14 "really pulled the rug out from under me in a lot of ways," Danny told Hettinger, but he was doing his best to move ahead: an album of Windsor vocal songs was due, he promised.

Jensen stands virtually alone in insisting that the impact of Windsor's death has been overstated. "People want to make more of it than it was," he says. "He missed him, he grieved over it, but I don't think it was a personal turning point." Bobby Jones also says he observed no outward changes in Danny's demeanor, though he's reluctant to use that as a measuring stick. "I think there probably was lot of feelings held inside with that, so that had to have some negative impact on him."

The number of projects on the table promised to keep Danny busy for a long time. An album with R&B keyboardist Tommy Lepson and a proposed "Lost Highways" tour with Arlen Roth loomed largest on the priority list. He and Ed Eastridge were also branching into co-production, having worked up demos for Robert Gordon's sister, Jackie, and country vocalist Mary Ann Redman. Although neither project got picked up, Danny had no shortage of potential collaborators, with Kentucky guitarist Scotty Anderson another promising candidate.

Locally, Danny's reputation remained unassailable. The 30 Wammies he'd taken home since the mid-'80s were one sign of his prominence, and he remained a top club draw. There was interest outside the area, too; Danny had agreed to do an Arizona wedding gig for $8,000 on October 22, according to the *Washington Post*. Only a couple of weeks before he died, Danny had even talked of hitting the road "with the clubs that treated us good and paid us right," Brent says. "We were thinking about doing that. Needless to say, that never came to be."

Work continued fitfully on the addition to Danny's Newburg home, which had taken on the dimensions of an epic project eight years after its beginning. "He loved that 14 acres—it was all flat and beautiful," says Jan. "But the farmhouse was a mess." Not that Jan could do much about it: the carpenter and his son didn't come every day, and Danny wasn't always around to supervise.

Jones found the addition a source of amusement, because it was "castle-like"—almost as large as the house. He recalls Danny being scared that everything would fall down before the work ended. "We had a lot of thunderstorms that summer," he says. "I remember how relieved he was when he got it under one roof. The inside wasn't finished yet, but now it wouldn't blow over."

The four garage bays remained as busy as ever, with Brent often joining his brother. Holly didn't welcome this development, which came after Brent's divorce from his first wife. "Dad and grandma sunk all this money into the garage, to put this addition on. Brent would come and be crying in his beer, and they'd sit out there drinking together, not doing anything productive. I think it was distracting and depressing to have this guy moping around."

Her father had begun spending more and more time in the garage, Holly says, often not eating dinner until midnight. "He'd just eat food out of the pan, wouldn't bother to put it on plates or anything." She also noticed that he was drinking a 12-pack of beer a day "and maybe a couple more on top of that. He had always liked to drink beer, but it wasn't like that. Even when he would drink that much, he didn't act drunk. It was just like water to him. It just took the edge off, I guess."

She also found him extremely controlling. "He listened in on my phone conversations a couple times, and caught me saying things he didn't want to hear his 14-year-old daughter saying. It was just stupid stuff, but I felt like there was a complete invasion of what little privacy I did have. He was just trying to protect me, but he was going about it all the wrong way."

Holly says that for the last few months of her father's life it was "like living with a ghost." And tension was running high. "We were fighting a lot more. It was painful: I didn't want us to be like that. You know how it is when you have hormones, but he just didn't seem to understand. I had these mood swings, and he didn't get it, and we'd just end up blowing up."

Things grew more tense on the celebration of Danny's 49th—and final—birthday on September 4. "We had to go out there and practically drag him in to open his presents," Jan says. "He opened two and went back out: 'I'll come in later.' I said, 'Yeah, but we've got a really big surprise for you, and you've got to come in soon.'"

Knowing how much Danny loved raccoons, Jan and Holly had gotten him a baby ferret. "Finally, he came in—and he was really sad," Jan recalls. "He said, 'You didn't buy this for me.' I said, 'Yes, I did.' He said, 'No, you bought this for Holly.'" The next day, Danny wanted to get rid of the ferret, "because it gets into everything," Jan remembers him saying. "I said, 'Dan, your raccoons destroyed the house! It doesn't matter.'" In the end, Danny decided to keep the animal after it began sleeping on his chest.

Billy Poore witnessed none of these moods when he saw Danny for the last time on September 8. Poore brought his friend Marge Coffy, whose husband had booked Danny in 1972–73 at the Back Alley Lounge in Glenburnie, Maryland. Poore wanted Danny to provide a foreword for his book *Rockabilly: A Forty-Year Journey*, which they'd pull together by recording some of Danny's thoughts and stories onto a cassette. It would be the final music-related project that Danny would complete during his lifetime.

The conversation took a freewheeling tack as the trio laughed, talked, and drank beer from 5:30 to 11 P.M. "He was in good spirits, sitting on that old 1930s pickup truck he was working on," Poore says. "He was all by himself. I thought back after he died—all the friends he had, and he didn't have nobody there with him." Danny seemed a little more reflective than usual, and they agreed that people cared more about each other in the '50s. "Danny was really into nostalgia," Poore says. "Simple things pleased him."

The conversation took a strange turn when they discussed Danny's admiration of '50s guitarists like Scotty Moore, James Burton, and Gene Vincent's ace, Cliff Gallup. "Yeah, what they did what was great, but I just think they should have thought to take it farther," Poore recalls Danny saying. Such a premise seemed impossible to fathom, even for a rock 'n' roll diehard like Poore. "I said, 'Danny, these guys were in their early twenties, and they didn't know what they were doing! They were inventin' this stuff!' I very rarely would jump up like that."

Danny persisted: "I guess you got a point, but I would have thought of it." Poore wasn't having any of it. "I said, 'No, you wouldn't have thought of it, either. You always have to get something from somewhere, too.'"

The subject dropped, they listened to some tapes that Poore had made in the early '90s, which prompted Danny to remark: "Man, all the money you wasted on Seaton, LesLee, and all them other artists—you should have spent it on yourself. You sound as good as they do on that [rockabilly] stuff."

Knowing how much Danny loved his guitar work on "Runnin' Wild," Poore was willing to let him have the track—if they could record some rockabilly covers and originals together. "He said, 'I just want to get that track back, so my mother can put out the best stuff I've cut for other people.'" All Danny had to do was pick up the expenses. "It's not just that we could have fun in the studio," Poore says. "He was going to get that track back, and get it back for nothing. It was nothin' for him to find a studio and pull out three or four guys to back me up as a singer. I would just pick obscure rock 'n' roll songs that he knew, and the other guys would pick right up on it." They tentatively planned on beginning in January 1995.

The next night, Danny played one of his favorite venues, the Birchmere; a recording of the evening became the posthumous *In Concert 9/9/94* disc on Big Mo (which this author reviewed in *DISCoveries*, October 1998 issue). As ever, the listener's ride was exhilarating and demanding. The band began with a driving, rock-accented exploration of Sonny Rollins's "Sunnymoon for Two," then nodded to the *Redneck Jazz* era with "Land of Make Believe," capped by a truly tribal drum solo from Biery.

Danny in Washington, D.C., 1994.

Danny stretched out farther still on a glistening, 16-minute "Blues Newburg" that bore little relation to its *88 Elmira St.* cousin. His double-neck guitar allowed him to bolster whatever Previti did while making melodic statements. Small wonder that Danny informed the crowd, "I think 'Free-for-all' is a pretty good name, because that's what we do here." Indeed: Previti got plenty of finger-popping room on Duke Ellington's "Caravan," while Biery carried his thunder on a fiery "Apache/Surf Medley." They closed with the inevitable coupling of "Linus and Lucy" and Danny's hundred-mile-per-hour showcase, "Orange Blossom Special."

Nobody found the gig particularly special, and it wasn't being considered for release in Danny's lifetime. "None of us thought we could hit our asses with our hands that night," Previti says. "I just felt like I was ruining everything." Having seen the new trio several times, Elliott agreed, although for other reasons. "It was too distracting, too busy. Danny played so much, he didn't need a drummer like that. You couldn't even pay attention to Danny, 'cause Tim was phenomenal."

Phil Zavarella saw Danny for the last time on the weekend before his death. They'd gone separately to a major car show in Carlisle, Pennsylvania, an event that had long occupied a prominent spot on Danny's calendar. "He would go every year with Jack Jensen, and they would stay there for the [entire] four days," Phil says. "I went only for one day."

The show itself went fine, and Danny returned "loaded with pieces of rust to put in his garage to look at," Phil jokes. Eastridge had also seen Danny in Carlisle. "I wanted his input on things, but he was a Ford guy and I was more interested in the Chevys and Mopars."

Jensen doesn't recall anything unusual about Danny's manner. "Believe me, I have searched for some kind of clue—nothing." Danny spent $1,600 on parts for his panel truck and '32 Ford, which led Jensen to say to him: "'I'll give you till Friday till you ask to borrow a couple hundred bucks.' 'Ah, bullshit!' Well, it wasn't Friday at noon, it was Friday at 2 P.M.!"

Back home, however, Jan found her husband's behavior increasingly disquieting. "Those last two days before he died, there was something very wrong, because he was just not reachable—he was just not Dan," she says. "He was making demands that didn't make any sense. He asked me to quit my job and become his manager." Jan didn't see quitting as an option, because she doubted the family finances could absorb the impact. Danny had just laid away for a $12,000 custom guitar and bought a new Ford cube van, she said.

Danny had also paid $10,000 for an antique car, as well as the $1,600 for the parts being shipped from Carlisle. Although the Elektra era had definitely improved Danny's earning power, something else struck Jan: what would happen if he couldn't play anymore? She found Danny's reaction utterly out of character, to say the least. "He was so angry that I wouldn't agree [to being his manager], it was scary. I couldn't do that. Then he got his car keys and left."

The subject flared up once more the next night, when Jan complained of feeling tired. "He got in a rage again: 'I told you to quit!'" she recalls. "He was off again on this tangent. I knew it was abnormal, but I just thought he was tired, very tired, and the third night..." Her voice trails off, and it doesn't take much imagination to tell where her memories are headed before she picks up her train of thought. "Of course, in retrospect, I thought, Oh God, I should have quit. I should have said yes—but I didn't know."

DANNY SPENT HIS LAST DAY—Tuesday, October 4—in the garage, where he and Brent worked on restoring the 1934 Ford that had figured so prominently in the Jensen trade and was valued at about $18,000.

According to Brent, he and Danny had interrupted their restoration work only to buy a 12-pack of beer between 3:30 and 4 P.M. He noticed nothing unusual, "except that he'd had an argument with Jan the night before. She normally stopped at the garage before going to the house [after work]. She'd sit there and smoke a cigarette, sometimes she'd drink a beer. But she would always stop. That day, she went right to the house—and that's when he told me about having a fight." From what Brent gathered, their argument had been about her job. "She was always bitching about her working conditions, and he'd get really upset about it—he couldn't do nothing about it."

Jensen was headed to Hershey, Pennsylvania, that day, but he had planned to get together with Danny before he left. However, Danny called between 4 and 4:30 P.M. to change their plans: could they meet later, he asked, so he didn't have to leave his restoration efforts behind just yet? "Sure, that's not a problem," Jensen said. Danny also asked him to pick up a 16-inch Kelsey wheel, if he saw one, to complete a set. They planned to get together after Jensen's return on the following Monday or Tuesday.

Brent would later tell police that he didn't detect anything amiss when he left the farm at about 6 P.M. Neither did John Previti, who talked to Danny on the phone at about 7 P.M. The conversation didn't seem unusual, though Danny voiced concern about some financial issues, the bassist said.

Holly was involved in planning homecoming activities at La Plata High School, which were set for the end of October; she had to attend a float-building meeting at 6 P.M. Unfortunately, Danny was too drunk to drive her there, so the chore fell to Jan, who'd been on her feet since 3 A.M. that morning. Jan got home around six o'clock and cooked pot roast, mashed potatoes, and peas. "Mom always managed to put together these awesome meals," Holly says. "She didn't just bring home pizza."

The logistics required Jan to immediately turn around and drive back to La Plata. "He was feeling really bad about that," Holly says, "and I don't know what happened during that period when I wasn't home. When we came in, he was eating dinner, but he was in a real bad mood." Mindful of the tension, mother and daughter tried to walk past Danny, since they "didn't want to upset the beast," Holly says. "It had always worked before when he was in a snit, but not this time. He said, 'What, you're not going to speak to me?'"

Holly had never seen her father behave this way. "There was something really wrong. He never directed his anger at us like that," she says. They tried to talk, but their attempt to be reasonable appeared to have the opposite effect. Jan watched as Danny tossed his dinner into the sink, breaking the plate. "Something had just snapped," she says. "It wasn't that we didn't speak, as Holly said; it was that *he* didn't speak. Then he took a swig of milk and stormed out of the house."

"I was so afraid—I thought he was going to do something," Holly says. "I knew he had the gun, and when he got angry I knew something was really wrong." She felt frightened enough of her father's temper to take a knife with her into the shower. Jan also found a temporary refuge from the night's pressures by taking a bath. But Danny still hadn't returned by the time mother and daughter had gotten ready for the night, so Jan called Brent. "I said, 'Did anything happen today? Was he angry? There's something wrong.' That's when I told Brent, 'I'll go try to find him.'"

Jan was uneasy, and her anxiety increased with every passing moment. "I was thinking, There's something very seriously wrong here. I don't know what it is, but it's scary. The door was locked. I knew where the key was, so he must have locked it from the inside." Jan found the key, opened the door, and walked into the darkened garage. She called out to Danny, but got no answer. "Then I walked around. He had his bench light on, and I saw him, and just ran out, calling for Holly."

Sometime after 9 P.M., Danny had left the house, saying, "I can't take this anymore," the *Post* reported. He entered the garage carrying a .22-caliber rifle, which he mounted in a vise on his workbench. The police received the first call at 9:30 P.M., and an emergency medical team responded. At 9:41 P.M., they pronounced Danny dead of a single gunshot wound to the head.

The next call to Brent was shorter than the first. "She called me, absolutely hysterical, so I came back and spent the night there," he says. Before leaving, he called Jack Jensen. "I can recall it like yesterday," Jensen says. "He said, 'Danny killed himself.' I said, 'Jesus!' And it went from there."

"We knew something was wrong," Holly says. "She went out there, found him, and came back in the house. She kind of crumpled and started bawling and moaning like a banshee." Her voice breaks; she pauses and then resumes her account. "She was just like a blob on the floor. All she could do was cry and kick and wail."

Holly gathered her wits and called the rescue squad. "It seemed like that conversation took so long, to get these people to understand what had happened. I guess I didn't say he committed suicide; I said he shot himself. 'Is he still alive?' 'I don't know, I didn't see him.'"

Jan furiously chain-smoked while the sheriff's deputies fanned out to investigate. "I can remember looking out the window and seeing the police taking their pictures, putting up crime-scene tape," Holly says. "[My mother] was pretty much like a vegetable. She wasn't making any sense."

Holly had lost her father just three weeks before her 15th birthday. A major force in her life had been violently ripped away, along with the family's veneer of normality; in its place came the cacophony of ambulance and police sirens, followed by curious neighbors and onlookers. Danny hadn't reached out for help this time, and his wife hadn't been able to pull the gun from his hand.

"That night, I ran outside—my hair was still wet from the shower," Holly says. "I just ran out there and screamed as loud as I possibly could, at God, at everything. I was so angry and so hurt. I just felt betrayed."

Ernie Gorospe was among the first people to arrive, as was 20-year family friend and local TV newscaster Doug McKelway. "Jan's sitting in the living room in tears—it was kind of an unusual situation," Ernie says. He found himself pressed into service as gatekeeper for the TV crews descending on Lloyd Point Road. "The first thing Jan said was, 'I don't want to talk to anybody. I don't want any of these people in here.' A couple of TV people came right up to the door. I went up to Channel Eight and said, 'Jan doesn't want any media on her property.'" If they wanted to take anybody's picture or get any comments, they'd have to go across the road, Ernie told the camera crew, who complied.

Jensen came over the next morning with a bag of groceries. Jan greeted him by coming out of the house, squeezing him vigorously, and saying: "Jack, we know you can fix anything. Bring him back." Jensen felt too overwhelmed to speak. "It was devastating to be confronted by that," he says.

DANNY'S DEATH WAS RULED a suicide after an autopsy on Wednesday, October 5, 1994. The official findings lent a hollow ring of finality to the story of the man acclaimed as "The World's Greatest Unknown Guitar Player." The suddenness of Danny's death hasn't stopped his family and friends from revisiting their last conversations or dealings with him, as if they'd find the one moment that might explain the whole tragedy.

For Danny's family, the most painful aspect of his death meant having to grieve amid speculation over his potential motives. "It was awful, because of his notoriety," Holly says. One classmate had a thoughtless reaction to the cancellation of Danny's planned La Plata homecoming gig. "'Oh great, now the main act is dead, who are they going to get now?' Needless to say, it wasn't funny. Again, it wasn't 'the world-class guitarist' who was dead. It was my father."

Jan was particularly enraged by a *Washington Times* story containing most of the same details as the *Post* account, with one key variation: an anonymous source claiming that the final events gathered speed after an argument over money. The unnamed source further claimed that Danny slapped Jan and threw some dishes into the sink, saying he wanted to shoot himself.

"The police in La Plata called me and apologized," Jan says. "I didn't know what they were apologizing for, and then I found out, in the *Times*, they said that he slapped me. I was pretty angry."

ALTHOUGH SHE COULDN'T PROVE it, Jan suspected one of the rescue squad's members of feeding that tidbit to the *Times*, which she made abundantly clear in a phone call several days later. "I was so furious: 'You know what? I was just sitting down here writing a check, but I read what was reported in the *Times* and I'm tearing it up right now.'"

Evan Johns believes that Danny's final desperate actions suggested an underlying problem. "Now that might sound to somebody else like he was having a bad day," he says, "but it was clear as hell to me when I ran around with Danny back in the '70s and early '80s there were a lot of 'bad days' back then. Every night he would walk off the stage, and at least one person—even if there was only six people there—would say, 'Danny, you're the greatest.' And then he would go home and be the guy who couldn't keep a job."

There was no easy explanation for anyone, least of all for his mother. "It was a real shock. I can't believe he did it," Norma says. She wonders if the pressures of maintaining the Lloyd Point Road Farm had anything to do with her son's death. "When he bought that place, it was a non-working farm that had these trashy little buildings all over it. He spent months with a tractor, pulling those buildings down, cleaning up the place as hard as he could. He worked his tail off."

Charles County Sheriff Jim Gartland had shared Danny's automotive passions for 20 years, and he was as bewildered as everyone else. He'd chatted with Danny just weeks before his death, but he had detected "no hint of any problems," Gartland told the *Independent*. Neither had booking agent Patrick Day, who'd talked to Danny no less than five times on October 4.

Dave Elliott saw Danny only two days before his death. "I was down at his house—just to sit around and shoot the shit—and it was no different than any other time," he says. "We had a great time, and everything was fine."

A phone call from Previti shattered the drummer's world at about 7 A.M. on the morning after Danny's death. "Within the hour, Channel Four [from Washington] called. It was just one of those numb feelings," Elliott says. He ended up doing an interview in the front yard of his Virginia home.

Ed Eastridge learned about Danny's death while waiting to take his son's second-grade class on a field trip. He stepped back into his home where his wife, Dixie, was on the phone with Norma. She was visibly upset, so he asked what had happened. Dixie responded by scribbling on a pad: "Danny shot himself." Dead? Dixie nodded. "I think he was just in a blind fury," Ed says of Danny's final night. "I was as close to him as anybody— you'd think I would have noticed. I think you have to have some sort of depression to take your own life."

Guilt led Eastridge to speculate for months about what might have happened if he and Dixie had remained in the D.C. area, though that hadn't apparently been an issue with Danny. He'd been planning to work as hard as ever at Timm Biery's Laurel, Maryland, studio, Eastridge says. Yet his knowledge couldn't prevent the emotional side from surfacing. "Maybe if I'd been there, it would have been different, because I think he felt deserted by everybody. Billy had died; I had left."

Roger McDuffie felt likewise; he hadn't seen Danny since Christmas 1993, when they'd bumped into each other at the mall. They'd discussed the idea of Roger writing some original songs, but he'd been too busy. "I didn't know Danny had a gun," he says. "I just wish I'd stormed up the day before with a case of beer and a handful of crabs—it would have changed the whole thing."

Steve Wolf was recording an album with his jazz band Swing Speak, which also included ex-Funhouse members Barry Hart and Bruce Swaim. Danny had discussed sitting in with them. "I have regrets that I didn't play with Danny in those [earlier] years now, because I'll never have the chance again."

Billy Poore had no idea anything was amiss until Marge Coffy called and began their conversation by asking if he was sitting down. "I was totally shocked. I couldn't write the book—I couldn't get it off my mind. My wife said, 'Danny was always the sensible one.' It didn't make sense."

Phil Zavarella wasn't surprised to get the news from Paul Tester (who would die himself of a heart attack that year). His immediate reaction was: "He never got to finish his '32 Ford," followed by, "What a waste." "I wasn't bereaved or went into any great mourning or anything like that," Phil says. "I thought of the 'relief' word for him, because of the turmoil he had to suffer his whole life—that curse, that artist mentality."

Robbie Weaver had been on federal business in New Mexico when he called Zavarella. Weaver says he felt "absolutely shattered," angry that "killing himself was higher on the list than calling me. I suppose, to some small degree, I'm still mad at him for that."

Steve Gorospe had seen Danny only a few days earlier at a nostalgic car race in Colonial Beach, Virginia. "That day, he just seemed like a kid in a candy store with all the street rods," he says. "I didn't actually quite believe it until a friend of mine said, 'Listen to this radio report.' That's when I realized it was the real deal."

Bobby Hancock last saw Danny when he and his wife, Liz, returned to Maryland for her 30th high school reunion. Danny signed an *88 Elmira St.* promotional poster for him. The message read: "Bobby, who'd ever have thought we'd have got this old? Your old pal, Danny Gatton." "I put it away, but Liz got it out and had it mounted for me," Bobby says. "When Danny died, it ripped my guts out. I couldn't look at it." He's put away the poster, and can hardly talk about what happened. "It's like I'm still in denial, like I can call him up and say, 'Okay, Danny, enough is enough.' I know that can't happen, but I still can't believe he's not there."

Now settled in Holland, Liz Meyer had last seen Danny between trips to Nashville and Washington. She'd caught him at the Birchmere in May. "They were doing all this shtick, and Danny was clearly very unhappy and bored. We visited backstage—had a nice visit and hung out for a couple of hours. It was good." They last spoke about three weeks before his death, to straighten out various credits for Meyer's solo album, where Danny had done a little picking.

"I phoned to ask what his label was, so I could get the album cover ready," she says. "And he said, 'Oh, I was just over there a few weeks ago.' I was so annoyed, because Belgium is three hours from Holland, but he had no sense of geography. He didn't know if he was 12 hours away or next door." (Danny had been referring to his appearance at the Peer Festival.)

After Gatton's death, Meyer recalled another conversation that she and Danny had had during their session. She'd compiled a tape of Danny's better live moments for a friend of fiddler Byron Berline—who insisted on getting his own copy. Thinking it might help Danny's reputation, Meyer made him the tape. "Danny said to me, 'You know, I'm still mad at you for making those tapes,'" Meyer says. "I said, 'Why? I thought it would be good for you.' He said, 'All those L.A. guitar players just copped my licks, and I don't have any new ones.' I thought, What a sad and telling remark—that he thought of himself as a bag of licks." But Meyer could also see why Danny felt that way. "A few months before he died, he was doing exactly the same thing [as] when I met him," she says.

Shannon Ford and Bill Holloman had just started working with the Gatlin Brothers at Myrtle Beach when a friend called them to the phone. Ford felt "completely numb, because of everybody in my life that I'd ever known, he was way at the bottom of the list for somebody that would do something like that." (Both missed Danny's funeral, because they'd just started working at Myrtle Beach and couldn't get substitutes on such short notice.)

Ford had last seen Danny with his new rhythm section at Tramps, and he was glad to see their friendship had survived whatever disagreements they'd had in the past. "He was doing the thing he always wanted to do, the jam thing from song to song. He seemed very happy doing that. I went backstage afterwards, and I'll never forget this—the last thing I said to him, right as we got through talking backstage, was: 'You sucked.'"

It was an in-joke they'd often shared, Ford says. "We'd get off a burning set, and we both knew we'd played our asses off. 'Man, you sucked.' And that's the last thing I said to him. It's strange, but I totally knew that he knew what I meant."

Holloman remembers another expression Danny would use after they'd finished a take: "That was almost good." It was usually said with a smile, but it reflected his uneasiness about his art. Like other people who'd known Danny well, Holloman sometimes sensed a nagging ambivalence outweighing the gleam in the eye. Being "The World's Greatest Unknown Guitar Player" might have been enjoyable at the NAMM show; otherwise, "he didn't want to have to play like that, go out and tour, all that kind of stuff you're supposed to do. It made him fairly miserable. You never got any feeling like, Boy, he really loves this."

Howard Thompson felt "gutted" on hearing the news. He wasn't invited to the service, because he realized how some people felt about the Elektra era, "so my being there would have been uncomfortable to the family or friends," he says. "I respect that, though I don't necessarily think the premise is true. I think he probably had gotten over the Elektra thing by that time." (Jan doesn't recall meeting Thompson, but she did receive a check and "this really sweet note" from him after Danny died.)

Pete Kennedy had seen little of Danny since the early '80s. He'd spent the decade leading his own roots-style band, Good Rockin' Tonight, which drew inspiration from Billy Hancock's work in that genre. Kennedy heard the news from Bias Recorders engineer Jim Robeson. Although Danny had been working at Big Mo, "he'd done a lot of work at Bias, too, and they found out about it right away. I was completely in shock."

Tom Principato was in Austin when one of his old bandmates called early in the morning. "It was really a stunning surprise." He felt helpless thinking about the events leading up to Danny's demise, which the media accounts that filtered down to Austin did little to illuminate. Neither did the bits and pieces that came in from various people who called afterwards. "Evan Johns called me in Austin, and he was really, really upset. There were a lot of rumors about Danny's personal life—none of them turned out to be true, really."

DANNY'S FRIENDS AND FANS said their goodbyes on Saturday, October 8, in Waldorf. A staggering number of people showed up, ranging from inner-circle stalwarts like Elliott, Monterose, and Previti to local fans and musicians who just wanted a chance to salute the person who'd fired up their imaginations.

A large photo greeted guests as they arrived, because Danny had been cremated. The funeral director said it was the second-largest service that he'd ever handled; extra rooms with a video feed had to be opened to accommodate everyone. Jan could barely speak or stand, leaving Holly to receive people as they came in. "As soon as she walked in there and saw the framed picture, she fell to her knees and started bawling and sobbing again," Holly says. "That was the only point at which I almost lost it. Watching her in that kind of pain—it was just crushing. I felt that to my core."

Holly has few memories of the service. "It's like I wasn't there," she says. "It was really hard, but it was obvious how many people's lives he'd touched. When I saw the flowers from the Gin Blossoms, I was like, 'What the hell?' Just one of those shocking things that I wasn't used to seeing."

Another emotional incident involved Ellis Duncan, who was escorted off the premises. Although he was scarred from the experience of working with Danny, nobody had ever questioned his dedication, least of all Jan. "I thought Ellis was so much in his corner—would have done it for nothing," she says. "That's my impression. As a matter of fact, he did do it for nothing, pretty much."

Jan did her best to make amends after she heard what had happened, but she wasn't able to reach Duncan, whose phone number had changed. "I was so angry about that—that somebody had gone up and escorted him out," she says. "I was just furious. I thought that was so tasteless. I don't think Dan would have liked it, either."

Joe Kogok found the funeral an amazing experience. "It was mobbed," he says. "When I got there, there were already lines that were [extending] way outside. Had somebody not let me in the line, I wouldn't have gotten inside in time."

Spike Ostmann says he had to wonder what had brought his friend to such a pass. "I'd have thought that if Danny was despondent and got down—and Billy Hancock said this, too—for his daughter's sake, he'd stick around." Then again, maybe Danny had just endured too many disappointments. As he had once said to Ostmann: "You're either a king or a bum in the music business."

Phil Zavarella says he spoke briefly to Jan at the service. "We had just made amends. She liked me off and on, because I would always go off: 'Gatton, you're not making any money,' and how she needed to make him get a job, or do something, instead of her carrying the whole load." At the same time, "she always saw me as somebody that took him away from the house when he was off. When he didn't have a gig, he'd call me: 'Let's go drinking' or 'Let's go eat crabs.' That's what we did. I left my wife and kids at home, too, which wasn't cool. But when you're that age, you don't think like that."

Some of the most unexpected gestures came from musicians outside of Danny's circle, like the Gin Blossoms, one of Holly's favorite bands. Fabulous Thunderbirds singer-guitarist Jimmie Vaughan sent $5,000 to help with Holly's college expenses, which reminded Jan of the time that Jimmie and his late brother Stevie Ray had seen Danny, but left before the set finished. "Danny said, 'They didn't like it. They didn't like my playing.' And I said, 'Gosh, how do you know that? Maybe they had to leave—it was great that they came to see you.' I thought, He wouldn't have sent the money if there hadn't been something there."

Arlen Roth had mixed reactions, since he didn't get to give a eulogy. "He had some connection to everybody down there, in a very big way. It was amazing," he says. "But if anybody knew him from the most angles, it would be me, from a professional and friendship standpoint. I didn't know who decided. I couldn't even get to talk to the right person. I felt so frustrated."

Some people avoided the funeral, such as Poore, who felt the event would be "a circus of people that wanted to get on television. I just knew it was going to be: 'Aw, I was his best friend.' Pete Kennedy also passed, preferring to keep his memories of playing live with Danny, "and he was happy-go-lucky at the gigs," he says. "I think he always saw himself as a misfit who wasn't cool, and that was fine with him. He was very comfortable with that. He didn't want people to pressure him." Bill Kirchen had to get another drummer for a wedding gig that he'd booked, because Elliott was going. "I wouldn't have canceled somebody's wedding for his funeral. I don't think he would have wanted me to do that," Kirchen says.

After the funeral, "everybody just disappeared," Holly says. "There was this initial flood of people contacting us, but it dropped off really quickly. I think they just felt strange. Nobody really knew what to say."

Peace proved to be an elusive proposition at Christmas time. Not wishing to stay on the farm where they'd lost Danny, Holly and Jan opted to spend the holiday in Ocean City, Maryland. "I remember watching MTV, and they were doing a little memorial for everybody that died that year—even then, I couldn't get away from it!" Holly says. "I started cursing a lot more after he died, and Mom let me. I felt like I deserved it. I was so angry."

DANNY'S ABRUPT EXIT LEFT a plethora of unanswered questions for those he left behind. What factor had been most responsible? Could anyone have foreseen what would happen? Could a taste of the mainstream success that eluded Danny throughout his lifetime have forestalled such an ending, or did his mood swings push him beyond the point of no return?

One theory that gained credence after Danny's death was a possibility that he'd suffered so-called "mini-strokes" during his final months of life, which may have affected his playing ability. Previti mentioned such a theory when interviewed for this author's April 1999 *Vintage Guitar* article. It also makes sense to Eastridge, who says, "He definitely had physical problems that could have had a lot to do with it."

Stories have surfaced of such problems being apparent at the Bayou, where Danny played one of his final gigs and allegedly had trouble getting through the performance. Neither Jan, Holly, nor Eastridge can vouch for the account—because they weren't there—but all say that disquieting signals of ill health had been evident before his death.

There had been an especially scary episode earlier that year, recalls Jan, which struck Danny in the garage. "He came inside in a hurry and described to me what had happened. The first word that came into my mind was 'stroke,'" she says. Danny had been complaining of one arm "falling asleep" and tingling, Jan says. (She doesn't recall which arm; Holly says it was the left.) For that reason, Jan insisted that Danny visit their doctor in La Plata, but she heard nothing more.

After Danny's death, she went to the doctor to find out what they'd actually discussed. "I said, 'Well, Dan had what I thought was a stroke. He came to you, and you didn't recommend anything. He said [that] you said everything was fine.' The doctor said, 'Dan never told me that. I don't have anything here.' I said, 'What did he talk to you about?' He said, 'We talked about music.'" (According to Eastridge, "[The doctor] said that Danny hadn't mentioned anything about his hand being numb. He just wanted a checkup.")

Holly didn't hear about the spring episode until much later, perhaps because Danny didn't want to frighten her. "I just remember hearing that his arm felt kind of weird—it didn't feel right. He kept talking more and more about how he was playing like shit, and he couldn't control [his playing]." Holly agrees with her mother that Danny would never have tolerated such a direct threat to his well-being. "He always talked about how, if he couldn't have a full life, he didn't want to live."

Others say the numbness is just a condition peculiar to guitar players. Billy Hancock suffers from a similar ailment, and Ed Eastridge says he notices similar problems whenever he plays classical guitar. "Your hand is up in the air, so the blood tends to run out of it, especially in the morning. I have to stop and shake my hand."

Poore takes no stock in the stroke theory. "I heard this much later, afterwards. It sounded like a belated 'take the blame off what the real reason might have been' or steer it away from that. I saw no sign of mini-strokes, no sign that Danny had any bad health."

Obviously, such questions cannot be answered without the benefit of an autopsy, and they would have fallen outside the scope of its main purpose: establishing the cause of Danny's death. Once the police had answered that question, all others—including the role that poor health may have played in his decision to shoot himself—would have fallen by the wayside.

Some speculate that the lost Elektra deal had tipped the balance against life. Pete Kennedy has no time for that notion; Danny was simply too suspicious of the music industry to imagine a record deal as the ticket to solving all of his problems, he believes. "Record deals meant nothing to Danny. It was to get to some money, but it wasn't a life-or-death thing at all." Elliott agrees. "The music business didn't have anything to do with what he did. I'm sure he was suffering from clinical depression, and he just didn't address it." Principato sensed a deep skepticism in Danny about his chances for greater recognition, even when he tried to meet the industry halfway during the Elektra era: "After some of the realities of the times and the business set in, I wouldn't be surprised if he was saying, 'Oh shit, I can never do this.'"

The effects of Danny's long-standing depression cannot be overestimated, especially when coupled with his sensitive streak. "Nobody ever knew that Danny was 'fragile: handle with care,'" Jan says. "Holly and I are the only ones who heard and saw those kinds of dark, lonely times that he had, in the valleys of depression."

The emotional ups and downs could be triggered by the most trivial matters, as seen by his reaction to the comment about wearing a clown suit—or being called "Pops." "Maybe he was feeling his age," Jan says. "We never talked about his retirement. I don't recall a time when he wasn't really active, some way or another."

Whenever Danny suffered one of his depressive episodes, "they would last a pretty good long time," Jerry Wallmark says. That's what made the support of old buddies like Billy Windsor so important; "if he got among a bunch of strangers, he felt very uncomfortable," the former Offbeats drummer adds. "He always had to have somebody that knew him—that touch of home. Then he felt better about himself and better about life." John Broaddus agrees: "No matter what happened that day, that wouldn't have happened if [Windsor] was alive."

The notion of seeing a psychiatrist would have sounded absurd to someone who wouldn't even take a stress test, Holly believes. "He wasn't that kind of person. He'd probably jump down your throat and tell you, *you* had a problem, not him. He just wasn't the kind of person that would seek help."

Neither was Roy Buchanan, who died under mysterious circumstances in a Virginia jail cell in 1988. Although the official ruling of suicide by hanging remains hotly disputed, numerous associates interviewed for this book have no doubt that Danny was deeply affected by the death of the man considered his crosstown rival. "I'm surprised how [much] to heart Danny took that," Elliott says. "The last time Roy played with us, he got mad at Danny and walked offstage. They were trading fours, and he thought that Danny was trying to outplay him. But he was really upset that Roy would take his own life. He said, 'That's the worst thing you can do.'"

The irony of those words isn't lost on Holly. "That's what he said, but sometimes, I think he felt he deserved that. He would beat himself up, just being so self-deprecating."

Was Danny's action impulsive or premeditated? Holloman remains unsure, having fielded that question many times over the years. "My favorite is: 'Did you know he was going to do it?' I feel like saying, 'Yeah, I just thought it would be a Wednesday instead of a Tuesday.' No, I didn't know he was going to do it!" His mind circles back to the rifle set up on the workbench. "It was more than just having picked up the gun on a moment's notice and put it to his head. I remember thinking at the time, Well, that's more than just going over the edge."

In the end, Holly believes that no single factor was responsible for the tragedy of October 4—although she and her mother experienced a jolt after seeing a phrase scrawled on the garage's door jamb in Magic Marker: "THE BEGINNING OF GONE." Anyone passing through the garage would have had to crane upward to see the words, which assumed ominous significance to Jan and Holly—until the carpenter who pointed them out said they had been there for months.

"He never said anything like that, but that's a pretty weird thing to find on the door, huh?" Holly says. "I never even noticed it till after [his death]—how bizarre. I just think all the stars happened to align perfectly that night, and he took his moment, and did it."

When Jan saw the phrase, she suspected that Danny had considered suicide over a longer period than anyone had dared to guess. "To me, it said somebody was going to do something horrible in there. It didn't make any sense, otherwise. Why would the place where you like to play be 'the beginning of gone'? But that was the only real concrete indication of something like that." She dismisses the significance of the rifle's position on the workbench. "His arms weren't real long, so how else could he do it? I don't think it was a rehearsal; I think it was just the best way he could do it, physically."

Not surprisingly, Holly can hardly listen to her father's music anymore. "People talk about stupid stuff going on in their lives. I just want to shake them: 'Hey, would you like to be me? Would you like to relive this night? I don't want to hear about your petty little problems, bring me something big!' But everything's relative; everybody has their problems."

Jan says she barely remembers the service, let alone who arranged it, but she was touched by the visible outpouring that she observed. "I wasn't surprised. All sorts of people, not just musicians, loved him. He was just a very likable person, very charming, very nice to talk to. I had been to concerts where people reacted that way."

Friends and family members who spoke at the funeral—including Danny's cousin, whom Jan had never met before, as well as Barden, Previti, and Monterose—also recalled Danny's seemingly effortless ability to touch whomever he met, whether it was onstage, after a gig, or working on a street rod. One of the most moving tributes came from Monterose, who said, in part: "When I was at the deepest, lowest point of despair in my life, Danny reached his hand way down into the pit and got it dirty pulling me back out. He was always there for me. We kidded and joked all the time and made light of all that seemed dark in the world. He wasn't pumped up and didn't have a big ego. He treated everybody with honor and respect. His music was so incredible and beautiful. For a man who didn't have a lot of confidence and self-esteem, he sure passed a lot of it out to other people to help them. Maybe that's where his went. He was giving it away freely so other people could go on."

Elliott wondered afterwards if that assistance wasn't somehow being continued from the other side. A week to the day after Danny shot himself, he was playing a nightclub gig in Arlington, with Bill Kirchen. "All the house lights were down, and there was one light over the stage. It was on full blast. Our bass player reached up and unscrewed it." Just before they started playing, the light flickered on. "I thought to myself, Okay, Danny, I know you're here," Elliott laughs. "So, anyway, [the bassist] unscrewed it again. We started playing, and halfway through the first song it came on. This time, I didn't think about it: I got this instant feeling of calm about Danny's death. It was strange. It could have been in my head, but I don't think so."

The Legacy
(1995–2002)

15

Only weeks after Danny's death, a handful of his core associates and musicians paid tribute to him with a concert at the Bottom Line. Arlen Roth—who played with Previti and Biery at the Bottom Line—recalls the show as "certainly the most 'reactive' and perhaps the most emotionally raw night of all the tributes. This was largely due to the fact that we had just lost Danny, and that we were still reeling from the shock of it all."

Roth played for most of the show, either in a backup or leading role; the Hellecasters opened, while the Kentucky Headhunters' Greg Martin, "a dear of friend of mine, played 'Sleepwalk' with me," Roth says. "But what I remember most about the evening was the sheer emotion the musicians were feeling."

Biery was so distraught, says Roth, "that he could only muster enough energy to play for a couple of minutes at a time. There were songs where he actually threw his sticks down in disgust, and would storm off the stage. John Previti seemed to be constantly trying to get Tim back onstage, sometimes gently, and sometimes not so gently!"

But Biery seemed most upset, Roth says, at seeing other performers "selfishly taking advantage of Danny's loss to further their own careers, even though they barely knew him. There were some incredibly obnoxious, self-important types who seemed to want to control the off- and on-stage patterns, but this was not to be."

Roth, Biery, and Previti hunkered down with Monterose in the stage-left dressing room, "where the real emotion seemed to live," Roth says. They spent time "trying to deal with this mess on a minute-by-minute basis: 'What should we play next? Can we play at all? Who should we let play with us?'"

What Roth calls the "slightly more 'Hollywood' side of the show" occupied the stage-right dressing room "and never the twain really met that night. It was a tough, snowy night to be out, for sure, but everyone seemed to come from nowhere, and filled the hall with good feelings."

Meanwhile, the void left by Danny's departure created two distinctly opposing ripple effects. For many rock fans, the *Rolling Stone* or *New York Times* obituary likely marked the first time they'd heard of him—if they were paying attention, following the suicide of Nirvana's star-crossed frontman, Kurt Cobain, who'd used a shotgun to end his life in April 1994. Even the December 1993 self-inflicted death of singer-guitarist Doug Hopkins had drawn more attention, coming on the heels of his sacking from the Gin Blossoms (for whom he'd written the hits "Hey Jealousy" and "Found Out About You").

Behind the media coverage, however, another story began gathering momentum: paying tribute to the fingers that had burned up so many frets and inspired so many players. Surely if anybody needed more evidence of the man's formidable talent, why not hear from the people who'd gotten fired up by playing alongside him? A former student of Danny's determined that's just what should happen, and that the job should be done right.

Mac Wilson first became acquainted with Danny's style through his friendship with Liz Meyer's fiddler, Jeff Wisor, in 1973. "I had seen Roy, and when I heard Danny play, I knew that I was in the presence of greatness," he says. "He was putting some chicken-pickin' spank on some really tough fiddle music—and I loved that. That's what impressed me. Danny was light-years ahead."

Once lightning had struck, Wilson rarely missed a chance to hear Danny's playing, even though he lived in the Shenandoah Valley. One time, he drove 95 miles to a town in Maryland, only to discover Danny playing bass. "I said, 'What's *this* about?'" Wilson laughs. "He said, 'Well, you know, things got changed.' I said, 'Well, change 'em back, goddamn it!' And he did pick up the guitar for me."

In 1978 Wilson began taking lessons from Danny at his Accokeek home. After one lesson, Danny made a surprising suggestion: "He said, 'Why don't you make it easy on yourself? Come on down to the Psyche Delly, and I'll take you backstage during a break.' And then he wouldn't take any money. He said, 'Hell, I'd just be out drinking a beer.' That's how generous he was with his time and talent."

The informal relationship continued through the '80s, as Wilson recounted in a June 2002 letter: "As a music business client and as the manager of Virginia Entertainment, I represented Danny and his band Red Neck Jazz Explosion [*sic*] during the 1982 NECA convention in Chicago. Again, in 1983, I booked Danny as a headline act at the Wax Museum nightclub in Washington. Additionally Danny did some demo work of us at our studio in Virginia."

In 1986, "I called and asked him to headline a benefit concert I was producing for fellow musician, cancer patient, and fan Jimmy Hodge," Wilson wrote. Best-known for playing pedal steel guitar in the Patsy Cline tribute movie *Sweet Dreams*, Hodge had been diagnosed with Hodgkin's lymphoma. "Danny said, and I quote, 'This is the least I can do for you and Jimmy.' Danny and bandmate Dave Elliott drove 190 miles round trip to West Virginia to ensure the success of the concert." The show was held at a large nightclub in Bunker Hill, West Virginia, Wilson recalled. "As you can imagine, it was a great time for all involved."

Wilson last saw Danny and his band on New Year's Eve 1994 at the Sheraton in Ocean City, Maryland. Wilson had meant to take one more lesson. "If Danny Gatton was nice to you as a guitar player, you had to feel pretty special," he says. They'd been scheduled to get together shortly before Danny's death, but Wilson had to cancel because he was attending music-business school in Nashville. And then Wilson's best friend called to tell him that Danny had shot himself. Once he'd gotten past his initial shock—and anger—Wilson called Jan, saying that he'd help however he could, but only when the time was right. "We had a very serious business meeting. She realized that I was articulate and very capable of doing this, and I would do it right."

Tramps owner Steve Weitzman organized the first Gatton tribute, which took place at his club on January 10–12, 1995. A second Tramps tribute took place a year later. Les Paul and Albert Lee appeared with Arlen Roth and the Uptown Horns on the opening night, which *Rolling Stone's* John Swenson rated "some of the fiercest playing of the tribute." The Guitar Guys from Hell, Mark Bosch and Arthur Neilson, saluted Danny with their own version of Santo & Johnny's "Sleepwalk," which had made such a compelling case for his eclectic artistry on *Unfinished Business*.

James Burton and Warren Haynes also lent their guitars to the cause, as did the redoubtable Bill Kirchen, whose take on "You Can't Catch Me" struck another nerve among the crowd, Swenson thought. "John Sebastian sang an old Lonnie Johnson blues," Kirchen recalls. "It was nice to hear someone not try to be a guitar hero." Kirchen felt moved to take the same route on "A Going-Away Party," "a beautiful Cindy Walker song that was written as Bob Wills was dying," the former Cody guitarist says. "It was good to see everybody out. I can't lie to you—it was a good place to be. I wanted to walk away fairly confident that I did it out of love for Danny."

Some guests sensed a difference between those who'd known Danny and those who hadn't. "It was nice to be around people who actually knew him, and a little unnerving to be around people that didn't," Shannon Ford says. "Nothing against them, but it was kind of invasive. And I'm not sure that all was forgiven, as far as the conflicts that we had, but who knows? I was happy to be able to help out however I could." In the end, Ford says, "The way I pay tribute to Danny Gatton is to play my absolute best, and to find situations that are honest and true and fun. That's the way I like to leave it: play like he taught me to play."

Evan Johns—who'd later organize a couple of Gatton birthday celebrations—agreed to play after Weitzman called. "I said, 'Holy mackerel, man, I just got out of detox!' 'Evan, I need you up here.' I said, 'Well, goddamn, I'm there.' I got to follow James Burton and Les Paul: *whoo!*" Johns coped with that task by making jokes; as he told the crowd, "It's clear to me now that I'll follow anybody!"

JAN SPENT THE NEXT few years struggling to avoid being consumed by anger and guilt. She didn't go to the Tramps benefit, although she was glad to have the money to help finish the house." I was really pleased that people were remembering him," she says. "I just couldn't work up a great amount of enthusiasm. I was still very angry, and angry that music took him away, so I didn't like the music aspect of it—which is the only aspect there was."

"For four years, she was crying every day," Holly says. "She'd come home from work and cry while she was feeding the dog. I could hear, even from inside the house, this wailing. Some people can bounce back from stuff like that, but this was so devastating, there's not even a word for what it's like."

Reminders lay all around the property, like the '73 Grand Prix that needed restoration. "Danny was gracious enough to let me leave it sitting in the yard with his other cars," Steve Gorospe says. "I always felt bad about that, but he told me my car looked a whole lot better than his did—it added value to the property. That was Danny."

Ernie Gorospe could hardly bear to look in the garage when he came down. "Everything was just the way it was on the day it happened," he says. "There were still cassette tapes sitting on the counter, and some in the cassette player. The calendar, of course, was open right to that month. It was like that for a long time. It was strange."

Dave Elliott says, "If I see Danny when I get to Heaven, the first thing I'm going to do is give him a hug, and then I'm going to punch him in the face." Jan has heard similar lines from others, which reflect her own despair at not seeing his talent fulfilled. "Everything seemed for nothing: all the years that I worked; all the things that we tried to do; all the years that we stayed there in squalor, trying to make it better; all the suffering Holly had to go through living in that mess, and the things that she didn't have."

Some cracks began to show within the family's relationships. Fissures that hadn't been evident while Danny was alive appeared after his death, without his presence to smooth them over. Brent had a falling-out with Jan and Holly over what he considered their enthusiasm for "the good life." "Danny had a cow right before Holly went to school one year, 'cause Jan took her downtown and got her hair cut," he recalls. "It was 200 bucks, and he wasn't happy." Such anecdotes constituted Brent's reading of Danny's troubled domestic life, which they never discussed. For her part, Holly didn't care to see much of Brent. "He just wasn't charismatic and funny and interesting, like my father was," she says.

The dicey relationship between the two families further complicated matters. "When [Jan] first got married to him, they were very cold and very rude," Holly says, speaking of Danny's parents. "It was only in the last two years [of his life] that [Norma] and my mother managed to put their animosity aside and started talking. Whether it was out of genuine affection, I can't say. I can just say that they made an effort."

Norma says she often found herself put off when she'd call her son. "I was always telling her that he was doing something else," Holly confirms, "because he didn't want to talk to her. She was trying to get him to do stuff for the fan club and things he didn't feel like doing—kind of always nagging."

THE LOCAL MUSIC COMMUNITY paid tribute to Danny on November 13, 1995, by honoring him at the Washington Area Music Association's tenth annual awards ceremony at northwest D.C.'s Hard Rock Café. On this occasion, Norma and Jan stood together for a photo that Steve Gorospe snapped for his website; other notable attendees included Ernie Gorospe, Brent Gatton, John Previti, Jay Monterose, and Donna Windsor. Bill Kirchen handled the program, whose notes summarized Danny's life and the many "Wammie" awards that he'd won: "From the bands Fat Boys to Funhouse, Gatton traveled from Nashville to L.A., but always returned to his Charles County farmhouse."

In Arlen Roth's opinion, Phil Zavarella organized the most down-to-earth tribute in January 1996, at Sam's Crab House. (Once again, Jan didn't go, although Holly did.) "That was like *It's a Wonderful Life*: Here's Danny Gatton's world without him—a world thrown into utter chaos, people fighting in alleyways, girls fighting in the bathroom, people just beating each other up," Roth says. "I waited through 20 groups. They had me headlining, and I didn't go on till three in the morning." Roth had to drive straight home after he'd finished, "so it was insane," he adds. "But that was the most real one, in the sense that it was his home area, and it was when people were still very much angry, very much upset over it."

Arlen had always shared a love of Tele playing with his late daughter, Gillian. "She also knew his daughter, Holly, from our Maryland visit," Roth says. "One of the true highlights of my life was when she performed with me at the Tramps Gatton tribute in 1996." (Gillian played with Shannon Ford and Paul Ossola, who play in Roth's current band.)

"Gillie had the silver-sparkle Tele I gave her, and she ripped through 'Suzie Q' and 'Day Tripper' and sang and played slide on 'Not Fade Away'— she brought the house down," Roth says. "Her guitar playing was amazing, considering she had just turned 12 years old."

The following year Gillian was offered a role on *The Gunks*—a Nickelodeon TV show patterned after *The Monkees*—and on February 16, President's Day, 1998, she recorded the show's theme song. "She sang and played so beautifully on that track," Roth says. "When we left the session she jumped up and punched the air out of sheer joy." But disaster struck two days later after Gillian had gone to New York City for an audition for a print ad. "On the way home my wife lost control of the car on the Merritt Parkway, and I lost both of them. The sense of loss is, of course, immeasurable, and the tragedy and heartbreak never ends."

Arlen Roth with his late daughter, Gillian, at the second Danny Gatton tribute show held at Tramps in New York City, February 11, 1996.

But Arlen will never forget how Gillian "brought joy to all during a time of great emotion over the loss of Danny. This father and his daughter had the best night onstage together ever, and my darling child, who never lived past 14, helped raise money to put Danny's daughter Holly through college."

The survivors gathered on January 8–9, 1998, for a larger tribute at the Birchmere, where Danny had impressed so many local crowds. Tickets ran $65 per night, with the aim of raising money for Holly's college education, as well as honoring Danny's music and memory through those who'd played with him.

Mac Wilson spent nine months organizing and promoting the Birchmere show, for which Fender was the main sponsor. The manufacturer donated two guitars for a silent auction to raise money for a scholarship fund for Holly and St. Jude's Children's Hospital in Memphis. Additional sponsors included Big Mo, BASF tape, *Guitar Player*, Gorospe Associates, Inc., and country station WMZQ. "Our relationship with Danny is one that we will always cherish," Fender vice president of product research and development Dan Smith said in a press release issued before the event. "Fender is proud in seeing that his unique spirit lives on, not only in his music and the instrument he played but fortunately with his daughter, Holly, whom he loved so much."

Wilson would later win a "Wammie" for his work in putting the event together. The two nights raised $77,000 for Holly's education and easily generated enough business to have justified a third night. Steve Gorospe set up a simultaneous webcast that drew 40,000 hits. The silent auction— which included such items as a portrait of Danny and a Gibson J-200 Custom Shop guitar with his name on it—further bolstered the final tally. *Vintage Guitar* dubbed it the "Guitar Event of the Decade."

Jan and Holly appreciated Wilson's efforts, but had little personal involvement. "I didn't really have much to do with that," Holly says. "I'm grateful that he did it, but we were just trying to keep ourselves together emotionally. We weren't really concerned with that kind of thing." Jan says she felt "pushed along" by the momentum of the event. "I felt like I had to agree, but I just didn't care. I was really in a bad state—very bad—so [Wilson] did everything."

Brent declined to be involved or even attend. He no longer spoke to Jan and Holly, and he wasn't convinced that they needed the money, citing the installation of a satellite-dish system as one of his many misgivings. He would have preferred to see the money used for school music programs. "I told [Wilson] that right from the jump: 'You know what? If you want to start a scholarship or something in Danny's name, I'll be right there to support this. But if you're going to give one penny of this to [Jan and Holly], forget it. I don't want nothing to do with it.'"

Wilson said that everyone knew up front that the primary goal was to raise money for Holly's education, with proceeds from the filming and taping earmarked for a scholarship in Danny's name at Boston's Berklee College of Music. Since Holly was a Maryland resident attending college in Virginia, she was subject to paying out-of-state tuition, "and [her mother] didn't have that much money," Wilson says. "In addition, they couldn't finish their house after Danny died. The bottom line is that Janet Gatton told me that the need was there, and I filled it. I did my job."

The headliners included Vince Gill, Rodney Crowell, Arlen Roth, Steve Earle, Radney Foster, Albert Lee, Brent Mason & the Nashville All Stars, and John Jorgenson. For Jan, Gill's appearance brought out a bittersweet memory of how her late husband had sometimes perceived himself. After Danny returned from a TNN appearance with Gill, "I went out to the garage, because he didn't come in the house," she says. "He was sitting out there, saying what a terrible job he did. And Vince Gill had told me—before he became famous—how he used to spend the money he made on his gigs on taxi rides to go see Danny. I was thinking, 'Wow, does Danny know this?' But he didn't think that—or if he thought it, he didn't want to admit he thought it or didn't believe it."

The special guests represented a cross-section of the many genres and styles that Danny drew from. Eddie Adcock, Ray Flacke, and John Jennings upheld the bluegrass and country side. Roots styles came from a reunited Fat Boys that paired the Elliott-Hancock rhythm team again, Amos Garrett, the Good Humor Band, Robert Gordon, and Evan Johns. Steve Wolf appeared with his jazz band, Swing Speak, and Arlen Roth joined forces with Bill Holloman and Joe Dalton. Bill Kirchen brought his band, Too Much Fun, and Pete Kennedy played with his wife, Maura.

"It all fit together nicely," Roth says. "I don't know who it was, but someone said, 'Out of such a terrible tragedy, something good has got to happen.' And that's exactly what we went ahead and started doing, because we all loved Danny so much, and we thought of Danny as such a positive force, that you can't help but do something good when you've lost him."

Tom Principato hadn't gone to the funeral, though he'd appeared at another fundraiser for Holly in Wheaton—and two birthday celebrations, including one organized by Johns. "It sure was a great weekend," he says. "It was kind of a drag, too, because—for me—it was like being at the funeral that I never attended." He noticed a difference in mood between those who'd known Danny and those who hadn't. "I think it was all honest tribute and love. But for the people who knew him, it was more like a wake."

"Put all of us together, we weren't as good as Danny," Pete Kennedy says. "But it was still great having everybody get together. It was in the spirit of Danny, too: everybody joked around and had fun." Eddie Adcock found the event to be "a joyous celebration over a man who everybody there had been extremely affected by—and not just a little. It was emotional at times, no doubt about it." An album compiled from the tribute performances remains unreleased at this writing, although Wilson says he'll issue it eventually.

Wilson personally delivered the check to the farm in Newburg. "[Jan] said, 'Danny would want you to have money.' I said, 'That's not the purpose. This is not about me—I don't want any of this money. I will have an opportunity as an executive producer of the record to realize that money later on.' And she said that was fine."

HOW DANNY'S RECORDED LEGACY will be finally resolved remains an open question, now that Jan and Holly have formed their own label to make his albums readily available again. No longer will *Blazing Telecasters* and Rhino's *Hot Rod Guitar* anthology be the major exceptions.

Ed Eastridge hoped to distribute the family's new label, and reactivated Big Mo to sell Danny's work through its website (www.bigmo.com) and its Yahoo! Stores affiliate. Eastridge has also retrieved hundreds of hours of tapes from Jan and Holly to review for unreleased gems. "They want to put out some new CDs and remix some of the out-of-print masters," he says. (Billy Hancock has also announced plans to reissue *American Music*.)

But first, there was an unpleasant detour when Jan and Holly sued NRG in U.S. District Court in Baltimore. Harold Walter represented Jan and Holly, while Barbara Gorinson handled NRG's case, according to Spike Ostmann, who had tried to help both sides settle the dispute, to no avail. He declines to discuss the case, except to say that Jan had expressed dissatisfaction with NRG's handling of Danny's music. The case went to arbitration, and the settlement gave Jan and Holly the rights to 31 songs that Danny had recorded for NRG.

Not surprisingly, the dispute aroused strong emotions in Washington's musical community. Orpheus Records owner Rick Carlisle—who had numbered Brawner Smoot among his most faithful customers 20 years ago—stopped selling Danny's albums after hearing about the lawsuit. He laughed when this writer explained both sides' positions, saying "I'm still waiting for you to defend what Jan's doing." Displayed high on a wall behind him was the red vinyl version of *Redneck Jazz*, priced at $100.

Brent says the lawsuit fails to meet the standard that he and his wife, Sherry, would expect anyone safeguarding Danny's legacy to uphold: "Would you do the same thing if he was sitting right here?" He adds: "Holly's running the show. Holly's always run the show. Nobody will admit it, but she is." Sherry is even more outspoken. "You ask why people don't like Jan too much?" she says. "She sued Danny's mother, and over nothing. All that time Danny was gone, Norma not only paid Jan royalties but she gave extra [money], at the drop of a hat."

Other friends have expressed astonishment that someone who'd worked so tirelessly to promote her son was being sued. "Poor Norma—she's an awful nice lady, been through a lot, and she was extremely supportive of Danny," Joe Kogok says. "I know she paid for a lot of [studio time]. I think that's just a shame. Norma turned Danny's music into a good business deal, and I don't know what started the battles."

Evan Johns raises another potentially nettlesome issue. He recalls that the Danny Gatton Band worked without contracts during his stint there, and all earnings were split equally. But Johns says he has seen nothing from *Redneck Jazz*, despite his prominence on it: "Three out of the eight songs are 100 percent mine. I was a featured vocalist—ever see the 'Ugly Man' single?—[and] featured guitar soloist. I was the arranger of all my songs proven by previous recordings."

Norma won't discuss the lawsuit in any detail, except to note that she sent royalty checks of $8,000 to $10,000 to Jan, who also received periodic gifts (including a blender). Jan says the amount averaged closer to $5,000 per year, although she did receive $10,000 on one occasion.

Jan and Holly say that those who condemn their actions don't know the whole story. Holly started wondering if it made sense for Norma to continue overseeing the music when she wasn't being invited into the studio or approached for input on the reissues of *American Music*, *The Humbler*, *Unfinished Business*, *Untouchable*, and *Redneck Jazz Explosion: Recorded Live*. "We weren't sure about anything," she says. "We were just left out there floating without him. We felt like we were being manipulated, and that's not a good feeling."

Holly calls *Untouchable* a prime example of an album that could have used some additional input. "The mixes are horrible, and it's not just me that thinks that. It's not up to his standards. She was his mother, so he loved her, of course, but I don't think he respected her musical taste all that much."

Jan had initially expressed no interest in what was happening. She was still reeling from losing her husband. "I didn't care about the money. I was just in limbo. I didn't ask her to show me the books—which she never offered, not ever. I didn't ask how she got permission. I didn't ask anything, but Holly was questioning."

Smoot said he didn't know enough about the allegations made in the lawsuit to comment, but he has trouble squaring them with his recollections of the woman who seemed every bit as exacting as her famous son, if not more so. "She would do everything to a 'T': filing her taxes and paying royalties to musicians on the records," he says. "She didn't want anything to be wrong. Danny would tear up royalty checks because this lady was putting all her time and energy into promoting [his records]."

The *Caviar and Grits* album—which Smoot and Norma were compiling—remains in limbo. Some of the candidates included the "Psy-kaw-liga" that Danny and Bobby had so much fun doing back in the '60s, an acoustic "Remington Ride," a studio "Linus and Lucy," and a live version of the jazz standard "Yesterdays" from the Cellar Door, with an Echoplex-laden solo that ranks among Danny's prettiest moments, in Smoot's opinion.

Billy Poore didn't know what to think after receiving a "cease and desist" letter about the *Runnin' Wild* box set, whose $165 price raised eyebrows, as did Danny's star billing. Associates like Billy Hancock argue that the packaging is misleading, since Danny's contributions are as a session man, not the featured artist, and that he would never have sanctioned much of the material's release. Poore will happily argue those issues, saying that he set the price high in recognition of the inevitable bootlegging that would dog its release—and that, as far as he's concerned, *Runnin' Wild* fulfilled its modest, limited-edition promise by rounding up the unheard highlights of Danny's career. Poore says he informed Jan of his plans to release the material in the winter of 1997–98—shortly before his house burned down—and recalls her voicing no objections.

Poore does feel that the lawsuit disrupted the one business best geared to serve Danny's legacy. "I think that Jan is following instructions," he says. "I think she unjustly took advantage of Danny's mother. I think she's fouled things up, in a business way."

In better circumstances, Holly says, she would have liked to find a way to work with her grandmother, whom she often visited in Georgia along with Danny's sister and her husband, Donna and Tom Oliff. "Out of all her grandkids, I was the one most like her, but she kept me at arm's length because of whose daughter I was, being that she didn't like my mom. We could talk for hours and hours about stuff that we liked. We had a lot in common, which is why it was sort of sad for me to have to [file the suit]."

Jan and Holly say they lost faith in the NRG regime after hearing that the Oliffs were taking a greater role when Norma's health problems surfaced—an issue that would loom even larger if she died or became incapacitated. "I was scared that if something happened to Norma and [the Oliffs] had power of attorney, I'd have a huge battle to unravel all of that business," Jan says. "I thought, 'This is not safe anymore. I can't do this.'" (The Oliffs did not respond to the author's request for an interview.)

Jan learned that no written contracts had existed between Norma and Danny, "except for three songs, and they had expired before his death," she says. Norma concedes that the lack of agreements eventually proved to be an issue, although she had never imagined it would be, because "he was my son."

In the end, the settlement awarded half of Norma's earnings from January to June 2000: $75,000. "They wouldn't go back any farther than that," Jan says. "I didn't get it, because I still owed the lawyer. I never saw a penny of it. I didn't care, because I thought what was important had already been done."

As harsh as the reaction was to the lawsuit, Jan and Holly say they'd do it all over again, because they saw no other way of preserving their rights to Danny's music. "If we could have talked, Norma and I, things could have been worked out in a better way," Jan says. "Or maybe not, because she seemed to be very bossy about the music. Brent was very angry, and I'm sure he felt he had a right to be angry, but if it was his daughter and something that belonged to him, anybody's bound to [feel differently]."

While Holly isn't proud about alienating the other side of the family, she believes the bottom line is simple. "I know [Norma] worked hard, but he worked harder." Although communications had been strained, "they brought it on themselves," she says. "It didn't have to be like that, as far as we were concerned."

JUDGING FROM THE MAY 19, 2001, auction of Danny's 15-acre property, the cultish fervor that had surrounded him during his life still burned as brightly as ever. For Jan, the event was just a way of clearing out the knick-knacks she and her husband had accumulated, as she prepared to move. His most ardent admirers saw it as their last chance to take home whatever keepsakes of their hero still lay within reach. One came all the way from California for the opportunity.

An open house was held on May 12, to preview the items listed for sale. Monte Reel's account in the *Washington Post* provided a vivid glimpse of the curiosities on display in the garage: "It might be an antique telephone, an old guitar, a neglected 60-cycle motor. It might lack key components. It might coat your fingertips with dust. Maybe it looks worthless. For Danny Gatton, the man who once owned all these items now up for sale, such objects brimmed with possibility. With a little work, that old telephone might produce a dial tone. That old motor might spark and whir."

Anywhere the eye roamed could reveal a treasure: the old Texaco gas pump that stood outside; vintage signs emblazoned with beer brands or gas station logos, or advertising past concerts; boxes of guitar pickups and hot rod magazines going back to the '60s, crammed into rusty filing cabinets. There were stacks of cassette tapes, compact discs, and records, while workbenches overflowed with spare parts, tools, and the inevitable clutter of amplifiers, guitar parts, and oddball instruments like the Castle accordion tucked into its dusty red-satin case.

Dave Elliott got the oversized "Danny Gatton Band" banner from the March 2, 1990, Roxy Club video (thanks to a successful bid from Andy Funt, who knew that his friend wanted it). Jan and Holly naturally held onto the most valuable guitars, though they offered some for sale—such as an old amp-in-case Silvertone, "an inexpensive model that served as a starter guitar for a generation of players in the 1960s," the *Post* noted. There was also an old Stratocaster that Danny had partially customized. Among the non-musical items, there was a dizzying array of old refrigerators, gas and wood stoves, and '50s-era collectibles like Marilyn Monroe dolls and James Dean posters. As Jan told the paper: "We were both very eclectic in our tastes. But after a while, you run out of room."

Phil Zavarella professes astonishment that anyone would want some of these things, as if Danny's DNA would magically rub off on the buyers and turn them into master guitarists. "Why did people want to go to that auction?" he says. "Everything he got, he adjusted it, he drilled it, he beat it, he did something to it. He did not leave it alone, because his mind was going 1,000 miles an hour, and he had to occupy it."

Tom Principato couldn't make it to the auction, because of commitments that kept him in Texas. But he got an unusual keepsake anyway. "I was at a gig, and a guy that I don't even know came up. 'Hey, man, did you make it to the Danny Gatton auction?' I said, 'No, but I regret it, because I really would have liked to have some kind of memento of Danny.'"

No problem, the stranger assured him—he'd brought him something. "He pulled out this old, old, old tarnished eggbeater. It looked like it was from the '40s. He goes, 'I got this at the yard sale. I thought you'd like to have it.' We burst out laughing, and I said, 'Thanks!'" Some day, Principato jokes, he'll get around to making a little plaque for his surprise gift: "Danny Gatton's Eggbeater."

FOR JOE BARDEN, LOSING the friend he'd known for nearly 20 years caused him to say: "It's time to get a job. Dan's not here anymore, what's the point?" Danny's life story is almost the polar opposite of Aerosmith's Joe Perry, for whom Barden has also made pickups. "He could not have done

Joe's job," he says. "The natural instinct that where you belong is connecting with 20,000 people—Dan had zero interest in that. It just wasn't his bag."

Those who hear Danny with fresh ears will come away with something that's all but lost in today's media-saturated age, Barden feels. "If people do stumble across him, their jaws will hit the ground. They'll say, 'Oh my God, I had no idea something so amazing could exist.'" Jay Monterose expresses a similar feeling: "Danny was the greatest, to me, because he was the only cat who could mix it all up and make it work, every time. That cat played so many notes that people had to get their calculators out, but he'd never throw one away. I swear to God, he never threw a note away."

STEVE GOROSPE, who runs the www.dannygatton.com website, says that Danny's appeal reaches far beyond his old Washington and Maryland stomping grounds. He's gotten e-mails from such improbable locales as Kosovo and the Middle East. "They may be killing each other [in those places], but they're writing about Danny. There was something that united these people, and it was a little guy out of D.C." Gorospe says he may have as many as 150 messages awaiting his response if he hasn't checked the site for a week.

Gorospe also carries on the legacy by playing guitar in a group that includes Billy Windsor's son Stephen as the vocalist. "You really get to know Danny through listening to his music, and that's what so many people who didn't know him personally have missed out on. But they can still get it through his music, if they listen." Ernie Gorospe and John Broaddus sometimes join them, and Jerry Wallmark occasionally sits in. Joe Kogok and Jay Monterose have guested at various gigs, giving the sense of closing a circle that began nearly four decades ago with the obscure local single that introduced Danny's playing to the world.

Like many players who'd admired him so long from afar, Bob Margolin simply could not fathom the sudden hole created by Danny's departure. "I was blown away when I heard Danny took his own life," he says. "I didn't know him well enough to guess at the specific reasons, and nobody who knew him has told me anything illuminating. It's tragic because he was so special and super-humanly talented, and he should have been recognized more." In a business that primarily rewards image and style, "Danny was more about guitar playing and not much else as an entertainer," Margolin says. "That was enough for me to appreciate him, but maybe he wanted more."

Phil Zavarella offers a more basic explanation for Danny's lack of major success. "Stevie Ray Vaughan, Jimi Hendrix, Eric Clapton—these guys were nothing until they stepped in front of a microphone. If you don't sing in this business, forget about it. You're just a sideman, and that's all you'll ever be. Nobody wants to hear somebody playing 90,000 notes a second. It's as simple as that. I did the test many times, taking people to see him play. When I took laymen [non-musicians], in ten minutes they'd want to leave, because they didn't understand what was going on."

For all his travails, Danny remained true to his beliefs, Phil says, "which I totally respected. He never threw that out the window." He speculates that a lucrative session career might well have awaited Danny, if only he'd relaxed that stubborn grip on his artistry. "He took it to Nashville with him, took it to L.A., took it to New York, and they run him right out of town every time. With those places, you've got to use the guitar they want you to use, the amp they want you to use, and you play what they tell you to play. He would not do that."

In Phil's mind, the expression "unfinished business" summarizes the course of Danny's life, whether the conversation turns to music or that '32 Ford. When Phil began one of his own restoration projects, he recalls telling his family, " 'Now, I'm going to make this brand new, but I'm going to finish it.' I'm not going to be like Danny and just tear it apart, and sit there and drink beer and look at it—I want to actually finish this car and drive it down the road. Which I did, and I still have that car to this day." To Phil, Danny's command of the guitar is his most enduring legacy, no matter how much ambivalence he felt about the music business. "*Nobody could play guitar like that. Nobody.*"

Joe Tass recalls Danny as a great talent who never bridged the gap between desires and expectations. "Going to see Roy was like a pilgrimage, and going to see Danny was like going to see Bigfoot at a tractor pull," he says. "Danny had painted himself into that corner of playing more, more, more, and faster, faster, faster. 'Well, this is what the people want.' I don't think he knew what the people wanted. I think he knew what he wanted to do—what was good for him."

Cutting an individual figure in the profit-driven music business is often a lonely pursuit, yet Ed Eastridge feels that seeing Danny solely in that light is too simplistic. "He was definitely a rebel. He wanted to make money, though. He would not have minded having a gigantic hit record—but, at the same time, it would have to have been on his terms." He remains confident that someone will be trying to crack the essence of Danny's guitar style 50 or 100 years from now. Eastridge cites a maxim of the Russian composer Stravinsky: "Composition is just improvisation that's written down." "That made me feel better about my skills," he laughs. "I think I got that from Danny—he did a lot of spontaneous improvisation, but he was really into planning out shit to the minutest detail."

Former *Guitar Player* editor Tom Wheeler stresses that Danny's idealization among guitarists was a function of the pre-grunge era, when "we valued virtuosity in all forms of music," he says. "Many of us felt that the real players were the jazz players and the classical players, because they understood music and played with a complexity and intellectual depth that most of us could hardly aspire to, and we respected that. That was very cool." For that reason alone, Danny commanded his peers' respect. "Anybody who'd heard him, whether you were into this kind of music or not, could not fail to grasp that he was an astonishing talent."

For Bill Kirchen, nothing beat hearing Danny backing a vocalist. "He was so right, so tasteful, and so sublime. I think he'll be remembered as a major musician in America. He carved out a piece of the guitar where you just can't touch it. My favorite thing about him is, he had these blazing chops but he also had kind of a rock 'n' roll and hillbilly sensibility and tone. I'd just marvel at the combination."

In Eddie Adcock's view, many of today's six-string hotshots "took a tiny, minute portion of Danny Gatton—and made their whole style. The ones that don't admit it's his, stole it; the ones that admit it's his, borrowed it." To Eddie, Danny's combination of chops and emotion will always separate him from the rest of the pack. "I don't think he ever did 16 bars without putting something really soulful in it, something that would really knock you out of your seat."

The other obvious musical crossover has been to the jazzers who've incorporated Danny's unorthodox chording and harmonic approaches into their vocabularies, Eddie believes. Danny was way ahead of his time, and never got the recognition (or rewards) he deserved for those innovations. Eddie says that he and Danny once discussed what would happen if they ever hit the big bucks—and found they had reached the same conclusion. "We will know that we have stopped growing," he says, "and the audience finally caught up with where our heads were."

"Danny had everything lifted from him," Eddie asserts. "And it was those people that didn't give him credit that Danny didn't have any use for—he would try to blow their doors off if they were ever fool enough to get onstage with him."

Like many others who played with Danny, Shannon Ford isn't sure how time will treat his former colleague's high-octane blend of chops, harmonic adventurism, and daredevil improvisation. "I don't know if enough musicians in general will know about him. But guitar players will always know about him. Any guitar player worth his salt should certainly dig into what he did."

Then and now, Danny's lethal sense of humor separates him from his peers. "God, are you going to be able to get us out of this? And if you don't, so what?" Ford laughs. "Humor is a part of music, too, and that's something he totally adopted. So many guys take it so seriously and completely miss the point: that it's actually about *playing* music."

Bill Holloman soon realized that Danny 's drive for success only went so far. He recalls their conversation after *88 Elmira St.*'s release: " 'Danny, you've got to get out there, they've got to see you—that's how we're going to sell records.' But he didn't want to, because the money wasn't right. Another ironic thing is that we did the tour for the second record that we should have done for the first one. By then, it was too late." His assessment of the legacy is simple and succinct. "I don't think they're ever going to write a Broadway musical about him," Holloman laughs. "I think it's going to be a legendary guitar-cult sort of thing, more than anything else. I think his legacy is unfulfilled potential. There was so much potential there, but it was sidetracked by so many things—it was sidetracked by him."

Danny cast an uncommonly wide net, according to Obie O'Brien, who went on to work with New Jersey pop-metallers Bon Jovi. Vocalist Jon Bon Jovi and guitarist Richie Sambora may not spring to mind as major Gatton fans, but O'Brien knows otherwise. "Jon used to go, 'This guy is unbelievable!' And Richie—I made him a copy of the stuff that I got at the bootleg stores in Japan. He wanted a copy, because he really appreciates what Danny was able to do. These guys, they get it and they're fans."

That lesson was driven home to O'Brien at the A&M Studios parking lot, where he happened to be hanging out with another hot-rodding guitar enthusiast: Jeff Beck. "He's letting me drive his deuce roadster down Sunset Boulevard," O'Brien says. "At the time, Danny was still alive. I said I was friends with him, and Beck goes, 'Oh, that guy is unbelievable.' They all knew—his reputation got to the guys that are the guitar gods today."

Holloman says the "Gatton factor" helped him to break the ice with Guns N' Roses' guitarist Slash. "I was rehearsing with him, and he wasn't paying any attention to 'the horn guy.' " Then someone from *Rolling Stone* informed Slash of Holloman's links to Danny. "All of a sudden, it was: 'Damn glad to meet you!' We hit it off and became really good friends after that. Once he found out that I'd worked with Danny, I was in the club."

Pete Kennedy feels that Danny's preference for the comforts of home trumped what his audiences expected or desired, as exemplified by his response to the hand injury that sidelined the Redneck Jazz Explosion. "Danny would usually back off when some kind of big success was looming, and he would just disappear for a while until things calmed down.

Then he'd start back up in the local clubs." Playing "redneck" bars around D.C. may not have matched other people's definition of success, but Danny "could leave the gig knowing he'd played 'Misty' better than he'd ever played it before. He really wanted to be where he could continue to grow as a musician, and he knew that touring on the big rock circuit was not the place to do that."

To some extent, Danny's future status depends on whether guitar riffs become a prominent force again in pop music. Today's hip-hop tracks leave little room for actual playing, but influences seep through anyway—such as Andy Summers's deft revamping of Lenny Breau licks on Police records, Kennedy says. "You see that with Danny. I'm definitely influenced by Danny, and there's a whole bunch of guitarists who are. We know how high that standard is. It's way higher than any of us have ever reached, but at least we know what it is."

For Joe Kogok, losing his friend had one immediate impact on a self-described "music fanatic": he doesn't attend nearly as many shows as he once did. "I used to go out and see Danny all the time. I'm trying to get out a little bit more every once in a while and see something, but there's not always something around to see. When he was around, there was always something to see."

Kogok says that even Danny didn't know where some of his ideas came from. "One time on a break—I don't remember if I was playing with him or just watching—he asked, 'Do you ever go blank when you're playing?' 'What do you mean?' He said, 'You know, sometimes I'll be playing, and I'll come down off the bandstand and somebody will say, "Man, that's the most incredible thing I've ever seen you play—what was that?" And I'm just totally blank. I don't remember anything.' He would remember the names of the songs, but he had no recollection of what it was that he had played."

When Danny asked Kogok if that ever happened to him, Joe said, "No, I remember everything I play." "And then Danny said, 'What do you make of that? Is that like God?' I said, 'Man, I don't know—but I'll bet there's a million other guitar players that would like to experience that!' "

Poore, on the other hand, firmly believes that "it takes more than sheer, natural, God-given talent for people to know who you are." If Poore's neighbor has no clue about Roy Buchanan—who carried the bigger name in the rock 'n' roll marketplace—how will Danny get a fair shake? "I think Danny will be remembered only by the musicians," he says. "They'll all rate him, probably, above Roy Buchanan, but I don't think he'll be remembered by the masses."

Principato has a tougher time assessing Danny's impact, because he feels that more time needs to pass. "He's come to be known as one of the world's greatest guitarists, and more readily as another chapter in a peculiar Washington guitar tradition," he says. "He and Roy Buchanan—two of the most notorious guitarists from Washington—both died mysterious deaths." Danny didn't have to prove anything to his peers, who long ago found themselves awed by his mastery of different styles and his amazing technical proficiency. Whether the general public will ever embrace those qualities remains an open question. "At this point, it's going to be cultish—like it always was. I think what happens with his recordings and what the people in charge now do to perpetuate the legacy is going to make a big difference."

Principato considers the April 25, 1979, Cellar Door gig with Breau and Emmons as a representative snapshot, "because they were all flying by the seats of their pants and having a ball. You can hear Danny laughing between [songs]. Even though he loved fun, you rarely heard him busting out in an open laugh like that onstage." Many times, "some of the highest praise that you'd get from Danny was for him to just come up to you quietly offstage, at the end of the night, offer his hand, and go, 'Mighty fine.' Often that would be the most you'd get from Danny. But if he really was having so much fun that he just burst out into open laughter, you knew you were on a roll."

Yet former friends and colleagues are learning that Danny's reach extends around the world in unexpected ways. Bobby Hancock recalls his astonishment when he and his wife, Liz, took a cruise to Cozumel, Mexico. "I'm coming from dinner, walking down to the other end of the ship, and I hear 'Country Together Again' playing. It's this guy who's doing a one-man-band thing with a laptop computer with all these songs on it." A closer look established that the performer was using an old Tele with Barden pickups. "He goes, 'Yeah, I bought this guitar from Danny Gatton in 1975.' I said, 'Well, I'm a lifelong friend of Danny Gatton's, and I used to play in his band.'"

The performer turned out to be former Virginian Pat Moore, who'd been around the '70s scene but hadn't crossed paths with Bobby. "We knew probably 20 of the same people," Bobby says. "The guitar he had—I had played that guitar. I said, 'Under that pickguard, there's a great big hole where a Charlie Christian pickup used to be.' He said, 'That's right.'"

Bobby talked to Moore at length the next night, and they've stayed in touch. "It was like we'd known each other for 40 years, but I was just with this guy for a day." He reads a letter from Moore, which says, in part: "I know that you will always keep Danny in your heart, as I do, and all we can do at this point is pass what we know of him along to others. We must be keepers of the star."

Like many people who knew Danny, Bobby found the personal aspect of their relationship as important as the musical one. "He was who he was [as a musician], but he was also my friend at the same time. It didn't seem like a big deal at the time—but it sure seems like a big deal now."

Despite their conflicts, the members of the Gatton family are united in hopes that Danny will reach a broader audience. Brent thinks the best way of passing down his brother's legacy is through those listeners who become musicians themselves. "It may not happen as much as with some of the big-name people," he says, "but I guess it'll stay alive to some degree." Barring that connection, he knows that anyone who met Danny never forgot the experience. "The people that knew him knew who he really was, and what kind of person he was. He was a humble person that played guitar and loved to work on his cars."

Norma expresses a characteristically individual take on the question. "He had determination. I have a certain amount of determination, too. Anything I tried to do, I was determined to work out." She cites the day that she spent upholstering a car seat in red velvet. "I'd never upholstered a car in my life, but I got it done. I wasn't one who gave up too easy, either." She believes that her son's life reflected similar qualities. "It takes a lot of humility to bounce back all the time, doesn't it? And we all get humbled. 'Just a plain old southern Maryland tobacco worm'—that's what Danny used to say he was. He had a lot of wit about him. He was funny."

Holly finished her college education in December 2001. Although she graduated in biology, she hadn't decided where life will take her. Her science courses may lead to a career in entomology, forestry, or veterinary medicine—or her passion for music could win out. Holly remains interested in working with her father's music, which she'll have to juggle around graduate school. "I feel like it's urgent, and I need to do something quickly, because it has been almost ten years. How long can you wait, before people's minds start to fade? But it's still the great music that it always was, and I hope there's a future for it. That's all I can say."

Holly still finds listening to her father's music difficult, because of the emotions bound up in his death and his dictum that she not follow him into music. "I was just so mad he wouldn't let me express myself like that. Music is my passion. My mother has a thing for books, but I have hundreds of CDs. I'm obsessed with music. I'm always playing music—can't be away from it."

Jan suspects that Holly may find her creative niche, even though Danny wouldn't teach her more than the rudiments of fiddle. "She's got a really good ear. It was just super to watch her play. It wasn't any time at all, and she was just so good, and then he said, 'No more.'" To this day, Holly wishes that she could have fulfilled her desire to express herself during her father's lifetime. "I feel like I lost the greatest teacher I ever could have had, and it makes me angry that he refused to share that with me. But he was just so bent on turning me into this scientist person. So here I am—I feel like I did all this for him, but he's not around to see it."

Holly also realizes how closely she resembles her father, in many ways. "I knew he loved me, but he didn't understand what I was becoming. But if he was still alive now, we would be great friends, because—despite all his best efforts—I have turned into him." Although Holly has managed to let go of her original anger, "I just feel robbed, like everybody else, of this great person."

When those feelings threaten to overtake her, Holly thinks back to the good moments. She relishes O'Brien's anecdotes about Bon Jovi's admiration of Danny, having crank-called the singer when she was a child. "My friends would come over, call his answering machine, and play a little song on the keys. I don't know if it went through or not, but it was fun," she laughs. "Dad talked about him: 'I knew that guy when he was just a [studio] janitor.' And then, he's this famous guy." The unspoken flipside involved seeing the former janitor overtake her father, at least in pure commercial terms. "That was another thing where he was kind of bitter, although Jon's a cool guy. It was really nerve-wracking for somebody that's such a prodigy to get run over by these guys."

Such sentiments hark back to Phil Zavarella's belief that Danny often let his artistic side overrule his more practical nature. Danny's reluctance to embrace the barest show-business trappings is well documented by many of his associates; as a teenager growing up in the MTV era, Holly was keenly aware of that issue, too. "Mom was always trying to get Dad to punch up his outfits. She used to go to these expensive boutiques in Georgetown and buy him these nice suits and purple shirts, just to make him stand out onstage—much better than just wearing a black T-shirt, although that might have been how the crowd preferred him to look. I have no idea."

The notion of compromise never occupied a spot on Danny Gatton's radar, though Jan sometimes wonders if her husband should have given the issue more consideration. "When I hear his music, it sounds so much better than what's commercial. I just wonder why it didn't come about." As much as Danny loathed touring and studio sideman work, Jan also wonders why he didn't get into soundtracks, which would have let him stay home and work at his own pace.

Realistically, however, Jan is well aware that each disappointment or twist of fate only hardened her husband's resistance to whatever people expected from him. "I don't see Dan as ever, ever giving in, in any way. He did with Elektra, but that was a little different. He didn't really have a chance to be commercial, and he didn't really have a chance to be himself—it was somewhere in the middle."

Not everything that befell Danny can be attributed to a lack of compromise. One of the hardest things for any artist to accept—and for the public to understand—is how many factors fall outside anyone's control. No matter how talented the artist, a certain amount of luck and timing are crucial in determining if the big time is only a phone call away or eternally out of reach. A review of Danny's life reveals no lack of turning points that could have altered it forever: if Danny had won a spot on the PBS-TV special that featured Buchanan; if he hadn't rejected Atlantic's offer; if Heintze hadn't gotten terminally ill during the *Redneck Jazz* era; if Lowell George hadn't died; if he'd won a Grammy for *88 Elmira St.*; if he'd done more European touring; if he'd scored an Oscar-winning film soundtrack; if more concrete assistance had come from high-profile friends like Les Paul; if Billy Windsor hadn't died—any, or all, of these factors could have tipped the balance of Danny's life and career in a different direction.

Since that didn't happen, Jan believes that gauging her husband's accomplishments will be a tricky business. "If [future listeners] can appreciate it and understand it, there could be some kind of a rebirth for good music. I don't know; it's hard for me to say. I guess if there's something [that] can be discovered in all of this, and in all the music that we have, and it could be presented in a way that makes sense, I hope that something good could happen."

Few know the ups and downs of a musician's life better than immediate family members, but Jan doesn't really dwell on the issue. "Being married to a musician was very, very hard. There was a lot of bending, but I'm not going to go out and say, 'Hey, this was really hard. I had to do this, this and this,' because he gave so much back." In the end, she feels Danny would have been far more miserable if he hadn't done what he wanted to do, whether he finished every project or not. "I have to believe that. It's the only thing that keeps me going forward. I have to believe that he did do something, and there was an impact, no matter how minuscule. It was there."

Jan cites a passage from one of her books that summarizes how she came to feel about her husband's life and work, and that gave her the first real measure of peace she'd known in some years. When and where she read that passage isn't as important as the impact it had on her thoughts, as she looked back on life with that self-described "short, old, fat guy that don't even sing."

"I read something by John Steinbeck that helped me more than my therapist," she says. "He speaks about quality and quantity. That really affected my way of thinking tremendously, because he said he didn't really care about the quantity of his days, just about the quality of his days. And I thought, That's really a beautiful way of putting it."

A Danny Gatton Discography

Rounding up Danny Gatton's recorded output is no simple task, given his many appearances as both a featured artist and a sideman. The author gratefully acknowledges the assistance provided by Steve Gorospe's Official Danny Gatton Website (www.dannygatton.com) and the Telemaster Archives (http://community2.webtv.net/RUMBLETWEED/DannyGatton/), both of which were helpful in assembling this overview of Danny's recording career.

Albums/CDs

American Music   Aladdin Records ALPS 102   1975
Original album on label reactivated by Billy Hancock. Made *Billboard*'s "Top Album Picks" for week ending 1/10/76; "a superlative effort from this Washington-based band," reviewer concluded, with dealers advised, "seek this LP out."

Redneck Jazz   NRG Records NLP-2916; NR 9646   1978
First release on Norma Gatton's label, following Aladdin's collapse; Norma is credited as executive producer and lyricist on "Love Is What You Need." Liner notes by Brawner Smoot. Also issued on rare red and yellow vinyl pressings of 1,000 to 2,000 copies apiece, according to Smoot.

American Music   Ripsaw Records 102   1982
Reissue of Aladdin album on Washington indie label.

Unfinished Business   NRG Records NR 17235   1987
Album cover is idealized rendition of Gatton's original Accokeek, Maryland, home.

Unfinished Business   NRG Records NCD-0479   1989
CD version features bonus tracks "Nit Pickin'" and "Georgia on My Mind"; is dedicated to guitarist's father, Dan Senior.

Vintage Masters 1971–76, Vol. I   Hippo Records H8901   1989
Reissue of *American Music* tracks from the Fat Boys era; includes alternate
takes of the title track and tunes that didn't make the album, such as
"Quiet Village." Has brief summary of the Fat Boys' history; cover is a
sketch of the band.

Tom Principato/Danny Gatton

Blazing Telecasters   Powerhouse Records POW-4036   1990
CD reissue of original 1984 album; credits indicate sequence of solos, as
well as featured musicians.

Redneck Jazz   NRG Records NCD-2916   1991
CD reissue of original album with two bonus tracks, "Ode to Billy Joe" and
"Canadian Sunset."

88 Elmira St.   Elektra Entertainment 9 61032-2   1991
Billy Windsor credited as associate producer; back cover features a young,
formally dressed Danny Gatton, playing guitar.

New York Stories   Blue Note Records 98959   1992

Cruisin' Deuces   Elektra Entertainment 9 61435-2   1993
Features guest vocalists Rodney Crowell on "It Doesn't Matter Anymore,"
James Lewis on "Heat of the Night," Delbert McClinton on "Sun Medley,"
and Billy Windsor on "Satisfied Mind"; Bill Holloman sings "Thirteen
Women." One tune, "Puddin' and Pie," was featured in Quentin Tarantino's
film *Destiny Turns on the Radio*.

Danny Gatton/Joey DeFrancesco

Relentless   Big Mo 20232   1994

Danny Gatton's Redneck Jazz Explosion   NRG Records NCD 3070   1995
CD release of legendary 12/31/78 gig from Washington's Cellar Door, with
extensive Brawner Smoot liner notes.

Robert Gordon/Danny Gatton

The Humbler   NRG Records NCD 6842   1996
Official release of long-circulated bootleg tape from Berkeley Square nightclub, Berkeley, California, 1981; includes bonus track of "Fingers on Fire"
soundcheck with drummer Shannon Ford.

American Music   NRG Records NCD-3422   1997
CD reissue of original Aladdin release, with two bonus tracks: "TV Mama"
and "Opus de Funk."

In Concert 9/9/94 Big Mo Records 20282 1998
Recorded live at the Birchmere, Alexandria, Virginia.

Untouchable NRG Records NCD-1242-2 1998
According to Norma Gatton's liner notes, this album was recorded but un-mixed before Danny's Elektra Records deal. "Deep Purple" is from the Cellar Door, 12/31/78; also includes live "Sweet Georgia Brown" from a fan's cassette recording.

Portraits Big Mo Records 2030 1998
Compilation of previously unreleased recordings overseen by longtime producer Ed Eastridge.

Hot Rod Guitar: The Danny Gatton Anthology Rhino CD 75691 1999
Double-CD anthology focuses mostly on Danny's Elektra albums, with selections from other recordings, such as "Redneck Jazz."

Albums that Feature or Reference Danny Gatton

Bobby Charles

Bobby Charles Invades the Wells Fargo Lounge Fontana FS 321 1968
Danny featured on "Malagueña" on this out-of-print LP from Bobby Charles Review, with whom he toured Midwest lounge circuit for 18 months.

Big Al Downing

Big Al Downing Team TRA-2001 1983

Link Wray

Fire & Brimstone
Danny played bottleneck slide guitar on this out-of-print LP by famed '50s rock guitarist, though the project had an unexpected outcome, as he told Opsasnick: "I played slide guitar with a spoon on his 1910 Gibson guitar that he had in his kitchen. The song was 'Fire and Brimstone,' and it's on the album where he's in the caricature of an Indian on the cover. They didn't give me credit. People think it was Link Wray, but it was really me. I did get ten dollars, though."

New Commander Cody Band

Flying Dreams Arista LP 4183 1978
Danny played guitar on "He's in Love, He's in Trouble" and "Vampira."

Cindy Bullens

Desire Wire   United Artists A-933H   1978

Robert Gordon

Are You Gonna Be the One?   RCA AFLI 1-3773   1981

Too Fast to Live, Too Young to Die   RCA AFLI 1-4380   1982

Red Hot: 1977–1981   Razor & Tie 2061   1995
CD compilation of Gordon's late-'70s and early-'80s material, which includes tracks from Danny's tenure with him.

Are You Gonna Be the One?   Collectables CD 2821   2002
Reissue of 1981 album with nine bonus tracks, including live versions of
"Black Slacks," "Fire," and "Red Hot" that feature guitarist Chris Spedding.

Meco

Pop Goes the Movies   Arista 9598   1982

Johnny Seaton

Uptown Renegade   Rounder Records 101   1983
Danny is featured on eight tracks later reissued on Billy Poore–compiled
Runnin' Wild limited-edition box set.

Reaction   Rounder Records 9004   1986
Danny also contributed arrangements for this 11-track album.

LesLee "Bird" Anderson

Runnin' Wild   Renegade RR-LP 104   1988
Another Billy Poore–coordinated project. Danny often cited the title
track— on which he played guitar, bass, pedal steel, and banjo—as his best
session work ever.

New Potato Caboose

Promising Traveler   Rykodisc CD 10116   1989
Ed Eastridge served as assistant engineer on this project, which also featured Danny.

Robert Gordon

Black Slacks   Bear Family Records BCD1 5489
Reissue of rockabilly singer's *Are You Gonna Be the One?* and *Too Fast to Live,
Too Young to Die* albums; Danny appears on six of the 25 tracks.

Deanna Bogart

Out to Get You   Blind Pig Records BP 73890   1991

Danny appears on jazz-style instrumental "Ethyl's Place" with former Redneck Jazz Explosion bassist Steve Wolf; drummer Timm Biery, who was in last Danny Gatton Band, also played. Produced and mixed by Ed Eastridge.

Levi's 501

One of many sessions that Gatton took after Elektra dropped him; played guitar on a blue jeans jingle.

Virginia & the Blue Dots

Games of Love   V-Twin Records V8002

Danny played on two tracks of this roots-rockabilly band's CD.

Chris Isaak

San Francisco Days   Reprise CD 45116   1993

Delbert McClinton

Delbert McClinton   Curb CD D-2 77600   1993

Danny and Delbert reprised their version of "Sun Medley," also on *Cruisin' Deuces*.

Arlen Roth

Toolin' Around   Blue Plate CD 300   1993

Danny teamed up with the New York guitarist/Hot Licks founder for a remake of "Tequila." Roth plans to reissue this album.

Liz Meyer

Womanly Arts   Strictly Country CD 37   1995

Brooks Tegler's Hot Jazz

Hot Jazz...And Not Only That   Big MO CD 2024   1995

According to Tegler, Danny's contribution was a reciprocal deal, following the drummer's appearance on *Unfinished Business*. Danny played on title track and "Lullaby of Birdland," which also features John Previti on upright bass.

Joe Stanley

King of the Honky Tonk Sax   Wildchild! 03852   1996

One track, "Blues for Danny," is a Gatton tribute; liner notes discuss Stanley's musical history, including first meeting with Danny. Guests include Billy Hancock (vocals), Dave Chappell (guitar), John Previti (bass).

Cathy Fink & Mary Marxer

Nobody Else Like You   A&M CD 540214   1995
Reissued by Rounder Records as Rounder CD 8079, 1998; Danny played guitar on "Twins" and "Harry's Glasses."

Hooked on Instrumentals   KTEL 3273   1986
Danny plays a '50s rock medley in closing song, "Hooked on Guitars," on compilation project arranged and conducted by Meco.

Everybody Loves to Slide   Rykodisc CD 10344   1996
Danny played "Notchco Blues" on this slide-guitar compilation that also features Duke Robillard, Tinsley Ellis, and Tom Principato.

Legends of Country Music: The Best of "Austin City Limits"
Sony CD 65323   1997
Danny appears as sideman with Roger Miller on "King of the Road" on this live compilation drawn from PBS-TV show.

Dinorock: Great Dinosaur Mystery—Musical Fossil Fantasy
Rounder CD 8083   1998
Danny appears on this album inspired by a popular children's program.

Hooked on Instrumentals   K-TEL CD 6798   1998
Danny appears on recycling of "Hooked on Guitars" from previous release that adds material from BBC Concert, London Symphony, and Royal Philarmonic orchestras.

Johnny Seaton

Runnin' Wild: The Renegade Years 1981–88   Renegade Records
RENCDX 430A   2001
Sprawling four-CD box set of mostly rockabilly-flavored material released by Billy Poore; includes 86 unreleased live and studio tracks that feature Danny's work with Seaton and vocalist Leslee "Bird" Anderson.

Good Humor Band

Good Humor Band   Permanent Records   2001
Danny plays slide guitar on "DWI," which also features Evan Johns (guitar/vocals); recorded 6/3/78 at Desperado's, Washington, D.C.

Ronnie & the Offbeats

"Beggar Man" b/w "Trouble in Mind"   Norwood Records   1961

Some sources cite the release date as 1962. Lineup features Danny with John Broaddus, Dick Heintze, Ronnie MacDonald, and Jerry Wallmark; band re-formed in the '80s as the American Music Company, with Billy Windsor on vocals.

The Soul Mates

"How's Your Sister" b/w "Moonlight Cruise"   Wilson Line Records 45-101-A   1966

Sold on tourist boat that cruised the Potomac River. A-side is a Gatton collaboration with keyboardist Dick Heintze; B-side is a MacDonald-Koslin tune.

Danny Gatton & the Fat Boys

"American Music" b/w "Harlem Nocturne"   Aladdin Records 5551-B   1974

A-side has vocal backing by the Memories; album version features backup by the Clovers.

Danny Gatton Band

"Ugly Man" b/w "Love Is What You Need"   NRG Records MR341922A   1977

A-side is by Evan Johns; B-side is by Chuck Tilley. Different take than *Redneck Jazz* album version.

Johnny Seaton

"Uptown" b/w "Get with It"   Renegade Records 408   1982

Billy Poore–produced single, which he remixed for *Uptown* album on Renegade.

Danny Gatton & the Naturals

"Love Them Hogs" b/w "Redskin Fever"   Medical Records MR 1818A   1983

Danny played guitar and earned a production credit for this tribute to the city's professional football team. Label reads: "Music That Soothes the Soul"; both songs written by Roger McDuffie.

Steve Simonds

"I Got a Lot to Say but That's OK" b/w "My Baby Gives Me Too Much to Eat"   Simonds Records   1984
Another one-off project featuring Danny and drummer Dave Elliott; Simonds wrote both sides and co-produced the single with Danny.

The Big Boss Band

"He's the Boss" b/w "Take a Chance on Rock & Roll"   Renegade 409 1986
Limited-edition single; A-side is parody of Bruce Springsteen, while B-side is Billy Poore–penned song recorded on 4/26/84. Marketed through the Springsteen fan club magazine, *Backstreets*.

Danny Gatton & Billy Windsor

"Diggin' the Dirt" b/w "Honky Tonkin' Country Girl"   NRG Records MR 9445   1985
A-side done at Big Mo, Kensington, Maryland; B-side at Bias Studios, Springfield, Virginia; Ed Eastridge's first production work with Gatton.

Ace Smith

"Birds of the World"* b/w "Remember Me"**   Cracktroop Music CT1243S2B   1987
First of several singles that feature Danny, according to Brawner Smoot. Taken from *Ferriswheel* (*) or *Burnin' Up the Ends* (**) albums. Asterisked material touts Danny's participation.

Others are:

"Little Miss Whip"* b/w "Down at the Clinic"**   Cracktroop CT 1244S2B   1988

"So Desperate"* b/w "The Worst of Me"**   Cracktroop CT 1244S5B   1988

"Livin' in a Suitcase"** b/w "Long Hot Summer"*   Cracktroop CT 1243S0B   1988

"Listen Julie"** b/w "The Suicide Bop"**   Cracktroop CT 1244S1B   1988

CD Singles

"Funky Mama"/"Blues Newburg"/"In My Room"/"The Simpsons" Elektra Records PRCD 8305-2   1991
Promotional-only CD single for the *88 Elmira St.* album.

"The Simpsons"   Elektra Records PRCD 8303-2   1991

Bootleg CDs

Live at Desperado's 1977
Taped at famous Washington nightclub; no artwork. "Wild show where Danny jumps from style to style and from tune to tune," according to one seller's eBay comments. "Danny's Magic Dingus Box is in full effect on this rare set."

Set list: "Irish Jig"/"Orange Blosson Special"/"Zorba the Greek"/"Steel Guitar Rag"/"Orange Blossom Special—Nutcracker Suite"/"Mr. Lee"/"Boogie Woogie"/"Big Boy"/"Mickey Mouse"/"Malagueña"/"Killer Joe" (bass solo)/ "Little Rock Getaway"/"How High the Moon"/"Quiet Village"/"So What"/ "Rock Candy"/"Harlem Nocturne"/"Fingers on Fire"/"Linus and Lucy"/ "Sitting on Top of the World"/"Beer Bottle Blues"/"Canadian Street"/ "Working Man Blues"/"Foggy Mountain Breakdown"/"Homage to Charlie Christian"/"Orange Blossom Special"/"Guitar Boogie"/"Mr. Lee"

Orphans   MA 990100 1/2
Three-CD set billed as Cellar Door shows with Redneck Jazz Explosion, 12/30–31/78. Cover photo features later-era Danny and Holly holding Teles. Contents have also turned up on bootleg videos.

Live in Milwaukee 1992
Two-CD set; no artwork. "This set kills the other live releases from Danny," according to comments posted on eBay. Disc One: "Funky Mama"/"Memphis"/"Blues Newburg"/"Sun Medley"/"Red Label." Disc Two: "Mustang Sally"/"Pretty Blue"/"It Doesn't Matter Anymore"/ "Harlem Nocturne"/"Perry Mason Theme"/"Guitar Solo"/"Jazz Jam"

Bootleg Videos

Maryland Inn   1989
Ebay comments: "Great second set of that night with lots of audience banter and a horn section; quite a few jazz tunes, killer turned-up version of 'Notchco Blues' and stellar take on 'Sleepwalk.' Cool take on 'Red Label' with the horns playing the guitar melody from '88 Elmira.'" Set also includes "One for Lenny" and "Take the A-Train."

Falls Church, Virginia   (50 minutes)   1991
Single-camera shoot mostly focused on Danny.

Bridgeton, Pennsylvania   (60 minutes)   1992
One of the most common videos that turns up on eBay; show features *Elmira St.*–era lineup.

Unreleased Videos

Club Soda, Washington (60 minutes) 1990
Not a bootleg video, because it was originally intended for commercial production; five-camera shoot used to capture Funhouse-era band at local club. Three songs from this show, "Seven Come Eleven," "Linus and Lucy," and "Orange Blossom Special" were released on Big Mo's *Portraits* compilation.

Sheldon Hall, St. Louis (60 minutes) 1993
Five-camera master shoot of summer show from *Cruisin' Deuces* lineup of Danny, John Previti, Shannon Ford, and Bill Holloman; Delbert McClinton guests to reprise the album's "Sun Medley."

Videos

Licks & Tricks for Guitar Pro Video Corp. 1987
Danny's first venture into the instructional video market; '53 Tele is prominently featured. The company reached settlement with Arlen Roth to avoid confusion with his company's "Hot Licks" brand name.

Danny Gatton: Telemaster! Hot Licks VGG 144 (90 minutes) 1990
First of two Hot Licks instructional videos; topics include banjo-style rolls, B-3 organ effects, jazz/country styles, and chord progressions, Les Paul–style fills/harmonies, new blues progressions, rockabilly echo effects/styles. Danny primarily playing solo, sitting on stool with '53 Tele.

Danny Gatton 2: Strictly Rhythm Guitar Hot Licks VGD 178
(73 minutes) 1994
Danny breaks down his rhythm and lead approaches on his own, then in a band context with the Previti-Biery rhythm section and Arlen Roth on lead guitar; guitar tech Jay Monterose also joins in closing jam. Danny plays black-and-white "Moto" Tele through blackfaced Vibrolux Reverb, plus Gibson J-200 acoustic guitar.

The Guitar Show featuring Danny Gatton (Recorded in 1989)
Front Row Music (30 minutes) 1999
One of the less-common items that pops up on eBay; Danny is interviewed and plays "Secret Love," "Sugarfoot Rag," "One for Lenny," and "Boot Hill Drag" with Previti. '53 Tele is prominently featured.

Hot Licks Among Friends: The Making of Toolin' Around Hot Licks
(approx. one hour) 1993
Features footage of Danny and Arlen Roth recording "Tequila" in the studio.

Notable TV Appearances

Maryland Public Television (PBS-TV)   (60 minutes)   1979
Program features Redneck Jazz Explosion's 1978 Cellar Door shows; also includes footage of support act, Tom Principato–Pete Kennedy guitar duo.

Austin City Limits (PBS-TV)   (60 minutes)   **Recorded 1/24/83; aired in March or April 1983**
First of two notable appearances on famed concert show; Danny is a sideman in Roger Miller's band, but gets to solo on three songs. Show also features special guest Willie Nelson. Danny also appeared with Miller on *Country Music Jamboree.*

Maryland Public Television (PBS-TV)   (60 minutes)   5/23/84
Danny appears with Tom Principato for set that covers similar territory as *Blazing Telecasters* album, which was culled from separate show at Adam's Rib club in Washington, D.C.

The Guiding Light (CBS-TV)   (60 minutes)   8/21/89
Another collectors' must-see that features Danny and the Elliott-Previti rhythm section in performance with country-pop vocalist Reba McEntire, who sings Randy Newman's "Guilty."

Finger-Pickin' Good—Nightwatch   (15 minutes)   1990
Local D.C.-area program hosted and produced by Jamie McIntyre; show features live clips of Danny performing with Bill Kirchen and driving with Holly in his 1934 Ford.

Late Night with David Letterman (NBC-TV)   1991
Danny sat in with the "World's Most Dangerous Band," led by keyboardist Paul Shaffer.

Austin City Limits (PBS-TV)   (30 minutes)   Recorded 10/24/91
Danny's second appearance, which remains widely circulated in collectors' and eBay circles. Emphasis is on newly released *88 Elmira St.* material like "Funky Mama" and "Red Label," though show also features Danny's beer-bottle slide trick on "Honky Tonkin' Country Girl." Danny plays '56 Gibson ES-350.

American Music Shop (TNN)   (50 minutes)   1993
Danny appears with Vince Gill and Albert Lee as part of all-star jam session; he also appeared on "Nashville Morning Show" that year to promote *Cruisin' Deuces* with performance that included versions of "Blues Newburg" and "Big Boss Man."

Late Night with Conan O'Brien (NBC-TV)   (5 minutes)   1/12/94
Danny appears with guitarist/Hot Licks founder Arlen Roth for a version of
"Tequila" off the latter's *Toolin' Around* album. Danny plays Fender Custom
Shop doubleneck guitar; band also includes Timm Biery, John Previti, and
"Late Night" band member Jimmy Vivino.

Awards/Honors

Guitar Player   **Cover story by Dan Forte, March 1989**
On cover Danny holds mask to his face, in keeping with story's portrayal
of him as "The World's Greatest Unknown Guitar Player"; issue came with
Soundpage recording, "Nit Pickin'." Danny also won four awards in magazine's annual readers' polls for "Best Country Guitar Player."

***Washington Area Music Awards* ("Wammies")**
Formed in 1985, the Washington Area Music Association holds an annual
ceremony to highlight local musicians' achievements. Danny won the following awards:

> Rock/Pop Instrumentalist   1986
>
> Jazz Instrumentalist   1987
>
> Jazz/Country Instrumentalist; Jazz Recording; Roots Rock Recording
> and Instrumentalist   1988
>
> Danny Gatton's Funhouse: Jazz Small Ensemble   1988
>
> Danny Gatton Group: Jazz Artist   1989
>
> Blues, Country/Rock, and Jazz Instrumentalist   1989
>
> Blues, Country/Roots Rock, Jazz, and Rock/Pop Instrumentalist; Blues
> and Jazz Recording, *88 Elmira St.*; Album of the Year, *88 Elmira St.*; Artist
> of the Year; Musician of the Year   1991
>
> WAMA Hall of Fame, inducted   1995

Tribute Concerts

***Tramps,* New York City, October 10–12, 1995**

***Sam's Crab House,* Clinton, Maryland, January 1996**

***The Birchmere,* Alexandria, Virginia, January 8–9, 1998**

***The Bottom Line,* New York City, Fall 1994**

Bibliography

Books

Carson, Phil. *American Axe: The Life and Times of Roy Buchanan.* San Francisco: Backbeat Books, 2001.

Jones, Alan and Jussi Kantonen. *Saturday Night Forever: The Story of Disco.* Edinburgh, Scotland: Mainstream Publishing, 1999.

Michaels, Mark. *Rockabilly Riffs for Guitar.* New York: Amsco Publications, 1985 (includes brief biography and breakdown of Danny's main guitars and techniques).

Opsasnick, Mark. *Capitol Rock.* Philadelphia: Xlibris Corp., 2002.

Poore, Billy. *Rockabilly: A Forty-Year Journey.* Milwaukee: Hal Leonard Publishing, 1994.

Periodicals

Adde, Nick. "Gatton Gears Up to Go Again." *Prince William County Journal*, February 26, 1982.

Anderson, John. "Whaddya Mean He Doesn't Practice: Danny Gatton, the Guitar Man." *New York Newsday*, August 10, 1989.

Bloom, Steve. "Wanted: Fame for a King," *New York Newsday*, February 26, 1989.

Brace, Eric. "A Wellspring of Gifted Guitarists." *Washington Post*, December 8, 2000.

Crowley, Kimberly Y. and John D. Johnston. "Gatton Found Dead at Newburg Farm," *Maryland Independent*, October 7, 1994.

Culbertson, D.C. "On the Cover...:Unknown? Not Anymore." *The Music Monthly*, May 1991.

Dolan, Michael. "Give the Drummer Some." *City Paper*, November 27–December 3, 1992.

Drozdowski, Ted. "Redneck Jazzman: Six-String Addict Danny Gatton Plugs In and Takes Off." *Pulse* (no date).

——————. "The Case of the Exploding Fretboard." *Pulse*, March 1991.

Eastridge, Ed. Booklet notes: *Portraits* compilation (Big Mo Records 2030) 1998.

Forte Dan. *Unfinished Business* album review. *Guitar Player*, March 1988.

————. "He's Been Called 'The World's Greatest Unknown Guitarist,' but What Famous Guitarist Could Possibly Outplay Him?" *Guitar Player*, March 1989.

Gatton, Norma. Booklet notes: *Untouchable* (NRG Records NCD-1242-2) 1998.

Gahar, Chelsea. "Billy Hancock: Hey! Little Rock & Roller." *Northern Virginia Rhythm*, November 16, 1993.

Gill, Bruce. Booklet notes: Good Humor Band compilation CD. Reprinted from *Live Bait Monthly Magazine*, Fall 1995.

Gill, Chris. "Danny Gatton: At Last! The Great Gatton Album." *Guitar Player*, July 1993.

————. "Remembering 'The World's Greatest Unknown Guitarist': Danny Gatton, 1945–1994." *Guitar Player*, January 1995.

Groce, Larry. Program notes: *Mountain Stage/On Air* (distributed by National Public Radio) May 1989.

Hadley, Frank. *Downbeat/Jazziz* review of *Relentless* (Danny Gatton and Joey DeFrancesco); reprinted in CD booklet (Big Mo 20232) 1994.

Harrington, Richard. "The Fastest Guitar in the East." *Washington Post* Sunday Magazine, August 11, 1991.

————. "Danny Gatton." *Unicorn Times*, Vol. I, No. 12 (year unlisted; appears to be 1974).

————. "Spotlight: The Roots of Rock." *Washington Post*, March 15, 1983.

————. "Gatton: Hot Property." *Washington Post*, May 3, 1989.

————. "Gatton Dead of Gunshot Wound." *Washington Post*, October 6, 1994.

————. "While Their Guitars Gently Weep." *Washington Post*, January 14, 1995.

Harrison, Joel. "Playing Hard." *The Washingtonian*, October 1998.

Heibutzki, Ralph. *In Concert 9/9/94* review, *DISCoveries*, October 1998.

————. "Unfinished Business: The Life & Times of Danny Gatton." *Vintage Guitar*, February 1999.

Hettinger, James. "Guitar Heaven: Rural Living Suits Danny Gatton." *Maryland Independent*, February 25, 1994.

Himes, Geoffrey. "Gatton, Watson Bopping the Blues." *Washington Post*, October 30, 1992.

————. "Gatton, Going for the Gold" (*88 Elmira St.* review). *Washington Post*, March 29, 1991.

Holley, Glenn. Booklet notes: Robert Gordon & Danny Gatton, *The Humbler* (NRG Records NCD 6842) 1996.

Howe, Desson. "Leaving the Blues Behind." *Washington Post*, April 25, 1984.

Joseph, Frank. "Danny Gatton: Robert Gordon's Redneck Jazzer." *Guitar Player*, September 1983.

Joyce, Mike. "Danny Gatton at the Cellar Door." *Washington Post*, July 30, 1981.

————. "Danny & the Fat Boys." *Washington Post*, December 21, 1982.

————. "Danny Gatton: Pickin' a Mood." *Washington Post*, December 20, 1987.

————. "Performing Arts: Danny Gatton." *Washington Post*, February 20, 1989.

Kernis, Mark. "Gatton, and All That (Redneck) Jazz." *Washington Star*, September 22, 1978.

Mazer, Dan. "Eddie Adcock: Renaissance Man." *Banjo Newsletter*, November 1996.

McKenna, Dave. "Pickup Artist: Joe Barden Wires the Monsters of Rock Guitar." *Washington City Paper*, December 13, 1991.

Milkowski, Bill. "Home-Grown Hero." *Guitar World*, January 1989.

Neufeld, Matt. "Guitarist Gatton Commits Suicide: Acclaimed Guitarist Had Money Woes." *Washington Times*, October 6, 1994.

Nitchie, Hub. "Eddie Adcock: Banjo Amplification." *Banjo Newsletter*, December 1978.

Poore, Billy. Booklet notes: *Runnin' Wild* CD box set (Renegade Records) 2001.

Reel, Monte. "Accumulated Stuff of a Music Legend Going On Block." *Washington Post*, May 11, 2001.

Rockwell, John. "Jazz: Danny Gatton's Guitar Plays 'Redneck' Style." *New York Times*, February 6, 1979.

Russell, Rusty. "The Humbler: A Tribute to Danny Gatton." *Guitar Player*, May 1998.

Santoro, Gene. "Picking Danny Gatton's Brain." *Musician*, February 1991.

Siegel, Eric. "Caviar and Grits: Danny Gatton, Prince of Redneck Jazz." *Baltimore Sun* Magazine, July 1, 1979.

Smoot, Brawner. "Danny Gatton: Waiting for the Sunrise (Brawner Smoot Explains Why Our Best Guitarist Is Not a Star)." *Unicorn Times*, September 1977.

————. "Gatton Hits the Road in Search of New Lease on Playing Life." *Unicorn Times*, July 1978.

————. NRG Newsletter, Volume 16; writeup of April 4–5, 1979, Redneck Jazz Explosion gigs at New York City's Lone Star Café; cites *Guitar Player* (May 1979) and *Washington Post* (April 30, 1979) reviews of *Redneck Jazz*.

————. "Danny Gatton: D.C.'s Best-Known Unknown." *Guitar World*, May 1982.

————. Booklet notes: *American Music* (NRG Records NCD- 3422-2) 1997; *Redneck Jazz Explosion: Recorded Live December 31, 1978* (NRG Records NCD-3760) 1995; *Unfinished Business* (NRG Records NCD-02479) 1987, 1989; *88 Elmira St.* (Elektra Entertainment 9 61032-2) 1991.

Souza, Alma. "Danny Gatton: The Legend Who's Local Aims to Tie Up Some Unfinished Business." *Maryland Musician*, August 1988.

Swenson, John. "Performance: Danny Gatton Tribute." *Rolling Stone*, February 23, 1995.

Tamarkin, Jeff. *Unfinished Business* review. *CMJ New Music Report*, March 25, 1988.

"The Doctor's Bag." No byline; preview of Danny Gatton's performance at Dave Elliott benefit. *Washington Post*, November 27, 1992.

"Top Album Picks." No byline; review of *American Music* by Danny & the Fat Boys. *Billboard*, for week ending January 10, 1976.

Unfinished Business review. *Rolling Stone*, "Hot Issue," May 19, 1988.

Warren, Tim. "Return of the Rock & Roll Redneck." *Washington Star*, September 22, 1978.

—————. "For Gatton Fans: Some Sterling Moments." *Washington Star*, September 23, 1978.

White, Slaton. "Gatton Rocks Glass Onion." University of Maryland *Diamondback*, September 19, 1977.

Yasui, Todd A. "Nine Wammies for Gatton: Guitarist Wins in Blues, Jazz, Country and Pop." *Washington Post*, November 11, 1991.

Yates, Bryan. "Mike McAdam: Good Times with Good Humor." *Vintage Guitar*, February 1999.

—————. "Guitar Event of the Decade." *Vintage Guitar*, February 1999.

Young, Charles D. "Gatton's Guitar Glitters Through Redneck Jazz." *Unicorn Times*, September 1978.

Young, Todd A. "Nine Wammies for Gatton." *Washington Post*, November 11, 1991.

Zibart, Eve. "Danny Gatton." *Washington Post*, September 23, 1978.

—————. "Funhouse, Full Houses." *Washington Post*, July 10, 1988.

Websites

Alpert, Brian. www.rhumba.com: "The Concert Tour" Drummer recounts brief tour with Danny Gatton. Also has anecdotes from other readers; recollections of interviewing Danny (February 1975); and audio clip of an April 9, 1989, National Public Radio interview with Danny (in which he discusses his influences, tone, and technique).

Barden, Joe. www.joebarden.com: Official site for Danny's pickup man; includes links to Stephen Gorospe's site (see below), artists who use Barden's gear, and other manufacturers.

Fender Players Club. www.fenderplayersclub.com: Manufacturer's "Hall of Legends" includes brief biography, gear list, and breakdown of the "Blues Newburg" solo.

Gorospe, Stephen. www.dannygatton.com: "Danny Gatton: The Definitive Website," the first major site dealing with the late Telemaster. Includes a brief history of the Offbeats; breakdowns of Danny's cars, gear, and guitars; assorted photo galleries and trivia.

Hosford, Larry. www.larryhosford.com: Official site of the man whose reputation lured Danny to California; "Guitar Wizards" section contains a brief summary of that period, with a photo of Danny.

Hot Licks Video. www.hotlicks.com: Website for ordering Danny's instructional videos.

Johns, Evan. www.evanjohns.com: Danny is referenced in the "Stories" section of Johns's official site.

Miles. http://community-2.webtv.net/RUMBLETWEED/DannyGatton/: "Danny Gatton: The Telemaster Archives" is the other major Danny-related site, aside from Stephen Gorospe's; includes a rundown on albums, gear, sessions, major TV and video appearances, as well as guest book for fans' comments.

Monterose, Jay. www.vintique.com: Site operated by Danny's friend and guitar tech, details the products and services he offers through his College Park, Maryland, business.

Simonds, Steve. www.fortunecity.com/tinpan/easy/142/: Onetime collaborator briefly describes his experience working with Danny in the studio. The songs "I've Got a Lot to Say But That's OK" and "My Baby Gives Me Too Much to Eat" are available for download on this "Simonds Says" site (motto: "Remember, It's OK Because Simonds Says!").

Unknown. www.rockabillyhall.com: The "Rockabilly Hall of Fame" site has a brief historical overview of Danny's musical career and a discussion of his musical influences (notably Lenny Breau). Also includes "Some Gatton History" by Steve Wolf, in which the former Redneck Jazz Explosion bassist discusses his role in Danny's late-'70s ensemble.

Interviews

John Adams (11/15/01)

Eddie and Martha Adcock (2/15/02, 3/13/02)

Laura Adkins, National Public Radio (4/27/88; this interview can be heard on the *Runnin' Wild* box set)

Joe Barden (10/7/01, 12/19/01, 2/28–3/1/02)

Paul Barrere (e-mail)

Chris Battistone (11/8/01)

Terry Benton (9/2/01, 9/5/01, 9/7/01, 10/7/01)

Ivan Brown (8/27/01)

Johnny Castle (11/9/01)

Dave Chappell (5/5/02)

Ed Eastridge (3/21/02, 3/25/02, 3/31/02, 4/2/02, 5/31/02, 6/11/02)

Dave Elliott (7/23/01, 7/25/01, 7/26/01, 7/31/01, 8/7/01, 8/21–23/01, 10/7/01)

Ray Flacke (7/2/02, 7/19/02)

Shannon Ford (3/15–16/02)

Paul Freeman (4/4/02)

Andy Funt (10/7/01)

Tony Garnier (10/26/01)

Brent Gatton (2/20/02, 5/7/02)

Danny Gatton: *Cruisin' Deuces* promotional interview, unedited cassette (90 minutes); provided by Howard Thompson

Holly Gatton (7/24/02, 8/2/02, and e-mail)

Jan Gatton (7/24–25/02, 7/28/02)

Norma Gatton (7/8/01)

Sherry Gatton (5/7/02)

Stephen Gorospe (5/6/02)

Tommy Gros (10/7/01)

Billy Hancock (5/7/02)

Bobby Hancock (2/24–25/02)

Richard Harrington (6/5/02)

Bill Holloman (1/2/02, 1/16/02, 3/19/02)

Jack Jensen (6/13/02)

Keith John (10/7/01)

Evan Johns (8/16/01, 8/25/01, 9/9/01, 9/16/01)

Bobby Jones (5/7/02)

Pete Kennedy (4/15/02)

Bill Kirchen (11/7/01)

Joe Kogok (11/27/01)

Mark Korpi (9/30/01)

Terry Lickona (7/26/01)

Ronnie MacDonald (5/6/02)

Bob Margolin (e-mail)

Mike McAdam (7/25/01)

Roger McDuffie (5/7/02)

Al McKay (1/31/02)

Liz Meyer (1/18–19/02)

Pat Moore (e-mail)

Obie O'Brien (10/27/01)

The Offbeats: John Broaddus, Ernie Gorospe, Jerry Wallmark (5/6/02)

James "Spike" Ostmann (5/6/02)

Billy Poore (4/24/02, 4/27/02)

Tom Principato (12/22/01, 1/15/02, 1/31/02)

Lance Quinn (10/27/01)

Arlen Roth (10/03/01)

Tex Rubinowitz (10/22–23/01, 10/26/01)

Brawner Smoot (5/8/02)

Jim Stephanson (10/10/01)

Fred Tackett (e-mail)

Joe Tass (5/9/02)

Brooks Tegler (5/5/02)

Jimmy Thackeray (4/16/02)

Howard Thompson (e-mail)

Rob Weaver (10/10/01)

Tom Wheeler (9/22/01)

Mac Wilson (6/2/02)

Steve Wolf (10/10/01)

Phil Zavarella (10/9/01)

Deborah Roth: *page x*

Courtesy of Jan Gatton: *pages 3, 15, 54, 112, 189*

Courtesy of Brent Gatton: *pages 9, 201, 205*

Evan Johns Collection: *page 74, 142, 143*

Wayne Eastep: *pages 80, 100*

Clayton Call: *pages 119, 203*

©Billy Poore Collection (Route 4, Box 161-A1, Linden, TN 37096-9804, (931) 589-3113, renegade@netease.net): *page 139*

Tom Principato: *page 146*

Guitar Player Archives, cover photo by John Peden/Onyx: *page 168*

Star File, photo by David Selig: *page 170*

Elektra Entertainment: *page 179*

Courtesy Arlen Roth: *page 210*

Jeromie Brian Stephens: *pages 217, 238*

All books reflect their authors' visions, but they are not produced in isolation. This is especially true when the subject is as complex as Danny Gatton.

As Arlen Roth notes in his foreword, separating the guitar virtuoso from the family man is impossible. I would have gleaned fewer insights about the latter aspect of Danny's life had I not had help from his mother, Norma; his widow, Jan, and daughter, Holly; his brother, Brent, and his wife, Sherry. They never turned away the questions I posed in countless e-mails, phone interviews, and visits, and they always extended a helping hand when I needed one. My warmest gratitude goes out to them for their honesty and responsiveness.

A similar attitude characterized Danny's friends, whether they played music with him or not. One gentle caveat before the credits roll: All the sources in this book made crucial contributions, whether their words got only a paragraph or were spread across several chapters.

That said, Eddie Adcock, Joe Barden, Ed Eastridge, Dave Elliott, Shannon Ford, Billy Hancock, Bobby "No Relation" Hancock, Richard Harrington, Bill Holloman, Jack Jensen, Evan Johns, Bobby Jones, Pete Kennedy, Bill Kirchen, Joe Kogok, Liz Meyer, Roger McDuffie, Billy Poore, Tom Principato, Lance Quinn, Arlen Roth, Tex Rubinowitz, Joe Tass, Robbie Weaver, and Steve Wolf underwent extensive phone and personal interviews—for which this book is so much richer.

The list goes on: Mac Wilson illuminated how he organized the 1998 tribute concert and suggested sources I might have overlooked. So did Arlen Roth, whose energy inspired me at the right moments.

Former Offbeats John Broaddus, Ernie Gorospe, Ronnie MacDonald, and Jerry Wallmark sat with me at Mama Stella's House of Italian Pasta in

Clinton, Maryland, to recall the teenaged Danny Gatton. They are gentlemen of the first order, as is Ernie's son, Steve, who pays homage through his website, www.dannygatton.com.

So is Dave Chappell, who drove from his Maryland home to my Falls Church, Virginia, motel room, and pulled out 20-year-old tapes of lessons he took with Danny—and enriched my knowledge.

Any project has its share of wondrous serendipity. I learned about Pat Moore from Bobby Hancock. Had they not met on a cruise, I would never have gleaned Pat's recollections of his encounters with Danny.

Brawner Smoot spent an afternoon at his Virginia home recalling the *Redneck Jazz* era's ins and outs, while his parrot, Lenny—named for the late jazz guitar phenomenon Lenny Breau, of course—squawked behind us.

Steve and Nancy Wolf took a couple hours from a hectic afternoon to proudly show landmarks at the home they bought from Danny in Accokeek, Maryland (immortalized on the cover of *Unfinished Business*).

Phil Zavarella interrupted the cleanup of his Arlington, Virginia, store to share his recollections with me, and he provided copies of relevant live CDs and one-off records like "Love Them Hogs." Brent Gatton, Evan Johns, Tom Principato, and David Tamarkin also provided information on or copies of tapes, videos, and one-off albums.

Austin City Limits producer Terry Lickona graciously sent edited and uncut tapes of the 1983 and 1991 shows that exposed Danny to a wider audience. Bill Holloman dubbed a tape of the oft-bootlegged 1993 St. Louis gig; Dave Elliott, Brent Gatton, Holly Gatton, and Brawner Smoot supplied me with press clippings to augment my own research. Thanks to them all for going the extra mile.

As always, several sources were unavailable for various reasons, led by Les Paul, whom Danny idolized so much as a teenager. For that reason, I've used other people's recollections to fill in the gaps, while trying to avoid putting words into anyone's mouth.

A similar approach held true for other notable omissions like Timm Biery, Jack Casady, Buddy Emmons, John Fogerty, Robert Gordon, Jimbo Manion, Jay Monterose, Delbert McClinton, Donna and Tom Oliff, John Sprung, and Donna and Stephen Windsor, among others. To those people I reached, I appreciate whatever advice or encouragement they gave behind the scenes.

Regrettably, two key sources did not live to see this book completed, including the Childe Harolde's irrepressible, free-spirited owner, Bill Heard, and Jack Jensen (of the Crazy Horse and Billy Jack's fame). Their roles in Danny's life are detailed throughout *Unfinished Business*.

Several people declined to participate; the author respects the various reasons they expressed to me. In Previti's case, I've used relevant quotes from his interview in my April 1999 *Vintage Guitar* article, and they are noted appropriately.

All books need a supportive editorial team, and *Unfinished Business* is no exception—beginning with my April 1999 *Vintage Guitar* article of the same name. Ward Meeker edited a sprawling epic into a cogent snapshot that inspired a larger whole, and I thank him for that.

At Backbeat, Dorothy Cox and Richard Johnston gave valuable advice and counsel, while Jim Roberts did a brilliant job of "filleting the fish" into a leaner, meaner, and more relevant manuscript. Nancy Tabor worked hard on following my photo leads, while Kevin Becketti, Nina Lesowitz, and Jennifer Steele led separate charges on marketing and endorsements.

My agent, Sherry Bykofsky, negotiated contractual thickets that would have bogged down others. I thank my old editor at *Goldmine*, Jeff Tamarkin, for introducing us to each other, which seems like a natural extension of his role in publishing my first feature in 1992.

As always, I remain grateful for the encouragement of those closest to me—starting with my wife, Lisa, who assisted with numerous research tasks and kept my spirits up when the workload seemed sky-high. So did the "old gang" of Tim Easterday, John Hilla, Anthony Salazar, Tani Spielberg, and Don Hargraves—who also poured considerable energy in designing a web page for this book.

Gene and Jane Humphrey, old friends of Lisa's family, allowed us to experience their hospitality by letting us stay at their Maryland home during my first research trip in October 2001.

Finally, I salute my parents, Herbert and Hildegard Heibutzki, both of whom died during the writing of *Unfinished Business*. They were one of the major forces in my life, and remain loved and missed by those who knew them.

—Ralph Heibutzki

February 1996 tribute to Danny, 236
gigs with Danny Gatton Band, 73–75
playing with Johnny Seaton, 139, 144
reaction to Danny's suicide, 222
Redneck Jazz, 72, 80–81
second split with Danny, 95
split with Danny Gatton Band, 77
Jones, Bobby, 136, 214
Joseph, Frank, 112
Joyce, Mike, 128–129, 165, 167

K

Kaukonen, Jorma, 167
Keith, Bill, 44
Kennedy, Pete
    on cause of Danny's death, 229
    on Danny playing with Front Porch
        Swing, 109–110
    on Danny's legacy, 249–250
    on Danny's unique style, 43
    on Fat Boys, 61
    on January 1998 tribute, 241
    meeting with Danny, 35–37
    passing up Danny's funeral, 227
    playing with Danny in the early '80s,
        135–136
    reaction to Danny's suicide, 225
    reviewing *88 Elmira St.*, 184
    on rift between Billy Hancock and
        Danny, 70
    on Roy Buchanan influence on
        Danny, 30
Kernis, Mark, 95
Kimmet, Ian, 182
Kirchen, Bill
    Gatton tributes and, 235
    meeting Danny, 55
    on missing Danny's funeral, 227
    playing gigs with Danny, 158
Kogok, Joe, 150, 242
    on Danny's funeral, 226
    on Danny's legacy, 250
    influence of Danny on, 65–66
    learning from Danny, 78
    Redneck Jazz Explosion and, 60
Korpi, Mark, 144

L

Late Night with Conan O'Brien, 209–211
Lee, Albert, 235
Leonard, Drake, 91
Lepson, Tommy, 214
Les Paul guitars, 51, 93
Les Paulverizer, 88, 110
Lewis, James, 197
Lickona, Terry, 186
Litt, Scott, 123
Little Feat, 84, 105, 106
Littleton, Bill, 75
Loder, Kurt, 175–176
Lofgren, Nils, 26

Lone Star Cafe, 99
Lover, Seth, 121

M

MacDonald, Ronnie, 90
    Drapes, 150
    friendship with, 148
    Naturals, 126
    Offbeats, 11
    Take Five Combo, 23
Magic Dingus Box, 79, 86, 99
    creation of, 88
    discarded by Danny, 112
    functions of, 89
Magruder, Robbie, 60
mandolin, 32, 42
Margolin, Bob, 97, 139, 246
Martin 00-18, 6
Martin D-28 acoustic, 25
Maye, Michael, 111
McAdam, Mike, 91, 112
McClinton, Delbert, 204, 207
McCloud, Tiny, 71
McDuffie, Roger, 136, 223
    Commander Cody experience and, 83
    Danny's death and, 137
    Fat Boys, 128–129
    Glass Wing gigs, 149
    Naturals, 126
    performance on *Unfinished Business*,
        157
McHugh, Jeff, 200
McKay, Al, 56–57, 83
McKelway, Doug, 221
media coverage, 234
Meyer, Liz
    band stories and tensions, 41–43
    breakup of band, 44–46
    country-rock style of, 38–39
    on Danny as musical prodigy, 7
    on Danny's West Coast trip, 84
    impact on Danny's career, 37
    on Jan's disinterest in Danny's
        music, 20
    meeting with Danny, 33
    members of her band, 38–41
    reaction to Danny's suicide, 224
    type of music played by her band,
        41–42
Milburn, Amos, 59
Miller, Roger, 115, 117, 122, 127, 129–131
Minor, John, 200
Monardo, Meco, 136–137
Monterose, Jay
    Cruisin' Deuces, 198
    on Danny's abandoning the Magic
        Dingus Box, 112
    on Danny's legacy, 246
    friendship with Danny, 32
    influence on Danny, 207
    playing with Johnny Seaton, 127
    tribute at Danny's funeral of, 231